MW00453449

THE FATHER'S SON

The Father's Son

by Rev. James T. O'Connor

Wipf and Stock Publishers
EUGENE, OREGON

Wipf and Stock Publishers
199 West 8th Avenue, Suite 3
Eugene, Oregon 97401

The Father's Son
By O'Connor, James T.
Copyright©1984 O'Connor, James T.
ISBN: 1-57910-848-2
Publication date: December, 2001
Previously published by St. Paul Books & Media, Daughters of St. Paul, 1984.

CONTENTS

APPENDIX — THE CREEDS

Preface

The Father's Son has been written primarily as a textbook, which hopefully will be of service not only to seminarians and college students but to anyone engaged in a study of Christology, the revealed mystery of Jesus of Nazareth, the eternal Son of God made man for our salvation. The book is the result of a need I myself have experienced as a seminary teacher of Christology over these past ten years. These years have witnessed the publication of a very large number of books about Jesus, many of them controversial and some of them clearly at variance with what the Scriptures, Tradition and the Church teach and have always taught about the Word Incarnate. Many of them, too, have been detailed studies about the historical development of Christian doctrine about Jesus and about the various "theologies" of the New Testament writers. More and more frequently such books have become "studies about studies" while Jesus Himself has receded, becoming an almost unknowable figure, unreachable in His historical immediacy, and hidden behind the real or imagined theologies about Him. Minutely studied and subjected to certain forms of critical analysis which often rests on unsubstantiated hypotheses, the truth and historical accuracy of the four Gospels have been called into question and even rejected. As a result, God's revelation of Himself in deed and word through Scripture and Tradition is a truth now undermined for many by the supposedly historical inaccuracy of the Bible, and of the Gospels in particular.

There can, at the present, be no return to a naive faith nor can the many problems raised by modern scriptural exegesis and studies in the development of Christological doctrine be ignored. I have tried to take account of these developments throughout the text, but especially in the footnotes. As a result the book is neither as simple nor as clear as I would want it to be. At times too much information is presumed as being already known by the reader—a presumption

1

which could be rectified only by a much longer book. There are times, as well, when my own conclusions are presented in much too tentative a manner. Such tentativeness is, in part, a personal reaction to the current tendency of some to present popular hypotheses as certain when in fact there is no real evidence to substantiate such pretended certitudes. Our certitudes about Jesus of Nazareth come from divine revelation, given to us in Scripture and Tradition, as these are interpreted by the Church. These certitudes, however, are supported by the historical reliability of the Gospels, a reliability which can be demonstrated with a reasonable application of the methods common to historical research. As I have noted elsewhere in the text, the various certitudes must not be confused. Historical certitude is, by its nature, often dependent upon a conjunction of probabilities and upon evidence which can be variously interpreted. The certitude about revelation as taught by the Church rests upon the divine gift of faith. The former is often tentative; the latter is never so.

No book on Christology—least of all this one—can say all that should be said about the Lord. Even the Gospels cannot do that, but it is to them that one must constantly turn if one wants to read something truly worthwhile about Jesus. Our age runs the danger of replacing them by commentaries and texts. I can only hope that what is written here will turn the reader to the Scriptures. To the extent that this book achieves its purpose, credit is due to many people, chief among them Fr. John Hardon, S.J., and Msgr. George Kelly, whose help has been invaluable; Sr. Loretta Josepha Conran, S.C. who read and corrected the original manuscript; my sister Mrs. Robert Creeden and Mrs. Joan McKee who typed the original, and Fr. Joseph Donachie of St. James, Milton, New York, whose hospitality made possible the book's beginnings.

I dedicate this book to my mother and father who first taught me about the Father's Son in word and in the example of a living faith. To the extent that I may have confused by abstractions and theological jargon the simple and vibrant faith they passed on and others fortified, I ask pardon.

INTRODUCTION

The Sources
and Understanding
What They Tell Us

Every theological study about Jesus of Nazareth must, directly or indirectly, refer to His appearance in Roman-controlled Palestine during the reigns of the Roman Caesars Augustus (31 B.C.-14 A.D.) and Tiberius (14-37 A.D.). The historical facts of Jesus' life and work are the foundation upon which Christianity has arisen, and the accuracy of these facts is, in part, the guarantee that Christology is not fable nor the elaboration of pious opinions which arose in early circles of Jesus' credulous followers. Such being the case, it is always important to return to the primary sources from which the historian must draw his information about Jesus. For the sake of convenience, those sources are normally listed as being 1) non-Christian or secular and 2) Christian.

1. Non-Christian Sources of Information About Jesus

If we limit ourselves to the time period previous to the year 125 A.D., the non-Christian references to Jesus are the following:

a. Flavius Josephus (37-c. 100 A.D.). Josephus was a Jew, born in Palestine, where, by his own account, he became a disciple of the Pharisees at the age of nineteen.[1] In 75 A.D. he published in Rome his account of the Jewish-Roman war, in which Josephus himself participated and which terminated with the destruction of Jerusalem in 70 A.D. Around 90-95, Josephus published his *Antiquities of the Jews*, covering the history of his people from creation to the reign of the Roman Emperor Nero. Book XVIII, chapter 3 of this work contains the following passage:

5

Now, there was about this time Jesus, a wise man, if it be lawful to call Him a man, for He was a doer of wonderful works—a teacher of such men as receive the truth with pleasure. He drew over to Him both many of the Jews, and many of the Gentiles. He was (the) Christ; and when Pilate, at the suggestion of the principal men amongst us, had condemned Him to the cross, those that loved Him at first did not forsake Him, for He appeared to them alive again the third day...and the tribe of Christians, so named after Him, are not extinct at this day.[2]

This *Testimonium Flavianum* can probably not be taken at face value. The majority of scholars accept it as being a version of what Josephus actually wrote, but "edited" by the Christian copyists who preserved the copies of Josephus' works.[3] Efforts to reconstruct Josephus' original comments have met with no general agreement.

b. Pliny the Younger (61-62 to c. 114 A.D.). This Roman governor of present-day Northwest Turkey (then Bithynia) from 111-113 has left us, in Letter 96 to the Emperor Trajan, a reference to Christians as practitioners of a "perverse superstition" who "sing hymns to Christ as to a god," and Pliny asks the Emperor what should be done about them.

c. Tacitus (56-c. 117 A.D.), Roman historian, published shortly before his death *The Annals of Imperial Rome*. Writing of the burning of Rome during the reign of Nero (ruled 54-68), Tacitus stated:

...neither human resources, nor imperial munificence, nor appeasement of the gods, eliminated sinister suspicions that the fire had been instigated. To suppress this rumor, Nero fabricated scapegoats—and punished with every refinement the notoriously depraved Christians (as they were popularly called). Their originator, Christ, had been executed in Tiberius' reign by the governor of Judea, Pontius Pilate. But in spite of this temporary setback the deadly superstition had broken out afresh, not only in Judea (where the mischief started) but even in Rome. All degraded and shameful practices collect and flourish in the capital.[4]

d. Gaius Suetonius Tranquillus (69-c. 140 A.D.). Writing of the reign of the Emperor Claudius (ruled 41-54 A.D.), Suetonius noted:

> Because the Jews at Rome caused continuous disturbances at the instigation of Chrestus, he (Claudius) expelled them from the city.[5]

Both Tacitus and Suetonius misspell the name of Christ, referring to Him as *Chrestos,* but no historian doubts that they refer to Jesus.

2. Christian Sources of Information About Jesus

Apart from the books of the New Testament, the earliest Christian sources for a study of Jesus are the letter of Clement of Rome to the Christians at Corinth (95-96 A.D.), the letters of Ignatius of Antioch (107-110 A.D.), and, perhaps, some of the fragmentary non-canonical gospels.[6] In all probability, however, the four canonical Gospels antedate all or most of these writings and thus remain our principal written witnesses to the life and work of Jesus. What evidence we have for the authorship and time of writing of the Gospels is to be gathered from external and internal evidence.

I. EXTERNAL EVIDENCE FOR DATING AND AUTHORSHIP OF THE GOSPELS

In the letter of Clement to Corinth, written about 96 A.D., there are two quotations from the sayings of Jesus *(Clement,* 13, 2-3 and 46, 8) which are found in the Gospels of Matthew and Luke, although Clement's Greek is closer to Luke than to Matthew, but not identical. Whether Clement is actually quoting loosely from the canonical text or is working from a non-canonical collection of the sayings of Jesus cannot be determined. However *Clement* 2, 1 and 59, 2 would appear to be references to Acts 20:35 and 26:18 respectively. While the evidence is too meager to be conclusive, there is at least some indication that the Gospel of Luke and the Acts of the Apostles were known in Rome by 96 A.D.

The letters of Ignatius of Antioch refer on several occasions to matter found only in the Gospel of Matthew. The remark that "a tree is known by its fruits" in Ephesians 14:2 is identical with the Greek of Matthew 12:33, except for the verb (Ignatius has *phaneron;* Matthew has *ginosetai).* The same epistle (19, 2) has a reference to the star of Bethlehem, an incident found only in Matthew 2 of the canonical Gospels. Ignatius' *Epistle to the Magnesians* 9, 2 reflects Matthew 27:52; the *Epistle to Polycarp* 2, 2 appears to be a citation of Matthew 10:16; the *Epistle to Smyrna* 6, 2 cites Matthew 19:12. In the epistles of Ignatius there are found as well, several possible references to the Gospel of Luke, the Acts of the Apostles, and to the Gospel of John (cf., esp., *Philadelphia* 2 and 7).

The first reference to the Gospel of Mark is probably found in the *Letter of St. Polycarp to the Philippians* (5, 2), along with references or citations of the other three Gospels and the Acts of the Apostles. Some would date Polycarp's letter around 110, shortly after his visit with Ignatius of Antioch, but this date is disputed on internal evidence. It is surely to be dated before 155.

The evidence offered by the *Didache* is consistent with what has already been cited. There is no clear reference to John nor Mark, but Matthew and Luke are amply cited. The dating of the *Didache* is disputed, running anywhere from 40 to 150 A.D., although parts of it, at least, are most certainly a good deal older than the later date.

An early testimony to the existence of the Gospels according to Matthew and Mark is found in the extracts of a work of Papias of Hierapolis, preserved in the *Ecclesiastical History* of Eusebius (c. 325 A.D.). Papias wrote that he had learned from the "Presbyter John" that Mark composed a Gospel based on Peter's preaching, and that Matthew had collected the sayings *(logia)* of Jesus in the Hebrew language.[7] By all the evidence we possess, Papias was a contemporary of Ignatius of Antioch, Clement of Rome and Polycarp of Smyrna. He wrote his remarks on Mark and Matthew at some indeterminate date between 100 and 135 A.D. St. Irenaeus, writing about 190, claimed that Papias had heard John the Apostle-Evangelist (cf. *Adversus Haereses,* V, 33); Eusebius later denied this, claiming that the Presbyter John mentioned by Papias was a person other than John the Apostle. The difference in view continues unresolved to our own day.[8] Likewise disputed is whether Papias' reference to the sayings of the Lord collected by Matthew constituted a Gospel.

St. Irenaeus of Lyons, writing his *Adversus Haereses* around 190, had the following to say about the Gospels.

> Matthew published a Gospel among the Hebrews in their own language, while Peter and Paul were preaching at Rome and establishing the Church. When they died, Mark, the disciple and interpreter of Peter, also passed down to us in writing what Peter had preached. Also, Luke, the disciple of Paul, wrote in a book the Gospel as Paul preached it. Later, John published a Gospel while he was living at Ephesus in Asia.[9]

The source or sources for Irenaeus' information are unknown. We do know from his own testimony that, as a youth, he had listened to Polycarp who, Irenaeus claims, had known John the Apostle and others who had known the Lord.[10] We know, too, that Irenaeus was familiar with the writings of Papias, the contemporary of Polycarp. It is from Irenaeus that we get the traditional ordering of the four Gospels: Matthew, Mark, Luke, John. He clearly mentions Matthew as the first written and John as the last. The chronological relation between Mark and Luke is imprecise, although Irenaeus seems to indicate that Mark preceded Luke. This indication was soon contradicted by Clement of Alexandria who, writing between 190-210, flatly stated that the "Gospels which contain the genealogies were the first written."[11] Clement cites the "oldest presbyters" as his source for this information.

To summarize the external evidence on dating and authorship up to the end of the second century:

1) It supports what today is a universally accepted conclusion, viz., that the four canonical Gospels were extant by around 100 A.D.

2) Attribution of authorship for the four Gospels is found, for Matthew and Mark, by 110-130 in Papias, and for all four Gospels by the end of the century in Irenaeus, Clement and Tatian, etc. By that time, the Matthew referred to is our present Greek-language Gospel, not the Hebrew sayings of Papias.

3) Citations from or references to matter found only in the Gospel of Mark are later and less frequent than similar references to the other three Gospels.

4) Irenaeus and Clement of Alexandria, and perhaps Papias, indicate that Matthew was the first written Gospel and John the last. There is disagreement on the order of Mark and Luke.

The external evidence suffers limitations. The dates for the writing of Clement to Corinth, and of Ignatius' seven letters, while not seriously disputed, are still imprecise. The dates for Polycarp and Papias are certain only within a period of thirty years. Furthermore, the sources for the information given by Papias, Irenaeus and Clement of Alexandria are not directly accessible, and are much disputed. Nonetheless, some of their most probable sources were immediate disciples and hearers of the Apostles themselves. Papias claims this to be such; Irenaeus implies it through his link with the Apostle John through Polycarp. Indeed, Papias' chief source for what he says about the Gospels may have been the Apostle John himself.

II. INTERNAL EVIDENCE FOR DATING AND AUTHORSHIP OF THE GOSPELS

The external evidence for dating and authorship carries little weight among many modern exegetes of the New Testament. One recent study of Matthew's Gospel brushes the external evidence aside as "nothing more than second century guesses."[12] What is then substituted, regrettably, appears to be little more than twentieth century guesses, supposedly drawn from indications contained within the Gospels themselves.

Now, internal evidence is an important tool for the literary and historical sciences. An author's style, his use of idiom, the items he stresses or underplays, his familiarity with the milieu he is describing, his use of sources (if any), the nature of his audience (if it can be discerned), comparisons made with other works he has produced or with other literature of the same period, etc.—all of these and many more are factors which must be utilized by the literary analyst or historian. Used well, they are invaluable. Many a documentary fraud has been unmasked by a critical use of the argument from internal evidence.

On the other hand, such argumentation from internal evidence is notoriously liable to manipulation and error. In the hands of some, internal "evidence" becomes merely a tool to buttress a thesis held on grounds other than evidentiary. The real evidence is juggled so that the "what it must have really meant" replaces the evidentiary fact itself. Charles Dickens has given us a satirical use of such argumentation when he set out to "demonstrate" that the great anti-hero of English literature and history, Guy Fawkes, was actually a member of the Chuzzlewit family.

> There was, within a few years, in the possession of a highly respectable and in every way credible and unimpeachable member of the Chuzzlewit family (for his bitterest enemy never dared to hint at his being otherwise than a wealthy man), a dark lantern of undoubted antiquity; rendered still more interesting by being, in shape and pattern, extremely like such as are in use at the present day. Now this gentleman, since deceased, was at all times ready to make oath, and did again and again set forth upon his solemn asseveration, that he had frequently heard his grandmother say, when contemplating this venerable relic, 'Aye, aye! This was carried by my fourth son on the fifth of November, when he was a Guy Fawkes.' These remarkable words wrought (as well they might) a strong impression on his mind, and he was in the habit of repeating them very often. The just interpretation which they bear, and the conclusion to which they lead, are triumphant and irresistible. The old lady, naturally strong-minded, was nevertheless frail and fading; she was notoriously subject to that confusion of ideas, or, to say the least, of speech, to which age and garrulity are liable. The slight, the very slight, confusion apparent in these expressions is manifest, and is ludicrously easy of correction. 'Aye, aye!' quoth she, and it will be observed that no emendation whatever is necessary to be made in these two initiative remarks. 'Aye, aye! This lantern was carried by my forefather'—not fourth son, which is preposterous—'on the fifth of November. And *he* was Guy Fawkes.' Here we have a remark at once consistent, clear, natural, and in strict accord-

ance with the character of the speaker. Indeed the anecdote is so plainly susceptible of this meaning, and no other, that it would be hardly worth recording in its original state, were it not a proof of what may be (and very often is) effected not only in historical prose but in imaginative poetry, by the exercise of a little ingenious labor on the part of a commentator.[13]

Since the grandmother was now dead and unable to be directly consulted, the statement, remembered and reported by the second generation after her, is re-worded to make it consistent with what she *must* have meant, i.e., with what the author thinks she *should* have said. Dickens' example is so patently unscholarly as to be facetious—and so he intends it. But, as in so much of his caricature, he is not far wide of the mark in respect to the reality at which he pokes fun. Witness what literary criticism has done at times to Shakespeare. Working from internal "evidence" in his plays and sonnets, and from a poverty of evidence in respect to Shakespeare's life, his works have been shown to have been authored by Christopher Marlowe and others, despite the widespread attribution of the works to Shakespeare himself within a century and a half of his death. Such "criticism" is today considered unsound and tendentious, but even yet books on Shakespeare use the argument from internal evidence to confound previous works using the same form of argumentation, a fascinating example of which can be found in R. Giroux's work, *The Book Known as Q.*[14] A sizeable volume could be written with what critics have thought Jesus of Nazareth (for whose life there is more substantial evidence than is the case for William Shakespeare) *must* have said or meant, after one has "scientifically examined" what the "second generation" of Christians claimed He actually said.

In connection with the difficulties involved in argumentation from internal evidence, the following example may prove informative. Imagine this quotation standing alone, i.e., with no external evidence available to situate or interpret it.

There are at the present time two great nations in the world, which started from different points, but seem to tend towards the same end. I allude to the Russians and the Americans. Both of them have grown up unnoticed; and while the attention of mankind was directed elsewhere, they have suddenly placed themselves in the front rank among the nations, and the world learned their existence and their greatness at almost the same time.

All other nations seem to have nearly reached their natural limits, and they have only to maintain their power; but these are still in the act of growth. All the others have stopped, or continue to advance with extreme difficulty; these alone are proceeding with ease and celerity along a path to which no limit can be perceived. The American struggles against the obstacles that nature opposes to him; the adversaries of the Russian are men. The former combats the wilderness and the savage life; the latter, civilization with all its new arms. The conquests of the American are therefore gained by the plowshare; those of the Russian by the sword. The Anglo-American relies upon personal interest to accomplish his ends and gives free scope to the unguided strength and common sense of the people; the Russian centers all the authority of society in a single arm. The principal instrument of the former is freedom; of the latter, servitude. Their starting point is different and their courses are not the same; yet each of them seems marked out by the will of heaven to sway the destinies of half the globe.

What can be said of the author of this piece and of its date of writing, using internal evidence? To begin with, it can be said that the piece reflects the "Cold War" mentality of the post-World War II era in Soviet-American relations. The use of the word "Russia" is not counter-indicative of this since, in common parlance, the Soviet Union continued to be called Russia long after the Communist Revolution. The author's tone is anti-Russian. This can be seen from the qualities he attributes to the two nations; liberty to the U.S.; centralism and servitude to the Soviet Union. It is possible that a rural audience is intended, since the author stresses not the industrial might of the United States, but its agricultural prowess, even using the archaic "plowshare" to romanticize and exalt. More likely, however, the agricultural imagery—as well as references to the wilderness and savage life, etc.—is simply an appeal to the "Frontier Myth" or motif so popular with Americans throughout their history, even into the 1960's and 70's with their cry for the "New Frontier." Since the author refers to "Anglo-Americans," he wrote before the Civil Rights movement of the late 60's. In short, the author was an American of Anglo-Saxon descent, writing political propaganda during the administrations of the American Presidents Kennedy or Johnson.

The analysis could be extended to the point of tedium, each point, however, buttressing the same final conclusion. On the other hand, at least two alternate arguments are possible, demonstrating different conclusions. In fact, of course, the piece being analyzed is semi-prophetic, written by a Frenchman in the 19th century. It is a 1960 translation of Alexis de Tocqueville's classic *Democracy in America*, published in 1835 in France.[15]

If we now look at some of the efforts to determine authorship and dating of the Gospels from internal evidence, we can witness many of the same difficulties evident in identifying the piece from de Tocqueville. Let us take, as example, the Gospel of Matthew. Of that work, the following are some of the more frequently used arguments from internal evidence for authorship and dating.

1. "A time of origin after 70 is surely to be inferred from the supplement to the parable of the wedding feast (22:7): 'Then the king became angry and sent his officer and condemned those murderers and burned their city.' Here obviously the destruction of Jerusalem is alluded to."[16]

What strikes one is the degree of certitude expressed: "surely" and "obviously." That certitude is based on the assumption that Matthew "expanded" the parable, since the reference to the destruction of the city is not found in the parallel text in Luke 14:15-24. The assumption, however, is gratuitous. It can as well be assumed that Luke abbreviated the parable as that Matthew enlarged it.

Another recent author, rejecting the notion that Matthew 22:7 reflects a post-70 date, writes:

> The burning of the city illustrates Matthew's habit of alluding to the O.T. Here the allusion is to Isaiah 5:24-25.... We know that Matthew was thinking about the O.T. passage, for he brought the parable closer to the text of Isaiah. The prophet's parable leads to a threat against Jerusalem that climaxes in 'fire' and 'flames' for they have rejected the law of the Lord

(cf. Matthew's preoccupation with the law).... On this account the anger (cf. the king's anger in Mt. 22:7a) has burned against his people...and their corpses (cf. the destruction of the murderers in Mt. 22:7b) were like refuse in the middle of the streets (cf. 'the outlets of the streets' in Mt. 22:9). We have no need then to suppose that Matthew is retrospecting the destruction of Jerusalem in A.D. 70.[17]

Yet another author notes that there is "small justification" for saying that Matthew 22:7 reflects a post-70 retrospective. "It is well to remember that the Zealots were founded shortly after 8 A.D. There is no reason to deny to Jesus in the explosive situation of the second quarter of the first century the insights of an Isaiah or a Jeremiah in like circumstances."[18]

Any certitude about which of these various opinions is correct can only be subjective since each of the explanations is possible, if not equally probable. In fact, Matthew 22:7 cannot truly help to establish the time of the Gospel's writing.[19]

2. A further effort at dating from internal evidence is produced by citing the fierce polemic against the Pharisees which is found in Matthew 23. It is noted that, after 70 A.D., Pharisaic Judaism purged itself of heretics and introduced into synagogue worship a prayer against Christians and other heretics. This happened, it is thought, around 85 A.D., and thus the strong polemic in Matthew would indicate the Christian-Jewish conflict at or after that date.[20]

The difficulties with this bit of evidence are varied. Luke in Acts 5—12 records the antipathy of the Jewish leaders toward the followers of Jesus in the late 30's and 40's, even to the stoning of Stephen and the death of James, the brother of John (c. 42 A.D.). Flavius Josephus records the following:

Ananus (the high priest)...assembled the Sanhedrin of judges, and brought before them the brother of Jesus, who was called Christ, whose name was James; and...he delivered them to be stoned.[21]

The death of James, brother of the Lord, took place in the early 60's. Paul's epistles, too, are replete with a form of polemic that directly or indirectly struck at the Pharisees. To presume, therefore, that the harsh words in Matthew 23 reflect a late first century Jewish-Christian conflict is to overlook much evidence leading to other conclusions.[22] Indeed, ultimately Jesus' death itself cannot be adequately explained without a marked antagonism between Himself and the leaders of the Jewish religion. There is, then, no need to look to a date in the 80's to explain the polemic found in Matthew.

3. More evidence for the (late) dating of Matthew is found "in his reworking of Mark" (which) "shows so clear a development of community relationships and theological reflection (e.g., 18:15 and 28:19) that a date of writing shortly after Mark seems less likely than a time between 80 and 100."[23]

Two presumptions are to be noted in this assertion: a) that the chronological and literary relationship between Matthew and Mark is an established datum and b) that theological "advances" are linear. In fact, the first presumption (a) is disputed, as we shall see below; the second (b) is an *a priori* construct. Were it true, Paul's Christology should be later than Mark's, which, of course, it is not.

4. Concerning authorship of the first Gospel by the Apostle Matthew, the most frequent reason given for a negative response is that it is inconceivable that an eyewitness (Matthew-Levi) should rely as he does on a non-eyewitness, Mark.[24]

A *priori* as it is in its reasoning, and presuming, as it does, the dependence of Matthew on Mark, the statement would have weight, if it could be determined:

a) that Mark is, in fact, prior to Matthew, and that Matthew relied on Mark, and

b) that the Gospel of Mark does not reflect Peter's catechesis which, given Peter's role, could be considered even by a fellow Apostle to be normative, at least as outline. The assertion also seems to presume that Matthew's Gospel is merely a "re-hash" of Mark, which it most certainly is not.

Such considerations about authorship and dating from internal evidence could be extended, and then applied to the other Gospels. In like manner, the counter-arguments, defending authorship by the Apostle Matthew at a date prior to A.D. 70 could be mustered. In all cases, however, possible and plausible alternatives and contrary arguments from internal indications and from "authorities" could also be presented. The conclusion from such a study can only be the perhaps unsettling fact that, from internal evidence, no conclusive arguments are to be had concerning the authorship or the dating of the four Gospels. The possibilities exist for various hypotheses, but historical hypotheses—helpful and necessary as they may be at times—are ultimately no substitute for "hard fact."

III. INTERNAL EVIDENCE AND THE INTER-RELATIONSHIP OF THE GOSPELS

The arguments from internal evidence take a different turn when one approaches the question of the relationship among the Gospels. Because of the marked similarities in the order in which events are narrated and in verbal and syntactical harmony among them, discussion on this matter has generally centered on the relationship among Matthew, Mark and Luke. Numerous hypotheses have been advanced to explain this relationship, but, of the many, four have predominated.

1. The Traditional or "Augustinian" View. This theory, dominant until the eighteenth century, held for the priority of Matthew. The Gospel of Mark, written in Rome, would have used Matthew, thereby producing a kind of catechetical synopsis of the earlier Gospel, while elaborating some things which rested on the eyewitness testimony of Peter. Luke would have known and used both previous works. John, in his Gospel, would have known all previous three works.

2. The Griesbach Hypothesis. In the middle of the eighteenth century, Henry Owen in England [25] and Johann Griesbach at the University of Jena in Germany put forth the idea that the Gospel of Mark was the third written of the Gospels, having used Matthew and Luke as sources. Griesbach himself produced the first of the modern Synopses of the Gospels.

3. The Two-Source Theory. This hypothesis owes its origin to Heinrich Holtzmann in Germany in 1863, but has been developed and modified in various ways, especially by B.H. Streeter in his 1924 work *The Four Gospels*. As developed, the Two-Source Theory replaced the earlier Griesbach Theory and has been, for most of the present century, the most generally used hypothesis to resolve the "Synoptic Problem."

Briefly put, the Two-Source Hypothesis holds that Mark is the first written of our canonical Gospels, and was used as a source by our present Gospels of Matthew and Luke. As a source, it was supplemented by another, the so-called Q (from the German *Quelle*, source). This Q would represent those things, mostly sayings of the Lord, common to Matthew and Luke and not found in Mark. In addition to Mark and Q, both Matthew and Luke would have had other sources—whether oral or written or both is disputed—which would explain in part those items peculiar to each of those Gospels.

4. Multiple Source Theories. These theories, too numerous and too complicated to be treated in detail, attempt to allow greater room for a continuing oral tradition, for a process of textual harmonization of the Synoptics by copyists of the manuscripts, and for the role of primitive Aramaic collections of sayings and deeds of Jesus. Most of these theories, however, are at one with the various modifications of the Two-Source Theory in maintaining the priority of Mark among the canonical Gospels.

Having long held the leading place among the various hypotheses, the Two-Source Theory, with its priority of Mark and postulation of Q, is presently under challenge. In the 1950's a strong case was made in defense of the traditional or "Augustinian" approach.[26] In the 1960's and 70's, significant efforts were put forth to re-animate the Griesbach Hypothesis,[27] and, in 1981, a new synopsis of the Gospels was published to support the Griesbach Hypothesis.[28]

An even more radical break with previous theories was made in a cogently argued work of John M. Rist in 1978.[29] Rist maintains that Matthew and Mark are independent works based on relatively fixed oral (and, perhaps, some written) traditions. After detailed analysis of the Greek of many of the parallel texts in the two Gospels, Rist concludes that:

> There is no evidence in the texts themselves which necessitates literary dependence of Mark on Matthew or of Matthew on Mark; and there is no evidence whatever in the early tradition to indicate that such dependence was ever thought to have existed.[30]

> The theory that Mark is the source of Matthew is a scholarly thesis with ideological overtones....[31]

My own view, therefore, is that Matthew and Mark grew up independently on the basis of a similar tradition. I should prefer to think that both of them (and Luke too) came into existence before A. D. 70, though my thesis does not depend on that.[32]

The challenge to Marcan priority has not gone unanswered, although whether it has been satisfactorily answered is moot.[33] At the present time, the discussion has taken on certain aspects of the Banezian-Molinist dispute in the 17th century concerning grace and free will in the mystery of predestination. There is an unhelpful amount of polemic, and each side is more adept at demonstrating the flaws in the opposing thesis than in demonstrating convincingly the adequacy of one's own position. The intractable nature of the problem is now admitted even by some of the adherents of the modified Two-Source Theory. In the introduction to his commentary on Luke, Joseph Fitzmyer has written:

> The relation of the Lucan Gospel to the Marcan and Matthean Gospels is part of the Synoptic problem—a problem that has thus far failed to find a fully satisfying solution. The main reason for this failure is the absence of adequate data for judgment about it.[34]

Although he grants the fact of there being no "fully satisfying solution" to the problem and admits its "practical insolubility," Fitzmyer, nevertheless, adopts a modified Two-Source Theory for his own exegesis, and, in addition to his own published defense of that theory, notes "one last extrinsic consideration" in its favor.

> Given the practical insolubility of the Synoptic problem, the modified Two-Source Theory has at least led to all sorts of advances in Gospel interpretation and has pragmatically established its utility.... For it has been the basis of Form-Criticism, Redaction-Criticism, and Composition-Criticism; and even granting that the connection between the Two-Source Theory and these advances in Gospel interpretation is not organic or necessary (because of any organic link), it is a matter of historical fact that they were born of studies conducted along the lines of this theory.[35]

Fitzmyer is not alone in continuing to use the modified Two-Source Theory as a starting point for his exegesis. The usual Catholic commentary in the United States today follows the same procedure. This approach is not without inherent difficulties from an historical and critical point of view—difficulties quite apart from that of canonizing Mark and the hypothetical Q as interpretative keys for Matthew and Luke.

There is an axiom of logic which states that a conclusion cannot be stronger than its premises. If the premises are uncertain or questionable, then the conclusion—to the extent that it is dependent on those premises—must also be regarded as uncertain or questionable. The axiom is valid for all historical-critical examination of a biblical text, and, when properly applied, will impose a certain humility on the theologian and exegete. Failure to respect the truth of the axiom results in a widely noted phenomenon: conclusions, markedly different or even contradictory to traditional Christian views or dogmas, are propounded as certain and claim the support of the "historical-critical" method of New Testament exegesis, whereas, in fact, the conclusions are dependent on hypotheses or theories which are taken as postulates no longer in need of critical re-examination. The lack of such critical re-examination has led to the charge that the "historical-critical method" has become, in practice, mere "dogmatic positivism"—and that charge from a man who uses the method carefully himself.[36]

Apart from the Synoptic Problem and the questions of authorship and dating, there are other premises of some forms of historical-critical exegesis which merit a caveat as part of an effort to make the method both more historical and more critical. To list only the more obvious:

1. There appears to be a presumption on the part of some authors that a "kerygmatic" or creedal proclamation chronologically precedes narrative, and thereby provides one with a more primitive stratum of tradition. Such a presumption must be seen to be no more than that, viz., a presumption, and one in need of demonstration. In fact, it would seem to run counter to all normal experience wherein the synoptic statement (which is what a "kerygmatic" or creedal formula is) is generally a summary in short form of a longer verbal or written narrative.[37]

2. A presumption closely allied to the previous one is that the more primitive an account is so it will be either shorter, or more "sober," or more vivid in descriptive detail, or less laden with aspects of the "miraculous" and "legendary." None of these conclusions is necessarily true as any student of literature knows. Nevertheless, one or another such statement is frequently used as a criterion to determine the relative age of a New Testament narrative (cf. Part II, note 54 below).

3. One must also beware of mixing literary and historical criteria of judgment. An important aspect of modern scriptural studies has been the awareness that various types or genera of literature are found throughout the Bible, and that an understanding of the literary type is important for the correct evaluation of what the biblical author is saying. However, it must also be noted that having determined the structure, the literary genus, and even the origins of a biblical statement does not in itself tell us anything about the historical truth of the statement, unless the literary genus is certainly parabolic or fictional. Thus, for example, the determination that the Annunciation account in Luke 1 is structurally or literarily of a pattern with other such types, or that Matthew's account of the stationing of the guards at the tomb of Jesus (Mt. 27:62 and 28:11) has an apologetic intent, etc., are matters touching upon literary structure, purpose, or genus. The question about historicity, however, must rest on other or additional material and criteria. An apologetic piece of literature does not necessarily contain historical mis-statement, nor does a similarity of literary pattern or structure necessitate the same historical judgment on the details contained in the similar types.[38]

4. There is also need to bear in mind the dangers involved in building an argument from what an author does not say—the famous argument from silence. If it can be demonstrated that what is not said should or had to be said in a given context, the argument is not without value. However, given the various possible reasons why something that *might* have been said is not said, such demonstration is difficult to produce. Normally, all that the silence of an author on a particular matter can be claimed, with certitude, to do is to remove that author as a corroborative witness to the point under discussion.

5. Caution must be exercised in any attempt to reconstruct the "life situation" of the early Church from a Gospel text, or in efforts to interpret a Gospel text by the presumed life situation of that same early Church.[39] At times, it is true, a piece of literature does reveal much of the milieu in which it was written. In turn, knowledge of that milieu can be placed at the service of those who wish to understand the literary work better. There are limits to the process, however, as experience proves. One may take as a case in point the great work of J.R.R. Tolkien, *The Lord of the Rings*, first published in the 1950's. As the popularity and influence of the work grew, it became fashionable among some reviewers to see in it reflections of the Second World War, the atomic bomb, and the economic situation of post-war England. In a foreword to the second edition in 1965, Tolkien explicitly repudiated such efforts to recreate the milieu from which his work developed. In doing so, he expresses a truth which should be well-remembered by all who are engaged in the business of literary or historical criticism which bases itself almost exclusively on internal indications.

An author cannot of course remain wholly unaffected by his experience, but the ways in which a story-germ uses the soil of experience are extremely complex, and attempts to define the process are at best guesses from evidence that is inadequate and ambiguous.[40]

Failures by theologians and exegetes to recognize the inadequacies and ambiguities in argumentation from internal evidence alone have led to frequent—and sometimes sharp—criticism of much current biblical exegesis. Such criticism should not be construed as negating the value of historical and literary criticism based on internal evidence, nor as denying the service rendered to biblical criticism by various hypotheses. What such criticism does call for is the recognition of the *tentative nature* of many of the conclusions drawn from this type of argumentation.

...Agnosticism is, in a sense, what I am preaching. I do not wish to reduce the sceptical element in your minds. I am only suggesting that it need not be reserved exclusively for the New Testament and the Creeds. Try doubting something else.[41]

That advice of C.S. Lewis to a group of theologians certainly merits attention: question not only your sources, but also your own methods of inquiry, and the certainty of your postulates.

THE ROLE OF THE CHURCH IN UNDERSTANDING THE SOURCES

A. The Church as External Evidence

No effort to understand the four Gospels and the New Testament in general can succeed unless one takes into account the Community which has always claimed those works as its own. That Community, the Church, holds as its exclusive right the authentic and authoritative interpretation of the written Gospel. Such a claim is binding on the Catholic exegetes and theologians as part of their Faith. In itself, however, that claim cannot enter into a study of the Gospel texts which is merely a critical historical and literary examination. On that level, the Church's right to be heard is of a different kind, namely that of external evidence or witness. This role can perhaps be illustrated by an analogy.

The last three decades of the 19th century witnessed, in England, the writing of the musical productions of Sir William Gilbert and Sir Arthur Sullivan. These works have become part of the cultural heritage of the English-speaking world and are performed into our own day even in media for which they were not originally written, movies and television. Over the last ninety years, countless musicians, directors, producers and actors have presented, interpreted and re-interpreted the musical scores and text of Gilbert and Sullivan. Like every written word and musical score, the works are susceptible of various understandings and adaptations. Someone approaching them for the first time can take them as they appear, or update them, or attempt to present them as faithfully close to the original as possible. If one chooses the last alternative, the inevitable question is: how does one know what the original was like? What kind of staging, what kind of costumes, what tempo to the music, what general sense of what the texts meant were manifested at the initial performances? Fortunately, until our own day, these questions could be answered because there was an unbroken tradition of not only text and score, but performance as well. Richard D'Oyly Carte had produced and directed the vast majority of the originals in collaboration with the authors themselves. He founded a company for the performance of the plays, the directorship of that company passing to his children and grandchildren, and the execution of the various roles passing from master performer to apprentice or understudy. Without doubt, there were changes and modifications, nuances of interpretation, shifts in emphasis, accommodations, etc. Nonetheless, the Savoyards (the D'Oyly Carte Company) were the recognized masters of the authentic Gilbert and Sullivan. Efforts to get behind the texts and scores in order to re-create the originals were always judged against the tradition of the Savoyards. The Savoyard tradition, not in detail but in substance, was the normative understanding of the original texts. The Savoyard tradition became an "external source" (i.e., a source apart from the texts themselves) for a proper understanding of Gilbert and Sullivan.

Although the analogy will limp, what was true of the Savoyards *vis à vis* Gilbert and Sullivan is true of the Church *vis à vis* the New Testament texts. With a remarkable consistency, the Church has manifested in "performance" a *global sense* of what the original works meant to say. Adjustments, re-readings, nuances and even conflicting interpretations of various parts or sections of the Gospel texts have been tolerated or even accepted and integrated. Indeed, the variety of interpretation of the New Testament by the Fathers, the Scholastics and present-day exegetes which the Church has tolerated is astounding. But, equally astounding, is the consistency with which the entire ensemble has been interpreted, and divergent views rejected. From her first conflict with Marcion who wanted his version of Luke to be the normative Gospel, through the controversy with Luther over Paul's grace and James' works, and into our own century, the Church has always rejected a "canon within a canon," as well as any effort to have one New Testament work contradict another on matters of substance. (One wonders whether efforts to do for Mark, although for different reasons, what Marcion desired for Luke are not fated ultimately to meet the same rejection.) From her conflict with the Gnostics who de-historicized the Incarnation to the conflict with the de-mythologizers who would do the same, the Church has defended the historical reality of the Gospel message. When some claimed that the Gospels do not indicate that Jesus is God, the Church responded that they do indeed. The examples could be multiplied at length. The point, however, is simply this: there exists, in an on-going Community, a particular and consistent understanding *in globo* of what the Gospels were written to say. Even without claiming normative value for that understanding, it must be seen as persisting as a datum for anyone who wishes to interpret the texts. Failure to weigh that datum would be foolish from a point of view of methodology. Of course, the assessment made of the datum will vary with the researcher. Consistency of interpretation does not guarantee accuracy of interpretation. From a historico-critical point of view, the Church's understanding of the Gospels is one datum among others, but a datum not to be passed over or dismissed out of hand. As a datum it has, moreover, the advantage of its consistency in the face of time and challenges, and of being no mere academic understanding but one that has motivated the lives of men, women and entire civilizations. It has understood, to take but one example, as historically accurate and literally binding Jesus' institution of the Eucharistic sacrifice-meal, and has defended that interpretation tenaciously. "Reason" has challenged that understanding, "logic" denied it, but men and women have died for it, and the Church has let nations leave her fold rather than change her understanding. And such reactions have not been the enthusiasms of a sect of forty years or a community of four hundred years, but rather the recognizable pattern of a major sociological world structure for almost two millennia. And all this because of the conviction that Jesus of Nazareth, God made man, had done and taught this matter during His course of time walking the earth. To reread the text in our own time and conclude (as some have) that, in fact, not Jesus Himself but rather some of His early followers were responsible for the Eucharist is certainly an option, a working-hypothesis, but surely not one tested as the interpretation it seeks to replace. In fact, there is a preponderance of historical probability in favor of the interpretation which has with consistency withstood the challenges of time and human opposition.

B. The Church as Authoritative Interpreter

The role of the Church is not limited to that of being a historical witness or external source for the critical historian or literary analyst. For the Catholic, she is also the "living gospel for all men to hear" (Preface for Apostles II). It is the life of the Church—her Tradition, her history, her preaching, the lives of her saints—which proclaims her Lord to the world and renders Him present, particularly through the Eucharist. As animated by the Spirit of Christ, the Church has always maintained that her knowledge of the Lord is not limited to the written word of the Scriptures. The Second Vatican Council taught this when speaking of the life of the Church and her Sacred Tradition:

> ...The Church does not draw her certitude about all that has been revealed from Sacred Scripture alone. As a result, both (Scripture and Tradition) must be received and venerated with an equal sense of piety and reverence.[42]

The Council was able to make this statement because there exists a *relative*, existential priority of the Church's life and Tradition over Sacred Scripture.

a) There is a historical priority. The Message of Christ is given, received and passed on as lived and preached and believed before it is ever written down.[43] The Scripture flows from life and expresses it, and not merely in the sense that all literature flows from a life situation of some sort. Scripture does so in a privileged sense. By the inspiration of the Holy Spirit, Scripture is guaranteed as adequately (and, perhaps in some sense, even comprehensively) expressing the Tradition. As privileged expression of the life and message, Scripture becomes, in a real sense, judge of future life and development, since growth, if it is to be organic, must occur in harmony with the origins of life. In this case the origin is Christ Himself and His Spirit.

But the position of Scripture as judge is not absolute. Scripture is the Church's norm, but Scripture only *lives* within the Church

and to the extent that it, through the Church, is animated by the
Spirit of Christ. Such is the meaning of the following remarks by
Karl Rahner.

> The teaching of the Church is inherent in the Church, and it
> may seem to authenticate itself by the very fact that it shares in
> the nature and spirit of the Church, in which humility and
> freedom are combined. But this is true only because this
> teaching is precisely an integral element in the Church herself,
> who can bear witness to herself because she has received her
> mission from Christ. Only in virtue of this fact is scripture the
> word which can command obedience. I cannot decide to check
> the Church's credentials, as it were, by taking scripture away
> from her...and by invoking it against her as a criterion apart. It
> is *she* who submits herself to the guidance of scripture.... If I
> wanted to take scripture alone as the sole concrete embodi-
> ment of the work of God which commands my allegiance, then,
> whether I realized it or not, only two alternatives would be
> open to me: either I would be entering into dialogue with a
> book which as such was incapable of defending itself against my
> wrong ideas or of offering any resistance to my false interpreta-
> tions, and in relation to which I must in the nature of things
> have the upper hand, or (the second alternative) I would have
> to have recourse to the Spirit of the Lord which gives this book
> its life and defends it. But in that case, once more, the question
> would have to be raised as to whether in the last analysis it was
> the book upon which the Spirit had descended and not rather
> the men whom that Spirit had sent to proclaim his message and
> so, amongst other things, to attest *a priori* to the fact that what
> they wrote had come from the Spirit himself. And when the
> question is put in this form as to whether the inspiration of the
> Spirit bears in the first instance upon the book or upon the men
> sent by that Spirit, the answer can only be: upon the men.

> The conclusion of all this is that he is truly a believer who
> hearkens to the Church and believes in the Church.[44]

b) From the above it can be seen that there is also a certain
metaphysical or existential priority of Tradition as regards Scripture. If one defines Tradition as the "true being and faith of the
Church,"[45] Scripture constitutes an absolutely essential part of that

being, but not all of it. It is the living Church that guarantees and authenticates Scripture, preserving and interpreting it. The establishment of the Canon of Scripture is clear enough evidence of this fact.

In light of these points, it follows that Scripture is not subject rightly to alien interpretation. Scripture flows from the Church, it forms part of the Church's Tradition, it lives because the Church lives. Indeed, the Church has expressed her life and faith in the Scriptures, much as an individual expresses himself in his words or actions. The Church knows herself progressively, of course, and under the direction of the Spirit. Moreover, in that progressive self-awareness, the Church is also ever more aware of her faith as expressed in Scripture. She reflects upon her own life and history and interprets them, including the Scriptural aspect of that life and faith. Recognizing the Scriptures as elements of her own life, the Church, in interpreting Scripture, is, in a sense, declaring, "This is what I (the Church) have written, and this is what I mean and meant then." In this way, the question about the veracity of the Scriptures comes ultimately to be, by necessity, the question about the Church's own veracity.

If one keeps in mind the Church's two-fold role as historical external source for information and as authoritative interpreter of Scripture for the Catholic believer, the Church's own understanding of the New Testament writings can be profitably examined. A brief summary of that understanding has been set forth in the *Dogmatic Constitution on Divine Revelation (Dei Verbum)* of Vatican Council II.

> The Church always and everywhere has held and holds that the four Gospels are of apostolic origin. For those things which the Apostles preached according to the mandate of Christ they themselves and apostolic men afterwards handed on to us in writing, under the inspiration of the Holy Spirit, namely the foundation of faith, the fourfold Gospel according to Matthew, Mark, Luke and John (cf. St. Irenaeus, *Adversus Haereses*, III, 11, 8: *P.G.*, 7, 885).

> Holy Mother Church firmly and most consistently has held and holds that the four Gospels just named, whose historicity she unhesitatingly affirms, faithfully hand on those

things which Jesus, the Son of God, really did and taught for the sake of our eternal salvation, while living among men up until the day He was assumed into heaven (cf. Acts 1:1-2). Indeed, after the ascension of the Lord, the Apostles handed on to their hearers those things which He Himself had said and done, and they did this with that fuller understanding which they enjoyed because they had been instructed by the glorious events of Christ and taught by the light of the Spirit of truth. Moreover the sacred authors wrote the four Gospels, selecting some things from the many handed on by word of mouth or already written, synthesizing some things, or explaining them in view of the conditions of the Churches, and preserving the form of proclamation, always in such a way that they would communicate to us things true and sincere about Jesus. For they wrote with the intention that we might know the 'truth' of those words in which we have been instructed (cf. Lk. 1:2-4), doing this either from their own memory and recollection or from the testimony of those 'who from the first were eyewitnesses and servants of the word.'[46]

Much of the Conciliar text is a synthesis of parts of the Instruction *Sancta Mater Ecclesia*, which was published by the Pontifical Biblical Commission in 1964 and which, in the words of Paul VI, "defends the historical truth of the holy Gospels in particular with a calm and vigorous clarity."[47] Certain aspects of the Council's teaching merit particular consideration:

1. *The four Gospels are of Apostolic origin, written by the "Apostles themselves and Apostolic men."*

This assertion has the unanimous support of Christian tradition and of all the external evidence presently available to the historian. Nevertheless, a few bishops at Vatican II were unhappy with the statement. They wanted it to say that the Gospels were written by the "Apostles *or* Apostolic men," instead of "*and* Apostolic men." This suggested change would have had the advantage, it was said, of leaving open the discussion about the actual authorship of Matthew and John. The suggestion was not adopted.[48]

2. *The Church recognizes that there are "sources" for the present Gospel texts.*

These sources are referred to as oral tradition or matters "already written down." The statement is circumspect, a witness to the fact that we no longer have direct access to such sources.

The Instruction *Sancta Mater Ecclesia* and the conciliar text recognize three stages of the Gospel tradition: a) the work and teaching of Jesus Himself, b) the preaching and catechesis of the Apostles, and c) the four written Gospels. The chronological relationship between stages (b) and (c) is imprecise, although, in some cases, it seems that the Council was saying that they over-lapped. This can be seen from the fact, noted in no. 1 above, that the Apostles themselves wrote Gospels, and by the subsequent assertion that the Gospel authors "drew from their own memory and recollection or from the teaching of those who were eyewitnesses." The point here is that the Apostles could draw from their own recollections in order to write. In that case, a chronological overlapping of stages (b) and (c) is evident. The assertion frequently made on the basis of argumentation from internal "evidence" that all four Gospels are the work of "second generation" Christians finds no support in what available external evidence indicates, nor in the teaching of Vatican Council II.

3. *The Gospels are no mere chronological recounting of the life of Jesus of Nazareth.*

The Evangelists were able to "select, synthesize and explain" those things which they drew from their own memory and recollection or from the testimony of others. In doing this they exercised considerable freedom, as any careful reading of the four Gospels makes evident. Frequently enough, words and deeds of Jesus were placed by the Evangelists in mutually variant contexts, while the chronological data is often only generic and sometimes purely literary.

The reasons why any author selects and arranges his material the way he does are many, sometimes conscious and deliberate, sometimes indeliberate and unconscious. The indeliberate and unconscious element is one to be remembered in the case of an interpreter's tendency to read too much into real or presumed redactional arrangement of source material. Nevertheless, an author's conscious purpose can truly be said to dictate—at least in

general—his use of material. In the case of the Gospels, Luke and
John make their purposes explicit:

> ...it seemed good also to me to write an orderly account—so that
> you might know the certainty of the things you have been
> taught (Lk. 1:4).

> These are written that you may believe that Jesus is the Christ,
> the Son of God, and that by believing you may have life in his
> name (Jn. 20:31).

These Gospels, then, are written to convince and, through
conviction, to promote faith. The implicit purposes of Mark and
Matthew are the same, and the Church recognizes this when she
notes that the Gospels "always preserve the form of proclamation."
The Gospels, unlike some (but not all) narrative history, were
written to beget conviction, not just record events. That effort to
convince and to promote faith moved the writers to arrange their
work in the manner they thought best suited to achieve their
purposes. It was those same purposes which caused them "to
explain some things in view of the conditions of the Churches."

The selecting, synthesizing and explicating of the Gospel
material has been produced not only by the outlook and purpose of
each of the human authors and by the situation and needs of the
particular Churches, but has also been accompanied by particular
theological conclusions and reflections, polemical and apologetical
material, and the various literary forms which must serve as the
structures for any written work. Since this is so, it is correct to speak
of the "theologies" of Matthew, Mark, Luke, John, Paul, etc.,
bearing in mind, however, that such "theologies" are, in their turn,
limited and shaped by the source material. It is the source material,
i.e., the life and work of Jesus and the Apostolic proclamation of that
life and work, which give unity and coherence to a theology and
which render the various theologies complementary, not discord-
ant, reflections of the same truth. The preeminent work of the
theologian—whether he be a New Testament writer or a modern—
is that of *reflection*, not creation. It takes nothing away from the
genius of the true theologian to claim that he is the servant of his
sources and not an originator. Nevertheless, there is almost a
perverse tendency in us which strives to highlight the differences

and overlook the fundamental harmonies. How many "Thomists" have attempted to exalt their master at the price of despising Augustine! As if Aquinas the theologian were not molded by Augustine, and both of them by what they had received from Revelation itself, and from others. That same tendency to stress the differences and downplay the harmonies can be noticed in some treatment of the New Testament "theologies." There is a craving to divide rather than to unite. The consequence is a divided Christ. Mark's Jesus is counterposed to John's Jesus; Matthew's to Paul's, etc. The unity of the Source, as well as of the sources, is destroyed in such a procedure. Reacting to this phenomenon, Hans Urs von Balthasar has written well:

> ...Jesus' entire being is one single Word. This perfect being becomes manifest only from the testimonies of faith: those of Paul which are as important as the ones in the Acts of the Apostles; John is as authoritative as the synoptics. They, all together, form a magnificent poliphony—not a pluralism in the contemporary sense. They can be compared to views of a free-standing statue that has to be observed from all directions to understand its self-expression. The more facets we can view, the better we grasp the unity of the inspiration.[49]

Each of the New Testament theologies, then, must be recognized for what it is: a partial perspective of its Source.

4. *The Gospels are historically accurate.*

While recognizing that the Gospel writers always maintain the form of proclamation (i.e., the intention to convince) and have selected, synthesized, and explained their source material, having in mind the needs of the particular Churches, Vatican Council II insisted on the historical accuracy of the Gospels.

> Holy Mother Church firmly and most consistently has held and holds that the four Gospels, whose historicity she unhesitatingly affirms, faithfully hand on those things which Jesus, the Son of God, really did and taught...while living among men.
> The intention of the Evangelists was to communicate to us things true and sincere about Jesus—so that we might know the truth....

For over a century, the question of the historicity of the Gospels has been acutely disputed. Because they were written by men who believed that Jesus is the Messiah; because none of these men (so it is claimed) were eyewitnesses; because they are works which are proclamatory in nature and flow out of the life situation of various Christian communities; because of internal inconsistencies which do not allow for plausible harmonization; etc., the historical reliability of the Gospels has been called into question. This scepticism led to the so-called quest for the historical Jesus, an effort to get behind the Gospel presentation and discern Jesus "as He really was" before post-resurrection faith in Him had, as if through a prism, re-read the events of His life and teaching.[50] In such an effort, the evangelists themselves and the early Christian communities increasingly tended to become a block between ourselves and Jesus. Instead of being mediated to us through the early Christian bodies and through the Gospels, the "Gospel Jesus," the "Christ of Faith," was seen as a creation of the communities and of the varying theological outlooks of the New Testament writers. As a consequence, Jesus Himself became relatively inaccessible to us.

The Instruction *Sancta Mater Ecclesia* referred to the attitude which would "exaggerate the creative power of the community" and found it "contrary to Catholic doctrine, devoid of scholarly foundation and inconsistent with the sound principles of the historical method."[51] The penultimate draft of *Dei Verbum*, no. 19, likewise contained a reference to the imagined creative powers of the early Christian communities. It read:

> ...And preserving the form of proclamation, always in such a way that they would communicate to us things true and sincere about Jesus, and not fictitious things flowing from the creative power of the primitive community.[52]

The remark was omitted, however, in order to keep the positive tone of the presentation and to avoid "giving recognition to an opinion which had seen its day."[53]

The Council had to move with caution between two positions. An excessive clinging to the literal meaning led to unreal results. On the other hand it was necessary to face the risks that arose from the questioning of the historical value of the Gospels as happens in various schools of contemporary exegesis. The Council considers that it was not enough to make a straightforward condemnation of this kind of dangerous skepticism. It is better to move beyond the present situation and treat the problem in its own right, while taking note of contemporary research. Negatively, it appeared necessary to avoid a terminology which is influenced by the infiltration of philosophical existentialism into the sphere of exegesis. If one uses the words "history" or "historical," it is easy to forget that the meaning of these words is controversial. The romance languages have no way of expressing the difference between the two words "Geschichte" and "Historia." In present terminology "Geschichte" is not the event itself, but what the proclamation conjures up in the mind, irrespective of its actual content. "Historia" is the grasping of the event through reason according to the laws of historical criticism.... Because of this kind of terminology the Council thought it better not to use these words, so as to avoid all ambiguity. The important point that it wanted to make was that Christian faith is bound up with a rational affirmation of the facts.[54]

The Council's assertion about the accuracy of the Gospel accounts was intended to be a statement of both faith *and reason*. To emphasize the reasonable aspect, the bishops said: "Holy Mother Church firmly and most consistently has *held* and *holds* (rather than "has *believed* and *believes*)...."[55] In this way, the Church states the conviction that the historical method, properly used, vindicates the Church's own awareness that the Gospels tell us what Jesus Himself "really did and said...while living among men."

It is, of course, a matter of faith that the New Testament writings are inerrant. Vatican Council II repeated this belief.

Since everything affirmed by the inspired authors or writers must be held as being asserted by the Holy Spirit, the Scriptures must be recognized as teaching firmly, faithfully and without error that truth which God willed to be consigned to the sacred writings for the sake of our salvation.[56]

The passage teaches that the *affirmations made for the sake of our salvation* are without error. It does not follow, of course, that everything affirmed by the human author—and therefore by God who inspires—is made for the sake of our salvation. Some things may be affirmed simply for the sake of "dressing up" the narrative or for "getting a point across," etc. On the other hand, what is affirmed for the sake of our salvation need not be what we call a religious or moral truth. If done for the sake of our salvation, scientific, historical and "profane" knowledge in general are affirmed as free from error.

As the footnotes to *Dei Verbum* no. 11 reveal, this doctrine is not new. Cited in the note are St. Augustine in his commentary on Genesis (*Gen. ad Litt,* 2,9,20) and St. Thomas' *De Veritate,* q. 12, a. 2 c, as well as Leo XIII in *Providentissimus Deus* and Pius XII in *Divino Afflante.* The citation from Aquinas contains within it the reference to Augustine and reads as follows:

> In all things which exist for the sake of an end the matter is determined according to the needs of the end.... But the gift of prophecy is given for the use of the Church.... Therefore all those things the knowledge of which can be useful for salvation are the matter of prophecy, whether they are past, or future, or even eternal, or necessary, or contingent. But those things which cannot pertain to salvation are outside the matter of prophecy. Hence, Augustine says: 'Although our authors knew what shape heaven is, the Spirit wants to speak through them only that which is useful for salvation.' And in the Gospel of John (16:13), 'But when he, the Spirit of truth, is come, he will teach you all truth,' the *Gloss* adds, 'necessary for salvation.'
>
> Moreover I say necessary for salvation, whether they are necessary for instruction in the Faith or for the formation of morals. But many things which are proved in the sciences can be useful for this.... Hence we find that mention of these is made in Holy Scripture.[57]

The meaning of the Council's teaching on inerrancy is clear. The difficulty, however, is this: how does one go about determining which assertions—whether they be historical or scientific or religious—have been consigned to the sacred writings for the sake of our salvation? How is one, that is, to differentiate between the truths included for the sake of salvation and those other assertions which are included for other motives? To that question there is no simple answer. The Council, repeating and summarizing Tradition and previous Church teaching, was content to set forth the methodology to be used in efforts to determine which assertions were made for the sake of our salvation. It did this by listing, in no. 12 of *Dei Verbum*, what may be called the presuppositions for a correct understanding of Scripture. These methodological presuppositions are as follows:

1. "Among other things, attention must be paid to the literary forms."

The elaboration of this sentence in *Dei Verbum* makes clear that theologians and exegetes must use every useful tool of historical and literary criticism as part of the effort to understand the intention of the inspired author. For a Catholic, the historico-critical investigation of the Scriptures—presuming that it has been purged of certain rationalistic presuppositions[58]—needs no justification. It is one requisite for the proper exegesis of Scripture.

As already indicated, however, the results of a historico-critical investigation of a text will frequently be only tentative or will be able to establish only various alternate interpretations. An adequate and correct understanding of the Gospel message cannot be dependent on tentative and/or partial viewpoints. The historico-critical method is one important tool, among others as the Council says, for interpretation. Its limitations must be recognized. As the Congregation for the Doctrine of the Faith pointed out in 1982:

...it is not possible for the Church to adopt as the effective norm for reading the Scriptures only what historical criticism maintains, thus allowing the homogeneity of the developments which appear in Tradition to remain in doubt.[59]

2. "No less attention must be paid to the content and unity of the whole of Scripture, taking account of the living Tradition of the whole Church and the analogy of faith, since Sacred Scripture must be read and interpreted according to the same Spirit by whom it was written" (*Dei Verbum*, no. 12).

There are several important elements in this statement: the unity of the Bible, the Tradition of the whole Church, the analogy of faith.

The unity and content of the Bible: No individual book of the Bible was inspired so as to stand alone. Each book is part of the whole and is properly understood only in the context of the entirety. This is the truth referred to by von Balthasar in the quotation cited above. Job cannot be adequately understood unless its questions about the suffering of the just be seen in the light of other aspects of Israel's faith; Mark cannot be adequately understood without John, and so forth. Each book is both a part and an aspect of the same revealed word in a unity which the Spirit has always intended. In the case of the Gospels, no one author has told us all we need to know about Jesus nor managed to capture all the various aspects of His personality as they manifested themselves before and after His resurrection.

The Tradition of the Church: On this there is no need to repeat what has already been said above.

The analogy of faith: This is a normal tool of Catholic theology and simply means that one truth helps to illustrate and explain another. Using the analogy of faith, one can better see how the doctrine of Christ's preexistence, for instance, and that of His virginal conception mutually illuminate and support one another.

It must be noted that the employment of all these elements is considered necessary for a proper understanding of the scriptural text and that their study is put on an equal level with that of the historico-critical investigation of the text: "no less attention must be paid... " is the way the Council put it.

The Council, in all that it says in no. 12 of *Dei Verbum*, is not speaking of two different ways of interpreting Scripture, one that would be "scientific" basing itelf on historico-critical tools, the other "dogmatic" resting on the postulates of faith and the Tradition and teaching of the Church. No such distinction is made in *Dei Verbum*, nor can it be legitimately made. The various norms for interpretation are complementary. The norm of the unity of the Bible and its content and that of the Church's Tradition, etc., are not to be used to impose on an individual book of the Bible a meaning that is not truly to be found there. Historical and critical analyses are not to be used in such a way as to imply that they are sufficient in themselves to grasp the full meaning of a Scriptural book or text. In practice, the historico-critical tools will, at times, be sufficient to determine the text's meaning. In other cases, they will be inadequate and need to be supplemented or even corrected. An example of the complementary functioning of the various norms can be seen below in reference to the question concerning the "brothers and sisters" of the Lord (cf. Part I, pp. 84-88).

It is in the light of the interpretative principles just presented and in light of her own long history of preserving and understanding the Gospels that the Church is able to affirm what she has always affirmed: that the four Gospels "faithfully hand on what Jesus, the Son of God, really did and taught." Ultimately a proper use of the historico-critical method will only substantiate that position. The Church is quite aware that the order of events cannot always be harmonized and that what Jesus taught is frequently recorded in different words by the four evangelists. The Gospels are not a "video tape" of His life and ministry. They are not, on the other hand, a pastiche of things which He actually said and did along with things that community traditions, post-Easter retrojections, Christian prophets,[60] and legend have said and done for Him. Assertions to the contrary, based on various suppositions, lack real evidence.

The fact that the Gospels are not a "video tape" presentation of the life of Christ should not be taken to mean that they are not "biographies" of Jesus. The statement, "They are not biographies" has become a truism of some modern biblical criticism. It is a truism, however, which is not true unless one takes a univocal understanding of what biography is. Secular literature knows many forms of biography. Unless one claims that the Gospels are a new literary genus invented by the evangelists (and, if they are, by what standard is one to judge from a historico-critical point of view?), they surely fall into the category generically called biography. The point is unimportant in itself, except for the fact that the connotations in the statement, "They are not biographies," seem to cast doubt on their historical worth.

THEOLOGICAL CONCEPTS AND LANGUAGE

Together with the problems raised in respect to the sources for a study of Jesus—and the correct understanding of those sources—Christology faces as well the difficult question concerning the nature and value of propositional truth in expressing the revealed mysteries. In this area, among the matters to be faced are: 1) the nature of language (spoken and written) as symbolic, and the adequacy of the symbolic to express what is transcendent in the Christian mysteries; 2) the influence of time, place, and culture on the symbolic expression of truth; 3) the possibility (and desirability) of replacing symbols which may no longer function as they were originally intended to do.

That language is symbolic or representational is an accepted fact. The particular problem of the mediatorial or symbolic use of language in expressing the Christian mysteries is not a new one (cf., for example, St. Thomas' treatment of how we use terms about God in *S. Th.*, I, q. 12 and q. 13), but has taken on new importance in our time. In theological discourse it is common to speak today of *models* (as in the statement: "The two-natures-one person model of Christology is outmoded and needs to be replaced"),[61] images, schema, symbol, even myth. Often enough these terms are used without any indication given as to what they mean or how they are being used. The impression can be conveyed at times—or is not infrequently assumed—that all models or symbols are or could be of equal value in mediating to us the reality which is other than ourselves, or that one model can readily be substituted for another. Such an impression or assumption must be recognized for what it is, viz., an assumption and one which, were it true, would lead to theoretical or practical skepticism or agnosticism because it would make language meaningless.

That some models or symbols are clearly not adequate or accurate mediators of reality has always been a Christian conviction. (The First Ecumenical Council at Nicea in 325 can be viewed as an exercise in the control of models. One model, the Arian, was rejected as being an unsuitable vehicle for conveying Christian truth.) That conviction was expressed by St. Augustine when he called for linguistic vigilance in respect to the Christian doctrines, "in order that a lack of caution in speech might not give rise to an irreverent opinion about the realities which are represented by the words."[62]

On this matter, it may be sufficient to summarize some fundamental Christian presuppositions without attempting to defend each of them, since in many cases the discussion belongs more properly to philosophy than to theology.

a) God as Transcendent cannot be known in this life by our natural human knowledge except insofar as He is mediated to us in deed and word, i.e., in sign.

We say "in this life" since in heaven He will be known immediately. We say "by our natural human knowledge" because we believe there is a knowledge in this life that goes beyond the mediate. As Jacques Maritain explains:

> The human and natural mode of knowing consists in knowing by ideas and concepts, and consequently, in matters that concern divine things, by analogy with created realities, for the manner in which our concepts signify is determined by them. That is why faith, even though it does reach God according to His very inwardness and His proper life, reaches Him thus only at a distance and remains a mediate knowledge, enigmatic, in the words of St. Paul; in the sense that faith has to make use of formal means, proportionate to our natural mode of knowing—concepts and conceptual formulas, analogical or rather superanalogical notions.[63]

There is, however, according to the same author, another type of knowing, that of mystical wisdom, "which judges the things of God through an affective experience which touches the very things that lie hidden in faith."[64]

It is the mediated knowledge of the Transcendent God which is the basis of the models or symbols used by man in his discourse about God.

b) God as Immanent is truly known by us in the symbolic deed or word, even though He infinitely transcends the sign. This truth is expressed by St. Thomas who says that in the act of faith we arrive at the reality and not simply at the concept or idea (or, as we would say today, at the model or symbol).

c) Certain conceptual and linguistic models or symbols have themselves been chosen by God and are thereby uniquely privileged symbols or models of divine self-revelation. In this sense, the definitive model is the humanity of God's own Word, Jesus Christ.

d) Not every sign or symbolic expression is equally or even adequately capacitated to manifest God and His revealed mysteries. The Church alone, under the Spirit, and authentically through the Magisterium, exercises normative control over our symbolic expression of the divine mysteries.

Points (c) and (d) give rise to a question: To what extent are the original symbols normative, given the fact that they reflect a time, a place, a culture, and thought patterns not necessarily those of 20th century man? This question was implicitly answered at Nicea when, in the case of the preexistent and divine Logos, it was determined that the New Testament symbols were *normative as to content but not necessarily as to expression*. Such is the meaning of the Council's debates over, and final use of, the term *homoousios*. As to the normative value of the models and symbols used by the Church to express the content of biblical teaching, the most explicit ecclesial response has been given in the Declaration *Mysterium Ecclesiae*, issued by the Congregation for the Doctrine of the Faith in 1973.

Mysterium Ecclesiae teaches that the *meaning or content* of dogmatic formulas or symbols "remains ever true and constant in the Church."[65] Summarizing the solemn teaching of the First Vatican Council, the declaration states that the meaning or content of dogmatic formulas is determinate and unalterable.

> The faithful must therefore shun the opinion, first, that dogmatic formulas (or some category of them) cannot signify truth in a determinate way, but can only offer changeable approximations to it, which to a certain extent distort or alter it; secondly, that these formulas signify the truth only in an indeterminate way, this truth being like a goal that is constantly being sought by means of such approximations. Those who hold such opinions do not escape dogmatic relativism....[66]

Although the meaning of such dogmatic formulas cannot be false and thus must ever remain a part of Catholic doctrine, it can happen that the meaning be only an incomplete expression of the particular aspect of truth involved. Therefore, it is capable of receiving a more complete expression when seen in a wider context of faith and/or human knowledge. Furthermore, the meaning of any particular dogmatic formula must always be viewed in the overall context of revealed truth. In this sense, the "analogy of faith" referred to by *Dei Verbum*, no 12, is again brought into play.

When one turns from the meaning or content of the dogmatic formulas to the formulas themselves (what we have been calling the symbols or models), the declaration states:

> ...even though the truths which the Church intends to teach through her dogmatic formulas are distinct from the changeable conceptions of a given epoch and can be expressed without them, nevertheless it can sometimes happen that these truths may be enunciated by the sacred Magisterium in terms that bear traces of such conceptions.[67]

Thus, the formulas or symbols are recognized as possibly bearing traces of outdated ways of looking at things. Because this is so, new terminology or new formulations, new symbols, can replace earlier ones provided that such newer models retain the full meaning intended by the earlier formulation and have been approved by the Magisterium.

Now in respect to updating the language or models or symbols, one comes across many complex problems. There is a tendency to think abstractly about this matter, almost as if the terminology or model could be easily changed while retaining the same meaning or perception of reality and/or the Christian mystery. Such is not, in fact, the case. The expression of meaning is intimately bound up with the meaning itself (this is the sense of Augustine's remark quoted above), much the same way as body and soul make the complex reality of the human person. Only those who think dichotomously will insist that the same meaning may be expressed in any form or model. This type of thinking is the intellectual equivalent of traditional gnosticism and its modern idealistic forms. A recognition of this fact is not meant to imply that the expression of the Christian mysteries must be "frozen" in the terminology or concepts or models of earlier times. Such is not the case. In fact, such would at times lead inevitably to a destruction of the truth intended to be signified. Nevertheless, the alteration of concepts or models is more complex than even the document *Mysterium Ecclesiae* seems to convey. Russel Aldwinkle's reflections on the ascent-descent language of the New Testament and the Christian creeds or symbols (as found, for example, in the creedal formula, "For us men and for our salvation he came down from heaven") may serve as an illustration of the difficulty.

> ...it is difficult to see what other language we can use than that of the temporal and spatial models, in this case the language of descent and ascent. That some Christians have interpreted this language in the most naïve sense does not mean that we are forbidden its use altogether. Nor does it help to call this language 'mythical.' There are passages in Bultmann which suggest that he considers all language of a metaphorical or symbolic kind to be mythical. This, however, is to stretch the meaning of myth to a point where it ceases to have any precise meaning. Since by nature of the case, all talk about God must involve metaphor, symbol, analogy, models, etc., then all language about God must be mythical. This, however, is bound to cause complete semantic confusion. Whatever the experts say, for most people myth is so closely linked with unexamined notions of the primitive in the sense of superstition, with legend, with obsolete science, etc., that to apply the word to all symbolic and analogical language is only to make confusion more confounded. The language of descent and ascent is not mythical in the technical sense.... For the Christian at least, it is the inevitable symbolic form in which the conviction is expressed that Jesus' coming into the world and His departure from it was the result of a prior initiative of the transcendent God.... The language is still saying something significant for Christian faith, and if we do not use it, we must find some other way of uttering the same truth, not a different truth.[68]

Aldwinckle highlights the difficulty well. What language or model would replace the ascent-descent model without being mere circumlocution or so technical as to be noncommunicative to most people? Consider as well the symbol "Mother of God." What model and/or terminology, while retaining all that Christians mean by the words, would be capable of replacing it?

Thus, while it is theoretically possible to change models and symbols while retaining the same meaning, it is, in practice, an enterprise of great difficulty. In fact, the classical models and symbols of Christological doctrine (*homoousios,* nature, person, hypostatic union, etc.) have never been successfully updated or altered. The fate of Karl Rahner's efforts to replace "person" with his "distinct mode of subsisting" in Trinitarian theology is a case in point.[69] For all the cogency of his argumentation, Christians in general are never likely to end up professing "There is One God in Three distinct modes of subsisting."

Without despairing in efforts to update models and symbols, the task of those who proclaim the Faith must be an effort to explain clearly what the classical symbols were intended to teach. Those symbols introduce us to the Reality itself, that is, in the case of the Christological symbols, to Christ Himself. The Church's knowledge of Him, of course, goes beyond dogmatic formulations and beyond even the Scriptures and Tradition. All these must serve as our guides, but ultimately He must be known and experienced in Himself as He lives and works in His Church, especially in and through the Eucharist. All who proclaim and study Him must realize that what they do is merely a preparation. "As a priest effaces himself before the Host he has just consecrated, they ought to efface themselves before the doctrine they proclaim."[70]

PART I

The Incarnation

I. ORIGINS

The human origins of Jesus Christ were described by St. Paul this way: "When the time had fully come, God sent his Son, born of a woman, born under the law..." (Gal. 4:4). That concept of being "sent" from the Father is described by St. John in terms of that Word which was God and was with God becoming flesh and dwelling among us (Jn. 1:1-14). It is St. Matthew and St. Luke, however, who give us in narrative form what we know of the details of this "coming forth" from the Father. Each of these, in his own way, highlights the Pauline and Johannine themes of origin from God and birth of a woman and under the law. This they achieve by recounting for us the virginal conception of Jesus, His genealogical roots in Israel (and even back to Adam) and the figure of His Mother, Mary, the betrothed of Joseph of the House of David.

In recent times, the so-called "Infancy Gospels" (i.e., Mt. 1:1—2:23 and Lk. 1:5—2:52) have been the subject of much study by exegetes of Scripture and by theologians, with no full consensus yet reached on even the more essential aspects of these accounts.[1] Since neither evangelist was a witness to the events recorded and since they do not identify the source or sources of their information, no certain conclusions can be reached as to sources. Logic, of course, compels the conclusion that—unless the accounts are fundamentally "theological constructs"—as some would hold[2]—(an hypothesis which must be considered unlikely)[3]—the ultimate source must be Jesus Himself, Joseph, or Mary who was "still on the scene" as the Gospel began to be preached (Acts 1:14). What does seem certain is that the accounts as we have them contain literary

47

material which considerably predates the composition of the Gospels of which they form part and that the important factual data which they share have been shaped or stylized distinctly in the process of composition.

It is the distinctive shaping or stylization of the material— prompted perhaps by different theological or pastoral purposes— which may account for some of the differences between the narratives in respect to details. The arranging of the genealogies, for instance, is peculiar to each evangelist, and the names included in those genealogies do not match in many cases. Likewise, some would see Matthew 2:22-23 as indicating that the evangelist presumed a Judean origin for Joseph and Mary, thus differing with Luke 1:26. A close examination of this last point, however, will reveal that the supposed difference between the two accounts is not nearly as clear as some would claim it to be—and such is the case on other items as well. Each would bear a more careful study than is warranted here. Whatever the case in the particulars, the narrative differences between Matthew and Luke should not be allowed to obscure the considerable area of agreement on items not of detail but of substance. In fact, these areas of agreement manifest themselves in the midst of differences, as well as among items peculiar to each evangelist. Among such items of substance which refer to the earthly origins of Jesus and are agreed upon by Matthew and Luke, may be cited the names of Mary and Joseph, i.e., His parentage or presumed parentage; place of birth; harmony in chronology as to date of birth; and the manner of His conception. Since each of these matters merits some consideration, we shall look briefly at each of them in turn, with the exception of Mary and Joseph to whom we shall return later.

A. Place of Birth

Both Matthew and Luke cite Bethlehem, the town of David, as birthplace of Jesus. The fact is not without theological importance because, along with the genealogies, it forms part of the background for the Messianic title "Son of David." Already by the year 57, when he is writing to the Romans, St. Paul will describe the gospel as the "Gospel regarding His (God's) Son, who as to His human nature was a descendant of David" (Rom. 1:3). Likewise, 2 Timothy 2:8 declares: "Remember Jesus Christ, raised from the dead, descended from David. This is my gospel." And the seer of the Apocalypse, in his turn, has Jesus proclaiming, "I am the root and offspring of David" (Rv. 22:16; cf. 5:5).

It is not only the early Christians, however, who recognize the Davidic connection of Jesus. Each of the Synoptics records the case of the blind man (or men) who appeals to Jesus with the cry: "Son of David, have mercy on me" (Mt. 20:31 and parallels). This, as well as other instances (cf. Mt. 12:23; 15:22; Jn. 7:41ff.), confirms what we know from other sources: that one current of Messianic expectation saw the Messiah as being Son of David. We know from the Church-historian Eusebius[4] that the relatives of Jesus treasured their Davidic connection. Citing the Jewish Christian Hegesippus who wrote in the middle of the second century, Eusebius records how the Roman Emperor Domitian (ruled 81 to 96 A.D.) sought out royal Jewish pretenders in order to prevent another uprising of the Jews. He thus came across the descendants of James and Simeon, the "brothers of the Lord." Although they indeed claimed descent from David, Domitian released them because of their poverty and obvious inability to cause trouble.

In short, everything that we know or can piece together tends to confirm the historical character of the Davidic connection of Jesus and His birth in David's town. At times it is pointed out that Jesus Himself appeared to deny the Davidic connection of the Messiah when He said:

How is it that the teachers of the law say that the Christ is the son of David? David himself, speaking by the Holy Spirit, declared: 'The Lord said to my Lord: Sit at my right hand until I put your enemies under your feet.' David himself calls him 'Lord.' How then can he be his son? (Mk. 12:35-36)

It can be noted, as well, that the Gospel of John cites, without refutation, the rejection of Jesus as Messiah by a crowd which uses as its reason the fact that Jesus comes from Galilee (i.e., Nazareth), not Bethlehem (Jn. 7:40-42).

What is at stake in both cases is the question of origins, and to that question neither descent from David nor birth in Bethlehem is a sufficient answer. The claims of the Messiah do not rest on human descent nor on place of birth. *He has His origin in God.* Jesus' answer to the scribes is an effort to get them to probe deeper, and John's report of the crowd's reasoning is ironic. He implies that they are doubly ignorant, aware neither of Jesus' human nor divine origin. The same chapter of the Gospel of John raises the very problem, but in a slightly different way, and Jesus Himself replies with irony, and then with the truth.

> 'We know where this man is from. When the Christ comes, no one will know where he is from.' Then Jesus...cried out: 'Yes you know me, and you know where I am from. I am not here on my own, but he who sent me is true. I know him because I am from him and he sent me' (Jn. 7:27-29).

Viewed in such a light, the statement of Jesus and the passage in John are not to be seen as questioning the historical nature of the birth in Bethlehem and the Davidic descent,[5] but rather as an invitation to go beyond the facts of this world and to realize that the origins in question cannot be answered by geography or genealogy.

B. Chronology

Both Matthew (2:1) and Luke (1:5) indicate that Jesus was born in Judea during the reign of Herod the Great. Because of the Gospels, he is probably one of the most famous rulers of ancient times. Thanks to Flavius Josephus, the first century Jewish historian, we know a good deal about the life and personality of this man who ruled Judea as a vassal of Rome. Herod became king on this side of 40 B.C., and ruled Judea—frequently with great cruelty[6]—until March of 4 B.C. We must therefore place the birth of Jesus before that date. It is difficult to be more precise than that since the other chronological reference of Luke, namely, the census taken while Quirinius was governor of Syria (Lk. 2:2), cannot be verified with certainty from secular sources. If, however, we use one further indication of Luke's which tells us that Jesus was about thirty when He was baptized by John (3:23), and that this event took place not long after John began his own career in the fifteenth year of the reign of Tiberius Caesar (Lk. 3:1), we can approximate the year of

His birth more exactly. The fifteenth year of the reign of Tiberius was either 26-27 or 28-29 A.D., depending on whether one counts the two years in which he shared full power with Augustus, his predecessor. If we choose the former date and place Jesus at the approximate age of thirty in the year 27 A.D., we can, by counting back, place His birth at about the year 5-4 B.C.

Such dates can be said to be certain within a year or two in either direction, and this type of chronological accuracy can be seen as a reflection of Luke's careful tracing of the whole sequence of events from the beginning (Lk. 1:3). It is a concern shared by the other evangelists as well, all of whom indicate in various ways (e.g., references to people, places, and events known to us from secular sources) that the Gospel message is firmly rooted in known history. For the New Testament writers, however, this chronology is not simply a matter of dating. It reflects the deeper mystery, viz., of the meaning God gives to time. It is saving time, even the last age of time. Variously they designate it as the "designated" time, the "fullness of time," the "final age" (cf. Gal. 4:4; Eph. 1:10; Hebrews 1:2, etc.), reflecting in this way the message of Jesus Himself that the "time of fulfillment" had arrived (Mk. 1:15). Later reflection would see it as the beginning of the new creation, a prelude to that "eighth day," as the Fathers of the Church called it, the day of resurrection which knows no tomorrow.

C. Manner of Conception

Both Matthew and Luke [7] testify to the virginal conception of Jesus. Matthew does so with emphasis.

> This is how the birth of Jesus Christ came about. His mother Mary was pledged to be married to Joseph, but before they came together, she was found to be with child through the Holy Spirit (Mt. 1:18) and:
>
> (Joseph) had no union with her until she gave birth to a son. And he gave him the name Jesus (Mt. 1:25).

As is his custom, Matthew sees this fact as fulfilling what had already been said in prophecy, citing Isaiah 7:14. (The fact that the original Hebrew of Isaiah can be understood as referring to a "young woman" and not necessarily to a "virgin" in the technical sense is of

interest only for the Old Testament or intra-testamentary development of the Isaian text, since Matthew is citing not the Hebrew
but a Greek version which employs the technical term for "virgin.")
Luke's treatment of the same mystery is made clear in the dialogue
between Mary and the angel.

> 'How will this be,' Mary asked the angel, 'since I am a virgin?'
> The angel answered, 'The Holy Spirit will come upon you, and
> the power of the Most High will overshadow you. So the holy
> one to be born will be called the Son of God' (Lk. 1:34-35).

Luke refers to this mystery again, as he begins the genealogy, by
writing: "Now Jesus himself was about thirty years old when he
began his ministry. He was the son—so it was thought—of Joseph"
(Lk. 3:23).

Apart from Matthew and Luke there is no explicit mention of
the virginal conception of Jesus elsewhere in the New Testament,
nor, it should be noted, is there recorded any statement made by a
believer to the contrary. This "silence" is readily understandable,
and really no more surprising than the omission of any reference to
the Eucharist in the Creed of Nicea, or in any number of the New
Testament epistles. A matter is simply taken for granted or is not in
the perspective of a particular author in a given circumstance. To
conclude from silence either a lack of knowledge or a disavowal of
the mystery or its relative importance is to venture beyond
reasonable evidence,[8] especially so considering the specific purposes of the epistles of the New Testament and of the book of
Revelation. The Gospel of John, where one might reasonably expect
to find reference to the conception, focuses on the eternal, not the
earthly origin of Jesus, making oblique—and probably ironic—
reference to the same. The Gospel of Mark, which begins with the
public ministry of Jesus, is somewhat enigmatic. It is the only
Gospel in which Joseph is never mentioned, even in the one case
where, from the parallels in Matthew and Luke, one might have
expected his name to appear (cf. Mk. 6:3 and parallels; Jn. 6:42). For
Mark, Jesus seems to be only "Son of God" (Mk. 1:1 and 15:39) and
"Son of Mary" (Mk. 6:3). To claim, however, that this is the evangelist's way of indicating the virginal conception is (like the arguments
from silence which imply that Mark knew nothing of or rejected it)
to argue for something which this evidence will not support.[9]

The mystery of the virginal conception of Jesus is a truth taught infallibly by the Church. The creeds of Nicea and Constantinople, the Roman or Apostles' Creed, the so-called Athanasian Creed, the *Firmiter* of Lateran Council IV in 1215, and the Creed of Paul VI in 1968 all teach and reaffirm the doctrine.[10] In the year 649, the Synod of the Lateran under Pope St. Martin I issued what by many is considered an infallible definition, stating that Mary "truly and in a proper sense conceived the Divine Word by the Holy Spirit without human seed *(absque semine)*" *(DS* 503), an explicitness in formulation which recalls that of the Christian apologist Aristides, writing around the year 140 A.D. ("and He was begotten of the Holy Virgin without seed and took flesh without defilement").[11] The same teaching, with the same degree of explicitness, is repeated by Paul IV in the Constitution *Cum Quorundam* in 1555 *(DS* 1880) as one of the doctrines he considers central to the faith.[12]

These statements of the Church's Magisterium can be viewed as a Spirit-guided judgment on two aspects of what Tradition and Scripture tell us about the virginal conception of Jesus: its historical and biological facticity. Along with Tradition, they reaffirm the obvious sense of Matthew and Luke and exclude any interpretation which would see the accounts of the Lord's conception as being merely symbolic, a "theologoumenon" of the evangelists or of the early Christians with the intention of conveying the "uniqueness of Jesus."[13] This historical and biological facticity of the virginal conception is, moreover, an invitation to a deeper study of the mystery. For, in asking the question "Why did it take place this way?" one is ultimately led to contemplate the purposes of God and, in His purposes the mystery of God Himself. St. Thomas Aquinas gives several reasons in response to the question "why." As a distillation of the tradition, they merit consideration.

> The Son of God assumed flesh and came into the world for the purpose of raising us to the state of resurrection, in which men 'shall neither marry nor be married, but shall be as the angels of God in heaven' (Mt. 22:30). This is why He inculcated the doctrine of continence and of virginal integrity, so that an image of the glory that is to come might, in some degree, shine forth in the lives of the faithful. Consequently, He did well to extol purity of life at His very birth, by being born of a virgin....[14]

Furthermore, Aquinas writes, this type of conception was fitting "because of the very purpose of the Incarnation, which purpose was to bring it about that men be reborn as sons of God, 'not by the will of flesh, nor by the will of men, but of God' (Jn. 1:13), that is by the power of God. And the type of this birth should have appeared in the very conception of Christ."[15] He says, too, in what may be the most profound of the reasons set forth, that such a conception was fitting "in order to preserve the dignity of the Father.... Since Christ is the true and natural Son of God it was not suitable that He have any father other than God lest the dignity of God be transferred to another."[16] Now, all of these arguments Aquinas brings forth as arguments from "suitability" or *covenientia*, not as being necessitated by the Incarnation itself. Nevertheless, in the last of the cited arguments, he touches on what is proper because of the very nature of God's own Trinitarian life—the relationship between Father and Son. It is possible that here he has touched on something which makes the virginal conception not only suitable but truly necessary inasmuch as it reflects the necessary relationships involved in intra-Trinitarian life.

The accounts of the virginal conception given by Matthew and Luke "fill in," as it were, some of the details of the Pauline proclamation "born of a woman" (Gal. 4:4). Their genealogies, traced through Joseph, parallel the Pauline "born under law" (Gal. 4:4), as do Luke's accounts of the circumcision of the Child and His presentation in the Temple (Lk. 2:21-35). Indeed, Luke's record of aged Simeon's prophecy prefigures the long struggle between the Law and Grace (cf. Jn. 1:17: "For the law was given through Moses; grace and truth came through Jesus Christ"), a tension begun in the ministry of Jesus Himself and carried on through the history of the early Church.

The origins of Jesus, however, go beyond the facts involved in being "born of a woman, born under law." As the virginal conception makes clear, the origins are ultimately hidden in the power of God, that is in God Himself. But it is to St. Paul and St. John and to the notion of "preexistence" contained in their writing that we must turn in order to probe the nature of this origin in God.

II. PREEXISTENCE

In his dialogue *Phaedo*, Plato (427-347 B.C.) depicts Socrates as saying: "So, Simmias, our souls existed long ago, before they were in human shape, apart from bodies, and at that time they had wisdom...our souls must have existed before our birth."[17]

Therein, a usable definition of preexistence is set forth, viz., the existence, in some form or another, which is possessed by an individual before his or her appearance within human history. With the conquests of Alexander the Great (356-323 B.C.), this idea became ever more common in the hybrid culture which marked the eastern Mediterranean after the third century before Christ—a culture often called Hellenistic but which was, in reality, an amalgam of many different influences.[18] It was within such an amalgam that the book of Wisdom was written by a devout Jew, probably in Alexandria, Egypt, in the first century before Christ. Describing the origin and qualities of wisdom, the author wrote:

> She is a breath of the power of God, pure emanation of the power of the Almighty;...she is a reflection of the eternal light, untarnished mirror of God's active power, image of his goodness (Wis. 7:25-26) (Jerusalem Bible).

The path for this passage had been paved, almost a century earlier, by Jesus Ben Sirach who, despite his anti-Hellenistic tone, likewise had personified Wisdom in terms reminiscent of the "ideas" or "forms" of Plato.

I came forth from the mouth of the Most High, and I covered
the earth like a mist.... From eternity, in the beginning he
created me, and for eternity I shall remain (Sirach 24:3-4, 9)
(Jerusalem Bible).

This movement toward the ever clearer personification of
Wisdom as a being proceeding from God and the mirror of His
active power reaches a certain plateau in the Alexandrian Jew Philo
(25 B.C.-50 A.D.) who, apparently using Wisdom *(Sophia)* and
Word *(Logos)* interchangeably, sees Logos as preexistent, active
and agent for God's creation of the world. It is also probable—
although disputed—that during the first century B.C. some form of
preexistence had begun to be attributed to the Son of Man figure in
Daniel 7, as well as to Wisdom and Word, and to the Torah or
Law.[19]

Very much remains obscure as to the nature and mode of the
preexistence spoken of in all these and similar instances, and the
connections among the various writings and their possible subsequent influences on the writings of the New Testament must still be
considered an open field for specialized study. What is significant,
nonetheless, is the general cross-fertilization which has gone on
between "Platonic" thought and Jewish belief, a cross-fertilization
which must be kept in mind as forming at least a general—but only
partial—background for the New Testament writing of the first
century A.D.

1. Preexistence in Paul

Among the writings of the New Testament, those of St. Paul
are the earliest in finished form, and already one finds the idea of
preexistence applied to Jesus of Nazareth, not only by Paul himself
but in Paul's use of material (perhaps liturgical) which predated his
writing of the epistles. In his first letter to Corinth, written about
the year 56 A.D., Paul writes: "...for us there is but one God, the
Father from whom all things come and for whom we live; and there
is but one Lord, Jesus Christ, through whom all things come and
through whom we live" (8:6). While the word preexistence is not

used—as it is nowhere in the New Testament—the idea is clearly contained in the statement which claims Jesus as the Mediator of creation ("through whom...and through whom...") even though, by historical birth, Jesus Himself only came to existence some fifty odd years before Paul writes.[20] Thus, we have verified what we saw above in the "common denominator" definition of preexistence: the existence of an individual before his appearance in history at his birth. In this specific case, we see the activity of Jesus previous to His own nativity in human history. By the year 56, this type of speaking about Jesus must have been clear to the people of Corinth—probably from Paul's own preaching to them in 50-52 A.D.—since no effort is made to explain the statement. What is more, Paul returns to the idea in the same letter:

> For I do not want you to be ignorant of the fact, brothers, that our forefathers were all under the cloud and that they all passed through the sea. They were all baptized into Moses in the cloud and in the sea. They all ate the same spiritual food and drank the same spiritual drink; for they drank from the spiritual rock that accompanied them, and that rock was Christ (1 Cor. 10:1-5).

Paul is here referring to the Jewish tradition that the rock of Exodus 17:6 followed the Jews through the desert as a continual source of water. For the Jews, of course, the rock was a symbol for Yahweh who Himself provided food and drink for the constantly grumbling Exodus community. But Paul identifies not Yahweh but rather the Christ as the source of this spiritual drink, thus pointing again to the activity of Christ before His birth in time, and simultaneously equating that activity with the divine activity of Yahweh Himself.[21]

Another aspect of Christ's preexistence is set forth when Paul compares the status or condition of Jesus before His birth in time with that of His earthly condition. Thus in 2 Corinthians 8:9 (probably written in 57), in an appeal for Corinthian generosity to the collection Paul was taking up for the community in Jerusalem, he writes: "For you know the grace of our Lord Jesus Christ, that though he was rich, yet for your sakes he became poor...." The same thought is contained in more elaborate form in the famous hymn in the letter to the Philippians (date of writing disputed, but the year 53 seems probable):

> Your attitude must be that of Christ: Though he was in the form of God, he did not deem equality with God something to be grasped at. Rather he emptied himself and took the form of a slave, being born in the likeness of men... (Phil. 2:5-11).[22] (NAB)

It is within this context of dual status or condition that one must read other passages in Paul which do not, in themselves, necessitate the idea of preexistence. This is especially true of those texts which speak of God sending His Son or handing Him over for our salvation. Thus, Romans 8:3: "Sending His own Son in the likeness of sinful man...,"[23] and 2 Corinthians 5:21: "God made him who had no sin to be sin...." Likewise, Romans 8:32ff.: "God did not spare his own Son, but gave him up for us all." And, of course, the text of Galatians 4:4.[24]

From such texts one can see that for Paul, Jesus, before His historical appearance, enjoyed an existence and activity comparable to that of God Himself. It is the existence and sphere of the "second Adam" who, unlike the first Adam is not from the earth but from heaven (1 Cor. 15:47). It is an existence and activity in apparent contrast to what was witnessed of His human condition which itself came about as a mission from the Father. It was a fulfillment of what the Father had promised to Israel, for, from Israel "according to the flesh" is Christ "who is above all God forever blessed" (Rom. 9:5).[25] It has already been noted that this attributing of preexistence to Jesus antedated the Pauline writings, thus placing it before 50 A.D.[26] Before that point, there is, of course, no textual evidence of an undisputed nature, and conclusions drawn as to the ultimate foundation for viewing Jesus as preexistent must remain either hypothetical or dependent on the historical value placed upon the answers which the Gospels give the question. To this, we shall return below. That the theme itself antedated the Pauline writings, however, is counter-indicative of those efforts which attempt to depict the development of the early Church's thinking about Jesus in a rather rigid linear fashion in which the preexistence theme would only appear as a relatively late—or even final—stage.

2. Preexistence in John

> Father, glorify me in your presence with that glory I had with
> you before the world began (Jn. 17:5).

In these words—and many similar passages—the Johannine
Gospel reflects the theme of Christ's previous exalted condition and
mission by the Father which we have seen in Paul. The Gospel
indeed begins with a formal statement of the theme of preexistence. In the powerful Prologue, Jesus is described as the
Logos, the Word, which was in the beginning, and was with God
and indeed was God. Through this Word all things came to be, and,
in time, the Word itself became flesh and lived among men. The
Prologue portrays the Word as the focal point of human history.
There are close parallels with the Pauline text in Colossians 1:14-18,
as well as with the epistle to the Hebrews 1:1-3 where Jesus, seen as
the definitive Word of God to our race—in comparison with the
fragmentary words of the prophets—is described as the "radiant
light of God's glory and the perfect copy of His 'hypostasis' (usually
translated in our versions as 'nature' or 'being') through whom the
Father made everything there is."

Whether the Gospel of John demonstrates an advance over the
earlier Church's reflection on the preexistence of Jesus is a
debatable point. In fact, it would seem that, given the differences in
language and context (due in part to the different literary forms of
Gospel and epistle), the same themes appear in both the Pauline and
Johannine references to preexistence. There is, however, one area
where John's Gospel appears to be distinctive in this regard, that,
namely, of the so-called use of the absolute "I am" statements by
Jesus.

There are times in the Gospel of John where Jesus uses the
statement "I am" in an absolute sense, i.e., without a predicate
nominative expressed or implied. The classical example is the
climax of the debate between Jesus and the Jews concerning
paternity and witness.

> 'Your father Abraham rejoiced to think that he would see my
> day; he saw it and was glad.' The Jews said, 'You are not yet
> fifty, and you have seen Abraham!' Jesus replied: 'Amen,

amen, I say to you, before Abraham ever was, I am' (Jn. 8:57-58). *(Jerusalem Bible,* with the original "Amen, amen" restored).

A like usage is found in John 8:24 and 13:19. The usage is a scarcely veiled reference to the divine name as revealed by God to Moses in Exodus 3:14, according to the Greek translation: "This," God added, "is what you are to say to the Israelites: 'I Am has sent me to you.'" Found on the mouth of Jesus, such "I am" statements are a claim to both preexistence and divinity, as is made clear from the sequel to the statement in 8:58 where the Jews attempt to stone Jesus for blasphemy. It must be observed, however, that the phrase is not without a certain ambiguity in some contexts since the Greek *ego eimi* may be translated either "I am" or "It is I," or "I am he" (i.e., "the one"). Such ambiguity can be seen in the different translations of the verses 8:24 and 13:19 as rendered by the *New American Bible* and the *Jerusalem Bible.* It is due to such ambiguity that similar passages in the Synoptic Gospels lack the clarity found in John 8:58. This is particularly true in Mark 6:45-52.[27] There Jesus, walking on the water of the Sea of Galilee, manifests Himself in an extraordinary way, and, to overcome the fear of the disciples, He says to them: "Take courage. I am (or, It is I). Do not be afraid." The words *ego eimi* in this context may be no more than the identification "It is I"; on the other hand, given the extraordinary nature of this manifestation of Jesus' power, they may be the same claim to divinity witnessed in the account in John 8. What makes the latter more likely yet is the fact that the words "I am" are found only three times in Mark's Gospel, always on the lips of Jesus and always in a particularly solemn context (Mk. 6:45-52;[28] 13:5-6 and 14:62).[29]

3. Preexistence in the Synoptics

The ambiguity just noted concerning the "I am" usage in the Synoptics and even, at times, in John, must be said to extend as well to the Synoptic treatment of Jesus' preexistence. Neither in Matthew, Mark nor Luke is there found an unequivocal expression of the preexistence theme. This fact undoubtedly explains in part the tendency of some to view the Marcan, Matthean-Lucan, and Johannine Gospels as presenting different answers to the question which touches upon Jesus' relationship to the God of Israel.[30] Such an approach, however, tends to posit differences where there is, in fact, only silence or lack of *explicit* agreement. While not pretending that an uncontestable answer is at hand, it does seem more probable to assert that, granting the lack of explicit reference to the preexistence theme, all the Synoptics presumed that teaching, accepted it, and wrote their Gospels within the context of a belief in the preexistence of Jesus. As indications confirmatory of such a conclusion, we may note the following:

1. There is no *explicit evidence* in any New Testament source that there was a time when the preexistence theme was unknown or rejected. On the contrary, we have already seen that the preexistence doctrine antedates the Pauline Epistles and thus the earliest writings of the New Testament (at least as we have them in completed form).

2. In view of the early Church's concern for unity in belief and practice (cf. 1 Cor. 1:10; Gal. 1:16-20; 2:6-7; Acts 15, etc.), one should presume harmony of doctrine unless there is clear indication to the contrary.

3. If the "I am" statements in Matthew, Mark, and Luke are truly parallels—even if guarded—to the absolute "I am" statements of John's Gospel, then preexistence may be presumed within that same context.

4. The beginning and inclusion of Mark's Gospel (1:1 "The beginning of the gospel about Jesus Christ, the *Son of God*" and 15:39 "In truth this man was Son of God") should, for the same reasons, be read in the context of Pauline preaching of Jesus as Son of God, a preaching which certainly included preexistence.

5. One finds in the Synoptics the language of mission or "being sent" (cf., for example, Mt. 10:40-41; 15:24; 21:27; Lk. 4:43; 9:48; 10:16; and Mk. 9:37) used by and of Jesus. Like the "I am" statements, these are ambiguous, but in Pauline and Johannine contexts such language falls within the preexistence theme (cf. Jn. 7:57; 6:44; 10:35; for Pauline references, see above, pp. 56-58 and notes). Can one conclude securely that such a context does not underlie the Synoptic usage? Solid criticism, it seems, should presume a harmony unless the opposite can be demonstrated.

As stated, the arguments are not conclusive. There is no doubt, too, that long habit prompts Christians to read the Synoptics in the preexistence context of Paul and John, thus yielding a "harmonizing" which is not explicitly present. Nevertheless, it would appear that such a "contextual reading" has greater probability than its alternative.[31] If someone two hundred years from now were to read a sermon (let us presume the only one extant) of the Bishop of Rome in 1984 in which he said "God sent Jesus into the world to save us" and "God sent John the Baptist to herald the coming Savior" and understand the word "sent" as meaning the same thing in both instances simply because the preexistence of Jesus was not explicitly mentioned, then that critic would be guilty of a "non-contextual" reading of the sermon in question. For, unless it could be clearly demonstrated to the contrary, it should be presumed that by writing "God sent Jesus, etc.," the said Bishop of Rome was speaking in the context of the general faith of the Church which does proclaim the preexistence of Jesus and not of John, even though the same word is used in both cases. That same presumption, we think, must be made when approaching the documents of the early Church. Moreover, such a presumption is in concordance with the Tradition and Magisterium of the Church on the matter of the Lord's preexistence, and it is the justifiable presumption which Christians have traditionally brought to the reading of the Synoptic Gospels. Nor can it be said in justice that such an approach vitiates the currently accepted view concerning the different "theologies" or approaches of the individual evangelists. Indeed, it may be said to presume such differences, but sees them as complementary, not contradictory, approaches to the Person and mission of Jesus. Any other presupposition would violate the accepted norms for scientific historical criticism.

III. TRADITION AND MAGISTERIUM
ON PREEXISTENCE

1. Ignatius of Antioch

Although St. Ignatius of Antioch (Bishop of Antioch in Syria from approximately the year 69 A.D. until his martyrdom in Rome c. 107 A.D.) in no way left us a systematic exposition of what he taught on the mystery of Christ, his seven letters to the churches in Asia Minor and Rome contain a wealth of Christological reflection. Among other items of importance, these works are the oldest extant Christian documents which consistently call Jesus God.

The word "God" is but rarely applied to Jesus in the New Testament.[32] That usage is evidenced in John 1:1 and John 20:28, and probably in Hebrews 1:8-9; Romans 9:5; Titus 2:13; 2 Peter 1:1; and Colossians 2:2. The scarcity should not be surprising, since until the word *Theos* (God) took on the rather generic sense which we normally give it, the Father was designated God while the relationship of Jesus to Him was expressed in other terms which, nonetheless, claimed divinity for Him. Thus, the "I am" statements, the hymns in Colossians and Philippians, the attribution to Jesus of the divine titles in Revelation 1:17 and 2:8 (cf. 1:8 where the title is applied to the Father) are all among the various ways of professing the divinity of the Christ.

By the time Ignatius was writing, however, the more generic use of *Theos* had become sufficiently common to use regularly both for Father and Son. Thus, Ignatius wrote to the Ephesians: "Jesus Christ our God was conceived by Mary of the seed of David and of the Spirit of God."[33] Again, to the Romans, he wrote: "All perfect happiness in Jesus Christ our God to you who are bodily and spiritually at one with all his commandments...."[34]

Our God Jesus Christ was, for Ignatius, eternally preexistent with the Father and has become manifest in time, born of the Virgin Mary and conceived by the Holy Spirit. Thus: "...let the deacons be entrusted with the service of Jesus Christ, who was with the Father from all eternity and in these last days has been made manifest."[35] This "manifestation" of the Eternal One is real, says Ignatius, not merely the insubstantial theophany of some pagan god. "I want you to be unshakably convinced of the birth, the passion, and the resurrection which were the true and indisputable experiences of Jesus Christ, our hope, in the days of Pontius Pilate's governship."[36]

The union of the doctrines of preexistence and of virginal conception occurs *explicitly* for the first time in Ignatius. Since he came from Antioch (frequently claimed as the origin of the Gospel of Matthew) and since he refers to the visit of the Magi,[37] it might be thought that he himself was the first to pull together the Matthean account of the virginal conception and the Pauline-Johannine doctrine of preexistence. What is evident, rather, is that he reads the Gospel traditions in a synthetic fashion, giving no sign that he is artificially harmonizing what were originally contradictory approaches.

A major contribution of Ignatius of Antioch was the development of what theology knows as the *communicatio idiomatum* (the interchangeability of attributes). This is a use of language whereby one can predicate of God an attribute which, properly speaking, is true only when predicated of a human—or the predication to a human of something which, properly speaking, is true only when said of God. For example, in his letter to the Ephesians, Ignatius wrote: "Taking God as your pattern...you have fulfilled to perfection the duties of brotherliness, with an ardor kindled into flame by the *blood of God* (Gk. *haima Theou*).[38] The deity as such does not have blood, but Ignatius is referring to the (Eucharistic) blood of Jesus who is God. A similar formulation is found in the letter to the Romans where he wrote: "Leave me to imitate the passion of my God (Gk. *pathos tou Theou mou*)."[39] Again, such a formulation is possible only because Ignatius recognized a duality in unity in Jesus, i.e., the fact that the same Individual was both God and Man—or, in later terminology, the unity of two natures in the One Subject or Person. This duality in unity is revealed in a remarkable passage in the letter to the Ephesians, where Ignatius wrote:

There is One Physician, Jesus Christ our Lord (who is)

flesh	and	spirit
born	and	uncreated
man	and	God (literally "God in man")
in death		true life
of Mary	and	of God
who has suffered	yet	is incapable of suffering[40]

As lined up here, the attributes mentioned in the column on the left belong to what is human, those on the right to what is divine. For Ignatius, both sets of attributes belong *properly* to the One Individual who is the Lord Jesus Christ.

The *communicatio idiomatum* has no direct parallel in the New Testament, apart from the disputed reading of Acts 20:28: *"Be shepherds of the Church of God which He bought with His own blood."*[41] However, even without this text, the claim by an (apparently mere) mortal to the divine Name ("Before Abraham was born, I am") is sufficient Scriptural warrant for what is a daring use of terminology. The most dramatic use of such language may have been achieved by Melito of Sardis, a little more than half a century after Ignatius. Melito wrote:

And so he was raised on a cross, and a title was fixed, indicating who it was who was being executed. Painful it is to say, but more terrible not to say.... He who suspended the earth is suspended; he who fixed the heavens is fixed; he who fastened all things is fastened to the wood; the Master is outraged; God is murdered.[42]

Not all of Ignatius of Antioch's writings are reflections of a growing synthesis of Christian doctrine about Jesus. He was compelled, as well, to engage in a certain amount of defensive polemic against the doctrine generally labeled *Docetism* (from the Greek *dokein*, to appear). This was one of the early manifestations of the philosophical current known as Gnosticism which, in almost all its many forms, depreciates matter and the body while exalting the spiritual, the psychic and the rational elements of creation. Even within the writings of the New Testament, there are indications that some form of Docetism appears to have been a problem for some believers (cf. 1 Jn. 4:2 and 2 Jn. 7). Since matter was base or evil, it was seen as unfitting that God should truly become flesh. Rather, he only "appeared" to do so, said the Docetists. They were, however, not totally consistent, since some admitted the reality of the Incarnation, while denying the reality of His sufferings. This doctrine may be seen as an attempt to maintain the transcendence of God while rejecting the scandal caused by the *kenosis* (cf. Phil. 2:7 "...he emptied himself" is *heauton ekenosen* in the Greek) contained in the doctrine of God becoming flesh, the Incarnation.[43]

In numerous passages in his letters,[44] Ignatius confronts this doctrine directly, emphasizing the truth of Jesus' flesh, His birth, His sufferings, His death, His resurrection in the flesh. It was, however, not a doctrine which died easily, and one sees Tertullian (died 220) mounting an attack on it in his classic work *De Carne Christi.*[45]

The specific development and disputes attendant on Christology after Ignatius must be left to the sciences of Patristics and of the history of the development of dogma.[46] What is important to note, by way of generalization, is the growth of two main theological tendencies and three basic theological questions. The theological tendencies are usually labeled the *Logos-Sarx* (Word-Flesh) and the *Logos-Anthropos* (Word-Man) theologies, respectively associated with the theological "schools" of Alexandria and Antioch. The Alexandrian School is marked by its use of the "spiritual" interpretation of Scripture and its stress on the unity and divinity of Christ; the Antiochean School by its emphasis on the "literal" interpretation of Scripture, and its stress on the humanity of the Lord. By way of action and reaction, these schools of thought dominate the history of Christology up to and including the Third Council of Constantinople in 681, and the tendencies which differentiate them are reflected in theology even in our own day.

The three theological questions facing the early Christian schools and finally the bishops in Council concerned: 1) the relationship of Jesus as Logos to God the Father; 2) the relationship of the Logos to the man Jesus; and 3) the duality in unity of Jesus. Three crises in Christian thought brought these questions to the fore, Arianism, Nestorianism and Eutychianism (Monophysitism), producing in time the Councils of Nicea (325), Constantinople I (381), Ephesus (431), and Chalcedon (451); Constantinople III (681). With each of these we must deal in turn.

2. Nicea

Reflecting on Jesus in terms of the Johannine *Logos,* the Alexandrian priest Arius and his followers denied the divinity of the Logos, maintaining that "there was (a time) when (the Logos) was not." For them, this teaching followed from the Christian belief that the Logos was begotten of the Father and thus, for them, not co-eternal with the Unbegotten Father who alone is God in the proper sense.

In Council at Nicea, called by the Emperor Constantine in 325, the bishops of the Church (mostly Eastern, although Hosius of Cordoba served as "legate" of the Pope) issued a rule of faith which, with the additions made when it was reaffirmed in 381 at Constantinople, we know as the Creed of the Mass.

> We believe in One God, the Almighty Father, Maker of all things visible and invisible. And (we believe) in one Lord Jesus Christ, the Son of God, born as the only-begotten of the Father, that is of the substance of the Father, God from God, Light from Light, true God from true God, begotten not made, of one substance *(homoousios)* with the Father, through whom all things came to be, both in heaven and on earth. For us men and for our salvation He came down, was made flesh and became man, suffered and rose the third day....[47]

There immediately followed the declaration that the Catholic Church anathematized those who said "There was a time when He was not" or "Before He was born, He was not."[48]

Several things are noteworthy in this first Conciliar Creed. First of all—and highly significant for all later thought—is the absolute identity presumed as existing between the Word or Logos and Jesus Christ. The Logos as such is not even mentioned. It is Jesus Christ who is confessed to be the One Only-Begotten of the Father, true God from true God.

Secondly, the phrase "Light from Light," like the anathema at the end of the Creed, is inserted to eliminate understanding the words "born" and "only-begotten" in any temporal sense. Once there is fire, there is light. So with the Father and the Son; Their existence is simultaneous and eternal.[49]

Thirdly, the *homoousios*. What the bishops meant by the word is that it is not a different reality or substance which constitute Father and Son. The Father and Son are one identical reality, one God, but are Father and Son nonetheless. The use of the word was innovative. It belonged to the *linqua franca* of philosophical and theological discussion in that age and was susceptible of various interpretations. The word was even capable of being used by those who viewed Christ as little more than an earthly form or mode of the Father Himself (hence the name *Modalists* or Sabellianists from the Roman priest Sabellius, c. 250 A.D., who propounded the doctrine), so that, for example, it was the Father Himself who suffered on Calvary in His mode or form as Son (from which theory derives the word *Patri-passionism*). The bishops of Nicea, however, shaped the word to suit their meaning by inserting it in a context in which the Father and Son are distinguished (Light from Light, God from God, etc.) while confessed to be one God, identical in substance.

The concerns of Nicea appear, at first glance, to be very different from those of the New Testament. At closer look, however, it becomes clear that the New Testament and, more fundamentally, Jesus Himself pose the questions which Nicea had to face. Who is this Jesus born of Mary by the power of the Spirit, and whom the biblical authors announce as One sent from God and as having existed before His appearance among us? Who is this One in whom the "fullness of the Deity lives in bodily form" (Col. 2:9) and what connection does He have with the God of Abraham, Isaac and Jacob, with the One whom He called Father and whose rule He proclaimed? Such questions were inevitable and essential, for ultimately the very nature of the salvation God has worked among the human race depends on their answer. Is it God Himself who saves us in Jesus? And, if so, in what sense is Jesus God? Far from betraying the Scriptures, Nicea is witness to the fact that Tradition, the primary (in a temporal sense) depository of Revelation, continued to reflect on what was its own, keeping it alive even once it had been consigned to writing at the Spirit's inspiration. Whether, in that process, the early Church calcified the Revelation by "Hellenizing" it is a question to which we will return below.

3. Ephesus

Nicea in its Creed identified Logos, Son, and Jesus Christ. This identification became a source of contention in the following century, although the point directly in question was a particular use of the *communicatio idiomatum*. It had become customary for Christians to call Mary *Mother of God* (Gk. *Theotokos*) and to invoke her under that name. Indeed, the familiar prayer *Sub tuum praesidium* ("We fly to thy patronage, O Holy Mother of God" etc.) was probably composed in Greek in the third century. Already in 107, Ignatius had noted how "Jesus Christ our God was conceived of Mary..."[50] and, before that, the Gospel of Luke had referred to her as "mother of my Lord" (Lk. 1:43). For Greek readers of the Old Testament in its Septuagint translation, *Kyrios* (Lord) was the common term for Yahweh, and so the transposition of terms was easily realized. "Mother of my Lord" and "Mother of my God" were, practically speaking, synonymous for them.[51] For the Patriarch of Constantinople, Nestorius, however, the usage was something of a scandal, and his rejection of it was accompanied by what many thought was a false concept of Jesus. What Nestorius actually believed is still a matter of some discussion, but at the time he was widely perceived as dividing Christ against Himself by explaining the union of the divine and human in Christ in such a way that the eternal Logos or Son and Jesus, Son of Mary, were distinct realities.

Nestorius' preaching against the *Theotokos* and his manner of explaining the union of the divine and human in Christ were vigorously opposed by St. Cyril, the Patriarch of Alexandria, in a classic confrontation between the theological "school" of Alexandria and an extreme form of the Antiochean "school." To settle the controversy, a Council met at Ephesus in 431[52] and, after considerable maneuvering on the part of the partisans of both sides, a decree was drawn up and confirmed by the papal legates when they arrived. The decree reads in part:

> We do not say that the nature of the Word became flesh through a change...rather we assert that the Word, having united to Himself, according to His *hypostasis*, living flesh with a rational soul, became man in an inexplicable and incomprehensible manner.... For, it was not that at first any ordinary man was born of the Virgin and that on him the Word of God later descended. Rather, united to the flesh in the womb, He is said to have been born according to the flesh.... And therefore, the holy Fathers have not hesitated to call the Holy Virgin *Theotokos* (Mother of God), not because the nature of the Word or of His divinity took the source of birth from the Holy Virgin, but because He took from her that sacred body with a rational soul in which the Word of God, united according to *hypostasis*, is said to be born according to the flesh.[53]

According to Catholic belief, no mother is responsible for everything which constitutes the child of her womb since the immortal soul is created directly by God. Nonetheless, she is called mother of the individual, not simply mother of so and so's body. So, in like fashion, in the case of Mary and her Son. She is not the cause of His divinity which exists with the Father from all eternity, nor is she the cause of His human soul. But since the Eternal Son has taken to Himself as His Own this body and soul, and is, in this way, born of her, she is *properly* called His Mother.[54]

The recognition of Mary as Theotokos did much to stimulate the already growing devotion of the Church to the Mother of Jesus. St. Cyril himself can be called one of the first great Marian theologians. In a talk given to the bishops at Ephesus in the Church of St. Mary, he used terminology of Our Lady which anticipated many later developments.

> Hail, O Holy and Mystic Trinity, Who have called us all together in this Church of the Mother of God. Hail Mary, Mother of God, Treasure who are to be venerated by the whole world. You are a constantly-shining light, the crown of

virginity, the measure of correct doctrine, an indestructible temple. You are the place which held Him who can be held by no place, mother and virgin. ...Hail you who have encompassed the Immense and the Incomprehensible in your virginal womb. Through you, the Holy Trinity is adored and glorified; through you the priceless Cross is celebrated and adored throughout the world. Through you heaven exults, the angels and archangels rejoice, the demons are put to flight, the Tempter has fallen from heaven. Through you fallen humanity is assumed into heaven...and all creatures have come to a knowledge of the truth.... You are the joy of the whole universe.[35]

What might almost seem excessive praise is actually but various and more limited ways of admiring the one great glory that is hers. She is Mother of God. Clearly the work of Ephesus, under Cyril's leadership, is a case of defending the dignity of the Mother for the sake of the Son. The fact that the *communicatio idiomatum*—in this case Mother of God—is not simply doxological (honorific) terminology but a reality stands as a safeguard against those who would so distinguish the divine and human in Jesus as to forget the unity which makes them inseparable. That unity, says Ephesus, exists "according to *hypostasis.*" That word, which basically meant an individually existing thing, had already been used by the author of the Epistle to the Hebrews 1:3 (cf. p. 59 above), and the Greek Fathers of the Church had come to use it to describe what there were "Three of" in the One God: Three hypostases in One Being. Thus, it is the *hypostasis* of the Son which assumes or takes a body and rational soul, so that these are united with divinity in that hypostasis. In this way, according to Ephesus, the divine nature and the human nature exist in the One Hypostasis, i.e., in the One Individual who is the Eternal Son. With these words, conciliar sanction is given to the doctrine called the Hypostatic Union (the Union of two natures, divine and human, in One Hypostasis or Individual) which would be elaborated in greater detail at Chalcedon.

It is noteworthy, also, that Ephesus rejects any form of adoptionism, by which there would have existed—even if only in the womb of Mary—an autonomous individual ("any ordinary man" in Ephesus' words) to which the Word united Himself later on in whatever manner one might explain such a theory.[56]

4. Chalcedon

In some respects, the decree of Ephesus could be viewed as a "victory" for the Alexandrian *(Logos-Sarx)* school of theology because of its strong reaffirmation of the unity of Christ and its defense of the *communicatio idiomatum*. On the other hand, it must be noted that Ephesus clearly stated that the Logos took to Himself a human body and soul, thus a full human nature, and that, in doing so, the divine nature underwent no change. Despite this teaching, the monk Eutyches so interpreted the doctrine of the Council and the writings of St. Cyril that, in effect, he denied the reality of the human in Christ by claiming that, after the Word became flesh, Christ had only one nature (thus the name *Monophysitism*), the human having been, in some way, absorbed into or divinized totally by the Union. Like Nestorius, who had pushed the Antiochean tendency to an extreme, Eutyches had now pushed the Alexandrian tendency to an unacceptable limit, both cases revealing how difficult theologians found it to live with a certain "tension" when thinking of Christ. Such a "tension" necessitated maintaining the unity of Christ without overlooking the difference in natures or of emphasizing one nature in such a way as to deny, implicitly or explicitly, the other nature. In fact, of course, the "tension" can only be maintained and defended; it cannot be explained. For that reason, most of the history of Christology is witness to a perduring "tug of war" between theologians who, in changed circumstances and from various perspectives, reveal a preference for one or the other of the original tendencies, the Alexandrian or Antiochean.

To meet the challenge posed by Eutyches, the Patriarch of Constantinople, Flavian, appealed to the Pope who, at the time, was St. Leo the Great. Leo responded to the Patriarch in a letter which is known to the history of dogma as the *Tome to Flavian*. The gist of that letter appears today in the second reading in the Roman Breviary or Liturgy of the Hours for the Solemnity of the Annunciation, the feast of the Incarnation, March 25. It reads as follows:

Humility was assumed by majesty, weakness was assumed by strength, mortality was assumed by eternity. In order to absolve the debt of our human condition, a nature which could not suffer was united to one which could suffer so that One and the Same Mediator between God and man, the man Jesus Christ, was able to die in the one nature while not able to die in the other.

Therefore, in the integral and complete nature of a true man, the true God is born—complete in what was His own, complete in what is ours. We say "ours" meaning those things in us which the Creator established from the beginning and which He assumed for the sake of their restoration. For those things which the devil introduced and which mankind lost by being deceived found no trace in the Savior. Although He undertook to share our human weakness, nevertheless, He did not become a sharer of our sins.... Therefore, He, who remaining in the form of God who made man, was made man in the form of a servant.

The Son of God entered the lowliness of this world, descending from His heavenly throne yet not leaving the glory of the Father. Thus, He is begotten in a new order and in a new birth. A new order because, invisible in what is proper to Himself, He became visible in what is proper to us...remaining beyond time, He begins to be in time....

He who is true God is also true man and in this unity there is no falsehood since both the lowliness of man and the greatness of the Godhead are His. Just as God is not changed by this act of mercy, so the man is not destroyed by the dignity of the divinity. Each nature performs what is proper to itself in union with the other; the Word doing what is proper to the Word, and the flesh what is proper to the flesh. The one nature shines with miracles, the other suffers injuries....

As it must be said frequently, He is One and the Same, truly Son of God and son of man: God because 'in the beginning was the Word, and the Word was with God, and the Word was God,' man because 'the Word became flesh and dwelt among us.

Without attempting to offer an explanation of the "how it can be," the letter is a striking summation of the various aspects of the mystery of the Incarnation. In a formula traditional since Ignatius of Antioch and Irenaeus of Lyons, the unity is stressed: the "One and the Same" is God and man. Jesus of Nazareth is the Eternal Logos; the Eternal Logos is Jesus. Leo rejects any "mythological" understanding of the Incarnation. Unlike the pagan gods of Greece and Rome, the Son does not "step out of heaven" to walk the earth. "Descending from His heavenly throne, yet He does not leave the glory of the Father," wrote Leo, again repeating an understanding of Revelation which has been traditional since Ignatius. In one simple sentence, he thus refutes an all-too-common picture of the Incarnation caused by the resonance of certain words (e.g., "descend," "become," "dwell among us," "came down from heaven") on our imaginations. The integrity of the human in Jesus is defended—"the flesh does what is proper to the flesh"—although here again the unity is asserted when Leo notes that each nature, doing what is proper to itself, acts "in union with the other." Eutychianism is refuted as Leo writes: "the man (i.e., the humanity) is not destroyed by the dignity of the divinity."

Leo's representatives, with his letter, were denied a hearing at a synod in Ephesus in 449 (the infamous "Robber Council") which was controlled by supporters of Eutyches and opponents of Flavian. The situation soon changed, however, and a general Council was called to meet at Nicea, but the site was changed to Chalcedon where the bishops did meet in 451. Leo's letter was read to them, enthusiastically received, and obviously influenced in decisive fashion the dogmatic definition which follows:

Following the holy Fathers, we teach in harmony that the One and the Same Son is our Lord Jesus Christ, the Same perfect in deity, the Same perfect in humanity, true God and true man, the Same from a rational soul and body, consubstantial *(homoousios)* with the Father according to deity, the Same consubstantial *(homoousios)* with us according to humanity, 'like to us in all things except sin' (cf. Heb. 4:15). Begotten of the Father before the ages according to His deity, the Same in these last days was born of the Virgin Mary, Mother of God (Theotokos), according to His humanity for us and for our salvation.

The One and the Same Christ, Son, Lord and Only-begotten is to be acknowledged in two natures which are unconfused, unchanged, undivided and inseparable. The difference of the natures is in no way removed because of the union. Rather, what is proper to each nature is preserved as they come together in One Person (Gk. *prosopon)* and one *hypostasis*—not separated or divided into two persons, but rather the One and the Same Son and Only-begotten God the Word, the Lord Jesus Christ, just as the prophets and our Lord Jesus Christ Himself taught us and as the Creed of the Fathers handed on to us.[57]

Although the Chalcedonian definition is unique and has served the Church for over fifteen hundred years as the touchstone for orthodox faith in Jesus, it was, nonetheless, a formulation of faith already traditional in its own time. To stress that the eternal Word *is* Jesus of Nazareth, the formula "One and the Same" is used three times, and five other times in the shortened version "the Same." This identity is likewise taught by the repetition of the term "one hypostasis" of Ephesus, to which—as an equivalent—the term "one person" is now added. Whereas the term "hypostasis" directly signified any individual thing existing by itself (e.g., a tree, a stone, a desk, a dog, etc.) the term "person" was more specific. In its Greek form *prosopon* it had originally meant the mask worn by the characters in Greek drama. Thence it had come to mean "face" and finally the rational or thinking individual. In its meaning as "face" and "rational individual" it is found in the New Testament (cf. Mt. 6:16—face; 2 Cor. 1:11 and Lk. 20:21—person; in Galatians, Paul uses it in both senses, Gal. 2:6 and 2:11). Along with hypostasis, it had begun to be used to describe what there are Three of in God. Thus, at Chalcedon, what there are "Three of" in God (Three Hypostases, Three Persons) is One in the case of the Word and Jesus of Nazareth. The eternal Word and Jesus of Nazareth are not two individuals or persons, but One only. As at Ephesus, the word "nature" is used to describe the divinity and the humanity. And, so, what there is "One of" in God (one nature) is twofold in Christ (two natures, the divine and human). By using the adjectives (they are adverbs in the Greek) "unconfused and unchanged," the bishops teach that the natures do not mix to form some third thing, but rather each remains what it was before the union in the sense that the divinity is not changed into the human nor is the humanity absorbed by the divinity. Jesus is declared—as at Nicea—*homoousios* or consubstantial with the Father, but, also, now at Chalcedon is described as *homoousios* or consubstantial with us according to His humanity. In this way, again, the fact that the divinity and the humanity each retain their integrity is taught. By adding "undivided and inseparable," the unity is reiterated lest the distinction of the natures appear to separate or divide the hypostasis or person. Mary is again called the Mother of God because the One and the Same who is the eternal Word is also her Son.

The teaching of Chalcedon was, in a sense, rounded out at the Third Council of Constantinople in 681 when the Church condemned *monothelitism* which held that, in Jesus, there was only *one will* and *one natural operation*. This heresy was a new form of monophysitism since it attempted to defend the unity of Christ by denying the duality of natures. At Constantinople, the bishops essentially repeated earlier teaching, saying that Jesus had two wills, the divine and human, and two natural operations (i.e., whatever flows naturally from the two distinct natures) which operate, however, in harmony. "The two natural wills are in no way opposed, as some impious heretics assert. Rather, His human will follows without reservation or holding back, and is submissive to His divine and omnipotent will. For it is necessary for the human will to act itself, obedient indeed to the divine will...."[58] What is being said, of course, is not that the human will of Christ lacks its proper spontaneity, serving only to put into execution a divine command. The human will, rather, acts in a manner proper to any human will, but in this case always in conformity with the divine will to which it is united in the One Person. The Greeks coined the word *theandric* (God-man) to express the duality in unity of Jesus' activity.

In our own time, the Church has found various occasions to reaffirm the teachings of the early Councils.[59] Most recently, through a Declaration by the Congregation for the Doctrine of the Faith, she has reminded Christians of three specific points:[60]

1. It has been revealed that the Son exists from all eternity distinct from the Father and the Spirit.

2. It must be held that Jesus is one Person, begotten of the Father before all time and born of Mary in time.

3. The humanity of Jesus did not exist of itself as a person, but exists as being assumed into the eternal Person of the Son of God.[61]

This declaration was prompted, in part, by renewed criticism of what is generally referred to as the Chalcedonian Christology of the Hypostatic Union. The "two natures in One Person" Christology has been charged with several faults. It is alleged that the doctrine is not biblical but rather a "Hellenistic" model which has little to do with the history of salvation and which presents the image of Christ in the static or essentialistic form of an outdated philosophy.[62]

The charge—frequently repeated—that the early Councils "hellenized" Christian theology is an accusation too unnuanced to be accepted in the light of historical research.[63] We have already noted that the New Testament itself was not only written in Greek, but also appeared in a cultural amalgum influenced by "Hellenistic" elements. That the early Councils took place in a Greek-speaking world and worldview, and that they employed, at times, terminology which was current in the philosophical thought and discussion of the time is undoubted. They did so, however—as did the authors of the New Testament—in such a way that the terminology was shaped and fashioned to express what the Church was convinced was contained in the original Revelation. The way that *homoousios*, hypostasis, person and nature were used clearly demonstrates this fact. In fact, as already noted, the terms hypostasis and person *(prosopon)* appear in the New Testament in usage at least analagous to conciliar usage. Far from being unconcerned with the history of salvation, their purpose was to defend the fact that, in Jesus of Nazareth, the eternal God Himself had come among us to effect our liberation, and that to do this He had to remain what He always is (infinite and transcendent) while taking to Himself what is ours so that what is ours could be saved in Him and by Him and through Him. This intent of theirs was made explicitly clear in their doctrinal affirmations: all was done "for us men and for our salvation."[64] In truth, the work of the early Councils is only a beginning,[65] but, nonetheless, a privileged one guaranteed by the infallibility which the Spirit grants the Church. For that very reason, while the conciliar doctrine may not be the end, it must always be the beginning; that is, the doctrinal content of the Councils must always serve as the starting point for the Church's continual and continued reflection on the mystery of Christ as found in Tradition and Scripture. If the Conciliar teaching appears to be static, essentialistic, a matter of words or philosophy alone, it will be because, in our time, we have failed to understand it and rethink it. On the other hand, the more closely we examine it, the more obvious it becomes that Nicea, Ephesus and Chalcedon are, each in turn, a defense of the "Gospel of Jesus Christ, Son of God" (Mk. 1:1) who, in often unpalatable words, challenged those who would no longer accept the testimony of their own tradition (cf. Lk. 16:31).

IV. GOD BECOMES MAN

The mystery of the Incarnation, defended time and again by the early Councils and by the Church down through the ages, finds its cause and explanation—as do all other things—in the mystery of God Himself. Working from Revelation and from centuries of Christian tradition (especially the writings of Athanasius, Cyril of Alexandria, Augustine, and Thomas Aquinas), the Council of Florence in 1442 set forth the mystery of God in the following terms:

> The holy Roman Church, founded by the word of Our Lord and Savior, firmly believes, professes, and preaches that there is One true God, all-powerful, unchangeable and eternal, the Father and the Son and the Holy Spirit, One in essence, Three in persons. The Father is unbegotten, the Son begotten of the Father, the Holy Spirit proceeding from the Father and the Son. The Father is not the Son nor the Holy Spirit; the Son is not the Father nor the Holy Spirit; the Holy Spirit is not the Father nor the Son. The Father is only the Father, the Son is only the Son, the Holy Spirit is only the Holy Spirit. The Father alone has begotten the Son from His own substance; the Son alone has been begotten of the Father alone; the Holy Spirit alone proceeds from both the Father and the Son. These three Persons are One God and not three gods because the Three are one substance, one essence, one nature, one divinity, one immensity, one eternity. All things are one (to the Three) where there is not present the opposition of relation.

Because of the unity, the Father is completely in the Son and completely in the Holy Spirit; the Son is completely in the Father and completely in the Holy Spirit; the Holy Spirit is completely in the Father and completely in the Son. None of the Three either precedes in eternity, nor exceeds in greatness nor is superior in power. The Son exists from the Father eternally and without beginning; the Holy Spirit proceeds from the Father and the Son eternally and without beginning; whatever the Father is or has, He does not have from another, but only of Himself. He is the principle which has no principle. Whatever the Son is or has He has from the Father. He is the principle from the principle. Whatever the Holy Spirit is or has, He has from the Father and the Son. But the Father and the Son are not two principles of the Holy Spirit, but only one principle, as the Father, Son, and Holy Spirit are not three principles of creation, but one principle only.[66]

The unity of the One God is stressed in the Decree by the principle of the *circumincession,* i.e., the total presence of the Three Persons in Each Other, and by the statement that "all things are One where there is not present the opposition of relation." This is to be understood as meaning that what distinguishes the Three from One Another are only the relations which the One God has to Himself.

In the reflections of St. Augustine and St. Thomas Aquinas on the Mystery of God—which reflections have become the common property of theology—God is and knows and wills (loves) Himself. Like His Being, His Knowing and Willing are perfect, eternal and one. In knowing Himself, He "expresses Himself" to Himself and for Himself. That Self-Expression is eternal and complete. It is neither more nor less than He Himself, but it is His Self-Expression which we know as His Word or His Son. And His love for Himself as Expressed and Expressing is no more nor less than He Himself— what we know of Him as Spirit. All that He is and has, the Father expresses and beholds in the Son. The Father exists for the Son; the Son from and for the Father while the "complacency" of the Father and Son in One Another is the Spirit.

For our sake and for our salvation, the One God has decided to enter the created universe which He Himself made from nothing; and to do so by becoming human. He did this not by the limited expression of Himself and His Will witnessed in creation itself and in the Revelation through word and deed which He made of Himself to Israel. He decided, rather, to express Himself completely, and so, in the final age of creation, He addressed us not by words but by Himself. At the consent of the Virgin, He created for Himself a human body and soul. This action is—as it has to be—the action of the One God, but in expressing Himself completely to us His self-expression is—as it is within Himself—His Word, His Son. Indeed, it would appear that the only way God expresses Himself is through His Self-Expression, His Son. And thus, the One God became man as Son, not as Father nor Spirit.[67]

The human body and soul of Jesus of Nazareth, from the first moment of His miraculous conception, is the *human* self-expression of God Himself. God, of course, does not "leave" heaven to come and be with us in human form. This the early Councils made quite clear. God cannot leave Himself, nor is there "anywhere" to leave, since He is always totally present to and in all He has created. The Hypostatic Union means—to the extent that we can even begin to understand it—that God takes to Himself or assumes a created body and soul which finds its individuality, its source of identity, not in itself—as we do—but in God Himself. What distinguishes myself from all other individuals or persons is the *created* individuality God has given me. What distinguishes Jesus of Nazareth from all other individuals or persons is the *uncreated* individuality of God Himself as Son. In philosophical, scholastic terminology we would say that, whereas each creature of God lives and operates because of a created participation in being, the humanity of Christ lives and operates by virtue of the uncreated act of existence of God Himself as that act of existence belongs to the Son.[68] This is the fundamental reason—so it would seem—why Jesus is said not to be a human person.[69] He is the eternal Person of the Son who has taken to and for Himself a complete human nature. This assumption by God of a human nature is, in itself, a unique, singular grace, *the grace of union,* a gift to the humanity completely surpassing the many ways God gives Himself to His creatures. By this gift, the man Jesus is *united in being* to God Himself—a union which uniquely molds and shapes the Lord's humanity. The person or hypostasis of the Son within the Trinity is *from* and *of* and *for* the Father; He is what He receives, and finds His own meaning in the Eternal Father from whom He originates. He is distinct and eternal only insofar as He is from, and of, and for the Father, so that it is His very relation to the Father which constitutes His Own Person, His being God. Since this "being from and of and for" is the very definition of personhood for the Son, so the humanity of the Son will resonate that which creates, supports and sustains it, namely that existence which is from, of and for the Father. As it exists in the Son, the humanity of Jesus is defined by relation to the Father. His humanity, like His divinity, is relational being, which means it is stamped by filial relation to the Eternal Father. As the Son is the eternal Image of the Father, so the humanity of the Son, His body and soul and their powers, is the human manifestation of what the Son is as the Father's Image.

Because of the grace of personal union with the Son and because of the abundance of created graces which came to His humanity as a consequence of that union, the humanity of Jesus is marked in a singular respect with an equilibrium and goodness theretofore unknown by a race separated from God by the original fall and steeped in personal sins. He Himself would ask the Jews who accused Him of excesses and sin (cf. Mt. 11:18-19; Jn. 9:24-25), "Which of you can convict me of sin?" (Jn. 8:46), and the author of the Epistle to the Hebrews would write of Him that "we have one who has been tested in every way that we are, though he is without sin" (Heb. 4:15; cf. 7:26-28). As the Church has always understood and proclaimed, Jesus was without sin of any kind, either original or personal. Indeed, because of the union, His humanity *could not* know sin; He was incapable of sinning. The Third Council of Constantinople (681) taught:

> Just as His humanity is said to be and is the humanity of God the Word, so too the will which is natural to His humanity is said to be and is proper to God the Word.... Just as His most holy and immaculate body and soul were deified but not taken away, but rather remained in their own state and kind, so His human will was deified but not taken away. On the contrary, it

was saved, as St. Gregory says: For the will which is
understood to be in the Savior is not contrary to God, but
completely deified.[70]

St. Leo the Great had already drawn the consequences from
this total sinlessness and impeccability of Jesus when he wrote: "His
humanity did not have anything contrary to His divinity; His bodily
senses were active without the law of sin, and His true emotions
were tempered by the direction of His deity and His intellect, and
so did not cede to illicit harms."[71]

In all of us, our natural desires and appetites, our human
emotions and affections naturally respond to what attracts or repels
them. These instinctual responses are intended to be guided by the
use of our reason in such a way that a harmony among the appetites
and instincts works to the good of the whole person. Vice occurs
when the proper harmony is disrupted. Thus, the body's instinctive
desire for food and drink, if not moderated by reason and will, yields
the vice of gluttony and ultimately illness to the body itself; our
instinctive fear of death, unless guided by reason and will, can yield
apostasy, treason, even murder. (One thinks of those who killed
others in concentration camps because of fear of being killed
themselves.) These instinctive, natural reactions were fully present
in Jesus, but, because of the union of His humanity with the divine
and because of the grace-filled operation of His mind and will, there
was a harmony preserved in Him unlike any which we have ever
experienced. We do not know what it is to have an equilibrated
personality. As a result, it is relatively easy to hail as spontaneity
what is merely unreasoned instinct, or to define freedom as the
power to choose that which is detrimental to ourselves. If that be
the way we define human freedom or spontaneity, Jesus was neither
free nor spontaneous in His actions.[72] But if we can imagine a
conjunction or harmony among our intellect and will and instinctive
drives which is fully integrated—and because of that, more richly
human—then we approach an understanding of the spontaneity and
human freedom of the Lord in His rational, emotional and
instinctive life.[73] In modern parlance, we would say that Jesus "had
it all together" in a way which we, not having, admire and spend so
much time trying to achieve. The Epistle to the Hebrews reflects on

the entrance of the Son into the world and on the conformity of His human will with that of the divine when it cites Psalm 40:6-7:

> Sacrifice and offering you did not desire, but a body you prepared for me; with burnt offerings and sin offerings you were not pleased. Then I said, 'Here I am—it is written about me in the scroll—I have come to do your will, O God' (Heb. 10:5-7).

1. Mary and Joseph

The harmony between the divine and the human will of Jesus—which one finds manifested through all His life's work—finds a reflection in the correspondence between the Divine Will and other human wills, which were prepared and chosen by God to make the Incarnation possible. The most important of these, of course, was Mary of Nazareth, called to be Mother of God. Mary's will was both prepared for and consulted in the role predestined for her. Conceived without sin herself in view of her Son, she had lived a life absolutely sinless and one filled with God's favor. Grace had predestined her role, prepared her for it, and effected her response when her consent was asked.

> The Father of mercies willed that the Incarnation be preceded by consent on the part of the predestined mother, so that just as a woman contributed to death, so should a woman contribute to life....[74]

That assent of Mary has always been viewed as part of her free and unique cooperation in the work of human redemption. Mary had to be given an understanding of the mystery in which she was to share so intimately. That she had an understanding befitting her role is clear not only from what is explicit and implied in the Annunciation account in St. Luke's Gospel, but also from Tradition. Along with numerous other Fathers of the Church, St. Augustine described Mary as having conceived the Word in her heart and mind before conceiving Him in her flesh.[75] To conceive in the mind is to understand; to conceive in the heart is to will and love, and this bestowal of that type of understanding and willing is both worthy of

God who does not move His creatures like blind or unthinking objects as well as it is necessary for an action which was to be a unique participation in human salvation.[76] Mary's consent, in order to be free and human, had to be an informed, not a blind consent. Such a consent was fitting as well, according to St. Thomas, because Mary, by her consent, acted in place of the entire human race.[77]

The free consent of the Mother was rewarded by God in ways explicable only by the magnitude of the event itself. A virgin conceived; "a certain spiritual marriage took place between the Son of God and human nature" in Mary's womb[78]; and the physical integrity of the Mother was preserved even in childbirth, as a sign that the recreation of the human race would sanctify, not diminish, what the first creation established.[79]

Since every human decision in some way affects others than the person immediately involved, so, too, did the consent of Mary. The first person touched by her decision was Joseph, to whom she was betrothed. Her obedient faith prepared for the faith of that just man who became the first to believe that what was born of her was conceived by the Holy Spirit. Their common response to the mystery confided to them was a virginal life. That Mary remained "ever-Virgin" in her marriage with Joseph is an infallible teaching of the Church as she interprets the evidence from Scripture and Tradition. We profess this faith each time we pray the Roman Canon of the Mass, saying: "we honor in the first place Mary, the ever-virgin Mother of our Lord and God, Jesus Christ." We do this despite the apparent difficulties offered to such a doctrine by certain texts of the New Testament.

Those texts noted for particular difficulty are Matthew 13:55 ("Isn't this the carpenter's son? Isn't his mother's name Mary, and aren't his brothers James, Joseph, Simon, and Jude? Aren't all his sisters with us?"); Mark 6:3 (the same as the previous one with the exception that it omits any reference to Joseph); also Luke 4:16-24; John 7:2; Acts 1:14; 1 Cor. 9:5, etc. From such texts we can be certain that, during His lifetime here on earth, various men and women were referred to as "brothers" and "sisters" of Jesus. This usage carried over into the books of the New Testament, and the Greek word *adelphos* was used to describe these people. The word normally means "blood-brother," although Liddell-Scott in their *Greek-English Lexicon* hold that it can mean a "near-kinsman."[80] The Greek translation of the Old Testament, the Septuagint (c. 180-145 B.C.) used *adelphos* to translate the Hebrew *'ah* which can mean either brother or kinsman (cf. Gn. 13:8, 11; 14:14 where *adelphos* is used even though Lot and Abraham were clearly not brothers in the sense of "blood brothers.") In the New Testament, as well, the word *adelphos* is not confined to blood brothers as can be seen in Romans 9:3-4 and Matthew 28:10 where it is used as we would use it in English to refer to a "brother" in race or faith, etc. *Adelphos* is also used when the words of Jesus Himself about the importance of spiritual relationship ("Anyone who does the will of my Father in heaven is my brother, sister and mother"—Mt. 12:50) are recorded. The word, therefore, while presenting a *prima facie* case for blood brotherhood, admits even in the New Testament of a meaning other than that and cannot be taken, philologically at least, as conclusive.[81]

On the other hand, it is worth noting that nowhere does the New Testament mention anyone other than Jesus as being the child of Mary or of Joseph, or of Mary and Joseph. Indeed there may be indications that some of the men called "brother" are in fact the sons of someone other than Mary, the Mother of Jesus. Matthew's Gospel, in the text quoted above, cites "James and Joseph" as among the "brothers" of the Lord. That same Gospel later (27:56) identifies one of the women standing near the Cross as "Mary, the mother of James and Joseph." The same occurrence can be found by comparing Mark 6:3 with Mark 13:55. These indications, although suggestive, cannot be claimed to be conclusive since it is not *absolutely* evident that the same men are being spoken of in the different instances.[82] It is at least theoretically possible that when Matthew attempts to identify the Mary who stood by the Cross by naming her sons who, presumably, were better known to his readers than she (as Mark, in 15:21, does for his readers by identifying Simon of Cyrene by noting that he is the father of Alexander and Rufus), he does not mean the same men he referred to earlier as "brothers of the Lord." Or, it is possible to claim that in each instance Matthew is simply reporting unconnected strands of tradition as it may be likewise in the case of the Marcan texts. While such possibilities hardly seem probable, they should at least be recognized as possibilities, thus leaving the identity of the "brothers"—like the word *adelphos* itself—uncertain, at least as far as what is ascertainable from New Testament evidence.

It is in just such a situation of exegetical inconclusiveness that Tradition and the Church's Magisterium serve their function as normative interpreters of Sacred Scripture. The evidence from Tradition and the Magisterium in this case is manifold and definitive. The oldest extant witnesses to Mary's perpetual virginity are the so-called *Protoevangelium of James*[83] which dates to approximately 150-180 A.D. and the *Gospel According to Peter*[84] which is already cited by Serapion of Antioch in 190 A.D. The historical value of both works is questionable, but what they do, nonetheless, is give testimony to the existence of a belief in the perpetual virginity of Mary by at least some Christians at a relatively early date. These testimonies were followed by those of Origen (c. 185-253) in his *Commentary on Matthew's Gospel*[85] and his *Seventh Homily on Luke*,[86] and by St. Jerome's classic work on *The Perpetual Virginity of Blessed Mary* (or, *Against Helvidius*),[87] published in the 380's. After that, the testimony of the Fathers is unanimous.

The expression "Ever-Virgin" has a long and ancient history in the Creeds and Magisterial statements of the Church. It is found in the Creed of Epiphanius (c. 374),[88] the *Firmiter* of Lateran IV in 1215 which is a conciliar definition of faith,[89] the *Creed of the People of God* of Pope Paul VI in 1967,[90] as well as in the teaching of the First Lateran Synod in 649,[91] the decree *Cum quorumdum* of Paul IV in 1555,[92] and Vatican Council II's Dogmatic Constitution on the Church, *Lumen Gentium*.[93]

It is only within the context of such abundant testimony that the New Testament references to the brothers and sisters of the Lord can be seen in a true perspective. These people are close relatives. The indeterminate Hebrew word *'ah*, seen reflected or translated in the Greek *adelphos* when referring to the brothers of Jesus, is akin to what we call, sociologically, the extended family (as opposed to the nuclear family with which we are so familiar). The Spanish language, which still retains that notion of extended family, has a verbal usage like that of *adelphos* in the texts speaking of Jesus' brothers. One can say in Spanish, "Somos primos hermanos" which literally means, "We are first brothers," but in reality means, "We are first cousins." St. Augustine was familiar with that type of linguistic usage when he wrote—in a context which makes no reference to Mary or to the brothers of Jesus: "…for even among ourselves cousins are called brothers and sisters because of their close relationship, and they are in fact the next thing to full brothers and sisters."[94]

The Second Vatican Council teaches that Mary, like her Son, chose and embraced a virginal and poor form of life.[95] Mary's choice, of course, must be said to have included the free choice also made by her husband. Nothing explains that choice on the part of Mary and Joseph except their own awe before the mystery entrusted to them and their decision to serve that mystery in the person of their Son with a total consecration of soul and body. Such a resolve—like Mary's at the Annunciation—necessitated not only freedom of choice but a knowledge commensurate with their roles and their decision.

V. THE HUMAN KNOWLEDGE OF JESUS

The awareness which Mary had of the Mystery virginally conceived in her, and the awareness of Mary and Joseph which prompted their choice of a celibate marriage naturally leads to one of the most controverted questions of recent times in Christology: what awareness or knowledge did Jesus have of Himself and of His mission? The question—at least for all those who accept the personal union of the divine and human in Jesus of Nazareth—concerns His human knowledge, since as God it is recognized that He knew all things. The Incarnation, however, leaves intact, even while elevating, His human nature and so His human intelligence and understanding. For that reason alone, the human knowledge of Jesus is finite, and, to some extent therefore, limited. What were the limitations?

St. Luke, as he records for us the finding of the twelve-year-old Jesus in the Temple, tells of perplexity on the part of Mary and Joseph in the face of His action and response.

> When his parents saw him, they were astonished. His mother said to him, 'Son, why have you treated us like this? Your father and I have been anxiously searching for you.' 'Why were you searching for me?' he asked. 'Didn't you know I had to be in my Father's house?' But they did not understand what he was saying to them (Lk. 2:48-50).

By way of comment, Luke adds: "His mother treasured all these things in her heart. And Jesus grew in wisdom and stature, and in favor with God and men" (Lk. 2:52).

Even at twelve, then, Jesus, according to St. Luke, knew that He was "from and for" the heavenly Father. That, in itself, is understandable, given the circumstances. Reared in that home, with parents who had chosen virginity because of Him, and made aware of the manner of His own conception, Jesus' concern with and for the Father—even apart from considerations flowing from the consequences of the Hypostatic Union—would be intelligible. Also, it was understandable to Mary and Joseph and, therefore, not likely a cause of perplexity. What would be puzzling is the independence He manifested in spite of such youth—an independence, or better a self-possession, which distinguishes His whole life and all its activities. That type of self-possession is grounded in a self-awareness which begets freedom and spontaneity in action. There remains, however, the question about the nature and extent of that self-awareness.

1. The Answer of Traditional Theology

The traditional answer to that question has been to distinguish—without artificially separating—three types of human knowledge in Christ: Beatific Vision, Infused Knowledge, and Experiential or Acquired Knowledge.

Beatific Vision was that aspect of His knowledge by which Jesus in His human intellect "saw" God "face to face." This "vision" was limited, of course, since as St. Thomas wrote: "The soul of Christ sees the whole essence of God; His soul does not, however, comprehend the whole essence of God since He does not see that essence totally, that is, as perfectly as it is capable of being seen (by the divine Intellect)."[96] Thus, although limited because no created intellect can completely comprehend the Infinite, the human mind of Christ, because it is personally united to the Son, sees God in His essence as do the saints in heaven but in a manner incomparably superior to the saints because of the union. It is essential to remember here that the words "knowing" and "seeing" when applied to a human intellect's knowing and seeing God are analogous concepts. We have no positive idea of what it means to know God *immediately* (i.e., not as a conclusion of reason or an act of faith or through His creatures) or "see" Him who is pure Spirit. Beatific knowledge of God is *like* what we call knowing and seeing but totally transcends anything we have experienced. It is certainly not a mental idea of God or an imaginative picture of Him. Nor, in the best of traditional theology, was it such for Jesus.

Infused knowledge was that aspect of His human awareness or knowledge by which Jesus was given to know all things necessary for Him in His mission of salvation—although in fact many theologians extended it to a knowledge of all things in general. Examples would be the gift of prophecy, the knowledge of the divine mysteries He came to teach, the ability to read the hearts of men, etc.

Acquired or experiential knowledge was that aspect of His human awareness or knowledge by which Jesus learned through daily experience all the many things we ourselves learn that way. Just as we learn things through experience which we already know in a theoretical way, so Jesus was capable of learning experientially things He knew by the particular gift of infused knowledge. In this way, He had to learn how to walk, talk, express Himself so as to be understood by others, etc., although, according to the traditional view, He already knew these things in a way we would call "theoretical."

Support for the traditional understanding can be found in the Scriptures. Jesus' prediction of the passion and resurrection, of Judas' betrayal, etc., are events common to all the Synoptics as well as St. John and would be examples of infused knowledge. Jesus' immediate knowledge of the Father and of His own eternal origins (e.g., Jn. 8:59; 14:10; 17:5) and of the coming Holy Spirit (Jn. 15:26ff.) would be examples of the Beatific Vision. His use of agricultural similies and the like in His parables would be given as examples of experiential knowledge.

However, not a few difficulties can be found with the traditional understanding of the Lord's human knowledge. Chief among them is that the true humanity of the Lord seems to disappear in an apparently non-human type of knowledge. If Jesus knew everything in the Beatific Vision or through infused knowledge, is not much of what the Gospels record of Him as being surprised, etc., really no more than a form of "play-acting"? St. John's account of the resuscitation of Lazarus seems to illustrate such difficulties. In John 11:11, Jesus announces, "Our friend Lazarus has fallen asleep, but I am going to wake him up." Jesus knew He would raise the dead man. Nevertheless, on arriving at the tomb (Jn. 11:36), "Jesus wept." What explains His tears if He knew He was about to raise the dead man? Indeed, some in the crowd question the tears, saying, "Could not he who opened the eyes of the blind man have kept this man from dying?" (Jn. 11:37) Furthermore, if He constantly possessed the Beatific Vision—source of unremitting joy to those in heaven—how is it He was able to suffer on Calvary—a difficulty realized even by proponents of the traditional theology.[97]

There are textual difficulties in the Scriptures themselves:

1) "No one knows about that day or hour, not even the angels in heaven, nor the Son, but only the Father" (Mt. 24:36; Mk. 13:32).

2) "During the days of Jesus' life on earth, he offered up prayers and petitions with loud cries and tears to the one who could save him from death, and he was heard because of his reverent submission. Although he was a son, he learned obedience from what he suffered..." (Heb. 5:7-10).

3) "...But we have one who has been tested (tempted) in every way just as we are, yet was without sin" (Heb. 4:15).

4) Luke 2:52 quoted above.

However, more than individual texts (which, it must be admitted, can be given a creditable interpretation by those who defend the traditional view concerning the Lord's human knowledge) are at stake here. How is it that none of the Synoptic Gospels record Jesus as speaking explicitly about His divine origins, His pre-existence, or of His identity with the Father the way the Gospel of John does? Again, why does Jesus as seen in the Synoptics appear so reluctant to claim that He is the Messiah, and how does one explain the apparent differences in the various recorded predictions of the end of the world, and of His passion and resurrection? Is it not likely that Jesus did not claim divinity nor messiahship, but rather that, with the fuller knowledge that came after the proclamation of His resurrection, the Early Church gradually came to understand these things, and that the Gospels (Mark being the most primitive, John the most developed) reflect that gradual growth in understanding of the primitive community rather than Jesus' own self-understanding?[98]

2. Current Tendencies

Because of such difficulties and because of some conclusions drawn by the proponents of the so-called "historico-critical method" of Scriptural exegesis, many theologians have abandoned the traditional view concerning Jesus' human knowledge. Indeed, it is common enough to find theologians who will defend some or all of the following conclusions concerning the knowledge or awareness which Jesus had of Himself and of His mission:

1) Jesus did not know He was God.[99]

2) The "worldview" of Jesus was fundamentally that of a first-century Jew whose teachings were time-conditioned.[100]

3) Jesus was mistaken in His views concerning the end of the world.[101]

4) Jesus did not see His death as having redemptive value, nor did He foresee it.[102]

5) Jesus did not found a Church.[103]

Rarely are such conclusions put in so bald a form, and frequently enough they are located in contexts which moderate some of the shock suffered by those Christians who find such positions offensive and even erroneous. The positions, however, are not imaginary, nor are they held by only a few. Put in such categorical form, they conflict not only with the views of traditional theology, but also with the general teaching of the Church's Magisterium as well. It is to that Magisterium we must look next.

3. Magisterial Teaching

It should be remembered that the following statements of the Magisterium of the Church were issued over a period of centuries and delivered in specific and different contexts, and have, as well, varying degrees of dogmatic significance. For the sake of convenience, however, they are here listed in chronological order without an effort to delve fully into the times and needs which occasioned them.

a) The Constitution *Inter innumeras sollicitudines* of Pope Vigilius in May, 553.

> If anyone says that the One Jesus Christ, true God and the
> Same true man, had ignorance of future things or of the day of
> the last judgment and that He was able to know only those
> things which the Deity revealed to Him, dwelling as it were
> within another, let him be anathema.[104]

This papal statement, included under an anathema, is
infallible, but its meaning is not totally clear. The Pope wrote in a
context where some were suspect of Nestorian opinions and thus of
separating Christ into two persons. Saying that "Christ was
ignorant" sounded as if "Christ" were someone different from the
eternal Son who clearly knows everything. Thus, the definition
attributes all knowledge to the One Person who is God and man,
but it does not greatly clarify the relation between the two natures
in respect to the question of the divine and human knowledge in
Jesus. It does, however, remind us that in speaking of the Lord's
human knowledge we cannot proceed as if His human intellect were
somehow separate from the unity of the eternal Person who knows
all things.

b) The Letter *Sicut aqua* of Pope Gregory I to the Patriarch of
Alexandria, Eulogius, in 600.

> ...Just as we speak of a 'happy' day not meaning thereby that
> the day itself is happy but rather that we make ourselves happy
> on that day, so the Almighty Son says He does not know the
> day of the last judgment, not because He Himself does not
> know it, but because He makes it to be unknown. The Father
> alone is said to know the day and the hour because the Son who
> is consubstantial with the Father also knew it from His
> consubstantial nature by which He is above the angels and
> knows what they do not.... The Only-Begotten who has
> become incarnate and been made man for our sake indeed
> knew *in* His human nature the day and the hour, but He did
> not know this *from* His human nature. That which He knew *in*
> the human nature, He knew not *from* the human nature
> because God the God-man knew the day and the hour of
> judgment because of the power of His divinity....
>
> It is clear that whoever is not a Nestorian cannot be an
> Agnoitae....[105]

The *Agnoitae* were those who attributed a lack of knowledge to Christ in His humanity. The position, at that time, appeared to border on Nestorianism or was, at least so it seemed, a psychological Nestorianism—one, that is, which separated the human and divine knowledge of Jesus. Gregory, despite what appears to be a contrived explanation of the words of Jesus in Matthew 24:36, is condemning such a separation. The letter is part of what is called the "ordinary papal magisterium" and, in itself, has no claim on infallibility.

c) The Decree *Lamentabili* of July, 1907, issued by the Congregation of the Holy Office. The following statements are condemned:

1) Jesus, while He was exercising His ministry, did not speak with the purpose of teaching that He was the Messiah nor did His miracles seek to demonstrate that.[106]

2) The natural sense of the Gospel texts is not able to be reconciled with that which our theologians teach about the consciousness and infallible knowledge of Jesus Christ.[107]

3) It is evident to anyone who is not led by preconceived opinions that Jesus either professed error about the proximate messianic coming, or that the greater part of His doctrine contained in the Synoptic Gospels lacks authenticity.[108]

4) The critic is not able to assert for Christ a knowledge circumscribed by no limit unless he makes an hypothesis, which historically is hardly able to be conceived and which is repugnant to the moral sense, namely, that Christ as man had the knowledge of God and nevertheless did not wish to communicate the knowledge of so many things to His disciples and posterity.[109]

5) Christ did not always have consciousness of His messianic dignity.[110]

6) The doctrine about the expiatory death of Christ is not evangelical but only Pauline.[111]

The positions cited were attributed to the Modernists, and
were condemned, but no specific theological note was attached to
them. One may say that they were listed as positions to be avoided,
at least in the unnuanced form in which the Decree presents them.

d) The Encyclical Letter *Sempiternus Rex Christus* of Pope
Pius XII, in September, 1951.

> Although nothing forbids a deeper study of the humanity
> of Christ—even by way of His psychology—there are, how-
> ever, some who...abandon the old more than is proper....
> These so stress the state and condition of Christ's human nature
> that it would appear to be a subject in its own right, as if it did
> not subsist in the Person of the Word Himself.[112]

Before its final publication as an official act of the Pope, the
above paragraph had been somewhat changed from the way it had
originally appeared. The original read: "that it would appear to be—
at least psychologically—a subject in its own right, etc." The reason
for the change is not certain, nor particularly important since the
meaning of the final document is the same. Pius, like Gregory long
before, is warning against explanations which tend to make the
human nature of Christ—which nature includes His human knowledge—completely autonomous, as if it were not inseparably united
to the divinity in the unity of the One Person.

e) The *Final Document of the Latin American Bishops at
Puebla* in 1980.

> We must present Jesus of Nazareth as someone conscious of
> His mission, as the proclaimer and realizer of the Kingdom and
> as founder of His Church, whose visible foundation is Peter....
>
> The Church cannot be separated from Christ because He
> Himself was her founder. By an express act of His will He
> founded the Church on the Twelve.... The Church is not a later
> 'result' nor a mere consequence 'set in motion' by the evan-
> gelizing activity of Jesus. It was born of this activity to be
> sure, but in a direct way....[113]

The positions set forth at Puebla are, practically speaking, a
positive restatement of some of the teachings of the *Lamentabili*.
They are papally approved (by John Paul II) and are the first major

Magisterial response to some of the more recent positions taken by theologians on the Lord's knowledge. Although they carry great weight, they are not a definitive teaching. They must be seen, however, in the overall context of previous Church teaching which—not frequently but periodically—has rejected efforts to set specific limitations on the self-awareness and knowledge possessed by Christ in His humanity. The reason for that rejection is also clear. One cannot treat the human knowledge of Christ as an "isolated unit." To do so runs the risk of a new form of "psychological Nestorianism" which would teach not only that His divine and human knowledge were "unconfused and unchanged" but also that they were "separated and divided" or even contrary to one another. Such an approach would vitiate—at least on the psychological level—what Nicea, Ephesus, Chalcedon, resting on the Gospels, have always held concerning the "undivided and inseparable" unity of the two natures in the One Individual. The One who is thinking and knowing and aware of Himself *in a human way* is the eternal Son. The "in a human way" must be stressed lest, avoiding Nestorianism, one tends again to Monophysitism (i.e., uniting the two operations of knowing in the Lord so as to confuse or mingle the divine and human). However one attempts to explain His human self-awareness and knowledge, one must do so in such a manner as to avoid the tendencies toward the two classical heresies.

4. *Critique* of Current Tendencies

As one examines some of the current positions concerning the human knowledge of the Lord, it becomes evident that certain of the conclusions set forth above were inevitable and form part of an almost necessary line of thought which will lead to even more radical positions. The methodology involved, as well as some of the hypotheses of the historico-critical school of biblical exegesis, leads almost by an inner necessity to the assertion that the "historical" Jesus was quite other than traditional theology has viewed Him. For some, the question of a Christology "from above" or "from below" has become, if only implicitly, a question of "either/or." [114] The so-called Christology "from above" is viewed as starting from the fact of the Incarnation of the preexistent Son and proceeding, at times, to an *a prioristic* understanding of how the divine and human natures functioned in the unity of the One Person. On the other hand, a Christology "from below," using as its chief tool the "historico-critical" approach to the New Testament, attempts to determine that which can be known of the Jesus who "lies beneath" the confessional documents of the New Testament. It is an effort to get at the "historical nucleus" of the New Testament account in order to reconstruct the gradual development of Christian thinking about Jesus, which development reached a certain culmination in the Conciliar teachings of the early Church. This approach—despite numerous efforts to get beyond the question—is still dominated by the 19th century quest for discovering the "historical Jesus" and presupposes some type of a dichotomy which must be bridged between that Jesus and the Jesus known as the Christ of Christian faith.[115]

The difficulties in such an enterprise are manifold. In many cases foundational positions must be accepted which, in fact, are highly tentative and seriously disputed. Some of these have already been referred to 1) the priority of the Gospel of Mark; 2) Mark and "Q" as the primary sources for the Gospels of Matthew and Luke; 3) the claim that none of the Gospels as we have them are the work of eyewitnesses; 4) the positing of a relatively long period of theological development which can then be traced through different strata of the New Testament traditions, etc. Given such presuppositions, there would almost have to be some form of conflict between the "Johannine" Jesus who publicly claims, "Before Abraham was born, I am" (8:58), and says to His disciples, "Anyone who has seen me has seen the Father" since "I am in the Father and the Father is in me" (14:9-10), and the "Marcan" (or "Synoptic") Jesus who is recorded in Mark and the Synoptics as making no such statements. If one presumes that Mark is closer in time to the actual events and that the Gospel of John reflects a more developed Christology, then the statements in John, since they find no parallels in earlier tradition, are "theological," not "historical." What is more, those statements in the Synoptics which approximate in tenor some of the statements in John (e.g., Mt. 11:25; Lk. 10:21-22) must also be understood as being not the words of Jesus, but of tradition, or must be "re-worded" to fit what the "historical" Jesus was capable of saying.[116]

Theoretically, the conclusions from such an approach *could* be accurate. However, they presume an ability "to get beyond" the present sources—which are the only written sources we have—to a degree that cannot be substantiated by what one must call the "hard evidence" of historical and literary criticism properly understood. Moreover, the approach does not do justice to the faith of the Church which "firmly and most consistently has held and holds that the four Gospels, whose historical character she unhesitatingly affirms, faithfully hand on those things which Jesus, the Son of God, really did and taught...." [117] Nor does it deal adequately with the repeated assertions to be found in John's Gospel (whether they are found elsewhere, as well, we will examine later) that Jesus did know who He was, whence He came, where He was going, and that He indeed claimed to be divine. Such assertions, the Church affirms, "must be held to be asserted by the Holy Spirit," whence it follows that "the Scripture must be recognized as teaching firmly, faithfully and without error that truth which God willed to be consigned to the sacred writings for the sake of our salvation." [118] More to the point yet is the fact that, in many recent efforts to understand the human knowledge of Jesus, areas of information as well as critical facts are not taken into account. Our certitude about the Lord and thus about His human understanding cannot come from the tentative results of an "historical-critical" exegesis alone (it is not even from the "Sacred Scriptures alone that the Church draws her certitude about everything which has been revealed" as *Dei Verbum,* no. 9 teaches). The understanding of Tradition, the teaching of the Magisterium, as well as other indications, must be "building blocks," along with a critical exegesis, in any effort to come to grips with so complex a theme as the humanity of God Incarnate. Among the "other indications" we must list: 1) the virginal conception of Christ and the meaning it must have had for the family of Nazareth; 2) the freely willed celibacy of Mary and Joseph as part of their own understanding of the mystery; 3) the "Abba" relationship of Jesus with God; [119] 4) Jesus' awareness of His power to forgive sins, definitively interpret the Law, perform miracles (e.g., raise the dead, walk on water), etc. Indeed, all these facts must be "edited out" of the Gospels or seen as post-resurrectional theophanies or reflections of a mythic tradition if one is not to be faced with the inevitable conclusion that the self-awareness possessed by Jesus of Nazareth was absolutely unique.

Any successful beginning to the understanding of the human psychology of Jesus cannot succumb to an either/or when faced with the approaches of a Christology "from below" and a Christology "from above." Rather, the certain data offered by both approaches must be used. Admittedly, the nature of the "certain data" will differ somewhat. In some cases, one will be working with what is "historically" certain or "scientifically" certain. Given the nature of the historical sciences, all that will be able to be offered in some cases will be that relative certitude which comes from a concurrence of probabilities, because, by their nature, the historical and literary sciences must work from the limitations placed on them by the nature of the source material (in this case the Gospels) and the unanswered and perhaps unanswerable questions touching upon that material. In other cases, the certitude involved will be the certitude which flows from faith and not from historical evidence in the strict sense. For example, it cannot be scientifically verified (on an historical or literary level) that Jesus of Nazareth is God become man. That is a certitude of faith, prompted by the Holy Spirit and supported by the historical evidence of written documents and the ongoing history of the Christian community. If, because it does not meet the canons of strict historical proof, one were to leave out of consideration the "faith-fact" of the Incarnation, one could not hope to achieve an accurate view of the human psychology of Jesus.[120] It is only by using all the facts, i.e., all the known and knowable truth, about Jesus that one can begin to understand Him. Such facts will have to include, then, the following:

1. The truth of the Incarnation and the resultant consequences which this has for the human nature which God has taken as His own;

2. The assertions made by the divinely inspired authors of the Gospels, particularly those of the Gospel of John which attribute to Jesus a self-awareness of His divinity, etc.;

3. The various facts and words of Jesus' life which find their *most reasonable* explanation in a divine self-awareness on His part. This must include a willingness to deal with His words and deeds as we have them without artificially attributing some of them to a theological rereading of His life on the part of the early community. It

must, as well, deal with the positive contributions of recent exegesis, realizing that the evangelists did write from a faith-inspired viewpoint, with an understanding enriched by events and years subsequent to the Lord's public ministry, without, however, leading them to distort the words and events they record;

4. The agelong unwillingness of the Church's Magisterium to tolerate any form of "psychological Nestorianism" in Christ;

5. A recognition that the Lord's humanity was indeed human, i.e., at least in general terms subject to the evolutionary laws of growth, development and maturity, all of which is attested to in the various sources along with their attestation to the unity of the divine and human in Him. This must include, however, the recognition that we are not in a position to determine *a priori* what all truly human development must be. If one has determined, for example, that it is not truly human to be born of a Virgin, or to know that one is God, one can end up only imposing on Jesus one's own limited ideas of what is possible for humanity;

6. A sober respect for earlier theological reflection, eschewing any notion that most of the valid Catholic insights on this difficult matter originate after 1930 or 1942.

The existence and functioning of the human nature of Jesus of Nazareth are understandable only in the order of gift or grace. St. Augustine has written well on this point:

The clearest light on predestination and grace is shed by the Savior Himself, the Man Jesus Christ, the Same who is Mediator between God and men. What was there by way of preceding merits or works or of faith in His human nature which made that nature what it is? How is it, I ask, that this man merited to be assumed by the Eternal Word of the Father into the unity of person whereby He would be the Only-begotten Son of God? Was there any kind of good on the part of His humanity which preceded this event? What did it do beforehand, what did it believe, what did it petition in order to arrive at such ineffable excellence? Was it not rather by the operation and assuming power of the Word that this humanity (lit., this man), from the moment it began to be, began to be as the only Son of God?

...That grace by which man becomes a Christian from the
moment of faith is the grace by which this Man was made the
Christ from His very beginning; from the Same Spirit by which
the Christian is reborn, Christ was born; by the Same Spirit by
whom it comes about that our sins are remitted it came about
that He should have no sin.

This lifting up of His human nature was predestined to be so
great, so lofty and so marvelous that there would not be
anything which could raise it higher, just as divinity itself could
not make itself more humble than by taking on human nature
with its infirmities—even to the point of dying on the cross.[121]

This humanity is predestined and graced from the moment of
its existence to such an extent that it is in "unity of person" with the
eternal Son. What that humanity, in the natural operation of its own
intellect and self-awareness, knew of the union was itself a grace—a
grace, moreover, which flowed directly from the unity itself. The
Savior's humanity was created by the union, and thereby fashioned
or molded in such a way as to reflect in a truly human way God's
own being as Son. As is evident from the Scriptures and from the
early Councils, that fashioning or shaping of the human will of
Christ was such that "without reservation or holding back" it was
"submissive to His divine and omnipotent will" even while acting
according to its own natural powers. It was a human will "tempered
by the direction of His divinity" so that it operated and acted in a
human, free manner, always in a total harmony with the divinity to
which it was, from its creation, inseparably united.[122] What was true
of the one faculty of His humanity (namely His human will) must
also be said of the other faculty of the humanity, His human
intellect. He knew and understood Himself in a human fashion
which was in conformity with who He was and why He had come as
man. To assert anything less would be not only to separate His
divine and human knowledge, but to separate, as well, the manner
of operation of His human will from the manner of operation of His
human knowledge. Both human will and intellect, by their very
existence and operations, manifested a sublime harmony with the
divine will and understanding.

Trying to understand this harmony between the divine and
human awareness of Christ, we must be aware of how anachronisti-

cally we pose the question. We ask: Did Jesus, in His humanity, know He was God? Did He know He preexisted? The way of putting the question is ours—even though God has given us the concepts through Revelation. The question is more complicated than we normally tend to think. If we leave aside for the moment the question of His human knowledge and reflect on the divine knowledge and self-awareness of the Son, what can we say? Does the Eternal Son know He is God? Does He know He is pre-existent? The questions are almost silly for they presume that God knows and understands Himself in our terms. If what we know from Revelation and theological reflection gives us any insight at all, we must say that the Son only knows Himself in knowing the Father. It is as from, and of, and for the Father that He is aware of Himself or knows Himself. Is He God? Yes, in our terms; but in His own terms (and it is arrogance to pretend to know such things) He is who He is in relation to the Father, and that alone. The question of knowing preexistence is a non-question for the eternal Son. It can only mean, for Him, the awareness of always—in the eternal now—receiving Himself from the Father.

If such thoughts even begin to approach the truth, then we must say that the harmony between the divine Intellect and the human self-awareness of the Son can be understood properly only in similar terms. Jesus, in His human knowledge and self-awareness, knew and knows Himself as from the Father, and of the Father, and for the Father.[123] Such is the human reflection of His divine self-awareness. The stamp or seal of the divine understanding was present to and tempered His human awareness from the first moment of His existence. It manifested itself in His human words and actions. From the age of twelve, when St. Luke gives us the first insight and the word "Father" is first recorded on His lips, until "Father, into your hands I commend my spirit" and "I go now to my Father and your Father, my God and your God," it is relation to the Father which identifies Him and by which He identifies Himself. When He teaches us to pray, it is the same. We are to pray using His word, "Abba," but even there He never includes us directly with Himself when speaking of the Father; it is always "My" Father and "your" Father or "My Father in heaven" and "Your Father in heaven"; "when *you* pray, say 'Our Father,'" not, "when *we* pray, let us say, 'Our Father.'" He never says with them in any instance recorded: "*our* Father." (Augustine noted this long ago.) His Sonship is unique. He is not only from and for, He is of the Father. Thus He knew Himself and let us know Him. This—at least as a minimal understanding—is what Tradition has always meant when it ascribes to the humanity of the Lord the grace of the Beatific Vision.[124] This truth is grounded not in one or two or several citations of Scripture used as "proof texts" to demonstrate an *a priori* conclusion. Rather, it is the certain conclusion based on all the evidence given us by Revelation in Scripture and Tradition, as the Church, through her Magisterium, has always understood it.

The knowledge Jesus had of the Father is, in a sense, reciprocal. Jesus knows Himself in knowing the Father, and the Father Himself alone fully knows the Son as His own perfect expression.

> All things have been committed to me by my Father. No one knows the Son except the Father, and no one knows the Father except the Son and those to whom the Son chooses to reveal him (Mt. 11:26-27).

If, then, we return to the direct question—Did Jesus, in His human awareness, know who He was and whence He came?—the answer must be an absolute yes, for no other answer will correspond to all the facts of faith and history which we know about Him. He knew He was from the Father, and of Him, and for Him. If we insist on putting the question in our terms—Did He know He was God?; Did He know of His preexistence?—the answer must again be an unqualified affirmative since the negative would mislead and therefore lie. But we must remember that, in this case, both the question and the answer are our way of thinking about Him, not His way of thinking of the Father and of Himself.

It is our insistence in putting the question in our terms which is partly responsible for our inability to understand various aspects of the Scriptures. We look at Matthew or Mark or Luke—and, yes, even at John—and want to find Jesus saying unambiguously: "I am God" or "I am the Second Person of the Blessed Trinity" or "Before I became a man, I created the world with the Father and the Spirit." Such expectations are our own version of the remarks of the Jews who said, "If you are the Christ, tell us plainly" (Jn. 10:24-25). Now, very few are so naive as, upon reflection, to indulge in such expectations, but they are often there nonetheless, for our minds find complacency and security in certitude. By the nature of the case, however, such declarations on the part of Jesus should not be expected. Even so introspective an age as our own witnesses only the few who spend their time analyzing themselves for themselves and for others. Most of us indicate who we are and what we are about by the way we speak and act and the way we live in relation with others—all without explicit analysis, at least to begin with.

Relevant here is an insight of St. Thomas Aquinas in his treatment of the gift of wisdom and its effects on our intellects.[125] He noted that we can discern two types of knowledge: one works through ideas and reasoning to draw conclusions; the other is "instinctual," clear and certain but not the result of ideas and reasoning. This latter he called "co-natural knowledge." It is like the knowledge which those in love have of one another when they are so "attuned" that they "sense" or "know" about the other even things which they have difficulty conceptualizing or putting into words.[126] It is the ability to intuit surely because of a certain harmony existing between them. In the case of the Christian who, by grace, has been made a "sharer of the divine nature" (2 Pt. 1:4) this type of knowledge reveals itself in the instinctive awareness one has of God and of His will, and is the foundation for mystical experience even in the unlettered and simple.[127]

Such co-natural knowledge belongs in a unique way to the humanity of Christ. United to the divine nature in the Person of the Son, the humanity *knows* in a fashion that surpasses the knowledge which comes through concepts or ideas. It is a knowledge that is immediate, experienced in the depths of one's being and is thus more certain than any form of knowledge derived from a process of reasoning. For Jesus such knowledge touches directly upon His own identity, His being of and from and for the Father. In conceptual form, Jesus' human mind would express this immediate awareness, this Beatific Vision, in terms suitable to His own age and to the needs of those to whom He preached.

It is, however, not enough to recognize that Jesus was humanly aware of Himself as the Father's eternal Son. His human intellect also had to know all those things necessary for the adequate fulfillment of His mission as Redeemer and Revealer. The specifics involved in such knowledge can still be called infused or prophetic knowledge.

There is what the Greeks call an *ekonomia* in the mystery of the Incarnation, by which is meant that God reveals Himself as He knows best, in the way and to the degree that He knows best. The *ekonomia* was present even in connection with the sacred humanity of the Lord.[128] That humanity could not know or do, in and of itself, all that the divinity knows and can do. Therefore, God, who ordains all things powerfully but gently, graced the Lord's humanity in ways suitable to its age, condition and circumstance, not leading it from the unknown to the known in relation to itself, but rather deepening, enriching, completing, maturing His humanity.[129] What such growth meant concretely is relatively unknown to us. We do not know *how* we will experience the Beatific Vision, nor do we know *how* the Beatific Vision (Jesus' awareness of Self as Son in knowing the Father) and infused knowledge operated in the case of the Lord's humanity. We can see some of its effects in His way of life, His words and deeds. We can see how, on the level of experience, His immediate awareness of being the Father's Son was confirmed for Him. It was confirmed by His parents at Nazareth. He was theirs, but virginally conceived—from God that is. It was a reality lived in a virginal home, experienced most profoundly in His own prayer and in His reflections on creation and the Revelation of the Old Testament. His immediate awareness of Self and His awareness of His mission manifested themselves in a mode of acting and teaching which scandalized many because of the self-assurance such awareness gave Him (cf. Mt. 13:53-54; Mk. 6:2; Jn. 8:13, etc.). What remains beyond such indications is a mystery in the strict theological sense of the word: something which totally surpasses the capacities of human understanding. Try as we may, we are not capable of plumbing the depths of another's personality—nor even our own for that matter. Much less are we capable of fathoming the depths of His personality nor its human development, rooted as it is in the Infinite.[130]

Not only does the humanity of Jesus share in the *ekonomia* of divine revelation: it exercised that *ekonomia*. Jesus, it would appear, was often deliberately vague or allusive in speech and deed. He would suggest rather than state directly; He would intimate or educate by parables, symbols and prophetic gestures. The "ambiguities" apparent in some of His words and actions are not simply the result of "various traditions" meshed together ineptly, or of evangelical relocations and confusion of primitive material. There is an enigmatic quality or allusiveness about Him which leaves so clear an impression in the Gospels that it can only reflect an aspect of how He acted and how He was perceived. His statement, for example, that He did not know the day or the hour of judgment is surely no more difficult to explain than His statement about the difficulty encountered by the rich in entering heaven (Mt. 19:23-26) or His response to His brothers that He was not going to Jerusalem for the Feast of Tabernacles, when in fact He did go (Jn. 7:1-10), or His cursing of a fig tree for not having fruit, even though it was not the season for fruit-bearing (Mk. 11:12, 14, 20). This enigmatic quality in word and action caused puzzlement and wonder on the part of His relatives, friends and enemies. It persists for us, making it difficult, if not impossible, to "read" Him with the precision and order we would like to find. It is necessary to remember this fact as we look at His ministry and at more of the critical judgments made about what are perceived as examples of His lack of knowledge. In the *ekonomia* He revealed and used, it is more likely our lack of knowledge than His which must be called into question.

PART II

The Ministry

In his great work on the Gospel of St. John, Augustine aptly sums up the ministry of the Incarnate God when he comments on the passage: "And, Jesus, being tired from His journey, sat down at the well" (Jn. 4:6):

> Now begin the mysteries. For it is not without purpose that Jesus is weary; not without purpose that the strength of God is weary; not without purpose that He is weary by whom the wearied are refreshed; not without purpose that He is weary, by whose absence we are wearied, by whose presence we are strengthened.
>
> Jesus was weak, being wearied by His journey. And His journey is the flesh assumed for us....[1]

The "mysteries" of God's journey in the flesh begin, of course, with the Incarnation itself, but, as Augustine noted, the mysteries began to be manifested generally when the Lord began His public ministry. For the Fathers and the greatest theologians of the Church, each deed and word of Christ is not simply action or speech, but also the expression of the mystery of His Person and of the Revelation He had come to bring. Those mysteries and the public ministry itself began where Mark begins his Gospel: the baptism of Jesus by the prophet John in the River Jordan. Indeed, each of the Gospels refer to this inaugural event, although John does it obliquely (cf. Mt. 3:13-17; Mk. 1:9-11; Lk. 3:21-22; Jn. 1:29-34).

It is Luke who, typically, gives us the chronological details.

> In the fifteenth year of the reign of Tiberius Caesar—when Pontius Pilate was governor of Judea, Herod tetrarch of

Galilee, his brother Philip tetrarch of Iturea and Trachonitis,
and Lysanias tetrarch of Abilene—during the high priesthood
of Annas and Caiaphas, the word of God came to John son of
Zechariah in the desert (Lk. 3:1-2).

Having thus set the time for the beginning of the Baptist's
ministry, Luke records the baptism of Jesus and continues:

> Now Jesus Himself was about thirty years old when He
> began His ministry. He was the son—so it was thought—of
> Joseph (Lk. 3:23).[2]

Luke's dating is not as clear for us as it must have been for him.
With certitude we know that Pilate was procurator in Judaea from
26 to 36 A.D. We also know that Tiberius succeeded Caesar
Augustus who died in August of 14 A.D. However, Tiberius had
been made "co-emperor" with Augustus in 12 A.D. and it is that fact
which causes some difficulty for us since we do not know whether
Luke counted the fifteenth year of Tiberius Caesar's reign from the
death of Augustus or from the time that Tiberius became co-
emperor. Depending on which date is chosen for the beginning of
the rule of Tiberius, John the Baptist began his ministry in the year
26-27 or 28-29 A.D. John the Evangelist, writing of events at the
first Passover after the Baptism of Jesus, records the Jews as saying
that the Temple had been forty-six years in the rebuilding begun by
Herod the Great about 20 B.C. If the remark is accurate, it would
harmonize fairly well with an understanding of Luke which sees the
year 26-27 as the fifteenth year of Tiberius' reign and the year of the
beginning of the Baptist's mission. From what can be gathered from
the Gospel accounts, Jesus' baptism is associated with the beginnings of John's mission, and so one can say with some probability
that Jesus was baptized and began His own preaching during the
year 27 A.D. He was at that time, says St. Luke, "about thirty years
old" (Lk. 3:23).[2]

The length of Jesus' public ministry is impossible to determine
from the Synoptic Gospels. If one reads them superficially, it would
appear that the ministry was relatively short and centered mainly in
Galilee. Then, after an initial period of success, Jesus would have
faced increasing opposition to His message, leading Him to turn to
Judea and Jerusalem where He was apprehended and killed. What
helps to support such a view is the fact that Matthew, Mark and

Luke only mention one visit of Jesus to Jerusalem, the one during which the events of His Passion occurred.[3] In the case of St. Luke, at least, the movement from Galilee to Jerusalem may be deliberately artificial in order to give a "dramatic" and theological flow to his narrative (cf. Lk. 9:51; 10:1; 13:22; 17:11). Indeed, Luke stays so close to this format that he depicts Jesus' lamentation over Jerusalem as having happened before Luke explicitly puts Jesus within the capital (cf. Lk. 13:34-35 and 19:28ff. and compare with Mt. 23:37 where Matthew, more logically, places the saying within the context of Jesus' presence in the city). The picture, however, is not as neat as it first appears in the synoptics. All of them, Luke included, mention the presence of people from Jerusalem among those come to hear Jesus (Mt. 4:25; Mk. 3:7-8; Lk. 6:17), and even the presence of Pharisees and scribes from the capital city come to hear Him (Mt. 15:1; Mk. 7:1; Lk. 5:17-21), a fact made more intelligible if Jesus had already preached there. The Gospel of John assures us, in fact, that He had.

It would appear from John that Jesus spent the first Passover after His baptism in Jerusalem (Jn. 2:13ff.) and then spent some time evangelizing near the capital (3:22). Indeed, the Gospel of John portrays a ministry which alternated between the capital and its environs, and Galilee and Samaria (cf. Jn. 4:1-3; 5:1; 6:1; 7:10, etc.). It is a ministry, moreover, during which at least three celebrations of the Passover occurred (Jn. 2:13; 6:4; 11:55), the last of them being the Passover of the Passion. There is no sufficient reason to discount these Johannine indications; indeed the items noted above from the synoptics may be read so as to confirm them. If this is so, then it may be said that the public ministry lasted at least two and a half to three years, probably from an undeterminable date in the year 27 to April of the year 30, when He was crucified.

The Gospel of John makes us explicitly aware that the evangelists do not give us a daily or yearly *journal* of the public ministry of Christ (cf. Jn. 20:30-31; 21:25)—a fact we will be aware of below as we attempt to approach thematically some of the words and deeds of the public years. What they have done is to record what each of them individually thought was sufficient to convince us that "Jesus is the Christ, the Son of God, and that believing" we might "have life in his name" (Jn. 20:31). Both Luke and John, however, point out that chronology and order (cf. Lk. 1:1-4; Acts 1:1; Jn. 1:29, 35, 43; 2:1—the record of the "first week," etc.) were important to them, as were the testimonies of eye-witnesses and other trustworthy sources (cf. Lk. 1:2-3; Jn. 19:35; 21:24). In this they—and there is nothing which indicates that this was not true for Matthew and Mark as well—reflect the concern expressed by Peter when he listed the criteria for a suitable replacement for Judas:

> ...It is necessary to choose one of the men who have been with us the whole time the Lord Jesus went in and out among us, beginning from John's baptism... (Acts 1:21-22).

I. THE FATHER'S KINGDOM

"Then Jesus came from Galilee to the Jordan to be baptized by John…" (Mt. 3:13ff.). The baptism, as told to us by the Gospels, is one of the three great manifestations of the Father during the public ministry of the Son. The Father's voice addresses Jesus, saying: "You are my Son whom I love; with you I am well pleased" (Mk. 1:11; Lk. 3:22; Mt. 3:17 records the words as a proclamation: "This is my Son whom I love; with him I am well pleased"). The second manifestation comes at the Transfiguration, in almost identical words, but all of them proclamatory: "This is my Son whom I love…" (Mt. 17:5; Mk. 9:7; Lk. 9:34). The third manifestation is recorded only by John:

> The hour has come for the Son of Man to be glorified…. Now my heart is troubled, and what shall I say? 'Father, save me from this hour'? No, it was for this very reason I came to this hour. Father, glorify your name! Then a voice came from heaven, 'I have glorified it, and will glorify it again.' The crowd that was there and heard it said it had thundered; others said an angel had spoken to him (Jn. 12:23-29).[4]

Each of these three theophanies, occurring at significant points in the ministry of Jesus, has several layers of meaning both historically and theologically. It would seem, however, that the primal level—and the one from which all other aspects must flow— is that which is directly concerned with Jesus Himself and His relationship with the Father. Jesus prayed (cf. Mt. 11:25; 14:23; Lk. 6:12; Mk. 6:46; Jn. 17:1ff., and many other places). His prayer sprang from the uninterrupted contemplation of the Father which was His because of the hypostatic union, and from the intimate awareness of the eternal Father which originated in that union. This unique form of "contemplative prayer," the beatific vision, was, as seen above, co-natural to Him, but was also, like all truly human prayer, capable of periods of greater intensity and degree. St. Luke highlights this truth when he writes:

> At that time Jesus, full of joy through the Holy Spirit, said, 'I praise you, Father, Lord of heaven and earth, because you have hidden these things from the wise and learned, and revealed them to little children' (Lk. 10:21).

That same notion of joy in contemplative insight can be seen in His exclamation to Simon.

> Blessed are you, Simon son of Jonah, for this was not revealed to you by man, but by my Father in heaven... (Mt. 16:17).

The manifestation of the Father at the Baptism, at the Transfiguration and in the voice from heaven recorded by John are moments of such intensity of prayerful experience on the part of Jesus. Whatever its other theological implications or its connections with Old Testament texts, the "You are my beloved Son" is fundamentally the earthly expression, in biblical words, of the eternal delight of the Father in the Son. Such manifestations came to the Son during His earthly life not as something new, nor even less as a revelation of what was previously unknown to Him, but rather as particular "highpoints" in His human experience of sonship.[5] The Gospels allow us only glimpses of such prayer, understandable enough since a person's prayer is ultimately a secret, hidden in the depths of an individual's relationship with God. It is only the Gospel of John which develops for us at any length what the synoptics sketch.

> Father, the time has come. Glorify your Son, that your Son may glorify you.... I have brought you glory on earth by completing the work you gave me to do.... That they may be one as we are one; I in them and you in me.... Righteous Father, though the world does not know you, I know you... (Jn. 17).

Whatever order or form John has given to the prayer, it is clearly the prayer of Jesus, congruent with the insights given by other evangelists. Such prayer, of course, exists like moments of ecstasy, as it were, in a life constantly lived in awareness of the Father and of His own relation to the Father. And, as the greatest of contemplatives, His teaching flowed from what Jesus Himself constantly contemplated (the *contemplata tradere* of St. Thomas).[5] Above all else what He taught was the Father.

He instructed the disciples to pray as He did: "Abba, Father" (Mk. 14:36). The intimacy and novelty of the word left such an impression that the early Church retained the original Aramaic itself, as if a translation could never capture its particular flavor. St. Paul twice reminded his hearers that it is only the Spirit of the Son which enables one to pray "Abba" (cf. Rom. 8:15; Gal. 4:6), and the liturgy of the Church conveyed the unheard-of nature of this daring form of address by introducing the Lord's Prayer with the words, "Urged by divine command and formed by heavenly instruction, we *dare* to say: Abba, Our Father in heaven, hallowed be Thy name."

The confidence toward God captured by the intimate "Abba" was inculcated by Jesus in innumerable parables and similies:

> Look at the birds of the air; they do not sow or reap or store away in barns, and yet your heavenly Father feeds them. Are you not much more valuable than they? (Mt. 6:26ff.)
>
> Which of you, if his son asks for bread, will give him a stone? Or if he asks for a fish, will give him a snake? If you, then, though you are evil, know how to give good gifts to your children, how much more will your Father in heaven give good gifts to those who ask him? (Mt. 7:7ff.; cf. parable of the judge and widow in Lk. 18:1ff.)
>
> ...Your Father in heaven is not willing that any of these little ones should be lost (Mt. 18:14).
>
> Do not be afraid, little flock, for your Father has been pleased to give you the kingdom (Lk. 12:32).

One has simply to cull the Gospels to find such quotations and many more like them. To them must be added the figure of the Father in the parable of the Prodigal (Lk. 15:11ff.) and what is implied of the Father in the parable of the lost sheep (Lk. 15:4ff.)

and the lost drachma (Lk. 15:8ff.) and of the owner of the vineyard marked by His generosity to all (Mt. 20:1ff.). In knowing this Father, all other fatherhood fades to insignificance. That truth, as well as Jesus' own Father-centeredness, can be heard in the injunction: "And do not call anyone on earth father, for you have one Father, and he is in heaven" (Mt. 23:9). As Jesus knows Him and reveals Him, this Father is all-powerful and all-knowing. From the sparrows of the air to the hairs of one's head, there is nothing too small to escape His attention and concern. But His power and knowledge are provident, that is, they are intent on our good, directed to giving and forgiving with a divine patience which extends to good and bad alike.

There can be no doubt but that Thérèse of Lisieux was a faithful mirror of the Teacher and reflected His teaching in the images she gave of God.

> Suppose a father with two sons, mischievous and disobedient, coming to punish them, he sees one shaking with terror and trying to get away from him—yet admitting in the bottom of his heart that he deserves punishment; while his brother does the opposite, casts himself into his Father's arms, says that he is sorry for having caused him pain, that he loves him and that he will prove it by being good in the future. Then, if this child asks his father *to punish him* with a *kiss*, I do not think the heart of the delighted father could resist the filial confidence of his child, for he knows his sincerity and love. He is, of course, perfectly aware that his son will fall, not once but many times, into the same faults, but he is ready to pardon him every time his son *takes* him *by the heart*....[7]

> That, Brother, is my idea of the good God's justice. My way is all of trust and love. I don't understand souls who are afraid of so loving a Friend. Sometimes, when I read spiritual treatises, in which perfection is shown with a thousand obstacles in the way...my poor soul grows very soon weary ...and I take the holy Scriptures. Then all seems luminous, a single word opens up infinite horizons to my soul, perfection seems easy; I see that it is enough to realize one's nothingness, and give oneself wholly, like a child, into the arms of the good God.[8]

Thérèse may be said to have captured the heart of Jesus' message: filial relationship to God as a loving Father (cf. Mt. 18:3-4; 19:13-15). When it is understood and experienced, it becomes an insistent invitation, like a magnet of attraction felt so keenly by saints like Ignatius of Antioch.

> ...My yearning is for death. My Love has been crucified, and I am not on fire with the love of earthly things. But there is in me a Living Water, which is eloquent and within me says: 'Come to the Father.'[9]

Those words of Ignatius echo Jesus' own: Come to the Father. And it is only within the context of that message about the Father that one can properly understand Jesus preaching on the *kingdom of God* (or, in the terminology of Matthew's Gospel, the *kingdom of heaven*). Jesus spoke of it so frequently that many would see the message of the kingdom as being central to His proclamation. Such an assertion is correct as long as one realizes that the emphasis is to be placed on the fact that it is the *Father's* kingdom or rule, not merely an abstract state or condition. Indeed, in Jesus' explanation of the parable of the weeds as found in Matthew, the "kingdom of heaven" and the "kingdom of the Father" are equivalent terms (cf. Mt. 13:24 and 13:43). In the message of Jesus, this kingdom or rule of God is intended, like other similies, to reveal the Father.

The parables and similies used by Jesus to describe the Father's kingdom are manifold. It is, He says, like a treasure hidden in the field, the pearl of great value, a dragnet cast into the sea, the mustard seed, a leavening yeast which produces good (compared with the "yeast" of the Pharisees and Sadducees in Mt. 16:5ff.), etc. Indeed, in one way or another, the word kingdom was so often on His lips that He was ultimately charged and condemned—at least in part—as a royal pretender (cf. Mt. 27:11, 37; Mk. 15:2, 26; Lk. 23:3, 38; Jn. 18:33ff.; 19:19ff.).

Of the many questions attendant on Jesus' preaching of the Father's kingdom, two are especially important: who are those called to the kingdom, and when does it come?

1. The Called

In response to the centurion at Capernaum who pleaded for the cure of his servant, Jesus replied:

> Nowhere in Israel have I found faith like this. Moreover, I say to you that many will come from the east and from the west to take their places with Abraham and Isaac and Jacob at the feast in the kingdom of heaven, but the subjects of the kingdom will be turned out into the dark... (Mt. 8:5ff.; cf. Lk. 7:1-10) (Jerusalem Bible).

The words of Jesus are universalistic, that is, they indicate that even the Gentiles (those from the "east and west") will have a share in the Father's kingdom. A completely different context finds the same idea set forth in the Gospel of Mark where, having cleansed the Temple of those who were buying and selling, Jesus explains His action by saying: "Is it not written: 'My house will be called a house of prayer for all nations'?" (Mk. 11:17-18; cf. Is. 56:7. As Matthew and Luke record the incident, the "for all nations" is omitted from the quote from Isaiah.) The nations here are the *ethnoi*, the Gentiles again, a point clear from the citation. The Gospel of John likewise records the same universalistic concept when Jesus is described as having other sheep than those who belong to the fold of Israel (Jn. 10:16). And the great scene of the Judgment (Mt. 25:31ff.) indicates, as well, that "all the nations" will be assembled before the Son of Man, their fate depending on charity, not on ethnic makeup.

It would seem only logical that the One hailed by the aged Simeon as "a light for revelation to the Gentiles" (Lk. 2:30-31) should, in the time of His ministry, hold open the kingdom He preached to all peoples. Nonetheless, there are some who would contend that He envisioned no such thing, and saw His mission exclusively in terms of the Jewish people.[10] Indeed, there are texts which seem to substantiate such a view. Jesus instructed His disciples, "Do not go among the Gentiles or enter any town of the Samaritans. Go rather to the lost sheep of Israel" (Mt. 10:5). And, in the dialogue with the pagan woman who sought a cure for her daughter, He uttered those harsh words, "It is not right to take the children's bread and toss it to their dogs. I was sent only to the lost sheep of Israel" (Mt. 15:21ff.). It is argued as well that, if a universal invitation to the kingdom had been preached by Jesus, there would be no logical explanation (other than disobedience to His word) for the fact that the early Church experienced such great difficulties in accepting the Gentiles. On the basis of such indications, it is suggested that those universalistic texts, admittedly few in number, which are found in the Gospels reflect not Jesus Himself but rather the fuller understanding achieved by the primitive community, or that they are revelations of the Risen Lord, not the teaching of His earthly ministry.

There is no compelling reason for accepting such a solution, however, and there are various reasons to choose against it. The Gospels, as seen from the texts quoted above and others,[11] assert that Jesus did in fact have a universalistic viewpoint concerning His mission, and furthermore they assert that He had that viewpoint before His resurrection. How such an assertion, were it wrong, could be reconciled with what must be believed concerning the veracity of Scripture is very difficult, if not impossible, to see. In addition, since it is their assertion, and since it is those same documents which include the apparently contrary indications, one should at least begin with the presumption that the evangelists did not see the difficulty, and then ask whether the problem may be ours, not theirs. And a deeper consideration yields the following:

1. Even some of the prophets of the Old Testament preached a universalistic concern on God's part. Thus the text cited from Isaiah in Matthew, Mark and Luke:

Let no foreigner who has joined himself to the Lord say, 'The Lord will surely exclude me from his people....' Foreigners who bind themselves to the Lord to serve him, to love the name of the Lord, and to worship him...these I will bring to my holy mountain...for my house will be called a house of prayer for all nations (Is. 56:3-8).

Likewise, the Book of Jonah, quoted by the Lord in a different context (cf. Mt. 12:38ff.; Mk. 8:11ff.; Lk. 11:29) is, by explicit purpose, universalistic in its teaching:

But the Lord said, 'You have been concerned about this vine, though you did not tend it or make it grow. It sprang up overnight and died overnight. But Nineveh has more than a hundred and twenty thousand people who cannot tell their right hand from their left, and many cattle as well. Should I not be concerned about that great city?' (Jon. 4:10-11).

Universalistic, too, are the famous *Servant Songs* in Isaiah (42:1-9; 49:1-6; 50:4-11; 52:13—53:12) to which we shall return later. Now it is inconceivable that God Incarnate whose own home was Galilee of the Gentiles (Is. 9:1; Mt. 4:15) should have a narrower view of His mission than did the Old Testament writings He inspired or that He was less than Jonah. Or are we to presume that, in His humanity, the Christ was incapable of appropriating for Himself one of the higher ideals of the Old Testament?

2. That Jesus envisioned a universal mission is, furthermore, consistent with other statements of the Gospels. John says the Lord Himself preached in Samaria to Samaritans (Jn. 4:39-42).[12] Luke agrees (9:51-56) and tells us Jesus used a Samaritan as an example to the Jews of charity (10:29ff.) and gratitude (17:11-19) and as recipients of God's favor, in contrast to Israel (cf. Lk. 4:25-27). The Gospel of Mark depicts Jesus as preaching in pagan or semi-pagan territories (Mk. 7:24-25, 31-32), and Matthew and Luke portray Him as comparing pagan towns favorably with the Jewish towns of His ministry (Mt. 11:20ff.; Lk. 10:13-15). What is more, even in the case of the pagan woman whom His words included among the "dogs," Jesus did not refuse to extend His salvation—just as He had done in the case of the centurion.

3. All of the texts cited against Jesus' universalistic vision of His mission admit of another reasonable explanation. He claims His *own* mission is limited even while proclaiming a kingdom open to all. No one, not even the Lord in His humanity, could do all things at one time; each is to be done in proper order and according to the divine plan. In the plan of God, salvation for mankind was to come from the Jews (cf. Jn. 4:22-23), and Jesus limited His immediate mission—and that of His disciples—to them. That limitation does not mean—especially in the light of contrary evidence—that He limited the ongoing effects of His mission simply to the Jews.

The objection posed by the conduct of the early Church really does not touch upon the issue at hand directly. The question there was not "Who can become a follower of the Christ?", but rather, "How or in what way is a follower of the Christ expected to live?" What was not clear to the Apostles and other first believers was whether the pagans could receive the Gospel without embracing the Jewish Law as well. All we know of the early Church shows that the Apostles understood that Jesus' offer was made to all; what they did not see at first was that it was made to all without the encumbrance of the Law. That conclusion is the only one which a reading of the Acts of the Apostles and the Pauline letters will warrant (cf. Acts 8:26-40; 10:34—11:18; 15:7-12; Gal. 2:11-14). It was this point alone which Jesus had apparently not spoken to during His ministry. He came to inaugurate salvation, not to codify law for every future situation His message would encounter. Sufficient for the day were the troubles thereof (Mt. 6:34).

2. The Coming of the Kingdom

What Jesus said and thought about the time sequence connected with the coming of the Father's kingdom has proven to be a problem for His followers until our own day. Paul had to deal with those who expected that the final consummation of all things was at hand (cf. 1 Thes. 4:13; 5:11; 2 Thes. 2:1-17, etc.)[13]; the second epistle of Peter (3:1-10) had to deal, on the other hand, with those who claimed it would never come; and the Apocalypse of John has offered sustenance to every Christian (sect) determined on predicting the day and the hour.[14] The Gospel texts as we have them, moreover, only seem to add to the difficulty. There are texts which:

1. indicate that the kingdom is here or very near at hand. As you go, preach this message: 'The kingdom of heaven is near.' Amen I say to you, you will not finish going through the cities of Israel before the Son of Man comes (Mt. 10:6-23; Mk. 1:15; Jn. 5:25).

2. indicate that it will come while the generation of Jesus' hearers survives.

I tell you the truth, some who are standing here will not taste death before they see the kingdom of God come with power (Mk. 9:1; Mt. 16:28).

3. indicate that it is connected with Jesus' own death.

Moreover, I tell you that from this time onward you will see the Son of Man seated at the right hand of the Power and coming on the clouds of heaven (Mt. 26:64; *NAB*).

4. indicate that no one knows the day nor the hour.

No one knows about that day or hour, not even the angels in heaven, nor the Son, but only the Father (Mt. 24:36; Mk. 13:32).

5. indicate that it will be considerably delayed.

Then John's disciples came and asked him, 'How is it that we and the Pharisees fast, but your disciples do not fast?' Jesus answered, 'How can the guests of the bridegroom mourn while he is with them? The time will come when the bridegroom will be taken from them; then they will fast' (Mt. 9:14-15; Mk. 2:14-22).

I tell you the truth, wherever this gospel is preached throughout the world, what she has done will also be told, in memory of her (Mt. 26:13; Mk. 14:9).

The coming of the kingdom—at least in its full manifestation, is also connected with the *eschata*, the last things. These are described in part as the "judgment" (Mt. 11:21-22; Lk. 10:13-14, etc.), or the "day of the Son of Man" (Mt. 24:37-39; Lk. 17:26-27).

The difficulties in making a coherent picture of all the various material are increased when one attempts to distinguish Jesus' own words from possible additions and interpretations which may have taken place in the process of oral or written tradition or from redaction on the part of the evangelists. Despite such difficulties, it is asserted with some frequency that the few texts which indicate a prolonged period between Jesus' own preaching of the kingdom and the day of judgment are to be understood as later material, not the teaching of Jesus Himself during His ministry. In such a case, Jesus would have thought and taught that the coming of the kingdom had begun with His preaching and that it would manifest itself fully either during that ministry or at His death or very shortly thereafter. It would mean, in other words, that He lived and preached in expectation of an imminent "end of the world."[15]

Now more is involved in such a view than a mistaken expectation on Jesus' part about the immediacy of the end of the world. Were such a view correct, the manner in which the Christian Church has generally understood His moral or ethical teaching would need to be altered. It would have to be understood as an ethics or morality of "crisis," an "interim ethic" which revealed how men and women should deport themselves while expecting the proximate end of all things.[16] Only with great difficulty—if at all— could one defend the assertion that such an ethic was the expression of a new way of life envisioned as applying to all people of future generations without qualification. Furthermore, if Jesus anticipated the proximate end of the world, His own intention to found a perduring community, the Church, with ministries and sacraments and with a universal mission would have to be called into serious question.

Realistically, a fully satisfactory solution to the problem cannot be given, if by "fully satisfactory" one understands a solution which will demonstrably lay to rest the various exegetical and theological problems. Two thousand years of study and reflection have not managed to do that. That fact alone serves to indicate at least one historical certitude: taken as a whole, the New Testament writings bear witness to the fact that Jesus never spoke of the coming of the kingdom and its relation to the end of the world in such a way as to obviate subsequent lack of clarity on these matters. It is Jesus Himself who is responsible for the ambiguity which has existed and persists. Given that fact, there are, nevertheless, various considerations which must be kept in mind.

1. Jesus' preaching about the kingdom of the Father and about the end of time was, for all its uniqueness, in line with the preaching and writings of the Old Testament prophets. Indeed, He often presented His teaching in the words and imagery of the Old Testament. It is, therefore, necessary to understand certain aspects of the prophetic activity of the great Jewish visionaries in order to appreciate the prophetic activity of Jesus. Among those aspects, the call to conversion is paramount. Oracles about future events were indeed delivered, but delivered so as to produce a change of heart in the here and now; in short, predictions about the future were

motivational, not primarily cognitive factors. For that reason, there is a marked tendency in prophetic statements to *compress time sequence*. What in fact is very remote is presented as being near at hand or in the proximate future. Witness the following:

> Pay attention to me, you peoples, listen to me, you nations.... I will establish my integrity speedily, my salvation shall come like the light, my arm shall judge the peoples.... The heavens will vanish like smoke, the earth wear out like a garment—but my salvation shall last for ever (Is. 51:4-6) (Jerusalem Bible). I mean to sweep away everything off the face of the earth—it is Yahweh who speaks.... Silence before the Lord Yahweh. For the day of Yahweh is near.... The great day of Yahweh is near and coming with all speed (Zep. 1:2, 7, 14) (Jerusalem Bible) The days are coming now—it is Yahweh who speaks—when harvest will follow directly after ploughing, the treading of grapes soon after sowing, when the mountains will run with new wine and the hills flow with it (Am. 9:13) (Jerusalem Bible).
> Know this, then, and understand: from the time this message went out: 'Return and rebuild Jerusalem' to the coming of an anointed Prince, seven weeks and sixty-two weeks, with squares and ramparts restored and rebuilt, but in a time of trouble. And after the sixty-two weeks an anointed one will be cut off and...the city and the sanctuary will be destroyed by a prince who will come. His end will come in catastrophe and, until the end, there will be war and all the devastation decreed.... He will put a stop to sacrifice and oblation, and on the wing of the Temple will be the disastrous abomination (abomination of desolation)... (Dn. 9:25-27) (Jerusalem Bible).

It should be clear that time ("speedily," "like the light," "now," "near," "coming with great speed," etc.), like the symbolic imagery, is a very fluid concept in prophetic preaching. Nor should it be thought that the constant emphasis on "now" and "soon" were simply mistaken notions about chronology. They were, rather, a technique of preaching, a device to provoke conversion, not a calendar for future events. It is in such a tradition that Jesus' own chronological details must be seen.

2. Jesus explicitly taught that He did not know the day nor the hour (Mt. 24:36, etc.). The fact that the saying appears to attribute a certain limitation to the Son is warrant enough that its content is authentic. What it means exactly is another question. That the Son in His divinity knows and knew the day and the hour cannot be questioned. Whether He knew it in His human awareness would have depended on what knowledge His divinity gave Him, along the lines of what is traditionally called "infused knowledge," that is, a form of knowing akin to the knowledge which the prophets had of facts and events beyond their immediate possibilities. Did the divinity withhold such knowledge in regard to this specific point from the human intellect of Jesus? Perhaps. There is certainly no teaching of the Church which absolutely prohibits such an under-standing; the statement of Pope Gregory I (cf. Part I, p. 94 above) was not infallible and the point has not been repeated since, although it should make one cautious. Nevertheless, exegesis which sees Matthew 24:36 (Mk. 13:32) as being a hyperbolic way of saying, "That is a fact which the Father has willed to be kept secret" should not be dismissed too readily. Jesus often spoke in hyperbolic language which very few would interpret as being His final or full word on an issue. "If your eye causes you to sin, pluck it out" (Mk. 9:47); "It is easier for a camel to go through the eye of a needle than for a rich man to enter the kingdom of God" (Mk. 10:24); "He went in and said to them, 'Why all this commotion and wailing? The child is not dead, but asleep'" (Mk. 5:39-40; in fact, she was dead). Do we have any certain indication that His word about the Son not knowing the day or the hour is any different a form of His speech than these and others like them? Rather, in the light of such statements, one should be slow in asserting that one logion of the Lord proves His ignorance on a specific point. At any rate, the logion is a reminder that Jesus did not consider eschatological chronology as forming part of His mission, whether the chronology was near or distant.[17]

3. In the light of His word about not knowing the day and the hour, the statements which seem to indicate an indefinite future before the final judgment should not simply be dismissed as being inauthentic. Such statements are found in all the Gospels, and in different forms. Some are direct statements, some are indications

given in parables and some are simply "presuppositions" needed to make other things intelligible (e.g., the question of fasting when the Bridegroom has been taken away). It is not a question again of one text or another being an authentic word of Jesus. It is the accumulation of indications which is significant—as well as the testimony of the evangelists. The attempt to discredit them all can only be called arbitrary or mistaken. Furthermore, the fact that He envisioned an indefinite future better harmonizes with the call of the Twelve as pillars of a new Community, with the institution of a commemorative Meal (what would there be to commemorate if He thought the end was at hand?), and the intention to call the Gentiles to salvation. Nor is the *a priori* argument without weight which would view as intrinsically improbable—or even repugnant—a position which would make the Incarnate God little more than a sectarian fanatic whose mission and work were shaped by a mistaken notion that the world was about to end—a man dominated by the type of apocalyptic fervor which time after time has led deluded disciples to gather and wait an end which did not come.

Christian thinking—especially the inspired word—must also be allowed to make its contribution.

> But do not forget this one thing, dear friends: With the Lord a day is like a thousand years, and a thousand years are like a day. The Lord is not slow in keeping his promise, as some understand slowness. He is patient with you, not wanting anyone to perish, but everyone to come to repentance. But the day of the Lord will come like a thief... (2 Pt. 3:8-10).

The day will come like a thief (cf. Mt. 24:37; 25:13); so repent because the kingdom is at hand. In line with all the Old Testament prophets—and like all good preachers since—Jesus preached in such a way as to prompt a decision *here and now*. To expect Him to have said, "The kingdom is at hand, but don't worry, the end won't come for two or three thousand years yet" is ludicrous. Human nature being what it is, such preaching would have amounted to an invitation to presumption. Certainly, it would have been misleading. The Father's will for man is always *now*, just as *now* is the moment of His action. The future, however real and long it be, is a gift, not a given. It is also meant to be the object of desire here and now. "Thy kingdom come" (cf. Rv. 22:17).

Jesus' own awareness of being the unique Son included the realization that the Father had, in Him, definitively acted in human history. The last word had been said; the Father is here, the kingdom is here because in Christ the Father Himself has drawn close. It would seem that the only way to present that message without diluting it was to stress what was near at hand. If one weighs all the factors, then, it would appear that the preaching of Jesus about the kingdom and the end of the world included a planned and salvific ambiguity directed to conversion and vigilance—a salvific ambiguity willed by Christ Himself, His own expression of the *ekonomia*.

This preaching of the kingdom was also the "good news," the Gospel. Because it involves a judgment, a "sifting out" and because it is intimately connected with struggle and suffering and a moral order, it is relatively easy to forget the focus of Jesus' teaching. In essence, that teaching is centered on the loving concern of the Father for mankind—a concern that wills good and does good for all. It is a love that had drawn God so close that He has taken on Himself our life, our history, our trials so that mankind may share His life, His eternity, His glory. God became man so that man might become God.[18] The Father revealed by Jesus is the penultimate manifestation of Israel's God who is slow to anger and rich in compassion, who is so close to His people as to have become One among them. The God revealed by and in Jesus is not One who changes the conditions of human history in order to find a suitable dwelling place, but One who takes on those human conditions to be with us before we can be with Him.

This nearness of God to humanity—source of abiding joy—is realized first of all and uniquely in the humanity of Jesus Himself. It is the point of reference for everything about Him, and He never ceases to direct man's attention to it. It is this "referral" which explains those texts of "subordination" of the Son to the Father which are sprinkled throughout the Gospels, and which are so especially clear in the Gospel of John. "If you loved me, you would be glad that I am going to the Father, for the Father is greater than I" (Jn. 14:28). Jesus says, in truth, "All that belongs to the Father is mine" (Jn. 16:15; cf. 17:10), for that is the very mystery of Their relation eternally, now imaged in the humanity of Christ.[19] It is that total unity which makes the Father's kingdom the kingdom of the

Son as well—a reciprocal giving, but one which finds, for the Son, its origin and end where He Himself finds His origin and end, in the Father. St. Paul captures this profoundly. "…Then the Son himself will be made subject to him who put everything under him, so that God may be all in all" (1 Cor. 15:28). There is no need to explain such texts by noting that, *in His humanity*, the Son is less than the Father, although that is true. The texts reveal the Son as He is, in divinity and humanity, as Self-Expression of the Father—from Him, and of Him and *for* Him. That unity is subordination without inequality of being or majesty. It is God's own life. As the last word, this is the "good news" brought by the Son: God will be all in all.

II. THE STRUGGLE FOR THE KINGDOM

After His baptism, "Jesus was led by the Spirit into the desert to be tempted by the devil" (Mt. 4:1). The fact of Christ's temptation in the wilderness is recorded by the three Synoptic Gospels, although Mark only refers to it (Mk. 1:12-13) while Matthew and Luke give us the more elaborated and basically identical accounts.[20] These accounts are rich in meaning and offer the opportunity for various approaches. The three evangelists indicate, at an initial level, that the ministry of Jesus is inaugurated with testing, and Luke remarks explicitly that, with the initial probation past, the trials did not end. "When the devil had finished all this tempting, he left Him until an opportune time" (Lk. 4:13). From the beginning of His ministry, then, there is no moment in which Jesus' proclamation of the kingdom is free from trial, misunderstandings, contradictions and malice. The ministry is begun not with glory, but with struggle.[21]

The chief antagonist in that struggle is Satan, the devil who is pictured throughout the New Testament as either directly involved in confrontation with Jesus, or indirectly involved via the human instruments who effect his designs. He is referred to as the "prince of this world" (Jn. 14:30; 16:11), a "liar and the father of lies" (Jn. 8:44) who has his own offspring (Jn. 8:44). Indeed, for Jesus, in the midst of this struggle with the evil one, there appears to be two paternities, that of the Father and that of the devil. Thus:

> The field is the world; and the good seed stands for the sons of the kingdom. The weeds are the sons of the evil one (Mt. 13:38; cf. Mt. 23:15; Jn. 8:44; 1 Jn. 3:10).

As was true in the case of Jesus Himself, the devil is seen as the tester of man (cf. Lk. 22:31; Mt. 16:22-23; Jn. 6:70; 13:27). This portrayal serves to remind us that "evil is not merely the absence of something, but an active force, a living, spiritual being that is perverted and perverts others. It is a terrible reality, mysterious and frightening."[22]

The existence of Satan, the evil one, and of the damned spirits associated with him—members, as Pope Paul VI said, of "a whole mysterious world, convulsed by a most unfortunate drama about which we know very little"[23]—is one of the biblical data apparently most amenable to re-interpretation or demytholization.[24] Without doubt, it is true that the teaching of both the Old and New Testaments about the devil has mythological parallels, and may even have been influenced in various ways by such mythology. Nevertheless, an awareness of that fact says nothing in itself as to the actual existence of such powers. That mankind has sensed the magnitude of evil and has, in myth, "located" the origin of this evil in personal powers does not mean, of itself, that mankind reached a wrong conclusion. On the contrary, Revelation assures us that the mythological instincts of the race in this regard arrived at a correct conclusion, at least in essentials. Tradition and the Magisterium of the Church are infallibly clear on this point.[25] We are faced in this matter with a case where the Church, without defining a particular text of Scripture, has given us an "in globo" interpretation of Scripture which is definitive, and thus set limits to any attempt at radical demythologizing. In doing so, she is merely reflecting the teaching and mode of action of Jesus Himself who invited all to believe that His very warfare with Satan was a sign that the kingdom of the Father had come.

> If Satan drives out Satan, he is divided against himself. How then can his kingdom stand? And if I drive out demons by Beelzebub, by whom do your people drive them out? So then, they will be your judges. But if I drive out demons by the Spirit of God, then the kingdom of God has come upon you (Mt. 12:27-28; cf. Mk. 3:22ff.; Lk. 11:14ff.; Jn. 14:30).

The struggle of Jesus with the evil one, against whom He taught His followers to pray[26] was so marked a feature of the Lord's life[27] that the Second Vatican Council, giving a brief synopsis of His mission, could say:

> He was crucified and rose again to break the hold of the evil one (Lt. *Malignus*), in order that the world might be made anew according to God's design and so reach its fulfillment.[28]

The Temptation Accounts, as given us by Matthew and Luke, indicate that Satan is ignorant of the true identity of Jesus. The "If you are the Son of God" (Mt. 4:6, etc.) has various levels of meaning. As reflective of Old Testament usage, "Son of God" can indicate no more than a special choice by God of an individual. Thus, in the Old Testament, the Davidic king, the people of Israel themselves and even the angels are given this title (cf. Ps. 2:7; Ex. 4:22; Jb. 1:6, etc.). For the Christian community, of course, it had come to mean the unique relationship of Jesus the Messiah with the Father (cf. Rom. 1:3; Acts 13:32-38; 1 Jn. 4:15; Mk. 1:1 and many others), and the questions of the devil are probably intended, by the evangelists themselves, to reflect the Christian meaning of the title. St. Mark's Gospel records that the demons claimed to know the identity of Jesus (cf. 1:25, 34; 3:12), but this is most likely to be understood in the sense that He was Messiah, not that He was the natural eternal Son of the Father. As to knowledge of that mystery, St. Paul comments:

> ...We speak of God's secret wisdom, a wisdom that has been hidden and that God destined for our glory before time began. None of the rulers of this age understood it, for if they had, they would not have crucified the Lord of glory (1 Cor. 2:7-8).[29]

It is this ignorance of the devil in respect to the mystery of the Incarnate One which Ignatius of Antioch referred to, in all probability, when he wrote:

> Now Mary's virginity and her giving birth escaped the notice of the prince of this world, as did the Lord's death—these three secrets crying to be told, but wrought in God's silence.[30]

Thus, even the intelligence of the demonic powers was inadequate to grasp the union of God and man in Jesus. All that any natural intelligence can understand of Jesus is the dimension of His humanity—graced, elect and mysterious. The devil's testing was an effort to reveal what more there was than met the eye. What that humanity manifested was hidden—at least during His life and ministry—to all but the eyes of faith, possessed by those to whom the Father had chosen to reveal it (cf. Mt. 16:17-18; 11:26-27; Jn. 6:65).

The text from St. Paul cited above indicates that it is the devil who is ultimately responsible for the crucifixion of Jesus. St. John conveys the same message in stark words when he writes:

> As soon as Judas took the bread, Satan entered into him.... As soon as Judas took the bread he went out. And, it was night (Jn. 13:27-30; cf. parallel in Lk. 22:3).

Of course, Paul and John are not alone in attributing to Satan and the evil spirits such malign influence over human action. The Lord Himself, in His famous rebuke to Peter, indicated the same conception of diabolical influence (cf. Mt. 16:22-23). That malicious influence must be viewed as "operating behind the scenes" in the stubborn resistance given to the Teacher's message by many among His hearers from the beginning of the public ministry. In a particular way, the instigation of the devil can be discerned in the struggle Jesus faced with the priests, the scribes, the Pharisees, the Sadducees and the Herodians.

Like the sect which lived at Qumran, called the Essenes, the Pharisees were the religious descendants of the Hasidim, those Israelites zealous for the Torah who had provided the backbone for the revolt against pagan domination in Israel at the time of the Maccabees.[31] They were the dominant religious party in first century Palestine, counting among themselves many learned and devout people. To this group Saul of Tarsus and probably his family belonged. Their paramount opponents for religious authority were the Sadducees whose origin likewise was in the period 200-100 B.C.[32] "Theological liberals" is the category often ascribed to them, although an argument can be made to demonstrate a certain reactionary traditionalism in their religious views. The New Testament notes their refusal to believe in the angelic order and in the resurrection of the dead. Over this last point, Jesus Himself rebuked them (Mt. 22:23ff.) and St. Paul afterwards used the disagreement between them and the Pharisees concerning the resurrection to his own advantage when he was on trial before them both for his teaching on the resurrection of Jesus (Acts 23:6-11).

The Herodians might be compared to the "Quislings" of the first century Palestine—those who aligned themselves to the political powers governing the nation, undoubtedly to their own social and material advantage.

The differences among these groups made them unlikely allies. Nevertheless, many of them appear to have been united in their rejection of John the Baptist (cf. Mt. 3:7) and certainly became progressively united in their opposition to Jesus whose teaching and mode of life seemed so frequently to be a deliberate counterpoint to much that they stood for (cf. Mt. 9:2-4, 11-13; 12:2, 24ff.; 15:1-9; 16:5-12 and parallels, and many other places). In chapter twenty-three of his Gospel, St. Matthew has probably grouped together various sayings of Jesus to highlight the intensity of that struggle. From the mouth of the One who had declared Himself "meek and humble of heart" (Mt. 11:29), the denunciation is scalding.

> Woe to you, teachers of the law and Pharisees, you hypocrites! You shut the kingdom of heaven in men's faces. You yourselves do not enter, nor will you let those enter who are trying to. Woe to you, blind guides....
>
> Woe to you, teachers of the law and Pharisees, you hypocrites! You travel over land and sea to win a single convert, and when he becomes one, you make him twice as much a son of hell as you are. Woe to you, teachers of the law and Pharisees, you hypocrites! You are like whitewashed tombs, which look beautiful on the outside but on the inside are full of dead men's bones and everything unclean.... Upon you will come all the righteous blood that has been shed on earth, from the blood of righteous Abel to the blood of Zechariah son of Berakiah whom you murdered between the temple and the altar. I tell you the truth, all this will come upon this generation (Mt. 23:13-39).[33]

While Matthew has apparently dramatized the denunciation, the vehemence of Jesus is well attested in the other Gospels (cf. Mk. 7:6-13; Lk. 11:37ff.; Jn. 8:55; 9:40-41, etc.). It is a sign of the reality of the human emotions in the God-man, and one of the many indications offered by the Scriptures that the recurrent tendencies to present to the world a "pallid" Jesus, one for whom the irascible emotions are nonexistent, is a betrayal of the multi-faceted richness of His personality. It should be observed, nevertheless, that such vehemence is not simply—as vehemence can so often be in us—the manifestation of frustrated anger. In all likelihood, it was partly didactic; like so much of His hyperbole, it was aimed not just at condemnation or threat, but at repentance and conversion—an effort to "shake them up" enough to allow His word a hearing.

The struggle to prepare a fertile ground for His preaching was not limited to the various elites among His audiences.[34] Repeatedly the evangelists remark at the astonishment and admiration of the populace at what He taught and how He taught.

> …The crowds were amazed at his teaching, because he taught as one who had authority, and not as their teachers of the law (Mt. 7:28-29 and parallels; cf. Mt. 15:31).

> …He began to teach in the synagogue, and many who heard him were amazed (Mk. 6:2; cf. Mk. 1:27).

> He taught in their synagogues, and everyone praised him (Lk. 4:15; cf. Lk. 8:25; 11:27; 19:48).

> After the people saw the miraculous sign that Jesus did, they began to say, 'Surely this is the Prophet who is to come into the world' (Jn. 6:14; cf. Jn. 4:42; 3:2; 11:45).

And Jesus Himself admitted that they had reason to marvel. "For I tell you the truth, many prophets and righteous men longed to see what you see, but did not see, and to hear what you hear but did not hear it" (Mt. 13:17; Lk. 10:23-24). But it was not universal acclaim that He received at any stage of His ministry. St. John summarizes what is clear from the synoptics when he writes: "Thus the people were divided because of Jesus" (Jn. 7:43). Some were pleased at nothing He said or did. His response to that varied—at times a lament, at other times condemnation.

> To what can I compare this generation? They are like children sitting in the marketplaces and calling out to others: 'We played the flute for you, and you did not dance; we sang a dirge, and you did not mourn.' For John came neither eating nor drinking, and they say, 'He has a demon.' The Son of Man came eating and drinking, and they say, 'Here is a glutton

and a drunkard, a friend of tax collectors and "sinners"'
(Mt. 11:16-18; Lk. 7:31-35).

Then Jesus began to denounce the cities in which most of his
miracles had been performed, because they did not repent.
'Woe to you, Korazin! Woe to you, Bethsaida.... It will be
more bearable for Tyre and Sidon on the day of judgment than
for you. And you, Capernaum, will you be lifted up to the
skies?... It will be more bearable for Sodom on the day of
judgment than for you' (Mt. 11:20-24; Lk. 10:13-15).

In short, many found Him "too much to take" (cf. Mt. 13:53ff.
and parallels; Jn. 6:59-66). Their reaction, of course, was probably
fairly typical of any audience at any time to a preacher; some for,
some against, some indifferent. Although He made no mention of it
that is recorded, the doctrine of original sin, already seminally
present in the writings of some Jewish authors of His generation[35]
and later elaborated by Paul and the Church, was witnessed to by
the Lord. As St. John remarks, "many believed in him.... But Jesus
would not entrust himself to them, for he knew all men. He did not
need man's testimony about man, for he knew what was in a man"
(Jn. 2:24-25; cf. Mt. 7:11).

What Divine Revelation makes known to us concords with
experience itself. For man, looking at his own heart, finds himself also inclined to evil and submerged in multiple evils which
cannot come from his good Creator. Frequently refusing to
recognize God as his beginning, man has disrupted his proper
relation to his final end, and simultaneously has disrupted his
relationship toward himself, toward other men and toward all
created things.[36]

Jesus well knew that no man was justified before God, not even
one, and that lack revealed itself regularly in the obtuse reaction to
His message and work. It is that obtuse hearing which must account
for the invoking of the difficult text of Isaiah 6:9-10.

You will be ever hearing but never understanding; you will be
ever seeing but never perceiving. For this people's heart has
become calloused; they hardly hear with their ears, and they

have closed their eyes. Otherwise they might see with their eyes, hear with their ears...and turn, and I would heal them (Mt. 13:14ff.).

All the evangelists cite it, as does St. Paul at the end of the Acts of the Apostles (Acts 28:26ff.). Mysterious as it is, it became an explanation in faith to the preacher who had to ask himself, "Why will they not listen?" The Lord Himself, the Gospel writers tell us, faced that same question when He encountered those who would not hear. That refusal to hear provoked in Him compassion for the multitude and a sense of the urgency of the mission (cf. Mt. 9:36-37). He was aware, too, that such obtuseness, such hardness of heart, could be permanent, and could frustrate the call to repentance. The consequence of that was eternal loss, the mystery of hell.[37] In salutary warnings, He spelled it out clearly.

If your hand causes you to sin, cut if off. It is better for you to enter life maimed than with two hands to go into hell, where the fire never goes out (Mk. 9:43-48 and parallels).

'Lord, are only a few people going to be saved?' He said to them, 'Make every effort.to enter through the narrow door, because many, I tell you, will try to enter and will not be able to' (Lk. 13:23-24; Mt. 7:13-14).

'I tell you the truth, whatever you did not do for one of the least of these, you did not do for me.' Then they will go away to eternal punishment... (Mt. 25:3-46).

Whoever believes in the Son has eternal life, but whoever rejects the Son will not see life for God's wrath remains on him (Jn. 3:36; cf. Jn. 9:41 and 5:28-29).

The words are stern and the doctrine itself is foreboding, reminding one that the "whole process out of which the New Earth is gradually born is an *aggregation* underlaid by a segregation."[38] It posits hell as a "structural element in the universe"[39] and one that points to the magnitude of the decision involved in the acts of free choice made by God's creatures. Its reasonableness and justice is ultimately to be discerned in the great love of the Father for all whom He has made His own—loving the world so much that He sent His only Son not to condemn but to save it (cf. Jn. 3:16-18).

The doctrine of hell and the possibilities inherent in the existence of such eternal loss for mankind in general and for individuals in particular are assuredly part of the explanation for the intensity and seriousness of the preaching of Jesus. Furthermore, they are one parameter of the struggle. Jesus envisioned no easy victory in that struggle. On the contrary, it is apparent that He expected the struggle to intensify, especially as the end drew near.

> Jesus answered: 'Watch out that no one deceives you. For many will come in my name, claiming, "I am the Christ," and will deceive many.... Then you will be handed over to be persecuted and put to death, and you will be hated by all nations because of me. At that time many will turn away from the faith and will betray and hate each other.... Because of the increase of wickedness, the love of most will grow cold, but he who stands firm to the end will be saved' (Mt. 24:4-14).

One may add to these words, the word of Jesus recorded by St. Luke, apparently taken out of its original context: "When the Son of Man comes, will he find faith on earth?" (Lk. 18:8)

As noted previously, the eschatological sayings of Jesus as recorded by the evangelists are most difficult to interpret. Each of the three synoptic writers has slightly different material, arranged in different ways. Not only the time sequences, but the subject matter as well presents a problem. Some of what is spoken of refers to the period antedating the destruction of the Jewish capital and its Temple; other parts of the sayings refer to the culmination of earthly history and the final judgment. Certain items, however, are relatively clear.

1. The future will be marked by false claims of messiahship, men claiming to speak with the sanction of God, but who are in fact false prophets, pseudo-Christs. Such claimants will appear not only at the end, but before the fall of Jerusalem as well. In a sense, there is nothing factually new in this. Israel's history, especially at times of crisis, had frequently been marked with false claimants (cf. 1 Kgs. 22:5ff.; 2 Chr. 18:4ff.; Is. 28:7-14; Jer. 23:9ff.). Such types, Jesus told His followers, will always be found, their claim all the more convincing because of the trials of those times. Some, it would

seem, will have the audacity to impersonate the Christ, but His Second Coming will not be hidden or obscure in any way (Mt. 24:26-28).

This doctrine on false claimants became in time the. theme of the anti-Christ (cf. 1 Jn. 2:18-22; 4:3; 2 Jn. 7; 2 Thes. 2:3-12). The fact that this figure appears, in the different references, to be at times one individual, while at other times a plurality of individuals—sometimes already present, at other times still to come—reflects the generalizing nature of Jesus' own imagery.

2. Jerusalem will be destroyed. What pain this prophecy must have caused the Lord can be gathered from the tender and sorrowful words He addressed to that city.

> O Jerusalem, Jerusalem, you who kill the prophets and stone those sent to you, how often I have longed to gather your children together, as a hen gathers her chicks under her wings, but you were not willing. Look, your house is left to you desolate (Mt. 23:37-39; Lk. 13:34).[40]

The Lord's prophecy on the fall of the city and its temple (Mt. 24:1-3; Mk. 13:1-4; Lk. 21:41-44) was fulfilled within some hundred years. The Roman armies moved on Galilee in 66-67, surrounded Jerusalem in March of 70 and burned the Temple in August of the same year. Flavius Josephus, an eyewitness to the events, described it in vivid language.

> While the sanctuary was burning, looting went on right and left and all who were caught were put to the sword. There was no pity for age, no regard for rank; little children and old men, laymen and priests alike were butchered.... The Temple Hill, enveloped in flames from top to bottom, appeared to be boiling up from its very roots; yet the sea of flame was nothing to the ocean of blood.[41]

Whatever may be the eventual outcome of the questions concerning the date of composition of the Synoptic Gospels, any contention that Jesus' words on Jerusalem's fall are a "prophecy after the event" or that His original words have been elaborated by the evangelists after the event is difficult to sustain from internal evidence. The prophecy of the Lord as it is recorded—even as recorded by Luke who is most frequently cited as having modified the words in light of what had already taken place—is almost totally drawn from Old Testament imagery and is completely lacking any of those specifics peculiar to the events of the year 70.[42] The prediction of the destruction of the city and its temple is the prophecy of Jesus Himself, not the work of an editor. That the Lord's warnings were not in vain, at least for His followers, can be gauged from the fact that prophets in the Christian community of Jerusalem, reading the signs, successfully warned the Christians in time to escape the coming destruction by fleeing to Pella, a town beyond the Jordan.[43]

The prophecy itself was only completely fulfilled in the year 135 when the temple area was leveled, and long after the Gospels were written.

3. The tribulations of the future—of which the fall of Jerusalem, though real in itself, was but a major sign—also included the suffering of the disciples of Jesus (Mt. 24:9-13 and parallels; Mt. 16:24-26 and parallels; Mk. 10:17-23). These prophecies, variously applied by the evangelists and probably resonating what the early Christians had already suffered and were suffering, are, in a sense, already contained in the Lord's words in the beatitudes.

> Blessed are those who are persecuted because of righteousness, for theirs is the kingdom of heaven. Blessed are you when people persecute you and falsely say all kinds of evil against you because of me. Rejoice and be glad, because great is your reward in heaven... (Mt. 5:10-12; Lk. 6:22-23).[44]

For Jesus, then, the tribulations of the end would appear to have been but an extension and intensification of what was evident in His own vocation from the time of His baptism. The kingdom of the Father does not come in power, but through testing, fidelity and perseverance. Human nature is such that even a good word—a word of liberation and peace, an assurance of the Father's love and the claims of that love—would not be received by all, nor even be perceived as being, indeed, a good word. For that reason, the devil's assault against the Lord in the desert was the proper beginning, for the message was to be met by opposition.

III. THE WAY OF THE FATHER

It should not be thought that the struggle for the Kingdom was merely one in which the forces of evil contended against Jesus. He Himself was an active agent, waging a campaign, as it were, on behalf of the Father's kingdom. It was a campaign waged in power through deed and word. The first of those deeds, says the Gospel of John, took place in Cana of Galilee.

> Three days later there was a wedding at Cana in Galilee. The mother of Jesus was there, and Jesus and his disciples had also been invited. When they ran out of wine...the mother of Jesus said to him, 'They have no wine.' Jesus said, 'Woman, what is that to me and to you? My hour has not yet come.' His mother said to the servants, 'Do whatever he tells you.' ...They did this: the steward tasted the water, and it had turned into wine.

> This was the first of the signs given by Jesus; it was given at Cana in Galilee. He let his glory be seen, and his disciples believed in him (Jn. 2:1-12) (Jerusalem Bible).

St. Thomas Aquinas, admitting the historical trustworthiness of the account, saw a symbolic meaning in the Johannine narrative. In the Old Testament, Yahweh is portrayed as having entered a nuptial covenant with Israel (cf. Hos. 2:7; Ez. 16:1ff.; Is. 62:4-5). Jesus also, undoubtedly evoking that imagery, spoke of the kingdom under the figure of a wedding banquet (cf. Mt. 22:1ff.; Lk. 14:16-24; Mk. 2:18-20), and Sts. Paul and John employ the bridal symbol to depict the nuptial union of Christ with His Church (2 Cor. 11:2; Eph. 5:21ff.; Rv. 19:7-9; 21:2, 9). What John narrates about Cana, says St. Thomas, can be understood within the framework of such images. At the Incarnation God weds Himself to humanity by taking our flesh as His own, man and God becoming one in the flesh. The consummation of that union will occur when the Church, as New Jerusalem, reaches perfection in heaven. The Mother of Jesus acts as the "go-between" (*"nuptiarum consiliatrix"*) in this mystical union "because through her intercession one is joined to Christ through grace."[45]

Whatever the various levels of truth to be found in the account may be—and John's Gospel is often to be read at various levels—the evangelist makes clear that the "sign" at Cana manifested the Son's glory, with the result that "his disciples believed in him." That the "signs"—what we generally call "miracles"—were meant to evoke belief is a frequent Johannine theme (cf. 2:23; 4:48-54; 11:15, etc.). Jesus, too, appeals to the signs as an indication that He is doing the Father's work.

> Do not believe me unless I do what my Father does. But if I do it, even though you do not believe me, believe the miracles, that you may learn and understand that the Father is in me, and I in the Father... (Jn. 10:38).

Indeed, it is the Father living in Jesus who performs the signs (Jn. 14:10) for, as Jesus says, "I am in the Father and the Father is in me" (Jn. 14:11).

Summarizing Tradition, Aquinas writes that the signs or miracles of Jesus reveal two purposes: first and "principally to confirm the truth which one teaches" and, "secondly, to manifest the presence of God in man through the grace of the Holy Spirit."[46] In that, he is fundamentally in agreement with the significance John stresses throughout his Gospel. That understanding must be completed, however, by another insight of Aquinas. The signs of Christ, Thomas wrote, were indications that by Christ's work "the whole world was to be changed for the better."[47] Studying St. Thomas' treatment of the miracles, one can say that he "asked the right questions": why did the miracles manifest themselves in relation to the devil and the demons, in relation to man, and in relation to inanimate matter?[48] In a word, was it not significant that the Incarnate Word touched all created realities in working His signs? Why did He do so?

Tradition and the New Testament give at least part of the answer to such questions. Creation had been made subject to sin and to the personal powers of evil. Jesus struggled with this dominion of evil on all levels. He came to liberate us from the power of the prince of this world (Jn. 12:31; Col. 2:15), from the slavery we experience in sin (Jn. 8:34), from the evils in creation consequent on sin: death, sickness, disunity, etc. To this Man, like us in all things except sin, was to be made subject again the creation man was made to dominate (Gn. 1:28-30; 2:19-20; Mk. 4:41); in this Man, the unity lost by mankind through sin was to be restored (Gn. 11; Jn. 17:21; Gal. 3:28-29); to this Man—and, in Him, to all who share His rule— the systems and institutions which have become sinful were to be made subject (Rv. 17:2, 13-14) because He had fought and overcome the evil one to whom the empires of the world were subject (Lk. 4:6). In Christ, literally all things were to be made new (Rv. 21:5). As universal as the rule of sin, equally universal is the saving work of Christ, the inauguration of the Father's kingdom. The miracles were a sign of all this. "...If I drive out demons by the Spirit of God, then the kingdom of God has come among you" (Mt. 12:28; Lk. 11:20).

The question of the historical accuracy of the wondrous deeds performed by Jesus as recounted in the Gospels has been much discussed.[49] There is today no serious scholar who will deny—in the light of the diverse and abundant New Testament testimonies—that Jesus performed at least some of the marvelous acts attributed to Him. The fact that His adversaries accused Him of working such signs by demonic power (Mt. 12:24-32 and parallels) is too unlikely a saying to have originated among His followers, and indicates that His renown as a "wonder-worker" had to be explained since denial was not possible. Whether each of the specific wonders recounted by the four evangelists is historically accurate would appear to be an insoluble problem, heavily dependent on how one evaluates the available evidence, the insights offered by literary, linguistic and redactional analysis, and the general historical reliability of the Gospel accounts. This can be illustrated by considering one of the most astonishing of the so-called "nature miracles": Jesus walking on the lake.

The incident is recounted in Mark 6:45ff., Matthew 14:22ff. and John 6:16ff. The narratives have much in common, including vocabulary. John's account is the shortest, Matthew's the most elaborated since it includes the episode of Peter going out to Jesus on the water, a fact not mentioned in the other accounts. In all three Gospels one can notice elements of a special epiphany or manifestation of the divine. Matthew even ends with a credal confession on the part of the disciples: "Truly you are the Son of God" (14:33). All three have the ambiguous but evocative "I am" statement on the part of Jesus (cf. Part I, pp. 59-60 above).[50] All of the accounts are narrated in conjunction with the multiplication of the bread, during what may be called the "middle period" of the Lord's pre-Easter ministry. In short, it is one of the best attested of Christ's miracles, common to the Synoptic (Matthew and Mark) and Johannine traditions, while maintaining certain items peculiar to each evangelist.

From the point of view of historicity, what is one to make of the incident? Some would suggest the possibility that it is a story which developed as a "result of a linguistic misunderstanding" since the Greek *epi tes thalasses* (Mt. 14:26; Mk. 6:47; Jn. 6:19) can be translated "on the seashore" as well as "on the sea."[51] Such a translation, however, must be judged totally improbable since it would rob each of the accounts as they now exist of their obvious significance,[52] or posit a development in the story which was unknown to the evangelists and for which there is no other evidence whatsoever.

Others would suggest that the narrative is a retrojection of the Easter experience into the ministry.[53] Evidence, either documentary or linguistic, for such a hypothesis is lacking—as it is for a similar solution for the transfiguration—and would appear to rest more on theological presuppositions than on any historical or literary evidence.[54]

In short, the "pre-history" of the three narratives—if they do not reflect the testimony of eyewitnesses (Matthew-Levi; Peter [Mark] and John of Zebedee)—is concretely unattainable, although open to conjecture. Much the same conclusion would have to be drawn in respect to the other miracle accounts. Despite the many contributions of literary and redactional analysis, one must recognize that the "hard evidence" necessary for resolving the historicity of the miracle accounts as a whole is still limited to the documents at hand and to how one evaluates their general reliability. That situation is not a completely unhappy one since it leaves a certain aura of ambiguity. Such ambiguity is, it would seem, native to the very nature of miracles. For in a miracle, there is always the possibility for a lack of comprehension or for a diversity of interpretations.[35] In His own lifetime, Jesus met such lack of comprehension and diversity of interpretation in regard to His works of power (Mk. 6:52; 3:22ff.; Mt. 8:27, 34; 13:54; 17:19; Lk. 5:26; Jn. 7:12; 9:24-34). Indeed, a certain openness was needed both to comprehend the significance of the signs and even to merit their occurrence (Mk. 6:5-6; Mt. 17:14-18; 15:21-28).

The mission of changing the whole world for the better formed the core of the Lord's preaching ministry. It was thus a mission manifested in the signs and proclaimed in the teaching. In that preaching it is again the Father who is set forth as the model.

> Be perfect, therefore, as your heavenly Father is perfect (Mt. 5:48).

Those words of the Sermon on the Mount are both the beginning and the culmination of the message of Jesus. Like so much of His teaching, the idea itself was not new, but rather a forceful restatement of the Revelation given to Israel. The reason given to the Israelites for observing the Law of the Covenant had been long before summed up in the book of Leviticus: "Be holy, because I, the Lord your God, am holy" (Lv. 19:2; cf. 1 Pt. 1:15-16). What was radically new, of course, when Jesus proclaimed that commandment was the fact that, in Him, it was being realized. Before Him, no man had been capable of living the injunction. Jesus alone, being who He is, was able to be among men what the Father is. That holiness was His by nature, but in Him our own flesh and blood were living the commandment, and so the very possibility of so doing had now been inserted into our race. Christ's own humanity had become the assurance that mankind could and would be the image of God, thereby enjoying Jesus' own privilege of calling Him "Abba" (Mt. 6:9; Lk. 11:2; Jn. 17:26; Rom. 8:15; Gal. 4:6). The realization that this was the case did not come to Christ's followers immediately, but when it did it would enable St. John to exclaim:

> How great is the love the Father has lavished on us, that we should be called children of God! And that is what we are!... Dear friends, now we are children of God, and what we will be

has not yet been made known. But we know that when he appears, we shall be like him, for we shall see him as he is (1 Jn. 3:1-2).

That love lavished by the Father has always been seen as the very heart of the message of Jesus. God loves us, so we must love one another. God forgives us, so we must forgive, times without number. God showers His benefits like rain on the good and the bad, so must we deal with all. The Father provides for the lilies of the field and the birds of the air, so must we provide for others, lending and giving without expecting a return, and without the anxious concern of providing for ourselves. The Father knows what we need and will provide it. Love even those who hate you; then you truly are children of your heavenly Father. Indeed, everything written in the Law and the prophets is summed up in "Love the Father and love your neighbor." It is such love and it alone which distinguishes the children of the Father from the children of the devil.

Love alone makes the difference between the children of God and the children of the devil. Everyone can sign himself with the sign of Christ's cross; everyone can respond 'Amen' and everyone can sing 'Alleluia'; everyone can be baptized and come to church, but only love will distinguish the children of God from the children of the devil. Those who have love are born of God; those who do not have love are not born of God.... You may have whatever else you will; if you do not have this, it all profits you nothing. If you do not have other things, but do have love, you have fulfilled the Law.... Love is the pearl of great price. If you have everything else but not it you have profited nothing. If you have nothing else, but have love, nothing else is necessary.[56]

What is so striking about love as lived and preached by Jesus is that it is a "doing-love," a "giving-love," not a feeling nor receptive love.

If you love those who love you, what reward will you get? Are not even the tax collectors doing that? And if you greet only your brothers, what are you doing more than others? Do not even pagans do that? (Mt. 5:46-47)

By a strict inner necessity, it is only a step from such love to the total giving of self.

The man who loves his life will lose it, while the man who hates his life in this world will keep it for eternal life (Jn. 12:25; Mt. 16:25; Mk. 8:35; Lk. 9:24).

Such a love is certain to terminate in the total dispossession of self, but one which has foreseeable consequences, for if the grain of wheat dies, it yields a rich harvest (Jn. 12:24). Already contained in what Jesus said on love was the message of the cross. It is in that fact that the true newness of the great commandment is to be found.

In an imaginative description of this type of love as it exists in the angels, C. S. Lewis wrote:

...It was terrifyingly different from the expression of human charity, which we always see either blossoming out of, or hastening to descend into, natural affection.... It was so unlike the love we experience that its expression would easily be mistaken for ferocity.[57]

It is a love that does not seek self and thus one that is not marked with certain forms of sentimentality which we so frequently tend to associate with love. As man, the Lord evidences clear, strong human emotions of love, sympathy, compassion, sorrow, anger. He is capable of and does weep openly for friends and over tragedies. For all that, there is in the Gospel picture a certain "hardness" in His love which at times comes close to the "ferocity" spoken of by Lewis. One can see it in His curt rebuke to Peter (Mt. 16:17-23), His reaction to the rich young man whom He had looked upon with love (Mk. 10:17-27), His harsh remark to the Syro-Phoenician woman (Mk. 7:24-30), His response to the women of Jerusalem who wept for Him on His way to Calvary (Lk. 22:28-32).

This love of Jesus—a love He lived and preached—with its depth of divine and human intensity and with its lack of sentimentality (which is not to be confused with a lack of sentiment) can be seen in His bearing toward and teaching on that primary "school of love" which is the human family. Rejecting the moral casuistry of the scribes and annulling the very concession of the Mosaic Law (cf. Dt. 24:1-4), He emphasized the rigorous demands of the love He preached by rejecting divorce and remarriage.

'It was because your hearts were hard that Moses wrote you this law,' Jesus replied. 'But at the beginning of creation God "made them male and female." For this reason a man will leave his father and mother and be united to his wife, and the two will become one flesh.... Therefore what God has joined together, let man not separate.'
'Anyone who divorces his wife and marries another woman commits adultery against her. And if she divorces her husband and marries another man, she commits adultery' (Mk. 10:1-12; cf. Mt. 19:1-9).[58]

The obligations of the covenanted union of husband and wife had already been indicated by God through the prophet Malachi (cf. 450 B.C.) in very strong terms.

> ...The Lord is acting as the witness between you and the wife of your youth, because you have broken faith with her, though she is your partner, the wife of your marriage covenant. Has not the Lord made them one? In flesh and spirit they are his. And why one? Because he was seeking godly offspring...do not break faith with the wife of your youth. 'I hate divorce,' says the Lord God of Israel (Mal. 2:14-16).

Malachi still spoke within the context of the Law of Deuteronomy, but his words hint (the textual difficulties of v. 15 must be noted) at the significance of the creation account in Genesis for the marriage union, and at its procreational orientation.[59] Jesus goes farther than any prophet would have dared. He abrogates the Deuteronomic Law in this respect (i.e., Dt. 24:1-4) and gives His own definitive interpretation to Genesis 2:24: God's plan for the sexes at creation itself meant monogamous union.[60] But the teaching of Jesus even went beyond a defense of the covenanted marriage union.

> You have heard that it was said, 'Do not commit adultery.' But I tell you that anyone who looks at a woman lustfully has already committed adultery with her in his heart (Mt. 5:27-28).

Both His word on divorce and His injunction against lust, while clearly aimed at strengthening and adding dignity to family life and the inter-relation of the sexes, are also norms of perfection, imitative of the Father's own perfection and demanding sacrificial love. By such words He does not idealize marriage; rather, He buttresses it by the exigencies of a love that goes beyond affection or the desires of the flesh by highlighting fidelity, discipline, and the implicit sacrifices entailed in both these virtues.

The obligations of marital love and the Creator's demands for the proper ordering of human sexuality must be seen within Jesus' overall view of how the life of man or woman is to be lived. It is a life shaped, in the first place, by complete faithfulness and obedience to the Father's will, to His call, to His purposes. For Jesus, the first commandment is always first.

> One of them, an expert in the law, tested him with this question: 'Teacher, which is the greatest commandment in the Law?' Jesus replied: 'Love the Lord your God with all your heart and with all your soul and with all your mind. This is the first and greatest commandment. And the second is like it: Love your neighbor as yourself. All the Law and the Prophets hang on these two commandments' (Mt. 22:34-40 and parallels).

It is this priority of the first commandment which helps to make intelligible some of the strong words and actions of Jesus in respect to natural family ties.

> Do not suppose that I have come to bring peace to the earth. I did not come to bring peace, but a sword. For I have come to turn a man against his father, a daughter against her mother, a daughter-in-law against her mother-in-law—a man's enemies will be the members of his own household. Anyone who loves his father or mother more than me is not worthy of me; anyone who loves his son or daughter more than me is not worthy of me (Mt. 10:34-37; Lk. 12:51-53; 14:26-27).[61]
>
> He said to another man, 'Follow me.' But the man replied, 'Lord, first let me go and bury my father.' Jesus said to him, 'Let the dead bury their own dead, but you go and proclaim the kingdom of God.' Still another said, 'I will follow you, Lord; but first let me go back and say goodbye to my family.' Jesus replied, 'No one who puts his hand to the plow and looks back is fit for service in the kingdom of God' (Lk. 9:57-62; Mt. 8:21-22).

The "ferocity" or harshness in such remarks is clear in the context of His message: the Father is first and the concerns of His kingdom take precedence over all. Only in such a context can even family ties be elevated to a type of love that surpasses and perfects the merely natural love which is common to tax-collectors, sinners, and even pagans (cf. Mt. 5:43-48). Jesus practiced what He preached; His own life modeled such an ordering of relationships. It was concern for the Father and His work that Jesus offered to His concerned parents as an explanation when they find Him in the Temple (Lk. 2:46-50). It is likewise the role of the "first and greatest commandment" in His life that contextualizes the apparently harsh sayings and gestures of Jesus in respect to His own family, and to His Mother in particular.

> Then Jesus' mother and brothers arrived. Standing outside, they sent someone in to call him. A crowd was sitting around him, and they told him, 'Your mother and brothers are outside looking for you.' 'Who are my mother and my brothers?' he asked. Then he looked at those seated in a circle around him and said, 'Here are my mother and my brothers! Whoever does God's will is my brother and sister and mother' (Mk. 3:31-35; Mt. 12:46-50; Lk. 8:19-21).

This scene as recorded by Mark can take on overtones of a more radical conflict between Jesus and His family, depending on how one relates it to verses 20-23 of the same chapter of Mark's Gospel. A literal translation of the Greek reads:

> And they came home; and again a crowd gathered so that they were not even able to eat. And when those who were his own heard this, they went to take hold of him. For they (or, some) were saying that he was beside himself. And the Scribes who had come from Jerusalem were saying that Beelzebub had him and that he drove out demons by the power of the prince of demons (Mk. 3:20-23).

Many understand the text to mean that "those who were his own" (hoi par' autou) refers to His family and that they were coming to take hold of Him saying that He was beside Himself (or, in a stronger reading, that He was "out of His mind").[62] If it is read that way and placed in conjunction with John 7:5 ("For even his own brothers did not believe in him"), one obtains a very negative reading on the family, including—in the case of Mark, but not John—His Mother, if Mary is seen as forming part of the *hoi par' autou*, and if Mark 3:31-35 is to be read as the actual sequence of Mark 3:20-22.[63]

Such is not, however, the only possible understanding of the text. It can be noted that Mark 3:31-35 is probably an isolated logion of Jesus which originally had no connection with the incident recorded in Mark 3:20-22.[64] Furthermore, the incident of Mark 3:20-22, which is not found in Matthew and Luke, is such that the Greek can be translated as referring to followers or friends of Jesus *(hoi par' autou)* who came to take Him away because *others* were saying *(elegon gar hoti exeste)* that He was "beside Himself" or "out of His mind."[65] Then, in the Marcan context, the friends would have acted because of the pressures on Jesus (inability even to eat because of the crowds, v. 20), because of what others were saying about Him (v. 21). All this would thus serve as a fitting introduction to what Mark intended to record the Scribes as saying (v. 22). One can add, as well, that Mark, if he intended the entire section to be read as a unit, did not explicitly include Mary among the *hoi par' autou*, nor does he state explicitly anywhere else in his Gospel that the Lord's brothers did not believe in Him. (Whether even the remark of John 7:5 is to be taken as a universal statement is questionable, since it is difficult to see why one of the very first resurrection appearances of Jesus would have been granted to James if he were previously one of the non-believing brothers [cf. 1 Cor. 15:7]).

However one understands what is admittedly something of an exegetical conundrum, it cannot be held that Mark is affirming a lack of faith on Mary's part. Such an interpretation would place one inspired author in direct conflict with another (i.e., with Luke, and probably with Matthew as well), and would contradict Catholic Tradition and doctrine on the absolute sinlessness of our Lady who, from her conception, has been the always faithful model of discipleship. It is also unlikely that Mark (and John) are indicating a lack of faith in Jesus on the part of *all* His family since the resurrection appearance of James and the presence of the mother of

James and Joseph (cf. Part I, p. 86) and of the Virgin Mary's sister
(Jn. 19:25) would seem to indicate that some family members were
faithful throughout His ministry and death. When all such factors
are taken into account, it would seem obligatory to leave the "those
who were his own" of Mark 3:21 as indefinite as Mark himself did;
he could, after all, have said "mother and brothers" had he
intended. Any other reading cannot be established with certitude,
and in such cases the Church's Tradition and doctrine must be the
norm for a proper understanding of the scriptural text.

Nevertheless, the Lord's saying about those who are truly
brothers and sisters and mother—at least as it is found in Mark[66]—
stands within the overall teaching and bearing of Jesus toward
family ties. It is fidelity to the Father which constitutes relationship
within the Kingdom, and that criterion includes even His Mother
and brothers. By that criterion, of course, Mary is His Mother in a
twofold sense—and thus uniquely, as St. Augustine pointed out
so well.

> All these relationships to Himself He manifests spiritually in
> the people whom He has redeemed. He regards holy men and
> women as His brothers and sisters because they are co-heirs
> with Him in the inheritance of heaven. The whole Church is
> His mother, because she most truly brings forth His mem-
> bers.... Mary, therefore, in fulfilling the will of God, is not
> merely the Mother of Christ in the body, but both sister and
> Mother in the spirit.

> ...She is evidently the Mother of us who are His members,
> because she has cooperated by charity that the faithful, who are
> members of that Head, might be born in the Church. Indeed,
> she is the Mother of the Head Himself in the body.[67]

It is the priority of the First Commandment—love of the
Father—which also helps to explain Jesus' teaching on money and
its use, as well as the special predilection He showed for the poor.
Having asked the rich young man to sell all he had and give it to the
poor, and then having seen him go away sad "because he had great
wealth," Jesus said:

I tell you the truth, it is hard for a rich man to enter the kingdom of heaven. Again I tell you, it is easier for a camel to go through the eye of a needle than for a rich man to enter the kingdom of God (Mt. 19:23ff.; Mk. 10:23ff.; Lk. 18:24ff.).

The remark astounded the disciples, but it was only one of the several such indications of the attitude of Jesus toward money (cf. Mt. 6:19-20; 6:24-34; Lk. 12:16-21; 16:19-26, etc.). In a particular way, the Gospel of Luke highlights this attitude as the evangelist juxtaposes the first two beatitudes and the first two woes.

Blessed are you who are poor, for yours is the kingdom of God. Blessed are you who hunger now, for you will be satisfied (Lk. 6:20-21; cf. Mt. 5:3, 6).

But woe to you who are rich, for you have already received your comfort.
Woe to you who are well fed now, for you will go hungry (Lk. 6:24-25).[68]

It should be observed that Jesus' attitude is not a rejection of those who had money. The family at Bethany do not appear to have been poor; He and His disciples were accompanied by women who "helped support them out of their own means" (Lk. 8:3); He saw the goodness of the rich young man and invited him to discipleship; He ate with the rich as well as with the poor (cf. Mt. 9:10-12; Lk. 7:36ff.). Nevertheless, the preference for the poor, the outcast, the sinners, and the simple marks the Gospel. His own words, in all probability, reveal the reason: it is difficult for the rich to be saved. They are not so readily aware of their own total dependence on a Father who will provide the necessities provided that the kingdom of heaven is sought first (Mt. 6:33). As was true with the "spiritually rich," the Pharisees and Scribes, a conviction of self-sufficiency tended to make them opaque to the light of the kingdom. According to St. Thomas, it is only when a man recognizes his own weaknesses, when he experiences the necessity of a liberator that he is able to cry out for grace or to be disposed for salvation.[69] The self-satisfied come to such a recognition only with great difficulty. Jesus

Himself, on the other hand, chose to have no place to lay His head (Lk. 9:58; Mt. 8:20), just as He chose celibacy out of love of the Father.

The demands made by Jesus' preaching of the Father's kingdom in respect to family life and sexuality and His attitude toward wealth and the poor are examples of the radicalizing element introduced into the religion of the Old Testament by His unique relationship to the Father. Nowhere do we find Him repudiating the Law of Sinai, the ten commandments. In fact, the evangelists have preserved two accounts of totally different situations where we are able to see Jesus reaffirming that Law (cf. Mt. 15:15-20 and Mk. 7:20-23; Mt. 19:16-19 and parallels). Even in those cases, however, He radicalizes the Law, indicating that the keeping of the commandments is good but not enough for the perfection expected of a disciple, and reminding His hearers that external conformity to the commandments is not enough. The heart must be purified, "for out of the overflow of the heart the mouth speaks" (Mt. 12:34). There is, moreover, more than a mere "personal ethic or morality" involved in all this. To proclaim the chosen status of the poor, while denouncing the danger of riches (and, with wealth, power since money makes for power); to heap abuse on many of the religious leaders of His nation—leaders at times closely allied with the civil rulers of the nation; to preach a kingdom which implicitly relativized the authority and power of an absolute State; to proclaim the equalizing power of love which would be seen as making even women and slaves co-heirs of men and owners in the Father's sight—all such things and more were parts of a message which was not only personal, but social and even "political." In an empire which was already heading toward deification of its Caesars,[70] and where the very standards of the emperors had been introduced into the Temple itself, the laconic "Give to Caesar what is Caesar's, and to God what is God's" (Mt. 22:21 and parallels) is a sword that cuts deeply. Few absolute States will tolerate a limitation of their authority—even by implication.[71] Little wonder that Herod, whom Jesus belittled when calling him a "fox" (Lk. 13:32), heard of Him, or that He would be labeled a "subverter of the nation" (Lk. 23:2), and "deceiver of the people" (Jn. 7:12-13).

The "social teaching" of the Church and even some aspects of the various "theologies of liberation" are correct in seeing in Jesus

Himself the source for a social and political ethic. His proclamation of the Father's kingdom was aimed at a radical change in man himself and in the situations in which man lived. Such changes were, properly speaking, revolutionary. Nevertheless, one thing must be clearly seen. To situate Jesus meaningfully in the social and political context of His times, to defend the relevance for ourselves of His relation *vis à vis* the "established powers," to admit that His message and Person were unsettling, transforming, liberating, is not to propound a claim that He was a first-century "revolutionary" in the sense we so often use that word.

> He was not a politician, a demagogue, an agitator.... He was no soldier,...nor a man of arms...much less was He a Zealot, a revolutionary, a contestator of the Roman Power.[72]

He did not have to be any of these since what He was in reality was quite as revolutionary as any of these.

> ...The figure of Christ presents—over and above the charm of His merciful gentleness—an aspect which is grave and strong, formidable, if you like, when dealing with cowardice, hypocrisy, injustice and cruelty, but never lacking an aura of love.[73]

Jesus' preaching of peace was a provocation to the violent; His preaching of love a provocation to those who hate. Having rejected the use of power to overcome evil and establish good,[74] He aimed at radical change by His full adherence to the Father's will, basing Himself on the sure conviction that evil destroys itself when it seeks to destroy the good.

Pope Paul VI rightly spoke of the "complexity of the figure of Jesus"[75]—a complexity evident to any who study the sources well. That complexity is seen readily enough in His relation to society, and to the civil and religious powers which dominated Palestine in His day. He was what we would call an "a-political" figure, but His preaching of the kingdom and His revelation of the Father were such that all authority—apart from the Father's—was "relativized" and all social relationships given a new orientation. The "political" overtones of such preaching and activity were apparent, and the outcome foreseeable.

IV. THE CHURCH AND SACRAMENTS

It is clear that the kingdom of God as preached by Jesus is marked by struggle, by a new experience of the Father as well as by a new way of praying to Him, by a universality of call and by a manner of discipleship modeled on the Father's own perfection, and finally, by a love which places the Father and His concerns first but which then is extended to all, even to one's enemies. The various parables about the kingdom also indicate something which was noted previously: the kingdom, while open to all, will in fact be marked by a segregation. Those who are unwilling to hear, or who are unworthy or tardy, will be excluded.

And he told them many things in parables saying: 'A farmer went out to sow his seed. As he was scattering the seed, some fell along the path, and the birds came and ate it up. Some fell on rocky places.... Other seed fell among thorns...' (Mt. 13:3 and parallels).

Jesus told them another parable: 'The kingdom of heaven is like a man who sowed good seed in his field. But while everyone was sleeping, his enemy came and sowed weeds among the wheat.... "Let them both grow until the harvest. At that time, I will tell the harvesters: First collect the weeds and tie them in bundles to be burned up, then gather the wheat and bring it into my barn"' (Mt. 13:24-30).

At that time the kingdom of heaven will be like ten virgins who took their lamps and went out to meet the bridegroom. Five of them were foolish and five were wise... (Mt. 25:1-13; Lk. 12:35-40).

As the parables indicate, the segregation takes place at the end, but it is prepared for by differing attitudes which exist beforehand, and sometimes even is anticipated from the start. Jesus proclaims the kingdom. Some accept His message and a group of disciples is formed. However, even within that group, further segregation will yet take place. This message of the kingdom, its distinctiveness from what has gone before, and, perhaps, even the aspect of segregation, can be summed up in another of Jesus similies.

No one sews a patch of unshrunk cloth on an old garment. If he does, the new piece will pull away from the old, making the tear worse. And no one pours new wine into old wineskins. If he does, the wine will burst the skins, and both the wine and the wineskins will be ruined. No, he pours new wine into new wineskins (Mt. 9:16-17 and parallels).

The newness of what He was doing was emphasized by Jesus in His choice of the Twelve (Mt. 10:2-3 and parallels[76]), the inner circle and leaders of those who accepted His preaching and became disciples. Like Jacob's sons, from whom sprang the tribes of Israel (Gn. 46:8ff.), these Twelve were symbolic of those who would receive the kingdom. Having trained them, Jesus sent them to preach (Mt. 10:5ff. and parallels; cf. Jn. 4:1-2), stressing, in a remarkable saying, the authority He gave them.

He who receives you receives me, and he who receives me receives the one who sent me (Mt. 10:40; Lk. 10:16; cf. Mk. 9:37; Jn. 15:20-21).[77]

The statement is also a testimony to the truthfulness of their preaching. They were to share in that authoritative proclamation of the Father's message which marked the teaching of Jesus and which was such an object of admiration on the part of His hearers (cf. Mt. 13:54; Mk. 6:2-3; Lk. 4:22, etc.). Indeed, the Gospel of John reveals to us that this gift of truth was an object of Jesus' prayer to the Father on behalf of the Twelve.

Sanctify them by the truth; your word is truth. As you sent me into the world, I have sent them into the world. For them I sanctify myself, that they too may be truly sanctified (Jn. 17:17-19).

The penalties for rejecting such preaching are severe (cf. Mt. 10:14-15; and parallels) while the reward for the preachers is a unique role in the final judgment (Mt. 19:28).

Among the Twelve, one is paramount, Simon, son of John, brother of Andrew. His character, with its strengths and weaknesses, and his role as spokesman reveal him as, after Jesus Himself, the most fully portrayed personality in the four Gospels. Simon is for all the evangelists, as he was for Paul (cf. 1 Cor. 1:12; 15:5; Gal. 1:18; 2:9, etc.), "Cephas," the Rock, Peter, a name given him by Jesus Himself. This preeminence of Peter is no longer seriously questioned, although its significance within the early Christian communities and for the subsequent structure of the Christian community are items still vigorously debated.[78] Discussion of those issues belongs more properly to the theology of the Church than to Christology, although Jesus' own choice of Simon and the role assigned to him as Rock must always be of fundamental significance.

Jesus' famous words to Simon as recorded in Matthew 16:18 ("And I tell you that you are Peter, and on this rock I will build my Church, and the gates of Hades will not overcome it.") are also the focus of much dispute. Not only their Petrine significance, but also the fact that here (as in Mt. 18:17 and nowhere else in the Gospels) Jesus was making explicitly clear His intention to form a community (church), are points which render their authenticity dubious to some.[79] Because of its heavily Semitic or Aramaic cast, most now admit that the saying is not a Matthean "invention," but it is variously attributed to the pre-Matthean Christian community in Palestine, to a post-resurrection appearance of Jesus, to Jesus in the Last Supper context, or even to the Caesarea Philippi scene where Matthew places it. Such disputes on one—admittedly important—text should not obscure, however, the central fact: it is Jesus Himself who inaugurated the Church.

"By an express act of His will He founded the Church on the Twelve.... The Church is not a later 'result' nor a mere consequence 'set in motion' by the evangelizing activity of Jesus. It was born of this activity to be sure, but in a direct way ...."[80] This assertion of the Magisterium[81]—like other previous assertions—is identical with the assertion made in Matthew 16:18. The Church is "*my* Church," i.e., the Church of Jesus. In fact, whether one calls it Church, or the New Israel, or a reconstituted Israel, or the sheep of the flock (Mt. 26:31; Mk. 14:27), or the "little flock" (Lk. 12:32) or simply His "family" (Mt. 12:48 and parallels), the reality is the same. Jesus preached the kingdom of the Father and gathered around Himself those who, because of His words and activity, accepted that message. Some He chose for a special function and mission. These He made the object of special training (Mt. 13:11; Mk. 4:11; Lk. 8:10), but the invitation was extended to all, even the non-Jew. To all who accepted, the kingdom would be given.

> Do not be afraid, little flock, for your Father has been pleased to give you the kingdom (Lk. 12:32).

The "founding" of the Church, then, is the work of Jesus Himself during His ministry. It was a work, of course, to be completed by the events of His passion, resurrection and the experiences which followed. Those events and subsequent generations would give His little flock a form, a structure, a growth and history which it was not His concern to spell out in detail beforehand. One looks in vain to His ministry in order to find Jesus organizing His followers the way we would expect a "founder" to organize a new society or a new political or religious association. He left no bureaucratic model. The future of His followers was in the hands of the Father.

> Who of you by worrying can add a single hour to his life? Since you cannot do this very little thing, why do you worry about the rest? (Mt. 6:27-34; Lk. 12:25-26)

Nonetheless, the essentials of the post-Easter community were put in place by the Lord Himself during His public ministry. This was true not only of the way of life and teaching that bound His followers together around Him and of the ordered functioning of the Twelve, but also of those particularly ecclesial activities which later would be called the Sacraments.

In a highly significant scene near the beginning of His public ministry, Jesus said to the paralytic who, having been lowered through the roof, was placed before Him, "Take heart, son, your sins are forgiven" (Mt. 9:1-4 and parallels). Unlike the prophets of Israel and unlike the work of the Baptist, there was here no mere call to repentance. There was, rather, the very forgiveness of sin. What was proper to God alone was now being done by one Man for another. In Jesus, salvation, God's own activity, was present as man among men. St. Paul would later say, "God was reconciling the world to himself in Christ" (2 Cor. 5:19). Sin was forgiven, the sick were healed. The primal institution of marriage was renewed and strengthened. Indeed, Jesus even used its symbolism to refer to His presence among His followers (Mt. 9:14-15 and parallels), a teaching Paul would develop (cf. Eph. 5:25-33). The baptism He had received from John He permitted His own disciples to use, although the context and content were certainly new (Jn. 3:22; 4:1-2).[82] And, in what was one of the most striking aspects of His ministry, He shared Himself at table with the unclean (Mt. 11:18-19; Lk. 7:33-34). This last trait of Jesus would receive its definitive meaning, of course, on the night before He died, but the meaning of that Last Supper was already implicit in what He had done before. To those who approached Him with trust, He was constantly giving of Himself, healing, forgiving, reconciling and strengthening. He would do it all ultimately by extending Himself through the ministry of others—as He did through the Twelve during those years of preaching (cf. Mt. 10:5-15; Mk. 6:8-13; Lk. 9:2-5; Jn. 4:1-2; 13:13-17). But this "ministry through others" would in fact always be His own. Commenting on the apparent contradiction between John 3:22 and 4:1-2, St. Augustine said:

> Are both statements true, namely that Jesus did and did not baptize? In fact, He did baptize because it was He who did the cleansing. On the other hand, He did not baptize, because He was not the one who touched. His disciples supplied the service to the body; He gave the aid of His majesty.... Jesus is still baptizing. As long as we continue to be baptized, it is Jesus who baptizes.[83]

Augustine's notion that it is Christ Himself who still administers the sacraments was picked up by later theology and became the dictum that the Church's ministers act *in persona Christi*.[84] This is the truth that also underlies the doctrine that the sacraments produce their results *ex opere operato*. It is why the moral condition of the minister does not substantially affect the essentials of the sacramental act. It is Jesus Himself who still administers the sacraments. This truth has a bearing on how one is to understand the notion of the "institution" of the sacraments by Jesus and His "foundation" of the Church. In neither case are we faced with a situation where an individual must provide for a future in which persons other than himself must perform or carry on a work after the founder or institutor has been removed from the scene. Normally such is the case. A founder must provide for what others will do in his place after his departure or death. Such provision usually entails specific directives or instructions or a fixed "constitutional" pattern. We look in vain for such specific instructions concerning His community on the part of Jesus. In His own awareness of the Father's presence in His work, Jesus formed a community around Himself, structured it, and performed His "works," doing each day what was demanded of the day. The future for Him was guaranteed by His "now" with the Father who would never undo what Jesus was now doing. The statement in John's Gospel fully captures that truth.

My Father is always at his work to this very day, and I, too, am working (Jn. 5:17).

As a result, there is no specific moment when the Church is "founded" or a sacrament "instituted." There is a continuum of action on the part of Jesus whereby He does now what He started to do then—calling a community of believers and acting on their behalf. The various "I" statements of all the earliest traditions ("Do not fear, I am," "It was written, but I say," "Before Abraham was born, I am," "I am with you all days") testify to at least one certain fact. Jesus was aware that, through Him, definitively and for all time, the Father was acting. That activity is the Church and the sacraments. Therefore, they are wrong who look to the ministry of Jesus to see what He set up to leave after Him. There is no indication whatsoever that He envisioned an "after Him" in the sense of "without Him." In her own way the Church has always reflected this singularity of Jesus; His coming in the "fullness of time," His resurrection as the "eighth day," each year a year "of the Lord," not "after the Lord." Even His seemingly ambiguous references to the end of the world reflect in some way His awareness that there would be no "after Him."

Because He is faithful to Himself or, as we would say, consistent, the Church looks to what He did "then" (i.e., during the public ministry) to discern what He does "now." The "norm" for the Church, her order, her sacraments, is fixed not because it is frozen in time but because it is consistent activity on His part.

V. JESUS REVEALED

St. John tells us that when Jesus said, "My Father is always at work...and I, too, am working" (Jn. 5:17), the Jews "tried all the harder to kill him; not only was he breaking the Sabbath, but he was even calling God his own Father, making himself equal to God" (Jn. 5:18). Matthew, Mark and Luke record a similar type of indignation toward Jesus when they recount the reaction of the Jewish Scribes as Jesus forgave the sins of the paralytic at Capernaum.

Why does this fellow talk like that? He's blaspheming! Who can forgive sins but God alone? (Mk. 2:7 and parallels)

This reaction—and others like it—inevitably leads to the question: what did Jesus say about Himself or what did He lead others to say about Him in order to cause such opposition? That question has led to numerous studies of the various titles applied to Jesus in the New Testament. They are many. Jesus is called "Rabbi-Teacher," "Son of David," "Son—Son of God," "Holy One of God," "Messiah-Christ," "Kyrios-Lord," "Apostle and High Priest" (Heb. 3:1), "Savior," "Logos-Word," and even "God." Although there has been much disagreement on the matter, it is probably fair to say that all these titles were applied to Him "according to the Scriptures," i.e., as applications of Old Testament titles or themes, as these titles and ideas had come to be understood in the first century B.C. and first century A.D.[85]

Some of the New Testament titles are clearly expressions of faith in Jesus as that faith was expressed after His resurrection. Among these may be placed Lord-Kyrios, Word-Logos, Savior, God, although the Kyrios-Lord (Aramaic *mari*, my Lord) may well have its origins in a title of respect used for Jesus during His ministry and which, after the resurrection, became theological and liturgical in the *Maranatha* prayer (1 Cor. 16:22).[86]

According to the Gospels, the titles Son of David (Mt. 20:31 and parallels), Son and Son of God (Mt. 4:3, 6; Lk. 4:3, 9; Mt. 14:33; Mt. 11:27; Lk. 10:22, etc.) and Messiah-Christ (Mt. 16:16 and parallels) are acknowledged by Jesus as referring to Himself, or are even used by Him when speaking of Himself. A difficulty arises, however, when one asks what such titles meant as acknowledged by Jesus. The title "Son of God," for example, is used in the Old Testament of Israel itself (Ex. 4:22; Hos. 11:1), of the Davidic king (Ps. 2:7) and of the angels (Gn. 6:2). In which of these senses, if any, would Jesus have acknowledged the title of Himself? Likewise, the title "Messiah-Christ," like its counterpart "Son of David," had various connotations—some of them markedly political. It is this variety of connotations which must account, at least in part, for Jesus' recorded reluctance to use the title or have it divulged (Mt. 16:20 and parallels).[87]

Like most people, Jesus generally spoke of Himself using the first person pronoun. How significant that was in His case will be examined below. He also used, however, the expression "Son of Man" to refer to Himself, and He did this frequently according to the testimony of the Gospels. The phrase occurs, always as spoken by Jesus Himself, almost seventy times in the Synoptic Gospels and thirteen times in the Gospel of John. Apart from those instances where it appears as spoken by Jesus, the phrase occurs only in Acts 7:56, Revelation 1:13, 14:14 and in the Epistle to the Hebrews where it is a quotation from Psalm 8:5. This would appear to indicate that, whatever the words meant for Jesus Himself, the phrase as a designation for Him never gained such popularity in the early Church as to make it a common way of referring to Him.

Examination of the various "Son of Man" sayings in the Gospels reveals that in about one half of the cases where it appears, one or another of the parallel texts has "I" instead of "Son of Man,"[88] thus making it difficult, if not impossible, to determine what the original was. It has also been noted that the "Son of Man" sayings can be categorized as falling into three basic types:

1. Sayings which refer to a Son of Man who will come in the future (e.g., Mt. 24:30 and parallels).

2. Sayings which speak of the Son of Man's activity as identical with the earthly activity of Jesus (e.g., Mt. 11:19; Lk. 7:34).

3. Sayings which speak of the Son of Man as suffering and rising (e.g., Mk. 8:31; Lk. 9:22; the Matthean parallel in 16:21 has "he" [Jesus] rather than Son of Man).[89]

The exegetical opinions on the "Son of Man" sayings vary widely. Indeed, it is probably no exaggeration to call them a "bewildering chaos."[90] Some have held that none of the sayings are authentically those of Jesus; others that Jesus Himself used all three types of the sayings; others still that He used only the first type and actually expected a coming Son of Man who was other than Himself.[91] Furthermore, the problem with the title does not stop once a decision has been reached *vis à vis* authenticity. Even if one grants—and it is surely the most reasonable conclusion on historical grounds alone[92]—that Jesus used the title to refer to Himself, there remains the difficulty as to what He meant by the phrase. The words, in their Hebrew and Aramaic equivalents, were not unfamiliar to the Jews. They are found frequently in the book of the prophet Ezekiel (2:1 and *passim*) where they simply mean "man"; they are found in the book of Daniel (written c. 170-160 B.C.) to describe an authoritative and powerful figure to whom God would give kingship and power and glory (7:13-14); they are found in noncanonical Jewish writings of the first century to refer to the preexistent and expected Messiah.[93] To which of these ideas or their variants—if to any of them—did Jesus wish to point when He used the term "Son of Man" of Himself?

An answer to that question is not easy. Indeed, an answer may not be possible if one approaches the question by starting with the titles themselves. Undoubtedly, each of the New Testament titles applied to Jesus or used by Him are rich in a content drawn from the Old Testament Scriptures and from contemporary Jewish thought and life. Those riches must be utilized. Nonetheless, an essential fact must be kept in mind: it is not the titles which give meaning to Jesus. As they are used in the New Testament, it is the Person Jesus who gives meaning to the titles, not *vice versa*.[94] Therefore the titles have only a relative importance. The reason for this relativity is clear, of course. Not one of them in itself was adequate. Because He is who He is, Jesus is truly the One who does not fit precisely into any title that was at hand. Each of them had to be "stretched," as it were, if it were to be made applicable to Him. In that sense, the titles are an example of old wineskins being forced to take new wine. They burst with an excess of meaning not previously there.

The recognized reluctance of Jesus to use any title of Himself (save the difficult-to-interpret "Son of Man") did not result from the fact that He did not consider Himself Prophet, Son, Messiah, etc., but rather from the fact that He knew Himself to be more than what any of these titles expressed. This "excess of meaning" in His own Person, He demonstrated in various ways.

First, one may consider His signs or miracles. They were indeed signs that the Father's kingdom which Jesus preached was now operative in power. But they were also a call to examine the relationship that existed between Jesus and that kingdom. They implied that something beyond the ordinary was present in this Man. That implication was not missed by those around Him, but the answers given were diverse.

> But when the Pharisees heard this, they said, 'It is only by Beelzebub, the prince of demons, that this fellow drives out demons.' Jesus knew their thoughts and said to them, '…and if I drive out demons by Beelzebub, by whom do your people drive them out? So then, they will be your judges. But if I drive out demons by the Spirit of God, then the kingdom of God has come among you' (Mt. 12:24-28; Lk. 11:15-20; Mk. 3:21-26).[95]

There is in that final statement a daring (from the hearer's point of view) equation made between God's activity and Jesus' activity. It is the same equation that is made when He forgave sins (Mk. 2:7 and parallels), fully justifying the thoughts that such a work is proper to God alone.

Like His actions, His words or teaching were provocative. He boldly interpreted or even changed the Mosaic Law, invoking no authority outside Himself (Mt. 19:3-9; Mk. 10:2-12; cf. Lk. 16:18; Mt. 5:21-48). In the same vein He violated the Sabbath, implying that His activity, like God's own, is never conditioned by any day no matter how sacred (Mt. 12:1-8; Mk. 2:23-28; Lk. 6:1-5; Mt. 12:9-15 and parallels; Jn. 7:23; 9:13ff.). Furthermore, the manner in which He proposed His teaching was distinctive. Unlike the Old Testament prophets who appealed to an oracle of Yahweh, or like the Pharisees and scribes who appealed to the authority of the Law, Jesus was more direct. The "Amen, I say to you" is an undeniable example of the very words of Jesus and it is truly an amazing display of self-assurance.[96] In the Synoptic Gospels the fact of that self-assurance is clearly evident while the ground or reason for it is never made explicit by Jesus Himself. Nevertheless, it must be seen as intimately connected with the self-assurance which dared to address Yahweh as "Abba" and taught others to do the same. In psychological terms, we might say that He got His self-assurance from the affirmation He received from the most important of His intimate relationships, namely from His relationship with the Father.

The combination of these various factors—the signs or miracles, the content and manner of His teaching, the intimacy He claimed with God and His readiness to act in matters which Jewish theology believed reserved to God alone—had the readily foreseen effect on those who came in contact with Him. They were amazed and astounded (Mt. 7:28; Mk. 1:22, 27; Lk. 4:32; Mt. 8:27 and parallels; Mt. 9:8 and parallels), angered (Mt. 12:14; Lk. 6:11; Mk. 3:6), scandalized (Mt. 11:6; Lk. 7:23; Mt. 13:57 and parallels; Jn. 7:15) and, perhaps above all, left guessing. It is recorded that the Baptist wondered (Mt. 11:3; Lk. 7:18), that Herod wondered (Mt. 14:1-2 and parallels), that the crowds wondered (Mt. 16:13 and parallels). Always it was the same things which provoked such wonderment. The scene in the eighth chapter of St. John, perhaps dramatically structured by the evangelist, captures in one great debate elements of a struggle evident throughout the Synoptics.

The Pharisees challenged him, 'Here you are, appearing as your own witness; your testimony is not valid.' Jesus answered, '...I am not alone. I stand with the Father who sent me.' Then they asked him, 'Where is your father?' Jesus replied, 'If you knew me, you would know my Father also.... If you do not believe that I am, you will indeed die in your sins.'

'Who are you?' they asked.

'Just what I have been claiming all along,' Jesus replied.

Every element of that dialogue has parallels in the Synoptic Gospels so there can be no legitimate claim that here we are faced with a Johannine creation *ex nihilo*. As in the Synoptics the matter at issue initially concerns Jesus' authority or His self-assurance (His "being witness to Himself"), but it invariably moves to become the question about His relationship with the One He calls His Father and whom the Jews call their God. Now, even though this chapter of John's Gospel ends with Jesus giving one of the clearest New Testament affirmations about His relationship with the Father (Jn. 8:58), the dialogue makes clear—as do other references in this Gospel (cf. Jn. 10:24, 34; 7:37-41; 6:29-30; 2:18-25; 18:33-37)—that on such questions it was very difficult to get an unequivocal answer from Jesus. Matthew points this out:

> Jesus entered the temple courts, and, while he was teaching, the chief priests and the elders of the people came to him. 'By what authority are you doing these things?' they asked. 'And who gave you this authority?'
>
> Jesus replied, 'I will ask you one question. If you answer me, I will tell you by what authority I am doing these things. John's baptism—where did it come from? Was it from heaven or from men?'
>
> ...so they answered Jesus, 'We don't know.' Then he said, 'Neither will I tell you by what authority I am doing these things' (Mt. 21:23-27 and parallels).

At other times He will even use His own exegesis of Scripture to avoid a direct answer.

> 'We are not stoning you for any of these,' replied the Jews, 'but for blasphemy, because you, a mere man, claim to be God.'
>
> Jesus answered them, 'Is it not written in your Law, "I have said you are gods"? If he called them "gods," to whom the word of God came—and the Scripture cannot be broken—what

about the one whom the Father set apart as his very own and sent into the world? Why then do you accuse me of blasphemy because I said, "I am God's Son"?' (Jn. 10:33-36)

Given the mentality of the people, there was little else the Lord could do than clothe His replies enigmatically.[97] One must see it as His own use of the *ekonomia* of revelation. Nevertheless, for all that unwillingness to make an unequivocal statement about the question of His authority and identity—and we must take that unwillingness to be a certain historical datum—it was clear to some at least that at times He was actually claiming equality with God. The remarks recorded by the Fourth Gospel (e.g., Jn. 5:18 and 10:33) should not—and need not—be taken as reflecting a later theological perspective.[98] We find there, not the reaction of the Jews to Jesus' claim of any particular title, nor even to any other bald assertion of His relationship to God. Rather, they should be seen as the reaction to the accumulation of His words, deeds and inferences. As some have noted,[99] there is no way to make His trial and execution intelligible unless one accepts the fact that during the ministry He gave some grounds at least for being charged with political messianism and even blasphemy (cf. Mt. 26:65; Mk. 14:63; Lk. 23:1-3; Jn. 19:7-12). Indeed, the Synoptics show that the type of blasphemy with which Jesus was charged at His trial had been anticipated when He forgave the sins of the paralytic, and the reason was that given by John: He was making Himself equal with God.[100]

To develop in greater detail the nature of Jesus' claim about Himself appeal could also be made to many other deeds and sayings: e.g., the miracle of the walking on the lake, the Transfiguration, the restoring of the dead to life, the text in Matthew 11:27, the predictions of the passion and resurrection, those texts in which Jesus identifies Himself and His cause with the manifestation of the glorious Son of Man (Mt. 10:32-33 and Lk. 12:8; Mk. 8:38), the implications of some of the parables (e.g., Mk. 12:1-12), etc., to say nothing of all that appears in the Gospel of St. John. All these instances, like much of the above, however, are contested. They are seen as being inauthentic, creations of the early Community, post-resurrectional happenings retrojected into the ministry, and so forth. All such attempts make it obvious that the Gospels must be rewritten or rearranged, or their historical value much discredited, in order to avoid what is evident in all of them: Jesus' way of acting and speaking before His trial and death were such that they invited either faith in Him as One who acted with the prerogatives of God or denunciation of Him as a blasphemous pretender. It is not the use of one or another title, nor the authenticity of one or another saying of Jesus which gives the historical assurance for the conclusion that He made Himself equal with God. Logic and historical coherency demand it because of the multiplication of the evidence which points to it. One or another of the pieces of evidence or the weight attached to it may be questioned, but the ensemble is what lends historical support to what the Gospel of John most explicitly asserts: Jesus claimed to be both Messiah and unique, eternal Son.

One can argue that the Johannine Gospel has sharpened the focus or made explicit what in Jesus' actual words and deeds was normally implicit, but such conclusions will often depend on how one has solved the questions about the disputed sayings in the Synoptics. Now, in fact, it can be admitted that some of these disputes cannot be solved definitively on the basis of an historical or literary evaluation. For example, the linguistic similarities between the "I am" statements in John and the Synoptics have already been noted. Can we conclude, therefore, that Mark and Matthew intended to give such statements a theological content similar to that of those found in John? Perhaps, but the linguistic ambiguity built into the "I am" expressions makes a definite conclusion difficult. Furthermore, if one does grant an equivalency in the Johannine and Synoptic "I am" statements, can one demonstrate that they reflect Jesus' own words or are they to be seen as a theological creation of the Christian Community? To such a question there can be no "historico-critical" answer because of the lack of real evidence. One must fall back upon the general historical reliability or non-reliability of the sources we have (i.e., the existing Gospels), or posit some hypothesis as an alternative. Much the same has to be said about the titles "Son of Man" and "Messiah." We are able to determine historico-critically the various types of sayings and that all the evangelists assert that Jesus used the various forms of the "Son of Man" sayings about Himself and that, at the minimum, He accepted the designation "Messiah" from others while trying to correct erroneous connotations the word might have. When we ask the question whether the evangelists are correct in their assertion, i.e., whether Jesus Himself actually did use or accept these titles, then one has passed beyond what can be *verified* by historical or literary science. One must draw conclusions either from the views one holds about the historical credibility of the documents or from some hypothesis which will give a coherent understanding of what facts one does have—the facts in this case being the assertions of the four evangelists.

Now, the hypothesis which attributes Jesus' use or acceptance of Messianic titles not to Jesus Himself but to a developing Christological awareness in that Christian community which predates our written sources can present a relatively coherent understanding of the sources as we have them. It suffers, however, from at least two weaknesses, one historical, the other theological. Historically, the hypothesis has no more "hard facts" to substantiate it than does its alternative, viz., that Jesus Himself did in fact use or accept the titles. Both positions must be argued from interpretations of the same source material. This truth is often overlooked. One speaks or writes, for example, of the "Matthean Community," the "Johannine Community," the "Q" document or community, and even of the early Community (i.e., the community as it preexisted the Pauline epistles and the other New Testament writings) as if one had knowledge about such entities from sources other than the New Testament. In fact, we have few sources, and the sources we do have offer no direct evidence at all for distinctive Matthean, Marcan or Johannine "Communities"—much less for "Q." What we can deduce of the early Community tells us nothing directly of its prowess in developing Christologies.[101] All of which is to say that these entities are in fact hypothetical constructs or inferences.[102] Their existence is an inference, not what one can properly call an historical fact. It is only the existence of the Christian Community in general which is directly attested to by Luke in Acts. In the other cases, the inferences may or may not be correct. However, once the inferences are posited as fact, one can get a very strange form of argumentation. To wit: by comparing the Gospel of Matthew with other New Testament writings, we infer the existence of a peculiar Matthean Community. This Community has a history of theological development, so it is inferred, and ultimately produces the Gospel of Matthew, some anonymous member of the community being its author. Subsequently, we can play the community off against the author, so that what the author of the Gospel attributes directly to Jesus we can attribute to the formative powers of the community. In this way, the hypothetical community serves as a control or interpretative aid for the only document which lends any credibility to the hypothesis itself. The danger in such reasoning is that the hypothesis becomes the norm against which the evidence is interpreted and such a process comes very close to being circular argumentation, if it is not that in fact.

The theological difficulty is posed by the nature of inspiration and inerrancy. If the evangelist asserts that Jesus Himself did or said such and such, whereas we conclude that it was not Jesus Himself but rather the hypothetical community which is the origin of such a word or deed, then we have constructed an assertion which is directly contrary to what the evangelist himself has asserted. How such contradictory assertions can be reconciled, while maintaining the Church's traditional understanding of inspiration and inerrancy, is far from apparent.

What is ultimately at stake here is the neuralgic point in modern studies of Jesus: how He humanly understood Himself and what He led others to understand. Now, in light of what must be said about His human self-awareness and His knowledge of His mission, and in light of the logical and theological difficulties just seen, it would appear proper to view skeptically those reductionist views which would attribute much of what the Gospels say about Jesus' self-awareness to the views of the early Community. Indeed such views are not demonstrable nor do all of them concord with reality once all the evidence (viz., the assertions of the evangelists, the Tradition of the Church and the Magisterium) has been taken into account. To claim, for instance, that Jesus expected and preached a Son of Man who was yet to come and who was other than

Jesus Himself is a position that cannot be reconciled with the Church's understanding of Jesus.

Jesus Himself must be seen as the source of the Christology of the New Testament. It was His own way of acting and speaking which gave rise to the titles applied to Him. During His ministry, the title "Son of Man," in all its forms was His own self-designation, although it is quite likely that an original "I" has been replaced by "Son of Man" in some of the sayings.[103] The title "Messiah" He accepted—reluctantly because of some of its undesirable connotations. Even the various forms of the "I" and "I am" statements are His own, with the ambiguity attendant upon them. The difficulty some scholars find in admitting such an "explicit" Christology on the part of Jesus Himself evolves, it would seem, from either a presupposition that Jesus did not know who He was or from a misunderstanding of how He used the titles. He never claimed to be "Son of Man" or "Messiah" in exactly the same sense as the Old Testament and contemporary Judaism understood those terms. The titles were not used to explain Him; rather He was forging a new understanding of the titles. This He did by putting all the references to Himself in the context of His relation to the Father. For it was in revealing the Father that Jesus was also revealing Himself, and it was His claim to reveal and act for the Father, and not any verbal designation, which gave scandal to some of His contemporaries.

Such an approach can help explain the subsequent history of the titles themselves. Titles were used, retained or discarded according to their ability to be adapted to the reality of Jesus. The designation "Son of Man" practically disappeared as a title in the early Church, while "Messiah-Christ" soon became little more than a surname, "Jesus Christ." "Lord" became the common title, allied with "Son of God," an Old Testament title which was now given a totally new depth of significance. In all probability this evolution of the titles and their meaning took place with great rapidity. A gradual evolution from a "low" to a "high" Christology among the first generations of Christians is a somewhat artificial construct which often develops from a too literalistic interpretation of a title or a phrase while forgetting the "excess of meaning" in the Person of Jesus which no formulation could then or has yet completely captured.[104]

In the light of all of the above, one can see the accuracy of the Magisterium of the Church when it condemned the two following propositions of the Modernists:

The divinity of Jesus Christ is not proved from the Gospels; rather it is a dogma which the Christian conscience deduced from the notion of Messiah.

The doctrine about Christ, as handed on by Paul, John and the Councils of Nicea, Ephesus, Chalcedon, is not that which Jesus taught, but rather what the Christian conscience conceived about Jesus. [105]

The New Testament's portrayal of Jesus is not exhausted by what we are able to find there of His relation to the Father. There is revealed, as well, aspects of what today we call personality, that combination of traits or characteristics which, viewed in interaction with people and events, manifest something of a person's "inner makeup." Such things are often impressions difficult to articulate or to capture in specific terminology. They form, nevertheless, a very important part of our overall understanding of Jesus and so, with the certitude of oversimplifying, some of those characteristics should be noted.

Perhaps the most striking impression made by the Gospel figure of Jesus of Nazareth is that which can be called His self-possession or independence. Jesus is the protagonist of events, never simply a reactor to them. One obtains the general impression of a Man who knew what He is about, what He is doing and intending, a Man of great self-assurance. That self-possession—a mark of great inner freedom—showed itself in relation to the norms of civil society, the religious traditions of His own people, and to human "traditions" (one need only recall His attitude toward women, the ritually unclean and the sinner, and the legalism of some of the leaders of His country). This independence or self-possession is allied with His "single-mindedness." The Father and the Father's will are the one great focus of His life and work—almost obsessive we would say if that word did not carry pejorative connotations.

There is also a marked seriousness or even sternness about His figure. Although our age tends to pass over this quality, it is an unmistakable datum of the Gospels. His words on hell, the difficulty of salvation, His condemnation of Scribes and Pharisees, together with the authority of tone, reveal a firm moral Teacher. For all that, the arrogance which so often accompanies great self-possession and moral earnestness is lacking in Jesus. There is, on the contrary, a profound humility which revealed itself in His refusal to seek grandeur or the spectacular, and in the total absence of pride of place or ostentation. There is no trace of the human vice of ambition, whereas a profound preference for the poor and the simplicity of children is evident, as well as the fact that He is a "country person." He is never recorded as using a favorable example of the city or city life, while His stories abound with examples from nature, agriculture, farms, fishing, etc. Humanly speaking, such humility came from origins in a simple family, but ultimately from an ever greater self-emptying.

The list of emotions or passions displayed by Him is a long one: anger, fear, patience, joy, sorrow, physical tiredness and hunger, courage, compassion and sympathy, to cite but the more obvious. Above them all is a love or concern for others which, although lacking in sentimentality and appearing at times even harsh, manifests itself in a constant sacrificial giving of self.

There is finally that prayerfulness which St. Luke especially sought to highlight (cf. Lk. 3:21; 5:15; 6:12; 9:18; 9:29; 11:1; 22:32; 22:41ff.) and which we are nearly incapable of understanding.

Such characteristics are the elements of a human personality inasmuch as they are all human traits. They are, of course, more than that. They are divinity itself "translated" into human terms since they are the human characteristics of the divine Person. They tell us, in ways we can recognize, what the Infinitely Other is like in Himself when He expresses Himself for us. As such, they too reveal the Father since "Anyone who has seen me has seen the Father" (Jn. 14:9).

Because they are not simply the actions and words of any man, but revelatory signs of the living God, the deeds and teaching of Jesus are historical facts and *an object of faith*. Pope Paul VI witnessed to this truth when, for the first time in a Creed of the Church, he included some of the aspects of Jesus' public ministry in the Creed.

> He lived among us full of grace and truth. He announced and set up the kingdom of God, manifesting the Father to us in Himself. He gave us His new commandment, that we love one another as He has loved us. He taught us the way of the Gospel beatitudes: namely, to be poor in spirit, and meek, to bear sorrow in patience, to thirst for justice, to be merciful, pure of heart, peacemakers, and to suffer persecution for the sake of justice.[106]

PART THREE

The Easter Triduum

I. THE PURPOSE OF HIS COMING

Catholic theology long ago raised the question whether God would have become man if the human race had not sinned. The current of thought which replies affirmatively to that question—traditionally called the "Scotist" position after the Franciscan theologian John Duns Scotus (1266-1308) has much to commend it. God is seen, in this point of view, as willing to communicate Himself to the human race in the most complete manner possible. Out of love He would have done this—even if we had not sinned—by taking a human nature as His own, thereby elevating and enriching humanity in a manner infinitely exceeding what was either necessary or owed to humanity. In the context of the theory of evolution, Christ thus becomes the purpose and goal of all material evolutionary development. In the personal union of divinity and humanity in Jesus, now raised from the dead and glorified, the created universe has reached its conclusion by anticipation.[1] Such a theological outlook opens a vast perspective, one richly Christocentric and one which offers manifold insights into the meaning of matter and a theology of the human body, as well as of the evolutionary process itself.

Considering the same question, St. Thomas Aquinas wrote that he was inclined to agree with those who would respond negatively. His reasons were partly "pragmatic." For him the "what-might-have beens" are uncertain grounds on which to found a theology. "We do not know what God would have done if He had not foreseen sin,"[2] he wrote when commenting on the Scriptural passage. "Here is a trustworthy saying that deserves full acceptance: Christ Jesus came into the world to save sinners (1 Tm. 1:15)." More theologically, he noted that God permits evil so that from it He may draw forth an even greater good, and citing the hymn for the blessing of the Paschal Candle ("O happy fault, O necessary sin of Adam which gained for us so great a Redeemer"), he presented the Incarnation as the chief example of this principle.[3]

Whatever might have been if our race had not fallen, it is clear that, in the actual order of things, the Incarnation was directed to our redemption. The great Latin poet, Venantius Fortunatus (530-609), in his hymn to the Cross, wrote:

Lustra sex qui iam peracta	Thirty years among us dwelling
tempus implens corporis	His appointed time fulfilled,
se volente, natus ad hoc,	*Born for this,* He meets His
passioni deditus,	Passion,
agnus in crucis levatur	For that—this He freely willed
immolandus stipite.[4]	On the Cross the Lamb is lifted
	Where His life-blood shall be spilled.

Natus ad hoc; He was born for suffering, a passion freely willed *(se volente)* for our sake. St. John records this as being Jesus' own understanding of His life when he writes:

Now my heart is troubled and what shall I say? 'Father, save me from this hour'? No, it was this very reason I came to this hour (12:27; cf. 18:11).

And Luke and Matthew write in like fashion.

He said to them,...'Did not the Christ have to suffer these things and then enter his glory?' (Lk. 24:26; cf. 9:22; 22:22)

Do you think I cannot call on my Father, and he will at once put at my disposal more than twelve legions of angels? But how then would the Scriptures be fulfilled that say it must happen in this way? (Mt. 26:53-54)

Jesus' own awareness of this destiny for which He had been born, as well as how He Himself interpreted that destiny, are elements of His life which have been minutely examined and discussed. It has already been noted that some go so far as to deny that He ever envisioned such a fate—or at least not until the very end—and that He ultimately accepted it thinking His work a failure.[5] Theology must come to grips with the exegetical and historical questions which raise even the possibility for such conclusions, but it must be able to do this within a wider framework than the parameters set by some exponents of literary and historical criticism. Within a wider framework, the historical problems can be approached somewhat differently while still doing justice to accepted scholarly norms. In such a framework, theology can and must work from what is a datum of revelation. That datum of faith is this: the human race has been saved by the freely-willed death of Jesus of Nazareth. This truth allows one to draw at least one conclusion which must serve by way of an *a priori* in examining the various historical and literary data. If redemption depends on the freely-willed death of Jesus, then it must be said that He foresaw—at least in general—both the death itself and its consequences. Without such knowledge, His death as redemptive could not have been freely willed and thus there would either be no redemption or there would be one which would have to posit the thesis that His humanity—through which the redemption was effected—was something akin to a mechanical, blind instrument in the hands of the Divinity. In other words, either Jesus freely willed His death to save us and thereby had an awareness commensurate with such a decision, or His humanity served as a virtually inert pawn through which God accomplished the restoration of the human race.

Christian Tradition firmly holds that Jesus gave Himself over to death freely for our sakes. For a Catholic, this Tradition may be summed up in two explicit statements of the second and fourth Eucharistic Prayers of the Mass. The Church prays:

When He was given over of His own will to His Passion... (*Qui cum Passioni voluntare traderetur...*)—Eucharistic Prayer II.

In order to fulfill Your will, He gave Himself over to death (*Ut tuam vero dispensationem impleret, in mortem tradidit semetipsum...*)—Eucharistic Prayer IV.

This liturgical expression of the Church's faith has been frequently confirmed by the Magisterium,[6] most recently in the Second Vatican Council.

Christ, as the Church has held and holds, in His great love freely underwent His passion and death so that all might attain salvation.[7]

Such teaching, of course, is no more than a reaffirmation of the explicit testimony of the New Testament writers who tell us that Jesus freely went to His death (Mt. 26:53-54; Jn. 10:17-18), as well as predicting both it and His resurrection (Mt. 16:20ff.; 17:22-23; 20:17-19, and parallels; cf. Jn. 3:13-14; 8:28; 12:32-33).

II. THE PREDICTIONS OF
PASSION AND RESURRECTION

As the Synoptics record it, Jesus first predicted His sufferings, death, and resurrection after the Petrine confession of faith at Caesarea Philippi (Mt. 16:13-20 and parallel). Immediately thereafter they also record the Lord's words on the necessity of following Jesus on the way of the cross.

> Then he called the crowd along with his disciples and said: 'If anyone would come after me, he must deny himself and take up his cross and follow me. For whoever wants to save his life will lose it, but whoever loses his life for me and the gospel will save it. What good is it for a man to gain the whole world, yet forfeit his soul? Or what can a man give in exchange for his soul? If anyone is ashamed of me and my words in this adulterous and sinful generation, the Son of Man will be ashamed of him when he comes in his Father's glory with the holy angels.' And he said to them, 'Amen, I say to you, some who are standing here will not taste death before they see the kingdom of God come with power' (Mk. 8:34; 9:1 and parallels).[8]

There are various historical questions raised by the predictions of the passion in the text cited. Did Jesus foresee and predict His death? If so, did He explicitly say it would be by crucifixion? And did He cite the cross itself as a model for discipleship? The answers to these questions run the usual spectrum of opinions. Some would say that the predictions are *vaticinia ex eventu*, prophecies after the event, which find their origin in the early Christian communities.

Others would hold that the Lord predicted His death in general terms, tradition filling in some of the specifics now recorded in the Gospels. The specific reference to the crucifixion (mentioned explicitly only in Mt. 20:19, the other predictions in Matthew and in all the parallels referring simply to Jesus' "being killed" with no direct mention of crucifixion) and the cross as a pattern for discipleship would be among such *post factum* specifications.

If one leaves out of consideration Jesus' infused or prophetic knowledge—which many seem to do when treating of this matter, reasonably enough if one is a historian, not so reasonably if one is a theologian—the question is twofold: 1) *could* Jesus have foreseen and predicted His own death and 2) *did He in fact* foresee and predict it? That He *could have* scarcely needs a defense. He would have been aware how the prophets of ancient Israel had suffered and how, according to Jewish legend,[9] some of them even met violent deaths. The fate of John the Baptist was evidence at hand for the danger He Himself faced as the opposition to His own preaching grew steadily. Matthew tells us that Jesus referred to this fact explicitly (Mt. 17:11-13, cf. Mk. 9:11-13).

That He did foresee and predict His fate is, of course, what the Evangelists report. The evidence goes beyond the mere recording of three predictions. There are a series of sayings which indicate His awareness of the outcome of His ministry.

> I have come to bring fire on earth, and how I wish it were already kindled! For I have a baptism to undergo, and how distressed I am until it is completed! (Lk. 12:49-50)

> Then James and John, the sons of Zebedee, came to him. 'Teacher,' they said, 'we want you to do for us whatever we ask.... Let one of us sit at your right and the other at your left in your glory.' 'You don't know what you are asking,' Jesus said. 'Can you drink the cup I drink or be baptized with the baptism I am baptized with?' (Mk. 10:35-38; Mt. 20:20-23)

> At the same time Pharisees came to Jesus and said to him, 'Leave this place and go somewhere else. Herod wants to kill you.' He replied, 'Go tell that fox, "I will drive out demons and heal people today and tomorrow, and on the third day I will reach my goal." In any case, I must keep going today and

tomorrow and the next day—for surely no prophet can die outside of Jerusalem' (Lk. 13:31-33).

One could add, as well, the parable of the wicked tenants (Mt.21:33-46 and parallel), Jesus' remark on the bridegroom being taken away (Mk. 2:18-19 and parallel), the sayings in Mk. 10:45 and Lk. 17:25. And all this without invoking the various testimonies in the Gospel of John (e.g., 7:19; 8:21-22; 10:11, etc.). In fact, in the face of the variety of the evidence, there can be no adequate reason to deny that Jesus did in fact foresee and predict His death.[10]

As to the specifics, and to the cross in particular, one does not find the same multiplicity of attestation. Apart from the Passion Narratives, reference to the cross is found only in the third prediction of the passion as Matthew reports it and in the texts cited above concerning the following of Jesus as well as in Matthew 26:2 and Matthew 23:34. It is plausible, therefore, from a historical point of view, to posit the thesis that the words "cross" and "crucifixion" in these contexts do not go back to Jesus Himself but are rather the form His words took after the fact and after His resurrection gave a new meaning to the cross. Plausible, however, would seem to be all that can be said for such a thesis since concrete evidence for it is lacking, and what appears to be substituted for that lack of evidence is frequently a theological-historical a priori, namely, that He could not have foreseen the specific manner of His death and that the idea of "carrying one's cross" would be intelligible only when its specifically Christian significance had been made manifest in Jesus' own life.[11] Such an a priori is itself questionable, and the question as to the specific references to cross and crucifixion should perhaps be classified as not admitting of historical certitude for or against.

Jesus' foreknowledge and prediction of His fate were not, of course, simply concerned with suffering and death. Each of the predictions of the passion—with the exception of the second prediction in Luke 9:44—also includes the forecast that He would be raised up in three days (or, as Mark puts it, "after three days").

The doctrine of bodily resurrection of the dead was not peculiar to Jesus in first century Palestine. When this idea clearly entered Israel's view is not certain, but one finds it reflected in the book of

Daniel 12:2-3 written around 150 B.C., while the imagery of resurrection is found much earlier (e.g., Ez. 37:1-14). By the time of Jesus, the Pharisees had accepted the notion while the Sadducees still rejected it. It was this cleavage in faith which led to the hypocritical question put to Jesus by the Sadducees, and which occasioned from Him a reaffirmation of the faith of the Pharisees. He said to the Sadducees:

> You are in error because you do not know the Scriptures or the power of God. At the resurrection people will neither marry nor be given in marriage; they will be like the angels in heaven. But about the resurrection of the dead—have you not read what God said to you, 'I am the God of Abraham, the God of Isaac, and the God of Jacob'? He is not the God of the dead but of the living (Mt. 22:23ff., and parallel). [12]

During His ministry, Jesus did more than confirm the Pharisees' belief in the resurrection of the dead. As the Father's emissary He showed His own power over death by recalling to life those already dead. Matthew, Mark and Luke record His raising of the daughter of Jairus (Mt. 9:18-26 and parallel); Luke records the resuscitation of the son of the widow of Naim (7:11-17); and John gives us the account of the reanimation of Lazarus (Jn. 11:1-44). [13] The self-assurance that Jesus had of His own power over death is made abundantly clear in each account. He says to Martha, "Your brother will rise again" (Jn. 11:22); to the crowd outside the house of Jairus, "Go away. The girl is not dead but asleep" (Mt. 9:24; cf. Jn. 11:11 for the same use of "sleep" for "death." We have here either a euphemism on the part of Jesus—which misled people—or a very different way of looking at death on His part); to the dead themselves:

"Talitha, koum" (which means, "Little girl, I say to you, get up")—Mk. 5:41.
"Young man, I say to you, get up!"—Lk. 7:14
"Lazarus, come out"—Jn. 11:43.

It is all done with a simple word of command. Only John explicitly reveals the source of such assurance.

Then Jesus looked up and said, 'Father, I thank you that you have heard me. I know that you always hear me, but I have said this for the benefit of the people standing here, that they may believe that you sent me' (Jn. 11:41-42).

The Father who is the God of Abraham, of Isaac and Jacob, the God of the living and not of the dead, is the source of all life and has constituted the Son as the source of life (cf. Jn. 5:26). The Son, in turn, uses His power over death as a sign to the Baptist (cf. Mt. 11:5; Lk. 7:22) and sends His disciples out with the power to "raise the dead" (Mt. 10:8). The parallel with Jesus' forgiving of sins is obvious enough. Only God can forgive sins; only God can give life. Appropriately enough, Luke sums up the reaction of the people to such wonders by noting:

They were filled with awe and praised God. 'A great prophet has appeared among us,' they said. 'God has come to help his people' (Lk. 7:16).

As was true of the Pharisees who had remarked that only God could forgive sins, so the crowd here did not realize the truth of their remark in saying that God had visited His people.

It is, then, within the context of Jesus' discussion with the Sadducees and His awareness of the power over death which was His that one must approach His predictions about His own resurrection. His awareness that the ultimate reward of the righteous was a resurrected life and His awareness of His own unique relation with the Father are factors sufficient in themselves to account for His predicting a glorious outcome to His own sufferings. But efforts to rationalize His understanding and His predictions in this way, helpful though they may be to put the prophecies in a context, are not adequate. They do not completely reveal the origins of the certitude He had about His own fate, nor are they capable of explaining how He knew that, unlike the fate of all who would arise at the end of the world as the Pharisees believed, His own resurrection would anticipate the general resurrection of all, that it would indeed occur within three days of His death. To explain that one must either impugn the historical veracity of the accounts and hold that He never said what is claimed of Him, or recur to Jesus' prophetic or infused knowledge. Although it is common enough to choose the first alternative,[14] there is no solid critical reason to do so. Indeed, the matter is all of a piece with the awareness He had of His relationship with the Father, with the assurance with which He forgave sin and with the surety that death could not hold its own when faced with His authoritative word. Jesus is singular in what He knew, in what He did, and in what He said.

There can be no certain historical answer given to the question which asks when or how Jesus became aware of His coming death and resurrection. Did that awareness come gradually, was it there already at the start of the ministry, was it always present? All these are interesting questions to which the Gospels offer no answer. However, since we do know that God became a man with this fate in view, it can be said that, in some way, His whole human nature was ordained to His death and resurrection. Such was the goal and purpose of His very being as man. He was born for this (*natus ad hoc*), not as part of some inexorable fate in the pagan sense, but as something known and chosen by the Divine Person to whom the human nature belongs. The passion and resurrection are not simply a "happening" in the life of Jesus of Nazareth. For them did He come, and so, in some way, His human awareness, just as it was always shaped by and reflective of His being "from, for and of the Father," was shaped by and resonated His personal decision for death and resurrection.[15]

III. JESUS INTERPRETS HIS DEATH

1. Background

In the apocryphal Fourth Book of Maccabees,[16] written early in the first century A.D. and before the destruction of the Temple in 70 A.D., we read:

> Eleazar prayed: You know, O God that though I might have saved myself, I die in fiery torment for the sake of the law. Be merciful to your people, and let my punishment be sufficient for their sake. Make my blood an expiation for them, and take my life as a ransom *(antipsychon)* for theirs (IV Mac. 6:27-29).[17]

After the heroic death of the Jewish martyr, Eleazar, it is written of him and the company with him:

> These, then, having been sanctified by God, are honored not only with this distinction but also by the fact that because of them our enemies did not prevail over our nation; and the tyrant was chastised, and our land purified—they having become as it were a ransom *(antipsychon)* for the sin of the nation. It was through the blood of these righteous ones, and through the expiation *(hilasterion)* of their death, that Divine Providence preserved Israel... (IV Mac. 17:20-22).[18]

These selections are a remarkable expression of the theme of vicarious suffering, wherein one makes up for or offers himself for the sins of others. The notion, at least in its general aspects, was common enough in the Mediterranean world of the period.[19] Within the religion of Israel, the origin of such an idea is diffuse and diverse. The Jews certainly had some notion of vicarious representation even at an early period in their history. In the Book of Genesis 18:16ff., one finds the amazing scene of Abraham attempting to strike a bargain with God in order to save Sodom. According to his proposed terms, the goodness of the few would serve to save the city which should have been doomed because of the wickedness of the many.

> What if there are fifty righteous people in the city? Will you really sweep it away and not spare the place for the sake of the fifty righteous people in it? (Gn. 18:24)

God agrees to the principle, although in fact the sufficient number of good people cannot be found. Now it is clear that the idea is still far from the notion of *one* good person "standing in" for the many evil and thereby saving them. But the seeds of such an idea are present.

The same general idea lies behind the Day of Atonement ritual of the Israelites. The scapegoat symbolically bears away the sins of the whole people.

> When Aaron has finished making atonement for the most Holy Place, the Tent of Meeting and the altar, he shall bring forward the live goat. He is to lay both hands on the head of the live goat and confess over it all the wickedness and rebellion of the Israelites—all their sins—and put them on the goat's head.... The goat will carry on itself all their sins to a solitary place; and the man shall release it in the desert (Lev. 16:20-22)

These ideas of the transference of sin and of the good of the righteous few "compensating" for the evil of the many were rooted in the Jewish notion of corporate solidarity and responsibility which, nonetheless, was balanced by the insistence of prophets such as Jeremiah 31:30 and Ezekiel 18:1-31 on the individual's responsibility. Even in the light of such a balancing, however, the theme of corporate solidarity reasserted itself, in a way unique in the Old Testament, in the figure of the Servant found in the later parts of the book of Isaiah.

The four "Servant Songs" (Is. 42:1-4; 49:1-6; 50:4-9; 52:13—53:12) were likely composed in the fifth century B.C. The Servant is a mysterious figure—unidentified in the poems except for Isaiah 49:3 where "Israel" is his name—who has been singularly chosen by Yahweh and who will have a special mission to the Gentiles (42:1; 49:6; 52:15) as well as to Israel. He will face opposition to his teaching but persevere in spite of insults (Is. 50:6-7). Finally, in the last of the poems—which the Church uses as her first reading for the Liturgy of Good Friday—the old themes of corporate solidarity and vicarious compensation are developed in a new and striking manner.

See, my servant will act wisely; he will be raised and lifted up and highly exalted. Just as there were many who were appalled at him—his appearance was so disfigured beyond that of any man and his form marred beyond human likeness—so will he sprinkle many nations, and kings will shut their mouths because of him. For what they were not told, they will see, and what they have not heard, they will understand.... He was despised and rejected by men, a man of sorrows, and familiar with suffering. Like one from whom men hide their faces he was despised, and we esteemed him not. Surely he took up our infirmities and carried our sorrows, yet we considered him stricken by God, smitten by him, and afflicted. But he was pierced for our transgressions, he was crushed for our iniquities; the punishment that brought us peace was upon him. We all, like sheep, have gone astray, each of us has turned to his own way; and the Lord has laid on him the iniquity of us all.... He was cut off from the land of the living; for the transgression of my people he was stricken. He was assigned a grave with the wicked, and with the rich in his death, though he had done no violence, nor was any deceit in his mouth.... Though the Lord makes his life a guilt offering, he will see his offspring and prolong his days, and the will of the Lord will prosper in his hand. After the suffering of his soul, he will see the light of life and be satisfied.... Therefore I will give him a portion among the great, and he will divide the spoils with the strong.... For he bore the sin of many, and made intercession for the transgressors (Is. 52:13—53:12).

Here, for the first time in the Old Testament, one who is just assumes a role like that of the scapegoat ("...the Lord laid on him the iniquity of us all") and, as a result of his sufferings and death (53:8-9), those who are not just are healed. ("The punishment that brought us peace was upon him and by his wounds we are healed.") In this we find the concept of vicarious suffering, wherein the just One takes on what was due to the unjust, namely punishment, chastisement and even death, and he does so with the consequent salvation of the unjust. Remarkable, also, is the idea that, although He died as a "guilt offering," the Servant will be vindicated and even "see the light" and "divide the spoils with the strong." In some fashion, life will be His despite the fact that He died, and even *"because* he poured out his life unto death."

This profound poem finds no subsequent development in the canonical books of the Old Testament, but its ideas surely underlie the picture of Eleazar as depicted in IV Maccabees, a fact which can be safely asserted without claiming any necessary literary connection or dependence.

While the fourth Servant poem may be the most exalted answer which the Old Testament gives to the questions of sin and suffering, it is not the only one. Parallel to it and probably not unrelated, although less profound in its thought, there appeared the idea of the suffering of the just man, one who is afflicted without cause. The book of Job raises the problem; Jeremiah reflects the theme in his own life and sufferings (e.g., Jer. 20:7-18). The book of Wisdom (late second century or early first century B.C.) developed the idea in a passage used by the Church on Friday of the fourth week of Lent.

Let us lie in wait for the virtuous man, since he annoys us and opposes our way of life, reproaches us for our breaches of the law and accuses us of playing false to our upbringing. He claims to have knowledge of God and calls himself a son of the Lord. Before us he stands, a reproof to our way of thinking, the very sight of him weighs our spirits down; his way of life is not like other men's, the paths he treads are unfamiliar. In his opinion we are counterfeit; he holds aloof from our doings as though from filth; he proclaims the final end of the virtuous as happy and boasts of having God for his father. Let us see if what he says is true, let us observe what kind of end he himself will have. If the virtuous man is God's son, God will take his part and rescue him from the clutches of his enemies. Let us test him with cruelty and torture, and thus explore this gentleness of his and put his endurance to the proof. Let us condemn him to a shameful death since he will be looked after—we have his word for it (Wis. 2:12-20) (Jerusalem Bible).

Similar sentiments are found in Psalm 22, a hymn which praises God for having delivered the just one from suffering and from the scorn of his enemies.

2. The Sayings

It is within the framework of such ideas, common in a general way to both the Jewish and pagan worlds of the first century, that Jesus, humanly speaking, must have interpreted the meaning of His own sufferings and death. To presume otherwise would be either to dehistoricize Him, abstracting Him from the religious milieu of His time, the very milieu which had been providentially prepared for His coming, or to presume that He went to His death simply as a fate destined by the Father, its consequences completely unforeseen. This last cannot have been the case. He foresaw one of the consequences of that death when He predicted that it would result in His vindication through resurrection. By way of a theological *a priori*, one must say that He also understood that His death would have saving significance for others. If such were not the case it would be impossible for Christianity to hold that He lay down His life freely *for our salvation.* Now, in fact, the Gospels do tell us that He interpreted His own death as a death for others, one which would benefit the many.

He said to his disciples, 'The time is coming when you will long to see one of the days of the Son of Man, but you will not see it. Men will tell you, "There he is!" or "Here he is!" Do not go running off after them. For the Son of Man in his day will be like the lightning, which flashes and lights up the sky from one end to the other. But first he must suffer many things and be rejected by this generation' (Lk. 17:22-25).

In that context Jesus is stating that His own suffering and rejection are a prelude to the victorious coming of the Son of Man. As such the text falls within the categories of the threefold prediction of the passion. It does not give particular insight into any causal connection which might exist between suffering and rejection and victorious coming. For that, one must look to a singular passage in the Gospel according to Matthew and Mark.

Whoever wants to become great among you must be your servant, and whoever wants to be first must be your slave—just as the Son of Man did not come to be served, but to serve, and to give his life as a ransom (lutron) for many (Mt. 20:27-28; Mk. 10:43-45; cf. Lk. 22:27).[20]

It can be noticed how similar the remark "to give his life as a ransom for many" is to the thought of Isaiah 52—53, and to the passages cited from IV Maccabees. The idea of ransom is used by other N.T. writers when speaking of the death of Jesus (cf. 1 Tm. 2:6; Ti. 2:14; 1 Pt. 1:18) and is the concept underlying Christianity's talk of the Redemption. As used by Jesus—and by later Christian writers—it is a metaphor to describe what His death achieved for us.[21]

As striking as the "ransom" text is in helping to understand the nexus between Jesus' death and mankind's salvation, it is perfectly in harmony with the rest of His life and teaching. Already He had said to His followers:

Do not be afraid of those who kill the body but cannot kill the soul. Rather, be afraid of the one who can destroy both body and soul in hell. Are not two sparrows sold for a penny? Yet not one of them will fall to the ground apart from the will of your Father (Mt. 10:28-29; Lk. 12:4-7).

For Jesus, all things, even death itself, fell within the Father's Providence and thus served His purpose in some way. To that general teaching He added the injunction:

Whoever tries to keep his life will lose it and whoever loses his life will preserve it (Lk. 17:33 and parallels; Jn. 12:25).

What the original context of this saying was is difficult to determine since the evangelists use it in various contexts. Indeed, by its nature, it is a saying capable of being variously used. But the fruitfulness of a life given for the kingdom of the Father is clear in the saying as it stands. In John, that fruitfulness appears explicitly.

> Jesus replied, 'The hour has come for the Son of Man to be glorified. Amen, amen, I say to you, unless a kernel of wheat falls to the ground and dies, it remains only a single seed. But if it dies, it produces many seeds. The man who loves his life will lose it, while the man who hates his life in this world will keep it for eternal life' (Jn. 12:23-25).[22]

These sayings of Jesus during His ministry, sayings which place a salvific interpretation on His coming death, although significant, are few in number. This should not be a cause of surprise. The Lord is the agent of salvation, not its theorist. Furthermore, His sayings—as well as the disputes over their authenticity—must be set in the framework of His entire life and preaching. That life, in its entirety, was one of self-donation, given first to the Father and His will and then to others in the preaching of the Father's kingdom. From the inception of the public ministry the preaching of that kingdom was marked by struggle against the devil and against human sin and inertia. In inviting His disciples and followers to accept the kingdom, Jesus never hid the fact that such an invitation was one that necessitated self-abnegation, a willingness to spend and to be spent. Such self-abnegation was never presented by Him as an end in itself. It was for the sake of the word and would yield fruit a hundred-, sixty- and thirty-fold (cf. Mt. 13:8 and parallels). In a very real sense, then, His life, His preaching, His death and the way in which He interpreted that death are all of a piece. It is inconceivable—apart from postulating that, despite His life and teaching, He approached His own death having lost confidence in the Father—that He did not see His own death as a prelude to growth.

His own definitive explanation of the meaning of His death He gave to His disciples the night before He died.

3. The Eucharist

> It was just before the Passover Feast. Jesus knew that the time
> had come for him to leave the world and go to the Father.
> Having loved his own who were in the world, he now showed
> the full extent of his love. The evening meal was being served,
> and the devil had already prompted Judas Iscariot, son of
> Simon, to betray Jesus. Jesus knew that the Father had put all
> things under his power, and that he had come from God and
> was returning to God; so he got up from the meal, took off his
> outer clothing, and wrapped a towel around his waist. After
> that, he poured water into a basin and began to wash his
> disciples' feet, drying them with the towel that was wrapped
> around him (Jn. 13:1-5).

Apart from the great beauty and drama of the scene as
described by John, these verses are important for at least three
categorical affirmations on the part of the evangelist. Two of them
touch directly on Jesus' awareness of His mission, its outcome and
His own origins. He was, says John, aware that the time was at hand
to leave the world and *go to the Father,* not simply to a meaningless
death.[23] He knew, as well, that He had come from God and was
returning to God. He was "of and from and for" the Father. Such
statements are direct theological assertions on the part of the
evangelist concerning Jesus' self-understanding and His understanding of His mission. Any theological effort to study the
psychology of Jesus must either find itself in harmony with these
assertions or deny the doctrines of inspiration and inerrancy as the
Church understands them. "Everything affirmed by the Sacred
Authors must be held to be affirmed by the Holy Spirit."[24] In fact,
there is nothing at any level of the traditions or anywhere in the
Gospels that contradicts these affirmations by John. Only hypothetical historical reconstructions of the traditions are available to
challenge the evangelist's assertions.

The third assertion of John is no less clear. Here at the Supper,
Jesus showed the full extent of His love.[25] Indeed, the Supper is
both the beginning and the summation of His passion and resurrec-

tion. Jesus summarizes His own life of service symbolically by washing the feet of His followers. Then, He explains His death, as well as His life, in the words spoken over the bread and the cup of wine.[26]

> While they were eating, Jesus took bread, gave thanks and broke it, and gave it to his disciples, saying, 'Take and eat; this is my body.'
> Then he took the cup, gave thanks and offered it to them, saying, 'Drink from it, all of you. This is my blood of the covenant, which is poured out for many for the forgiveness of sins' (Mt. 26:26-27; Mk. 14:22-24; Lk. 22:19-20; 1 Cor. 11:23-25).

The four accounts we possess of the words of Jesus over the bread and wine vary slightly and are normally grouped as the Matthean-Marcan, and Pauline-Lucan, supposedly reflecting the usage of two liturgical settings.[27] What is clear from the harmony of the essential elements in each account is that Jesus asks the Twelve to share in His body and blood which are (or are to be) broken and/or poured out on behalf of others ("for many"—"for you"—"for the remission of sins"). It is Jesus' own definitive interpretation of what was about to take place, the summation of His whole life. His giving over of Himself, even unto death, was what was needed to make the Father's kingdom a reality. His own blood would be the yeast which would produce growth.

The injunction to: "Take and drink. This is my blood of the covenant"—was a daring statement for a Jew. The law of Moses said:

> Any Israelite or any alien living among them who eats any blood—I will set my face against that person who eats blood and I will cut him off from his people. For the life of a creature is in the blood, and I have given it to you to make atonement for yourselves on the altar; it is the blood that makes atonement for one's life. Therefore I say to the Israelites, 'None of you may eat blood, nor may an alien living among you eat blood' (Lv. 17:10-12).

For Jesus, it was His own blood which would henceforth be the blood of atonement, but, instead of being sprinkled on the altar or over the people (as at the confirmation of the covenant in the desert, cf. Ex. 24:4-8), it would be drunk just as a communion or fellowship offering was shared (cf. Lv. 7:11ff.).[28]

Because of the sins of Israel against the covenant God had made with them in Sinai, Jeremiah had prophesied:

'The time is coming,' declares the Lord, 'when I will make a new covenant with the house of Israel and with the house of Judah. It will not be like the covenant I made with their forefathers when I took them by the hand to lead them out of Egypt, because they broke my covenant, though I was a husband to them' (Jer. 31:31ff.).

At the Supper and in anticipation of His death, Jesus fulfills that promise. He offers His blood as the "blood of the covenant." Underlying the interpretation of His death in the words He spoke over the bread and the cup are many O.T. themes. The suffering of the Just One, the vicarious suffering of the servant as He carries the sins of others, the sealing of the covenant in blood, the scapegoat of the Day of Atonement—all of these are elements discernible in the way He interpreted His death in the Eucharistic words at the Supper. To what extent these themes had helped Him, in His human understanding, to formulate the meaning of His death, we are not really able to know. Like the themes of Messiah and Son of Man and Suffering Servant—which had never been "merged" into one figure by the theologians of Israel—Jesus is the point of convergence for many O.T. themes. But the convergence was more than simply an amalgam or "composite picture" of all of them. They are intelligible when applied to Him, but He is not fully intelligible through them, even when a composite is drawn. There is still in Him that "excess of meaning" which necessitated the stretching of all the old categories. What is true of the various titles is also true of the way He interpreted His death. The themes can be made to "fit" Him and His giving of Himself, but He cannot be made to "fit" them. In that sense, the disputed question as to whether Jesus Himself had an "explicit Christology" or an "explicit soteriology" is, on the level at which it is normally posed, probably incapable of solution.[29] We can see how the various themes and titles are recognizable in the figure of the suffering Christ, we can see how some of them find an echo in His own words and how the early

Church used such themes and titles about Him, but we are offered little direct evidence as to how He Himself "theologized" about the various themes. What can be said is that they served as "material at hand" or as a context for Himself and His work. Even if we could know the extent to which He explicitly thought about them, we would still be left with the puzzle about the way He transcended them. Thus, here again, one is faced with the mystery of His Person and His own self-awareness.

The Supper and its events are reminders that prophetic or infused knowledge is not merely a scholastic invention, but a necessary condition for understanding the events, unless one chooses the alternative of stripping the accounts of much of their historicity. There is no merely natural explanation of the accounts of Eucharistic institution. A Man claims to share Himself, body and blood, with His followers as a sign of His freely-willed death for the sake of the many. In so doing, He changes the very reality of the signs He uses for such a sharing—the bread and wine—so that they become His body and blood. Of this reality, Cyril of Jerusalem (315-386) was to write:

> With full assurance let us partake...for in the figure of bread is given His body and in the figure of wine is given His blood.
>
> Therefore you must think of the bread and wine not as bare and common elements; for they are the Body and Blood of Christ, according to the Lord's own assertion.... What seems to be bread is not bread, although it is sensible to the taste; what seems to be wine is not wine, although it seems to be such to the taste. Rather they are the Body and Blood of Christ.[30]

The Church has always taught that the institution of this sacrament as a memorial of His passion, itself a sacrifice, with a real change in the elements of bread and wine, was done by Jesus Himself at the Last Supper.[31] She has defined, moreover, that at the same Supper, He commissioned the Twelve to repeat what He had done.[32] This Jesus did, not only by the words found in Lk. 22:19 and 1 Cor. 11:24, but also in the great prayer of the Lord as found in John's Gospel. There Jesus tells the Father that He has "sanctified" or "consecrated" or "set Himself apart for sacred things" (the Greek *hagiazo* in Jn. 17:19 carries all these ideas)[33] and asks that those with Him may be likewise set apart.

> Sanctify them by the truth; your word is truth. As you sent me into the world, I have sent them into the world. For them I sanctify myself, that they too may be truly sanctified (Jn. 17:17-19).

Both the mystery of the Eucharist (including Jesus' interpretation of His own death) and the commissioning of the Apostles are mysteries whose explanation must be sought in the hidden depths of Jesus' own self-awareness. They are mysteries, however, totally connected with His own mission, His very purpose for being as man, namely His being lifted up, through death and resurrection, so as to draw all things to the Father.

IV. ONE OF THE TRINITY
DIED ON THE CROSS:
GOD HAS REIGNED FROM A TREE[34]

1. The Suffering God

The Solemn Liturgy of Good Friday, during the veneration of the cross, addresses the following words to the Crucified One:

> Holy is God!
> Holy and strong!
> Holy immortal One,
> have mercy on us! (The Sacramentary)

There follows this Trisagion, the words of the Reproaches:

> I opened the sea before you,
> but you opened my side with a spear.

> I led you on your way in a pillar of cloud,
> but you led me to Pilate's court.

> I gave you saving water from the rock,
> but you gave me gall and vinegar to drink.... (The Sacramentary)

Throughout the Reproaches there is echoed the thought of St. Paul who identified Christ as the One who sustained the Jews in the desert (1 Cor. 10:3-4). Melito of Sardis was later to teach the same truth and draw its logical conclusion when, speaking of the crucifixion, he proclaimed "The Master is outraged; God is murdered." Although Melito's expression is stark, it is coherent with the

Pauline teaching and with the Reproaches. Linguistically, it is also
similar to two New Testament expressions, one of St. Peter, the
other of St. Paul. In his address to the Jews in Solomon's colonnade
of the temple, Luke records Peter as saying:

> You disowned the Holy and Righteous One and asked that a
> murderer be released to you. You killed the Author of Life, but
> God raised him from the dead (Acts 3:15).

In the Old Testament, God Himself is the "Holy One of Israel"
(Is. 54:5, etc.), and therefore it is not impossible that Peter is
transferring that divine title to Jesus. If that were so, it would then
be possible to understand the "Author of Life" in the same absolute
sense of divinity, and Peter would equivalently be making the same
assertion as Melito, namely, that the "Author of Life," the Creator
had been crucified. An examination of the other uses of the phrase
in the N.T. would seem to indicate, however, that the words are not
used in that absolute sense, but rather in the sense that, by His
death and resurrection, Jesus is the author of the new life of those
He has redeemed.[35] Nevertheless, the phrase is, at least, a
preparation for the terminology of the *communicatio idiomatum* as
it is used so strikingly by Melito and in the Reproaches.

More than linguistic similarity is found in the Pauline text in
1 Cor. 2:7-8.

> No, we speak of God's secret wisdom, a wisdom that has been
> hidden and that God has destined for our glory before time
> began. None of the rulers of this age understood it, for if they
> had, they would not have crucified the Lord of glory.

The "Lord of glory" here is so similar to the title given to God
Himself in Psalm 24:10 ("Who is he, this King of glory? The Lord
Almighty—he is the King of glory") that there can be little doubt
that Paul is applying a divine title to Jesus crucified.[36] Latent in such
usage is the notion of preexistence, found in that same epistle
(1 Cor. 8:6; 10:4), and thus both the terminology and the meaning
are very close to Patristic usage: One who is divine has been
crucified.

The idea of a "suffering God" was clarified for theology after the
Nestorian dispute when it was seen that the *communicatio idio-*

matum was not merely a matter of honorific titles being applied to Jesus, but rather was a way of referring to the unity of divinity and humanity in the One Person of the Eternal Word. In accepting the Twelve Anathemas of St. Cyril of Alexandria (*DS* 252-263), the bishops at the Council of Ephesus concurred in the notion that "if anyone does not admit that the Word of God suffered in the flesh" such a one was anathema (*DS* 263).[37] This teaching was further confirmed by Pope John II in 534 in a letter to the Senators of the Empire. The Pope defended the axiom that "One of the Trinity suffered" and that Christ was "God who suffered in the flesh." In this defense of the doctrine, the Pope used the two scripture texts cited above—as well as Acts 20:28, the Twelfth Anathema of Cyril and the Tome of Pope Leo—to support the doctrine. Indeed, the Creed of Nicea itself substantiates the position when it confesses that it is the "Only-begotten Son, God from God, Light from Light, true God from true God" who was "born of the Virgin Mary...suffered, died and was buried."

This Christian faith in a crucified God has never been free of those who accuse it of being an only slightly veiled form or variation of Monophysitism or Apollinarianism.[38] In reality it is no such thing, although it does highlight one of the "limit situations" in theology's understanding of the mystery of the Incarnation. That theology has always defended the truth that God Himself is incapable of change and that, as a consequence, He is impassible, incapable of suffering.[39] Indeed, the doctrine of God's unchangeableness is a dogma of faith,[40] and, in its definition of God *become* Man, Chalcedon made explicit the teaching that the divine nature (as well as the human) remained "unconfused and unchanged."

To defend this doctrine, St. Thomas Aquinas applied a distinction in his language about Christ which he had already used in describing God's relationship to the world. Since for Aquinas a real relation signified a reality in God Himself and thus that a real relation to creation would entail a change in Him, Aquinas called all such temporal relationships *real* from the creation's side but only *logical* from God's side. In respect to Christ, he wrote:

Now every relation which is said of God from a temporal point of view does not posit any reality in the Eternal God Himself....Therefore, the sonship by which Christ is referred to His Mother is not a real relation (in God) but only a relation of reason.[41]

This position is not well received in our day, even by theologians who in a general sense can be called Thomists. It is argued that, while it defends the immutability and impassibility of God, the position effectively eviscerates the doctrine of Faith about the Word *becoming* flesh. According to the critics of Aquinas, his theological position is actually saying that the human nature became united to God in such a way that all change (and thus all the experiences of the human life) took place only in the humanity, leaving the divinity completely unaffected. In such a case it would seem that the Word is no different after the assumption of a human nature than He was before the human nature came to be.[42]

The criticism would appear to have much merit—if not against the substance of Aquinas' position, then at least against the conceptual and terminological expression of the matter. The difficulty is more general, of course, than simply that of the relationship of the divine and human natures in Christ. The relationship involved in the Incarnation—the relation of the divine to the human—is a unique instance of the more comprehensive difficulty we experience in understanding how the unchanging Creator relates to a universe which He brings to be. Is He affected by His creative act, and, if so, how? In creating, is He more or different than when He was not creating? Involved, too, in that question is the relation between time, a created reality, and eternity, the simultaneous presence of God and His power to Himself.

As being itself, the very fullness of being, God neither diminishes Himself nor acquires in Himself anything when He acts, since His acting is not to be pictured as a process whereby He moves from the unrealized to the realized. There is never an actualization of possibilities within Him. He is all Act and Eternal Act. God does from His eternal present what for His creation becomes past, present and future. It is this truth that Aquinas defends by his terminology of "real" and "logical" relations. Furthermore, as fullness of being, God *gives* while creating, but does *not receive*. Since by definition, relation means point of reference or referral to something else, God exists and causes only in reference to Himself so that what is given or created refers to Him and not He to it. In that sense, as well, Aquinas' position is accurate, although the positive aspect of that truth cannot be grasped since that would entail an intellectual comprehension of the Divine Power, which type of comprehension is beyond any created intellect. In short, the truth in question involves absolute mystery.

On the other hand, what God does is "real" both for Himself and for the created effect. Therefore, the Incarnation is "real" not only for the created humanity of Christ but for the Son whose humanity this is. It is this aspect of the truth which Aquinas' terminology about "real" and "logical" relations does not seem to express well. Nevertheless, it is consistent with his "theocentric" approach to reality. God is the Agent, never the recipient.

In the case of the Incarnation, God creates for Himself a human nature which receives all that it is from His creative power. There is no actuality at all in the Sacred Humanity which is not immediately dependent on the existence given it by the Word. Truly, He, the Eternal Son, is born of woman, suffers and dies, but these are not events that *happen* to Him, at least not in the way we use the word "happen." He is the Agent of the events, the One doing the action. This is the deepest meaning of the words given us by St. John:

> The reason my Father loves me is that I lay down my life—only to take it up again. No one takes it from me, but I lay it down of my own accord. I have authority to lay it down and authority to take it up again (Jn. 10:17-18).

Sufferings, like being born and thirsting, are for us passivities. We endure them; they happen to us. God, on the other hand, *does* them. He does not experience them; He creates them. In His humanity the Son of God dies. He does it in His humanity, but it is *He* who does it. What happens is a reality not just for His humanity, but for Him, the Eternal God. How He can be doing what for His humanity is an enduring; how He can effect what for His humanity is a-being-affected; how He can express Himself as a Man and thus become One Individual in His own creation while still being the sovereign Lord of that creation, which does not act on Him but rather He on it, is the very mystery of His unchanging power and activity. It is a truth, nonetheless, and Thomas' unpalatable terminology can serve as a jolting reminder of our inability to make Him conform to any human pattern of thought. To say that His relation to us is "logical, not real" is saying that His activity—even or especially in the wonder of the Incarnation and in His human death—can be seen but not understood, can be conceptualized but not categorized. One of the Trinity died on the cross—but that truth will not be grasped by our notions of relation and change.

In such a framework, the agony in all its reality only becomes more awesome.

> Jesus went out as usual to the Mount of Olives, and his disciples followed him. On reaching the place, he said to them, 'Pray that you will not fall into temptation.' He withdrew about a stone's throw beyond them, knelt down and prayed, 'Father, if you are willing, take this cup from me; yet not my will, but yours be done.' An angel from heaven appeared to him and strengthened him. And being in anguish, he prayed more earnestly, and his sweat was like drops of blood falling to the ground (Lk. 22:39-44; Mt. 26:36-46; Mk. 14:32-42; cf. Jn. 12:27-28).

Such anguish and prayer are the eternal Son's own in His humanity. The paradox cannot be removed. The One who is incapable of suffering suffers.[43] Beyond the paradox there lies the question—why. Why did the Messiah have to suffer and thus enter His glory? (Lk. 24:26)

2. The Atonement

From what the Gospels tell us, Jesus saw the Father's will as being the reason for His passion and death. That will intended that Christ's death be offered "for the many," as a ransom, in which His blood shed for man would be a covenant between God and man. Essential in such ideas are the concepts of obedience and vicarious suffering wherein the freely willed suffering of the One who is just would benefit the many who are unjust.

In various ways and forms these ideas appear in the apostolic preaching and writings of the New Testament. The metaphor of ransom (Gk. *lutron, lutromai, lutrosis,* normally translated as some form of "redeem" or "redemption") appears frequently. We are redeemed, ransomed by Christ and by His death, the shedding of His blood. Typical of such descriptions are the following:

> For you know that it was not with perishable things such as silver or gold that you were redeemed from the empty way of life handed down to you from your forefathers, but with the precious blood of Christ, a lamb without blemish or defect (1 Pt. 1:18-19).
>
> ...We wait for the blessed hope—the glorious appearing of our great God and Savior, Jesus Christ, who gave himself for us to redeem us from all wickedness and to purify for himself a people that are his own, eager to do what is good (Ti. 2:13-14).[44]

Another usage was that of "propitiation" (Gk. *hilasmos, hilasterion)*—an offering made to placate or please God, an atonement offering. St. Paul uses both the idea of Redemption and atonement or propitiation in his epistle to the Romans when he writes:

> ...For all have sinned and fall short of the glory of God, and are justified freely by his grace through the Redemption (Gk. *apolutroseos)* that came by Christ Jesus. God presented him as a sacrifice of atonement (Gk. *hilasterion),* through faith in his blood (Rom. 3:23-25; cf. Heb. 9:5, and, for propitiation, 1 Jn. 2:2; 4:10).

The Fathers of the Church, in their own writings on the work of Christ, basically repeated the variety of New Testament concepts and terminology. It was only with St. Anselm of Canterbury (1033-1109) and his classic work, *Cur Deus Homo* (written 1092-1094), that an effort was made to systematize the teaching of Jesus Himself and the N.T. writers.[45]

St. Anselm's thesis in essence was this: Sin had violated the dignity of God's majesty by failing to give Him the honor which was due Him. That violation was an outrage which demanded satisfaction. However, because it was the infinite dignity of God which had been violated, no finite man was capable of making truly adequate satisfaction. Therefore, God became a man so that the value of the human actions of Christ would be that of a divine Person and thereby capable of adequately satisfying for the injury done to God's honor. As Anselm had his questioner summarize the doctrine:

> You showed by many conclusive arguments that the restoration of human nature ought not be neglected, and that it could not be accomplished unless man paid to God what he owed for sin. But the debt was so great that, although man alone owed the debt, still God alone was able to pay it, so that the same person would have to be both man and God. Hence it was necessary that God assume human nature into the unity of His person, so that the one who in His nature owed the debt and could not pay it, should be, in His Person, able to pay it.[46]

Anselm's views were significantly modified by subsequent theologians, especially by St. Thomas Aquinas, and the fundamental points of that synthesis remain the common property of Catholic theology.

Sacred Scripture frequently describes the human race as object of God's anger or wrath. As we read in St. John's Gospel, "Whoever believes in the Son has eternal life, but whoever rejects the Son will not see life, for God's wrath remains on him" (Jn. 3:36). Paul, too, refers to this wrath of God.

> But because of your stubbornness and your unrepentant heart, you are storing up wrath against yourself for the day of God's wrath, when his righteous judgment will be revealed. God "will give to each person according to what he has done." To those who by persistence in doing good seek glory, honor and immortality, he will give eternal life. But for those who are self-seeking and who reject truth and follow evil, there will be wrath and anger (Rom. 2:5-8; cf. Eph. 5:6).

As Paul makes clear in the context of the first chapters of that same epistle, this wrath of God is not to be understood as God's hatred of the human race. It is rather a way of describing what happens when God "gives them over" (cf. Rom. 1:24, 26) to their sinful desires and shameful lusts. Man's rejection of God brings its own consequences (Rom. 1:26-32), the greatest of which are igno-

rance, death, and the inability to change the sinful situation. Once
sin enters the world through Adam, so that all his descendants are
subject to sin and death because of him (Rom. 5:18-19), there is no
one capable of achieving that reconciliation with God which will
restore life and holiness. This incapacity is due, according to
Aquinas, not to the fact that finite man cannot satisfy for an infinite
wrong, but rather because of the *universal* scope of the sin.
Following Paul and Augustine, Thomas saw that the disobedience of
Adam lost for human nature the original goodness bestowed by
God.

> ...The privation of original justice is a sin of nature, in the sense
> that it has its origin in the inordinate will of the first principle in
> human nature, namely, of the first parent.... And so it is
> transmitted to all who receive human nature from him, for they
> are all, as it were, his members.[47]

> ...The reparation of human nature could not be effected either
> by Adam or by any other purely human being. For no
> individual man ever occupied a position of preeminence over
> the whole of nature; nor can any mere man be the cause of
> grace.[48]

In short, what was lost to the race because of its solidarity in a
now sinful nature could only be restored by the One who originally
created man good. Only God can freely give that condition of union
with Himself which we call grace. This He could have done, of
course, by a free bestowal of pardon. However, for reasons known
ultimately only to Himself, He decided to work according to the
mode of justice: He willed that the race make up or satisfy for its
evils and thereby be reconciled to Him.

This demand for justice—an adequate compensation for the
evil done—is able to be seen by us as maintaining an overall order
or harmony in creation. It is the restoration of a balance. Mankind
sins; mankind makes up for the evil committed. However, we are
also capable of discerning that God's plan ran deeper than mere
juridical balancing. By demanding adequate compensation and then
by giving the race the ability to meet the demand, God in fact
ennobled and dignified humankind. Becoming man Himself, He
gave us the power to do for ourselves what, of ourselves, we were

not able to do. Reconciliation with Him is achieved within the race. The Liturgy of the Eucharist describes His work in just this fashion.

> We see your infinite power
> in your loving plan of salvation.
> You came to our rescue by your power as God,
> but you wanted us to be saved by one like us.
> Man refused your friendship,
> but man himself was to restore it
> through Jesus Christ our Lord
> (Preface III for Sundays in Ordinary Time).

> You sent him as one like ourselves,
> though free from sin,
> that you might see and love in us
> what you see and love in Christ
> (Preface VII for Sundays in Ordinary Time).
> (The Sacramentary)

Man saves man. To make that possible, God Himself became a man so that what He achieved as man would be for the glory of man, would be to man's credit. "The work of divine justice always presupposes the work of mercy and is founded on it."[49] In writing those words, Aquinas set forth the reason why God demanded justice for the offenses committed against Him. The demand for justice was the condition for showing His mercy—a mercy which, in Christ, raised us to new heights when He called for justice while giving us the capacity to fulfill it. St. Paul describes it as a new creation.

> ...If anyone is in Christ, he is a new creation; the old has gone, the new has come. All this is from God, who reconciled us to himself through Christ and gave us the ministry of reconciliation; that God was reconciling the world to himself in Christ, not counting men's sins against them.... Be reconciled to God. God made him who had no sin to be sin for us, so that in him we might become the righteousness of God (2 Cor. 5:17-21).

The principle of solidarity, absolutely fundamental to a correct understanding of Christ's work, is evident in this passage from Paul. It is in Christ and through Christ that we become the new creation. Just as solidarity with Adam is the root of our sinfulness, so solidarity in Christ is cause of holiness and glory. What Christ did He did for us, and we did it in Him. As Paul points out, it was this solidarity with us that made Him, who was sinless, to be sin for us so that, in Him, we might become righteous. Appealing to the same notion of solidarity as seen in the vicarious suffering of the Servant, St. Peter writes:

> He himself bore our sins in his body on the tree, so that we might die to sins and live for righteousness; by his wounds you have been healed. For you were like sheep going astray, but now you have returned to the Shepherd and Overseer of your souls (1 Pt. 2:24-25).

This solidarity in Christ which ennobled the whole human race and made the race capable, in Him, of fulfilling the demands of God's justice is also what makes all who live in Christ associates with Him in the Redemption.

> Near the cross of Jesus stood his mother, his mother's sister, Mary of Clopas, and Mary of Magdala. When Jesus saw his mother there, and the disciple whom he loved standing nearby, he said to his mother, '...Here is your son,' and to the disciple, 'Here is your mother.' From that time on, this disciple took her into his home (Jn. 19:25-27).

That little group which remained faithful to Jesus during His passion is the first to be associated with Him as He bore our sins in His body on the tree. Of the association of His followers in Christ's work, the Second Vatican Council said:

> ...The Redeemer's unique mediation does not exclude but rather gives rise to a multiform cooperation among creatures—which cooperation is only a share in this Unique Source.[50]

Among such associations, the one which is preeminent and in itself unique, is the role of His Mother.

> Suffering with Him as He died on the cross, she cooperated by her faith, hope and ardent love in a totally singular manner with the work of the Savior in restoring supernatural life to souls. Because of that, she is Mother to us in the order of

grace. And this maternity of Mary in the economy of grace
...will endure without interruption until the eternal fulfillment
of all the chosen.[51]

The solidarity of the Son of God and our race in suffering
manifested itself in many ways during the passion. By the mystery
of the Incarnation, God had become a man, the Son of a nation
which suffered the status of what we today call a "minority" group.
Although innocent of any crime, He was judged guilty by the
dominant political, social and military elite (the Romans), was
libeled, tortured, bore the stigma of incarceration and "legal"
execution. To His executioners He was undoubtedly just another
insignificant Jew, a disposable commodity. In truth He was the chief
victim of the "Holocaust," whether that holocaust be the ones—up
to and including Auschwitz—that His nation has suffered historically or the ones that innumerable defenseless "minorities," including the unborn child in the womb, have and do suffer at the hands of
those who have power over them.

Christian thought has always had the task of setting forth
reasons for the "fittingness" or suitability of the mystery of the cross.
As the Church sings in the Liturgy of the Hours, there is a certain
"divine harmony" or symmetry in the mysteries of our fall and our
Redemption.

De parentis protoplasti
fraude factor condolens
quando pomi noxialis
morte morsu corruit,
ipse lignum tunc notavit
damna ligni ut solveret.

(He, our Maker, deeply grieving
That the first-made Adam fell,
When he ate the fruit forbidden
Whose reward was death and hell,
Marked e'en then this Tree, the ruin
Of the first tree to dispel.

Hoc opus nostrae salutis
ordo depoposceret,
multiformis perditoris
arte ut artem falleret,
et medelam ferret inde,
hostis unde laeserat.

Thus the work of our salvation
Was of old in order laid,
That the manifold deceiver's
Art by art might be outweighed,
And the lure the foe put forward
Into means of healing made.)[52]

The Fathers of the Church were fascinated by this "divine
harmony" (the *ordo depoposceret* of Fortunatus' hymn) and found

the cross prefigured in many Old Testament images. Aquinas summed up many of them when he wrote:

> This type of death corresponds to many figures. As Augustine says in his sermon *On the Passion*, a wooden ark saved the human race at the time of the Flood;...at the time of the Exodus, Moses put the wood into the bitter water and made it sweet (Ex. 15:23); by his wooden rod, Moses made saving water flow from the spiritual rock (Ex. 17:5; 1 Cor. 10:4);...the Law of the Lord was contained in the wooden Ark of the Covenant...etc. [53]

Death entered the world as a result of the sin of Adam's disobedience when he ate the fruit of the tree. In the divine harmony, Christ obediently took upon Himself the result of sin, namely death, and, by dying on a tree, undid the cause by enduring the consequence. To the disobedience of Adam (and, in Adam, all who sin) is counterpoised the obedience of Christ; to the tree of Eden is counterpoised the tree of Golgotha.

The fundamental element in such reasoning is the divine will which decreed that death should destroy death; that the freely willed death of Christ should destroy the death of sin and ultimately the physical death which has its origin in sin (cf. Gn. 3:2-3, 19; Rom. 5:12-21: DS 1512, 1521). Unlike Isaac, who was destined for sacrifice but was spared (Gn. 22:1-18), God "did not spare his own Son, but gave him up for us all" (Rom. 8:32).

The idea that Christ's death was a sacrifice, willed by God and freely offered by Jesus Himself in His human will, is a truth taught in the New Testament. Paul, in the text just quoted, compares it with the (incomplete) sacrifice of Isaac. Elsewhere he compares it with the sacrifice of the Paschal Lamb.

> Get rid of the old yeast that you may be a new batch without yeast—as you really are. For Christ, our Passover Lamb, has been sacrificed. Therefore let us keep the Festival, not with the old yeast, the yeast of malice and wickedness, but

with bread without yeast, the bread of sincerity and truth (1 Cor. 5:7-8; cf. Eph. 5:2; Ex. 12:1-20; Mt. 16:5-12 and parallels).

St. John alludes to the sacrifice in his reference to the Lamb of God who is slain as the Passover lambs are being prepared (i.e., killed) for the celebration (cf. Jn. 1:29; 19:28-37; cf. Rv. 5:6). The epistle to the Hebrews is a treatise on Christ's perfect sacrifice in comparison with the sacrifices of the Old Law. Using the theology of that epistle, the Council of Trent solemnly defined the sacrificial nature of Christ's death and the presence of that sacrifice in the Mass.

> Since there was no perfection in the Old Testament because of the weakness of the Levitical priesthood, it was necessary (because God the Father of mercies so ordained it) that there arise another Priest 'according to the order of Melchizedek,' our Lord Jesus Christ who would be able to perfect all those who were to be sanctified, and bring them to perfection (cf. Heb. 10:14). Therefore, He, our Lord and God, although He was to offer Himself to God the Father once and for all through His death on the cross in order to work the Redemption, was not to have His priesthood extinguished (cf. Heb. 7:24, 27). At the Last Supper, on the night He was betrayed, He left His beloved spouse the Church a visible sacrifice (visible in accord with the needs of human nature) by which that bloody sacrifice offered once and for all on the cross would be represented and its memory last until the end of time....[54]

Neither the Bible nor the Council of Trent attempted to explain what constituted a sacrifice in the general sense of the word. Human experience made that general meaning obvious: an offering to God (or, in the case of pagans, to the gods) to honor Him and show human dependence on Him, while seeking His favor. What is astounding in the case of Christ is that God who, throughout His revelation of Himself to Israel, had repeatedly rejected human sacrifice should, in this one case, will the sacrificial death of one Man, His own Son.

The scandal created by the apparent fact that an all-good and all-merciful God should will Christ's death to restore the human race was faced by St. Anselm in his *Cur Deus Homo*. Anselm's initial answer seems to offer "a way out" in the face of the many N.T. texts which speak of Christ's death as a necessity, or as a result of the Father's will (cf., for example, Lk. 24:26; 9:22; 22:22; Jn. 12:27; 18:11; Mt. 26:39 and parallels).

> As I see it, you fail to distinguish His doing something under the requirement of obedience, and His enduring what happened to Him, without obedience requiring it, because He persevered in obedience.

> Therefore, God did not compel Christ to die, there being no sin in Him. But Christ freely endured death, not by giving up His life out of obedience, but by obeying a command to preserve justice, in which He persevered so unswervingly that He endured death as a result.[55]

In this view, what is *directly* willed by the Father and by His Christ is faithfulness to a ministry of truth and goodness. However, given the nature of evil to strike out against the good, Christ's faithfulness in the concrete circumstances of His own life would only be preserved if He willingly submitted to the death His enemies prepared for Him. Thus, the Son's death would be indirectly willed by the Father or willed contingently or conditionally.

The answer is not truly satisfactory, as Anselm himself apparently saw. All of the elements which seem contingent or conditional to us were, in reality, part of God's plan. He knew the outcome, chose the time of the Incarnation, chose that is, the circumstances and the *dramatis personae* of His own life in human history—and chose it always foreseeing the outcome. In short, He could have arranged a different outcome, but chose the one which in fact happened. One is left with the truth already seen: the *natus ad hoc* of Fortunatus' poem. He was born to die; He became man to die the sacrificial death of the cross.

> ...When Christ came into the world, he said: 'Sacrifice and offering you did not desire, but a body you prepared for me.... Then I said, "Here I am—it is written about me in the scroll—I

have come to do your will, O God!" ' First he said, 'sacrifices and offerings, burnt offering and sin offerings you did not desire, nor were you pleased with them.... Then he said, "Here I am, I have come to do your will." ' He sets aside the first to establish the second. And by that will, we have been made holy through the sacrifice of the body of Jesus Christ once for all (Heb. 10:5-10).

The mystery of the Father's willed sacrifice of the Son has at times been portrayed in completely unacceptable terms. Appeal is made to one of the words of Jesus from the cross (the "My God, my God, why have you forsaken me?" of Mt. 27:46 and Mk. 15:34) to substantiate the thesis that Jesus died forsaken by God,[56] and that the Father had made Him "sin for our sakes": exacting from Him the penalty for sin. The text, however, will not bear the weight put on it. The words "My God, my God, why have you forsaken me?" are the first words of Psalm 22 which is a song of a man whose lament in misery is answered favorably by God. In no way is it a prayer of despair, but rather one where apparent abandonment by God serves as the occasion for the manifestation of God's love and mercy. Neither Jesus Himself, nor Matthew and Mark, can be credited with being unaware of the significance of a prayer which depicts sufferings so like Jesus' own, and which ends as thanksgiving for God's saving presence.

Of course, much Christian piety has appealed to these same words as evidence, not of the Father's abandonment, but of Jesus' own intense anguish in His passion. And, indeed, that anguish was real. Human nature could not face the prospect and then the reality of such a death without dread and intense physical and mental suffering. As Scripture makes clear, Jesus, too, experienced such forms of anguish (cf. Jn. 12:27; Lk. 12:49-50; Mt. 26:39 and parallels; Heb. 5:7-8). The death of Jesus of Nazareth was not the stoic and almost placid death of Socrates as described by Plato in the *Phaedo*. It was a death of great horror and pain, but not one without the consoling presence of God. In the passion of Christ, God was yet— and for Jesus—the "Father of compassion and the God of all comfort, who comforts us in all our troubles" (2 Cor. 1:3-4). As Paul makes clear in the very context of those words, the comforting presence of God does not wipe out the human emotions of "distress" (2 Cor. 1:6) and pressure so great that it seems beyond human power to endure, even to the point that life is despaired of (2 Cor. 1:8-9). The idea that abandonment by God is necessary to feel the fullness of human misery seems based on the false notion that God's presence is the antithesis of pain. Calvary proves that it is no such thing. Indeed, as we know from the mystics, in this life on earth a conscious awareness of God's presence can be the very crucible of pain.

Furthermore, to assert that Jesus died abandoned by the Father or that the Father exacted from the Son the bloody debt of human sin is to misunderstand both the mystery of the Hypostatic Union and the mystery of the Trinity. The One who died on the cross as Man is the eternal Son, God Himself. He cannot in truth be claimed to have abandoned Himself. Even the claim that it was in His humanity that He would have experienced such abandonment is but another form of the "psychological" Nestorianism which would divide the Incarnate One against Himself. It is God Himself in His humanity who dies—not merely a human nature ontologically or psychologically separated from the divinity. By similar reasoning, it cannot be said that the Father stood apart *vis à vis* the suffering Son. The early heresy of Patripassianism which held that it was the Father Himself who died on the cross was erroneous because it denied the reality of the Son and Spirit, except inasmuch as they were modes or manifestations of the Father. Like most heresies, however, there was something of truth in its position. It is the One God who gave Himself to humanity in the Incarnation. He demanded from our race that price for sin which, as one of us and to elevate us, He Himself would pay. Since, in His expression of Himself to Himself and to others, it is His Word that is expressed, it is as His own Word that He was incarnate and died. Nonetheless, it was Himself, the one God, who expressed Himself thus and gave Himself. In giving His Word, the Father gave of His very self, the fullness of His own Being. Jesus' words to Philip are as true of the mystery of the cross as they are of all the rest of Jesus' life.

Anyone who has seen me has seen the Father. How can you say, 'Show us the Father'? Don't you believe that I am in the

Father, and that the Father is in me?... It is the Father, living in me, who is doing his work (Jn. 14:9-10).

The cross is as full a manifestation of the Father's giving of Himself as it is of the Son's. Their mutual giving of Each to the Other is never interrupted, even as the Son died.

When you have lifted up the Son of Man, then you will know who I am and that I do nothing on my own but speak just what the Father has taught me. The one who sent me is with me; he has not left me alone, for I always do what pleases him (Jn. 8:28-29).

One need not claim a Trinitarian ontology for such a statement (although in fact every human statement presumes some ontology or metaphysic) in order to understand its main thrust: what Jesus says and does, the Father says and does in Him, since the Son is always *from* Him, and *of* Him, and *for* Him. The mystery of our atonement and the statement "One of the Trinity suffered" remind us not only of the immense evil of sin but of the Trinity in Unity who gave Himself for us. In His goodness, He raised up a human will, His own, to share in His work. The "Father, if it is possible, let this cup pass" is neither more nor less human than the "but not my will, but yours, be done." The suffering is real, the conformity of wills complete.

The events of Golgotha are, of course, inexplicable when viewed as an end in themselves. They were never viewed as such by God nor by the human mind and will of Jesus. It was "for the joy set before him" that He "endured the cross, scorning its shame" (Heb. 12:2). The cross—like the divine decree that satisfaction should be made for sin—was never willed for itself, but only for the sake of the glorification of humanity in Christ.

V. THE DESCENT INTO HELL

The glorification that the Incarnation and death of God achieved for mankind manifested itself in the consequences which these events had for other humans. The Apostles' Creed succinctly refers to this when it confesses: "He suffered under Pontius Pilate, was crucified, died and was buried. He descended into hell...."

The phrase about Christ's descent into hell was not contained in the earliest version of the Roman or Apostles' Creed, but is found there in the fourth century in a version of that same creed known to Rufinus—the Aquileian Creed upon which he wrote a commentary in the early 400's.[57] Reference to the theme, moreover, can be found in Eastern writing of a considerably earlier date.[58]

The Quicumque or Athanasian Creed mentions the descent into hell,[59] and the *Firmiter* of Lateran IV (1215) solemnly professes:

For the salvation of the human race He suffered and died on the wood of the cross, descended into hell, rose from the dead and ascended into heaven. He descended in His soul and rose in His flesh, and ascended in soul and flesh.[60]

While it is certainly part of Tradition, attested to by ancient authorities, and forms part of solemn and infallible professions of the Church's faith, the witness of the N.T. to the doctrine is obscure. Among the Fathers, various passages were cited (e.g., Acts 2:24; Mt. 12:39; Eph. 4:9) as referring to this mystery, but other and more convincing interpretations can be offered for each of them. Only a text in the first Epistle of Peter seems to offer any real possibility as a N.T. reference.

For Christ died for sins once for all.... He was put to death in the body but made alive in the spirit, through which also He

223

went and preached to the spirits in prison who disobeyed long
ago when God waited patiently in the days of Noah while the
ark was being built.

...This is the reason the gospel was preached even to those who
are now dead, so that they might be judged according to men in
regard to the body, but alive to God in regard to the spirit (1 Pt.
3:18-20; 4:6).

The text is certainly generally associated with Christian imagery about the descent into hell, but the meaning of the passage is
very obscure, with neither traditional nor modern agreement as to
its meaning.[61]

Fortunately, the meaning of the doctrine is clearer than the
question concerning its Scriptural origins. The earliest understanding of it may have viewed it as a statement equivalent to the "He
died and was buried" of the Creed.[62] Very early, however—perhaps
simultaneously—it was also seen as an expression of Christ's salvific
work in favor of those who had died before His coming. The Lord
had gone among the dead to apply to those who had longed for His
coming the fruits of His satisfactory death. It is this view that
predominates in the Church's beautiful second reading for the
Liturgy of the Hours on Holy Saturday.

There is a great silence on the earth—a great silence and even
solitude. A great silence because the King sleeps. The earth
feared and was quiet, because God slept in the flesh and raised
up those who slept from the beginning of the ages. God died in
the flesh, and earth trembled. He has gone in search of the first
parent, as though for a lost sheep. He wished to find those who
were sitting in darkness and the shadow of death. He who was
their God and their Son has gone to free from sorrow captive
Adam and captive Eve.... The Lord approaches them and says,
'I, your God, who for your sakes have become your son,...say
to you, Rise!... Rise, let us leave this place. The Enemy led you
out of the earthly paradise; I, however, will place you, not in a
paradise, but on a heavenly throne.'[63]

Fallen mankind is represented here in the first Adam as the
New Adam proclaims the salvation He has acquired for the race.
The scene is picturesque and filled with symbols. Indeed, the

mystery of the descent into hell would seem to cry out to be "demythologized." No such thing is needed, however, since the imagery is readily seen to serve the truth being proclaimed. One is not dealing here with the "geography" of man's life after death, but rather with a fundamental Christian truth: all who are saved are redeemed by the merits of Christ's death, and the effects of that death are not to be limited by space or time. Just as His Mother was preserved from all sin in anticipation of His coming, so the effects of His work are applied "retroactively" to those who had died anticipating His coming.[64]

The descent of Christ into hell, then, when it is not restricted in its meaning to a mere repetition of the truth of His death (a restriction which the Church does not countenance), is the foundational doctrine for the Church's proclamation of the possibility of salvation even for those who die not knowing the Christ.

> These, also, can reach eternal salvation who do not know the Gospel of Christ or His Church, through no fault of their own, but who sincerely seek God and, under the influence of grace, seek to do His will in their works as that will is known to them through the dictates of their conscience.[65]

Christ's activity among the dead as we profess it in the Creed can serve to remind us, also, of another allied truth. By the sin of Adam, the "gates of heaven" were closed to mankind, not "to be opened" until the victory of Christ. The language again is pictorial. As expressed by Aquinas, it means that "eternal happiness which consists in the full enjoyment of God" was unattainable to mankind until the race had expiated its guilt in Christ. St. Thomas makes his treatment of this fact a commentary on a text in Hebrews.

> When Christ came as high priest of the good things that are already here, he went through the greater and more perfect tabernacle that is not man-made, that is to say not a part of this creation. He did not enter by means of the blood of goats and calves; but he entered the Most Holy Place once for all by his own blood, having obtained eternal redemption (Heb. 9:11-12).

The first man to "see God in the face" was the Son of God become man and He did it as the "first fruits," the first among many brethren born from the dead.

VI. THE RESURRECTION

Men of Israel, listen to this: Jesus of Nazareth was a man
accredited by God to you by miracles, wonders and signs....
This man was handed over to you by God's set purpose and
foreknowledge; and you...put him to death by nailing him to
the cross. But God raised him from the dead, freeing him from
the agony of death, because it was impossible for death to keep
its hold on him. David said about him: '...therefore my heart is
glad and my tongue rejoices: my body also will live in hope,
because you will not abandon me to the grave, nor let your
Holy One see decay....' Brothers, I can tell you confidently
that the patriarch David died and was buried, and his tomb is
here to this day. But he was a prophet and knew that God had
promised him on oath that he would place one of his
descendants on his throne. Seeing what was ahead, he spoke of
the resurrection of the Christ, that he was not abandoned to the
grave, nor did his body see decay. God has raised this Jesus to
life, and we are all witnesses of the fact (Acts 2:22-32).[66]

The words are St. Luke's version of Peter's speech at Pentecost. As Luke presents it, the speech is the earliest proclamation of
the Christian message. It declares that Jesus was handed over to
death according to "God's set purpose and foreknowledge," that He
actually died, but that God "raised him" (Gk. *anestesen*), having
loosed the bonds of death. This raising was such that His body was
not abandoned to the grave, nor did it see decay—a freedom from
corruption already prophesied by Psalm 16 as Peter interpreted it.
It is clear that Jesus' body is not corrupting in any tomb—unlike
David's—and hence, there cannot be a place where reverence is

227

offered to the deceased Jesus. Indeed, Peter and his companions are "witnesses" to the fact that Jesus has been raised to life, although no reference is made to any appearances of Jesus.

The account of the resurrection in the Gospel of Mark, whose connection with Peter is attested to by Papias (c. 65-125 A.D.) and finds modern support,[67] bears certain similarities to the Petrine speech in Acts 2. As we have it, Mark's Gospel ends with chapter 16:1-8. Verses 9-19 of that chapter, inspired and canonical, were added later. In the first eight verses, the women are described as going to the tomb, finding the stone rolled away, and, on entering, being greeted by a "young man" (angel) with the words:

> You are looking for Jesus of Nazareth, who was crucified. He has risen: He is not here. See the place where they laid him. But go, tell his disciples and Peter, 'He is going ahead of you into Galilee. There you will see him, just as he told you (Mk. 16:6-7).

It is then noted that "trembling and bewildered, the women went out and fled from the tomb," saying "nothing to anyone because they were afraid" (Mk. 16:8). There, whether by design or accident (whether, that is, Mark intended to end at that point or whether his original ending has been lost) Mark's account ends. Like Peter's sermon in Acts 2, it tells of an empty tomb, explained by the proclamation, "He has risen." No account is given of appearances, although the "there you will see him" anticipates such appearances.[68]

This lack of stress on the appearances of the risen Lord finds a counterpoint, however, in St. Paul's first letter to the Corinthians, written in the mid 50's.

> For what I received I passed on to you as of first importance: that Christ died for our sins according to the Scriptures, that he was buried, that he was raised on the third day according to the Scriptures, and that he appeared to Peter, and then to the Twelve. After that, he appeared to more than five hundred of the brothers at the same time, most of whom are still living, though some have fallen asleep. Then he appeared to James, then to all the apostles, and last of all he appeared to me also, as to one abnormally born (1 Cor. 15:3-8).

The empty tomb plays as little part here as the appearances play in the texts from Acts and Mark. It is only later—so it is frequently said—that efforts are taken to "integrate" the empty tomb and the appearances so as to give a picture of what began to happen on the first day of the week which followed Jesus' death. (We speak here, of course, of "integration" in the sources we have at hand.) At this point, various questions may arise: What actually happened first? What form or forms did the original proclamation of the Easter message take? Was Paul unaware of or did he reject the fact of the empty tomb? And so forth.

There are almost innumerable solutions proposed to the historical and literary difficulties raised (or capable of being raised) by the various N.T. witnesses to the resurrection of Jesus. In outline form, a couple can be presented here just to indicate the complexity of the problems and the multiplicity of opinions.

Proposed Solution A.

If one may presume that Luke is substantially accurate in his presentation of the first proclamation of the resurrection as Peter gave it on Pentecost, and that Mark 16:1-8 is the conclusion of the first written Gospel and reflects the catechesis of Peter, then it is possible to speak of the "primitive Petrine kerygma." In that proclamation, the empty tomb is central, indicating the fulfilling of prophecy and the Father's reversal of the judgment passed on Jesus by those who condemned Him. The "Incorrupt One" has been proclaimed Lord and Messiah (cf. Acts 2:36) by the Father. The process which led Peter to this conviction is basically this. The "material" element, if one may put it that way, is his viewing of the empty tomb (cf. Lk. 24:12; Jn. 20:3-8);[69] the "formal" element is the appearance of the risen Jesus to Peter (cf. 1 Cor. 15:5; Lk. 24:34). Thus, the appearance serves the same basic function as the angelic proclamation, "He has risen"—a giving-of-meaning to the sight of the empty tomb.[70] In subsequent preaching, the "material" element is emphasized because the preaching itself acts as "formal" element; consequently, there is no elaboration of the appearances in Peter's first preaching or in the ending of Mark's Gospel which reflects that preaching. Later on, Paul, in order to substantiate his claim to be an Apostle, a witness to the resurrected Lord, and unable to do so by claiming a presence "on the scene" at the time of the empty tomb, will stress the appearances as that which constitute one an official witness. The later Gospels will strive to integrate both elements.

Proposed Solution B.

In this proposal, the original kerygma is viewed as best reflected in 1 Corinthians 15 and other Pauline references since they are the earliest testimonies we possess.[71] The accounts of the empty tomb are "secondary" or later elements of tradition.[72] Indeed, the story of the tomb may have developed from an early "cult" wherein believers went to the site of Jesus' burial in reverent "pilgrimage." Such "pilgrimages" would end with the proclamation that "He lives," "He has risen," "See the place where they laid Him." Whether the tomb was actually empty is moot.[73] With time, the account of the discovery of the tomb became a confirmatory and then an apologetic tool, a clear example of which is Matthew's account of the stationing and bribing of the guards (Mt. 27:62-66; Mt. 28:11-15).[74] In any case, the resurrection faith rests on the experiences of the risen One as described in the various appearances, whose number, location and "objective" quality are matters difficult, if not impossible, to ascertain.

The above "solutions" are a pastiche of opinions—certainly not comprehensive and not to be found in their "pure" form, although variations on "B" can be discovered in a relatively pristine state. Now, each of the various elements in either proposal has been or could be defended with much elaborate argumentation and, in many cases, the citation of many authorities. Likewise, an adequate critique of these and similar proposals would necessitate elaborate argumentation and numerous citations. Such not being possible, only some general observations can be made.

What is involved directly is not theology as such—although the impact on theology is great—but rather the logic or method to be followed in historical and literary criticism. Neither history nor literature develop according to the rules of logic, but the sciences of historical and literary criticism should.

The first "rule" of logic or methodology which would seem to apply is this: the criteria for literary criticism and the criteria for historical investigation must be kept distinct.

Literary criticism and historical investigation are two disciplines. They can be related and corroborative of one another, but an automatic transposition of methods and conclusions can be made only at the risk of destroying accuracy. As corollaries of this truth, the following should be noted:

a) Literary priority need not indicate historical priority. If someone is dealing with two works which treat, more or less, the same general matter, and if one can determine their relative dates of publication, it does not automatically follow that the *information* contained in the work more recently published is less accurate, or of a more recent date, or of less value than the information contained in the account written earlier. The dating and accuracy of the information contained in each work is a question in its own right, whose solution may be advanced by knowing the relative dates of publication but which may not be decided by that knowledge alone. Therefore, one must be cautious in speaking of "primary" or "secondary traditions," when what one is really speaking about is date of writing, not the dating of the contents. If, for example, Saint Paul does not refer to the empty tomb whereas Matthew, who wrote after Paul, does refer to it, one cannot conclude, on the basis of the date of the Matthean composition alone, that the accounts concerning the tomb are "secondary" in the sense that such accounts were known only after the time of Paul's writing. Nor can it be concluded logically that Paul's failure to mention something means he either did not know, or knew and rejected the item not mentioned. Paul, for example, never mentions John's baptism of Jesus in the Jordan. To conclude that he did not know the fact, or rejected it as a fact is an "argument from silence" leading to indefensible conclusions.

It is sometimes said that the relative date of a N.T. text can be judged by the type of Christology manifested in it. For example, the reference to Jesus as the "servant of God" in the Acts of the Apostles (e.g., 3:13, 26; 4:27, 30) is seen by some as an example of an early Christology, not nearly as developed as the notion of preexistence or the ideas contained in the titles "Lord" or "Messiah."[75] Therefore, since the "Servant Christology" is primitive, those texts in which it is found can be said to represent a primitive stratum of the traditions about Jesus. The conclusion in an individual case may be true, but it rests on dubious presuppositions. For it seems to be presumed that the title used in a particular context says all that there is to say or can be said about Jesus at a particular period, or says all that the author or speaker does or can say at a particular time. But that presupposition is often demonstrably wrong. Were I to give a sermon on Jesus as "Son of Mary" and never mention in it His eternal filiation from the Father or His Incarnation, it would certainly be a sermon which has not said all that could be said about Him, but it need not reflect an "adoptionist Christology." So it is in the New Testament. Many examples of supposedly "primitive" Christological titles can be found in works which also contain "more advanced Christologies." Peter, for example, who calls Jesus "Servant" also is depicted as calling Him Messiah, Lord, Holy and Righteous One, Author of Life (Acts 2:36; 3:14, 15), the "one chosen before the creation of the world and revealed in these last times" (1 Pt. 1:20), etc. Does the use of the one title reveal a "more primitive" stage in Peter's thinking than do the other titles? Perhaps so, but not necessarily so. Various factors, other than a "primitive" or "advanced" Christology, can influence the use or nonuse of a title.[76]

Similar cautions must be applied to the attempts to translate a text or phrase from the Greek New Testament back into a so-called Aramaic "original" and thus argue for the primitive nature of the text or phrase. All that process actually proves is that the text is *capable* of having come from Aramaic, or that the author may have thought in Aramaic patterns. Some of Joseph Conrad's works are susceptible of such a process *vis à vis* Polish, his original tongue, but the process is wrong if it concludes that his English masterpieces work from a Polish original.

b) Having determined a "literary form" does not necessarily mean that one has determined the historical reliability of what is contained in the form. We may take as an example Matthew's account of the stationing of the guards at the tomb and the subsequent bribing of those same. Here we clearly have a case of apologetic or polemic literature. Matthew 28:15 would seem to make that conclusion evident. However, to conclude that, because the literary form is apologetic or polemic, the facts stated in such a piece of literature are not true is to draw an invalid conclusion. Counter-argument based on fact or perceived fact is the normal form of apologetic. The form may be apologetic; the truth or facticity of what is contained in the apologetic form is a separate question.

As regards that separate question, one can argue that Matthew could not have known what actually took place between the chief priest and Pilate or between the chief priests and the guards. That may be true; it may even be probable. It is not, however, self-evident. We presently have no way of ascertaining what information Matthew did or did not have access to. The same must be said for his account of what took place between Pilate and his wife (Mt. 27:19). It is possible that there was greater access to such information than we imagine—access provided by people close to the "higher circles" of Palestinian society in the 30's, 40's and 50's of the first century. Indeed, there are indications that such was the case (e.g., Joseph and Nicodemus; Joanna, the wife of Herod's steward Chuza; Manaen).

c) The determination of literary forms tells us nothing, in itself, about the date of the matter contained in the forms. Thus, there is nothing in the nature of narrative which indicates it must necessarily precede in time that literary form called philosophical discourse. Likewise, there is nothing in the nature of kerygmatic or creedal proclamation which indicates that it must precede narrative. In fact, in this case, the opposite should be expected, although it cannot be shown to be so of necessity. The claim, for example, that the kerygmatic statement "The Lord has risen and has appeared to Simon" (Lk. 24:34)—or others like it—precedes a narrative account of the events cannot really be substantiated.[77] In truth, narratives can be constructed around such phrases, but it is also true that such phrases are already—at least generally—the summation of a yet earlier narrative form. "I came, I saw, I conquered" is a summation of Caesar's campaign in Pontus, not a phrase on which the history of that campaign is to be constructed.

The text in 1 Corinthians 15:3-8 is indicative of this point. As a written source of information about Jesus' resurrection it is undoubtedly early. General consensus dates it to the mid-50's, thus about twenty-five or so years after the resurrection. Furthermore, Paul claims that he is reminding the Corinthians of what he had told them previously. The form his reminder takes is quite certainly a synopsis, one which he is quoting (as some think) or drawing up on his own. That synopsis is the beginning of an apologetic-polemical argumentation, since he is attempting to counter the position of some in Corinth who have false ideas about the resurrection of the dead in general (1 Cor. 15:12ff.). His purpose, then, is not to reteach the apostolic message about Jesus. Rather, that message is summarized in order to draw further conclusions or arguments from it. The fact that he is giving no full presentation of the death and resurrection of Jesus is clear from the phrase—twice repeated— "according to the Scriptures." He does not present again the scriptural "proofs." These, he implies and we must conclude, the Corinthians had already heard. So it is with his list of witnesses. Behind the statements "he appeared to Peter," "he appeared to the Twelve," "he appeared to James," there lie narratives of events. We must conclude that each of the five hundred whom he mentions as being still alive had a "story to tell." What the stories were, and whether Paul himself or the Corinthians knew those stories are items of information we do not know, and probably never can know. Our sources are too limited.

In the same way, it must be concluded that a narrative or catechesis lies behind the summary "he was buried...he was raised on the third day according to the Scriptures." Whether and to what extent the narrative was like the other accounts we have of the passion and resurrection cannot be ascertained with any claim to historical certitude. All we can presume with reasonable certitude is that the formulas are a synopsis. Nor can we conclude rightly that, because he is using the synopsis apologetically, Paul is inventing the facts. Indeed, the mention of the five hundred, "most of whom are still living," is—at the very least implicitly—asserting that part of the summary he gives can be checked for accuracy.

The synopsis does not mention the empty tomb. Whether this is implied because of the narrative which lies behind the "he was buried...he was raised" is something about which we can form opinions, not historical conclusions.

The above leads directly to a second "rule" of logic or method for literary criticism or historical verification: extreme caution must be taken in respect to the results of "source reconstruction."

It cannot be doubted that various "sources" lie behind the various documents of the New Testament. The sources were many and multiform, written and oral. Unfortunately, none of our documents give a bibliography, and we have no direct access—at least none that is undisputed—to the sources used for any of them. Even in the cases where we know a source (e.g., the preaching of Peter is surely a source), we have no direct information as to the content of the source material (apart, that is, from what Luke tells us in Acts), nor how it influenced a given document. Efforts to reconstruct suspected sources—as with "Q" for example—are certainly legitimate, but good scientific method will view the reconstructed source with greater reserve than one views the document for which sources are being sought. Even when an attempted reconstruction can claim some success as a working hypothesis, it is never safe to presume that one has reconstructed all the information contained in the hypothetical source.

In the case of the resurrection, some of the source reconstructions have little claim to serious consideration. An example would be the hypothesis which posits an early Christian cult "pilgrimage" as the milieu from which the account emerged (cf. Proposed solution "B" above). This process of reasoning can only be described as proceeding from the problematic (viz., what is the precise origin of the accounts?) to the unknown (viz., the cult of hypothesis, for which there is no evidence whatsoever as a Christian phenomenon before the third century) and then using the unknown to rule out the more probable (viz., that the tomb narratives ultimately rest on the testimony of the various people mentioned in the narratives). Such a procedure defies logic. Even the fact that there is some evidence of a Jewish cult of the dead in the first century offers nothing more than a possibility that Jewish Christians could have venerated the tomb of Jesus in some analogous sense.

It must be noted, too, that the danger of circular reasoning is a very real one when dealing with source reconstruction. One uses the documents at hand to reconstruct their sources and then uses the sources to explain or interpret the documents. Little of value can be gained from such a process as far as historical evidence is concerned.

A third "rule" to be employed in evaluating the historical worth of documents would be: differences and even conflicts in detail, or an inability to harmonize what is reported in various documents, should not be allowed to outweigh the points of agreement, nor should the differences be ignored.

In the Gospel accounts of the resurrection there are many conflicts in detail and an apparent inability to harmonize all that is asserted. How many women went to the tomb, and what was their reason for going? Was there one angel, or two angels? Did the women say nothing to anyone, or did they run and tell the disciples? Did Peter go to the tomb alone, or did the beloved disciple go with him? Where did Jesus appear first, in Jerusalem or in Galilee? When did the "Ascension" take place—on Easter Sunday or forty days later? Where did it take place? A careful reading of the accounts readily provides such questions and others like them.

On the other hand, there is remarkable unanimity on other things. In all the Gospel accounts, the Magdalene goes to the tomb, it is found empty, a commission is given to inform the disciples, Jesus Himself appears (in the case of Mark, it is said that He will appear) to His followers. It is these common assertions to which we must now turn since it is they which form the core of the message.[78]

1. The Tomb

> This is what the Sovereign Lord says: O my people, I am going to open your graves and bring you up from them: I will bring you back to the land of Israel. Then you, my people, will know that I am the Lord, when I open your graves, and bring you up from them (Ezekiel 37:12-13).

Through Ezekiel God used these words to offer Israel hope for return from its exile in Babylon. What was figurative language then for the prophet and his people took on new depths of meaning on the first day of the week which followed Passover in the year 30. "You will know that I am the Lord, when I open your graves...." The emptying of the tomb is primarily a manifestation of God's power. He who creates from nothing brings life from death.

All four evangelists record the discovery of the empty tomb.[79] On what evidence they base their testimony is something much discussed and the subject of numerous and frequently contradictory theories. St. Luke tells us that both Peter (Acts 2:22ff.) and Paul (Acts 13:32ff.) preached it in the sense that Jesus' body was not left to undergo corruption. Paul, in his Epistles, never mentions it directly.

It is of some significance that when Matthew wrote his Gospel the non-Christian Jews with whom he had contact were not denying that the tomb was empty, but rather explained its emptiness by saying the body of Jesus had been stolen (Mt. 28:15). This admission by the opponents of the Christian message would be even more significant if we could know when and where it was made. Did it represent the general position of the Jews, or only of some in a localized area? And how soon after 30 A.D. did the Jewish counter-charge begin to circulate? However, since we do not know where and when Matthew wrote his Gospel, such questions cannot be satisfactorily answered.

The fact of the tomb's emptiness finds some support, too, from other subsequent historical events. That Jesus is Messiah and that God raised Him from the dead is a message first preached in Jerusalem within a short time of Jesus' public execution. It has frequently been noted that such preaching could have found little hearing if a tomb containing the deceased's body could have been pointed to.[60]

The charge that the body of Jesus was taken away still dead was a possibility that occurred not only to Jewish adversaries, but even to those Jews who had followed Jesus. John tells us that the Magdalene's initial reaction was just that (Jn. 20:13-15). Both cases are sufficient to remind us that an empty tomb is no proof that the one buried there had returned to life. Nonetheless, in the light of the subsequent appearances of Jesus, the empty tomb played a confirmatory role and an educative one. Without the empty tomb there would be a certain ambiguity about the appearances. The empty tomb is an assurance of the continuity between the body which was buried and the One who appeared. God may and does transform what He has created; He does not discard it. As distasteful as it is to a gnostic or platonist or an idealist, the empty tomb is a sign of the "fleshiness" of the resurrection. Ignatius of Antioch saw this already when he wrote:

As for me, I am sure and believe that He was in the flesh even after the resurrection. When He came to Peter and His companions, He said, 'Touch me and see that I am no ghost without a body.'[81]

The Church's Magisterium has repeated the same doctrine:

We confess that He freely suffered in the flesh for our salvation, that He was crucified in the flesh, that He died in the flesh, that He rose on the third day in the same glorified and incorrupt flesh.[82]

He rose in the flesh (*Firmiter* of Lateran IV).[83]

The same truth is recalled when the Christian venerates the body of Christ in the Eucharist. The Reality hidden there is hailed as the "True body, born of Mary":

Ave verum corpus natum	(Hail, true Body,
De Maria Virgine;	Born of Mary Virgin,
Vere passum, immolatum	And which truly suffered and
In cruce pro homine!	Was immolated on the cross
	for mankind!)[84]

When he made his prophecy about David's descendant, Isaiah said:

In that day the Root of Jesse will stand as a banner for the peoples; the nations will rally to him, and his place of rest will be glorious (Is. 11:20).[85]

That "place of rest" for Jesus was neither Jerusalem nor the tomb, but the eternal rest promised by God (cf. Ps. 95:11 and Heb. 3:15—4:8). The glory of the empty tomb is simply this: it is a sign that for His body there was a "place of rest" which was not death.

2. The Appearances

That which was not seen dead in the tomb was soon seen not "by all the people, but by witnesses whom God had already

chosen...who ate and drank with him after he rose from the dead"
(Acts 10:41). The evangelists and Paul refer to these appearances of
Jesus after His death.

Much has been written about the *opthe* of 1 Corinthians 15:5-8.
It is the passive voice of the Greek *horao* which is the English verb
to see. In the passive it means "was seen" or, in some cases,
"appeared." St. Paul uses it in the active and passive voices, when
he writes about his own experience of the risen Christ: "Have I not
seen Jesus our Lord" (Gk. *heoraka;* 1 Cor. 9:1); "...last of all he was
seen by me..." (Gk. *opthe;* 1 Cor. 15:8).

Since he uses both in the same epistle, it is doubtful he thought
of any significant distinction as existing between the active and
passive forms of the verb. He even uses another word to describe
what may be (but is not certainly) the same experience (cf. Gal.
1:16). Once he even calls the experience a "vision" (Acts 26:19). In
this case, however, it could be Paul's thought, but Luke's wording
since Luke's use of the verb *to see* can be applied to the appearances
of angels as well as to the appearances of the risen Lord (cf.
Lk. 24:23).

In short, the meaning of the word *to see* as used concerning the
risen Christ must be understood from its context, not from a
dictionary definition. In itself, the word allows for various types of
"seeing." When one looks for the context, St. Paul is not much help.
He tells us *that* Jesus appeared; he never tells us *how* or *in what
form* He appeared. St. Mark in 16:1-8 only tells us that He would
appear. It is Matthew, Luke and John who help us to contextualize
the "seeing" involved when Jesus manifested Himself after His
death.

St. Matthew tells us that Jesus "met" the women coming from
the tomb and that they "clasped his feet and worshiped him" (Mt.
28:9). Luke tells us that, when He appeared to the Eleven, they
thought they were seeing a ghost. Jesus had to reassure them by
offering Himself to be touched and then by eating before them (Lk.
24:36-42). John tells us that He showed the disciples "his hands and
side" (Jn. 20:20) and offered the same for them to touch (Jn. 20:27).
For these three evangelists then, the context of "seeing" is tactile.

There is no mere "appearance." The risen One has a body, can be touched as well as seen, can and does eat. John even says He bears the marks of His passion.

A claim is frequently made to the effect that, for didactic and/or apologetic reasons, these three evangelists have "filled in" details which did not form part of the original Easter proclamation as evidenced in Paul's epistles or in Mark 16:1-8.[86] The claim is arbitrary and lacking support. All that can be said reasonably is that Matthew, Luke and John are saying more than Paul or Mark say. Neither Paul nor Mark contradict what is asserted by the others. Whence the others drew their information is unknown to us, if one concludes that Luke is not accurately portraying Peter's preaching in Acts 10:41. Is it possible that the evangelists were giving an inspired "interpretation" of the resurrection appearances at a time when there was a tendency to mitigate or "spiritualize" their reality? Yes, it is possible, but one may not argue from a possibility to a fact and call it history.

We are not free to conclude from the emphasis placed on the reality of Jesus' risen body that the evangelists are guilty of a naïve materiality or are talking about the simple resuscitation of a corpse comparable to what happened to Lazarus, the daughter of Jairus, and the son of the widow of Naim. The Jesus who lives after His crucifixion is different. His appearances, for example, are capable of leaving some with doubts. Matthew says this explicitly:

> Then the eleven disciples went to Galilee, to the mountain where Jesus had told them to go. When they saw him, they worshiped him; but some doubted (Mt. 28:16-17).

Luke and John also make it clear that Jesus was not immediately recognizable or could not be recognized until He allowed it (cf. Lk. 24:15; Jn. 20:15; Mk. 16:12; and perhaps Jn. 21:4-7). All three relate that He came and went suddenly—even locked doors being no obstacle (Mt. 28:9; Lk. 24:36; Jn. 20:19, 26). It is clear, too, from the accounts of His return to the Father that Jesus no longer lived the type of bodily life we are accustomed to.

Some find a similarity between such indication and what Paul writes concerning the resurrection of the dead.

But someone may ask, 'How are the dead raised? With what kind of body will they come?' How foolish!... The body that is sown is perishable, it is raised imperishable; it is sown in dishonor, it is raised in glory; it is sown in weakness, it is raised in power; it is sown a natural body, it is raised a spiritual body.... The first man was of the dust of the earth, the second man from heaven. As was the earthly man, so are those who are of the earth; and as is the man from heaven, so also are those who are of heaven. And just as we have borne the likeness of the earthly man, so shall we bear the likeness of the man from heaven (1 Cor. 15:35-49).

For Paul, there is a continuity between the body which is buried and the body raised. But there is also a vast difference. He highlights some of the differences, and summarizes by calling one a "natural body," the other a "spiritual body." Here, as in other places, he refers to the risen Christ as the model of what our life will be. It must be observed, nevertheless, that in 1 Corinthians 15:38-58, Paul is not attempting to explain the kind of risen body which Jesus has, but rather the kind of body others who have died will have (1 Cor. 15:35). He is dealing, then, not with a resurrection on the third day after death, as he proclaims in the case of Jesus (1 Cor. 15:4), but with one postponed indefinitely. There is also no direct equivalent between the resurrection of Jesus and ours. The Lord's resurrection is firstfruits and model of ours; our resurrection will be like His. His resurrection will be the cause of ours. The cases are analogous, not identical. For such reasons, we cannot transpose what Paul writes about the resurrection of the dead in general to the resurrection of Jesus without making allowances for the differences. Although he never directly mentions the empty tomb, there is no indication either that Paul envisioned a "reconstructed" body for the Lord—or even some newly created body. With those cautions, it is probably fair to describe the body of the risen Lord as a "spiritual body" in the sense that, while still a real body and indeed the body which had been buried, it is not now subject to the ordinary laws of earthly bodies.

At times a distinction is made between the words "resuscitation" and "resurrection" in order to avoid a naïve materialism when considering the resurrected Lord. It is then stated that what happened to Jesus was not a "resuscitation." The distinction can be helpful, but it can also be somewhat deceptive. In the case of "resuscitation" we have some positive concept from experience of the reality being described—if only in the sense that we are aware of medical resuscitations, the recall to life of someone already apparently dead. Resuscitation means the resumption of those vital activities and forms of being and acting with which we are familiar.

Resurrection, on the other hand, is an analogous term. It is a comparison with something else with which we are familiar in order to give us an idea of something with which we are not familiar. The New Testament vocabulary itself makes this fairly evident. The usual words for resurrection are the Greek verbs *egeiro* and *anistamai* which mean "to waken" or "to rise," respectively. The noun, *anastasis*, likewise means a "standing up," a "raising up." Even before the time of the New Testament writings, these words were used to describe what was a "waking up from" or "rising from" the dead. In the New Testament, other words as well were used to describe what happened to Jesus after His burial. Peter, in the sermon from Acts quoted above, spoke of Him as being "exalted to the right hand of God" (Acts 2:33). Paul uses the same word in Philippians 2:

> ...He humbled himself and became obedient to death—even death on a cross! Therefore God exalted him...and gave him the name that is above every name... (Phil. 2:8-9).

Such language, and similar expressions, should not be viewed as an alternative to "resurrection language" in the sense of having a temporal or theological priority.[87] They are but different formulations for describing the same reality or highlighting various aspects of it. Analogous language, by its nature, is like what we know, but reminds us that what is being described is yet more unlike our point of reference. So, especially, with the resurrection It is certainly like a "raising up," a "waking from sleep," a "lifting up," etc. In that sense it is like what we know to be a "resuscitation." A dead body comes back to life. But it is unlike any of these descriptions because it is so much more. And, from that point of view, it is not a "resuscitation." We must strive simultaneously to balance the "like" and the "unlike," the identity between the body of Jesus which was buried and His body which was raised—as well as the differences in that body.

This identity between the body which died and was buried and rose, as well as the change involved, is what the Church teaches:

> Note two things. First: Jesus rose again with the same body He had taken from the Blessed Virgin, but in new conditions, vivified by a new and immortal animation, which imposes on Christ's flesh the laws and energies of the Spirit.... Second: this new reality...is so far above our capacities of knowledge even of imagination that it is necessary to make room for it in our minds through faith.[88]

VII. THE ASCENSION

When he had led them out to the vicinity of Bethany, he lifted up his hands and blessed them. While he was blessing them, he left them and was taken up into heaven. Then they worshiped him and returned to Jerusalem with great joy (Lk. 24:50-52; cf. Acts 1:3-11; Mk. 16:19).

Since St. John tells us that Jesus' words to Mary Magdalene on the morning of the resurrection were: "I am returning to my Father and your Father, to my God and your God" (Jn. 20:17), it is probably correct to conclude that the risen Lord entered heaven in glory on Easter itself.[89] It is from heaven, then, that He appears to the Twelve and to the others in that series of manifestations written about by Paul and the evangelists. These appearances, intended to confirm the faith of His followers and prepare them for their future ministry, came to an end, says St. Luke, after a period of forty days (Acts 1:3). Then, in a final appearance, Jesus is taken up from their sight, marking an end to one phase in the history of the Incarnate God. St. Paul recognized this fact when he describes the appearance made to him as having come outside of the proper time (1 Cor. 15:8).

The end of the Easter appearances was not the termination of Jesus' activity in human history. In various ways, all the evangelists indicate this truth. The Gospel of John, which in a sense has two endings (Jn. 20:30-31; 21:25) comes to a close without recording any departure of Jesus. Luke follows his Gospel with Acts, telling us thereby that the formation of disciples of the Lord continues. Matthew ends with the Lord's own promise to remain: "And surely I will be with you always, to the very end of the age" (Mt. 28:20).

And the canonical ending of Mark makes clear that it is the Lord
Himself who continues His work through the disciples.

> After the Lord Jesus had spoken to them, he was taken up into
> heaven and he sat at the right hand of God. Then the disciples
> went out and preached everywhere, and the Lord worked with
> them and confirmed his word by the signs that accompanied it
> (Mk. 16:19-20).

It is frequently debated whether Jesus' resurrection and
ascension are facts of the historical order.[90] The various answers
given depend to a very great extent on how one defines history and
on what criteria one will rely for historical verification. Normally,
the testimony of eyewitnesses is considered a fine historical source.
Now, the events in question claim to have the authority of
eyewitnesses. People claim to have found the tomb empty and to
have seen Jesus alive after He had been buried. Those witnesses
were so convinced and were so convincing that the historical reality
called the Church began to grow and continues to this day. The
leader of the group of witnesses, Simon Peter of Galilee, and many
others gave their lives as evidence.[91] However, what is being
witnessed to in this case is so far beyond the ordinary and is so
fraught with consequences that there never has been agreement on
what should be required for verification. In truth, once a person
accepts the fact that a human has risen from the dead and is
operative in earthly history two thousand years later the ordinary
notion of history has to be enlarged. Acute Jewish theologians
rejecting the terminology B.C. and A.D. and preferring to use C.E.
(the Common Era) and B.C.E. (Before the Common Era), implicitly
recognize the different view of history which logically follows the
acceptance of a risen Jesus.[92] The Christian message clashes with a
non-Christian view of history. For the sake of apologetics, the
Christian will continue to argue "history" and present arguments for
historical verification of what took place in the year thirty. In reality,
however, A.U.C. and all its variants ended that year.

> Christ, yesterday and today,
> the beginning and the end
> Alpha and Omega,
> all time belongs to him
> and all the ages.[93] (The Sacramentary)

VIII. JESUS CHRIST IS LORD

Jesus Christ "through the Spirit of holiness was declared with power to be Son of God by his resurrection from the dead..." (Rom. 1:4).

The exaltation of Jesus in His resurrection and ascension is not only manifestation and proof of His claims, but—as in all other events in His life—a revelation of the Father's glory. In Philippians, Paul writes:

> ...At the name of Jesus every knee should bow, in heaven and on earth and under the earth, and every tongue confess that Jesus Christ is Lord, to the glory of God the Father (Phil. 2:10-11).

So much is the resurrection to be seen as a work for the glory of God the Father that it is generally described in the New Testament as the Father's action. It is He "who raised Jesus our Lord from the dead" (Rom. 4:24). Only in St. John's Gospel do we find a direct statement on Jesus' own power to raise Himself (Jn. 10:17-18). That Jesus had the power to raise Himself is, of course, an article of faith. Pope Paul VI declares it so in his profession of faith.

> He was buried, and by His own power rose on the third day....[94]

The two ways of speaking about the causal power of the resurrection are but different manners of expressing the same reality. It is God who raises the dead to life. In His divinity and equality with the Father, the Son exercises that power. Anyone who overstresses one formula in preference for the other is picturing the

Father as "hoarding" a prerogative from the Son or *vice versa*. Such thinking is a total misunderstanding of the divine Equality and Power. Nonetheless, the more common terminology—the Father raised the Son—serves to remind us of the one great reality of Jesus' life, indeed of His divine Person: He is from, of, and for the Father. He does what He has learned from the Father; it is the Father who works in Him. It is the one God revealed to us in and through the eternal and co-equal Son.

So manifest is the Father's work in the resurrection that it becomes the great motive of belief. No longer do we believe simply in the God of Abraham, Isaac and Jacob, the God who led our fathers through the desert. We now "believe in him who raised Jesus our Lord from the dead" (Rom. 4:24).

The Father's glory is the glory of the Son, and the Son's glory is ours because He shares our humanity. In the hymn in Philippians, St. Paul reminds us that the Father has glorified the Son and has done it as a result of the Son's freely willed obedience unto death.

> ...He humbled himself and became obedient unto death—
> even death on a cross! Therefore God has exalted him...and
> gave him the name that is above every other name (Phil. 2:8-9).

Christian thought has rightly captured the force of the "therefore" when, as St. Thomas writes, it says that "through His passion Christ earned or merited His exaltation."[95] His human nature is exalted and glorified in the resurrection. That humanity is then given primacy of place, governance and jurisdiction over all of creation. Even the angels who, in themselves, were the highest realizations of God's creative power, the pinnacle of the ordered structure of the universe, are made subject to the God-man. Citing Psalm 8, the epistle to the Hebrews says:

> It is not to angels that he has subjected the world to come....
> Someone has testified: 'What is man that you are mindful of
> him, the son of man that you care for him? You made him a
> little lower than the angels; you crowned him with glory and
> honor and put everything under his feet.' In putting everything
> under him, God left nothing that is not subject to him. Yet at
> present we do not see everything subject to him. But we see

Jesus, who was made a little lower than the angels, now crowned with glory and honor because he suffered death, so that by the grace of God he might taste death for everyone (Heb. 2:5-9).

In the last verse of this citation, the author of Hebrews invokes the principle of solidarity. Jesus tasted death for everyone; the one for the many. The glorification of His humanity is likewise for everyone. In his exaltation, our human flesh reigns.

Tremunt videntes angeli	(The angels tremble when they
versam vicem mortalium:	see how changed is the lot of
culpat caro, purgat caro,	humanity. Our flesh had sinned,
regnat caro Verbum Dei.[96]	our flesh was cleansed, for the
	Word of God reigns in the flesh.)

What happens to our humanity in Him happens to us. "From the fullness of his grace we have all received one blessing after another" (Jn. 1:16).

In his proclamation before the Sanhedrin, Simon Peter proclaimed:

It is by the name of Jesus Christ of Nazareth, whom you crucified but whom God raised from the dead, that this man stands before you completely healed.... Salvation is found in no one else, for there is no other name under heaven given to men by which we must be saved (Acts 4:10-12).

This statement, an expression of what "exaltation" means when we speak of the exaltation of Jesus, is shocking in its ramifications. It highlights the awesome "particularity" of the Incarnation and Redemption. Creation has been made subject to a Jewish carpenter. God became man only once, in only one place, at only one time, and He took His humanity from only one people. His risen flesh is that same flesh, Israel's through Mary of Nazareth. The Lord's own saying, clear enough in itself, is not merely a reference to temporal origins. It is always true: "salvation is from the Jews" (Jn. 4:22). The resurrection and exaltation of His flesh guarantee this truth. It is truth enough to choke any anti-semite. "God's gifts and his call are irrevocable" (Rom. 11:29). The remnant of Israel which accepted their Messiah and ours is but the beginning, so that time might be given for the Gentiles to hear the word. "But if their transgression means riches for the world, and their loss means riches for the Gentiles, how much greater riches will their fullness bring! ...For if their rejection is the reconciliation of the world, what will their acceptance be but life from the dead?" (Rom. 11:12-15)

The "Jewishness" of it all is not the only particularity. "Salvation is found in no one else," proclaims Peter. Many have, do and always will see such a statement as the arrogance of Christianity. What of Buddha, Confucius, Mohammed and the great religious and philosophical movements initiated by their lives? What about the forms of prayer, the depth of thought, the riches of tradition found in non-Christian religions? In a society which for more than a millennium was Christian, it is easy to overlook or to be oblivious to the particularity, the exclusivity of Peter's claim. The early Church saw it. St. Justin (died c. 165) tried to answer the difficulty by showing how all good men, to a greater or less degree, participated in the Truth which is the divine Word. Aquinas repeated that answer, reminding us that every truth, by whomsoever it is spoken, is from God Himself, a share in His Truth.[97] The consequences of such an answer are manifold, the ultimate source of religious dialogue and ecumenism. But the particularity remains: Jesus of Nazareth is Lord; He is the Truth, not in partial form, but in the very fullness of God become man.

The temporal particularity is more manifest in our day than it was when Peter first proclaimed it. God became incarnate, lived, thought and spoke in a fundamentally agrarian society of the first century. In the twentieth century, his "You have heard it said...but I say to you" demands the same adherence it demanded then, because He is the same, yesterday, today and forever (cf. Heb. 13:8). How strong the temptation to "universalize" and "modernize" Him. The desire to "open our eyes and be like God" (cf. Gn. 3:4-5) is only blocked now by faithfulness to the very particularity of the Second Adam.

This particularity of the God-man raises a problem, moreover, from the point of view of mankind's solidarity with and through Him. We say that, in Him, our human nature has risen from its fallen condition, has been ennobled and given preeminence in the created order. All that is true of our human nature as it is found in

Him, but what of that nature as found in us as individuals? We share Adam's fall by descent. By propagation we inherit the nature which was Adam's to pass on, i.e., a wounded and sinful nature. How, though, do we "inherit" what our humanity has achieved in Christ?

One answer would be that of "juridical imputation." From this point of view, God would credit to us what had been accomplished by and in Christ. He would accept the many for the sake of the One. By faith in Christ, we would, in a sense, appropriate to ourselves what is proper to Him. In fact, the reality is much more profound. Our solidarity with and in Christ is not representative nor juridical, but real. To approach an understanding of that truth, one must examine the words of Jesus at the Supper when, speaking of His exaltation, He said:

> It is good for you that I am going away. Unless I go away the Counselor will not come to you; but if I go, I will send him to you (Jn. 16:7).

The work of our salvation was not completed on Calvary. Paul writes: Christ "was delivered over to death for our sins and was raised to life for our justification" (Rom. 4:25). The Lord, risen and exalted, is He who sends the Spirit and through that Spirit the work of our salvation is completed in Christ.

IX. THE SPIRIT

If we work from what the Creed of Nicea says about the Holy Spirit, and do so in reverse order, we find that He 1) spoke through the prophets, 2) is Lord and Giver of life, and 3) is He by whose power Mary conceives and brings to birth the Christ.

1. He Has Spoken Through the Prophets

One aspect of the Christian preaching of the resurrection of Jesus was that it happened "according to the Scriptures," i.e., according to what the Old Testament had foretold. This proclamation appears frequently in the New Testament in various forms (cf. 1 Cor. 15:4; Lk. 24:27; Jn. 20:19; Pt. 1:10-12; Acts 2:24-32), and in the Nicene Creed as well:

> "On the third day he rose again in fulfillment of the Scriptures."

It can be said with some justice that, before the Gospels were written, the Old Testament itself served as Gospel for the Christian community. The life, death and resurrection of Jesus were found recorded there. Not only do all the evangelists and St. Paul refer to such fulfillment of prophecy, but Jesus Himself is said to have done so (cf. Mk. 12:10-12; 14:27; Lk. 24:44-48, etc.).

Now it must be admitted that the New Testament authors use the Old Testament with a freedom in citation that is frequently quite amazing and even alien to us. St. Matthew, for example, tells us that the words of Jeremiah 31:15 are "fulfilled" when the Holy

Innocents are slaughtered by Herod (Mt. 2:17-18) and John tells us that Exodus 12:46 is "fulfilled" when the side of Jesus is lanced, His legs being left unbroken (Jn. 19:36-37). Such citations are likely to appear forced from our point of view. Others, however, are more readily seen. In all cases a cautious study must be made both of the original text and its application in order to understand what type of fulfillment is being written of. What is involved, however, is more than simply scientific exegesis. The scriptures are literature intended not only to convey facts, but also to stimulate the imagination, to form a life of prayer, and to nourish faith. They are, for a Christian, the work of one Author who sums them all up in Himself when He became man. The "according to the Scriptures" is an article of Faith which proclaims that Jesus, the Word made flesh, is the interpretative key for understanding the Bible. This traditional truth has been repeated by the Second Vatican Council.

> The economy of the Old Testament was most especially ordained to prepare the coming of Christ...and the Messianic kingdom, to announce this coming prophetically (cf. Lk. 24:44; Jn. 5:39; 1 Pt. 1:10) and to signify it by various types (cf. 1 Cor. 10:11).

> Therefore, God, the inspirer and author of the books of both Testaments, wisely arranged that the New Testament would be hidden in the Old and that the Old would be manifested in the New.[96]

This "according to the Scriptures" involves even more than Jesus being the interpretative key to the understanding of the Old Testament. The phrase reminds us the Spirit is our tutor in Christ and the one who causes us to know all things (cf. 1 Jn. 2:20). He is tutor because it is He who spoke through the Law and the prophets, leading to Christ. He causes us to know all things about Christ because He takes what belongs to Jesus and makes it known to us (Jn. 16:13-15). It is this prophetic role of the Spirit which partially explains the work of the Spirit. His work is Christo-centric; He leads history and individuals to Christ. This very fact is part of the difficulty Christians experience in knowing the Spirit Himself. He seems to have no "personality" of His own. In the mystery of God, we may say that this is the way it is intended. Emile Mersch wrote the following which touches on the point.

> ...We believe we should be in error were we to search for the place of the Spirit outside that of Christ, and to say, for example, that He comes to contribute the finishing touch....
>
> In reality, no separation may be made. The Spirit is all and accomplished all in His own way, just as the Father and Son are all and accomplish all in their way. But everything is summed up in the Incarnation and in the Incarnate Word, and the explanation of the Spirit's work has to be found within the totality of Christ.[99]

2. Lord and Giver of Life

Within the totality of Christ, the role of the Holy Spirit is analogous to His role within the Trinity. He is the "bond of unity." This role He fulfills in the union He effects between Christ and Christians, causing them to live Christ's own life, and, in Christ, making them "sharers of the divine nature" (2 Pt. 1:4). It is the Spirit who brings about that solidarity in Christ which makes Jesus' life and work something much more real than merely "standing in" for us.

The depth of the union which would exist between Christ and His followers was indicated by the Savior Himself during His ministry. He compared Himself as Bridegroom in relation to them (Mt. 9:14-15 and parallels); He said that anyone who received His disciples received Him (Mt. 10:40; Lk. 10:16; Mk. 9:37). In His preaching on the judgment, He makes the identity existing between Himself and others the norm for admission into eternal life.

> For I was hungry and you gave me something to eat, I was thirsty and you gave me something to drink, I was a stranger and you invited me in.... Amen, I say to you, whatever you did for one of the least of these brothers of mine, you did it for me (Mt. 25:35-40).

St. John tells us that, at the Supper, Jesus prayed for this union, while comparing it to the very union which exists between Him and the Father.

> I pray also for those who will believe in me through their message, that all of them may be one, Father, just as you are in me and I am in you. May they also be in us... (Jn. 17:20-21).

The Lord's first words to Saul of Tarsus, on the road to Damascus, were a repetition of the same truth (cf. Acts 9:4-5). Whoever persecutes a disciple persecutes the Lord. The truth struck deep roots in Paul and we find his epistles filled with references to the Christians living "in Christ." Looking for the reason for this union of life and being between the risen Lord and His followers, Paul found it in the Eucharist.

> Is not the cup of thanksgiving for which we give thanks a participation in the blood of Christ? And is not the bread that we break a participation in the body of Christ? Because there is one loaf, we, who are many, are one body, for we partake of the one loaf (1 Cor. 10:16-17).

The words are an expression of Paul's realization that the Eucharist effects a union between the flesh of Christ and His followers which has no earthly counterpart and for which the two-in-one-flesh union of marriage is but a sign (cf. Eph. 5:31-32).

> For my flesh is real food and my blood is real drink. Whoever eats my flesh and drinks my blood remains in me, and I in him.... I live because of the Father, so the one who feeds on me will live because of me (Jn. 6:55-57).

The union of Christ and His disciples is achieved in the flesh through Eucharistic Communion. The union is so intimate that the receiver shares not only Christ's body, but the very life which Christ receives from the Father. It is thus that what was achieved by and in the Lord becomes the "common property" of all who live in Christ. His obedience, His sacrifice unto death, the raising and exaltation of our nature in Him—all this becomes ours who live in Him. The Apostle could exclaim in truth:

For you have died, and your life is now hidden with Christ in God. When Christ, who is your life appears, then you also will appear with him in glory (Col. 3:3-4).

Commenting on the sixth chapter of St. John, St. Thomas wrote:

> He has eternal life who eats and drinks not only sacramentally but also spiritually. Indeed he eats and drinks sacramentally who receives this sacrament. He eats and drinks spiritually, however, who reaches the reality of the sacrament which is twofold: 1) the reality contained and signified, namely the whole Christ who is contained under the species of bread and wine; 2) the reality signified but not contained, namely the Mystical Body of Christ which exists in the predestined, the called, and the chosen.

> Whoever spiritually eats and drinks becomes a sharer in the Holy Spirit, through whom we are united to Christ by a union of faith and charity, and through whom we are made members of the Church.[100]

The risen Lord gives the Spirit of Life, and He does it normally through the instrument of His flesh in the Sacrament of the Eucharist. In this way the Spirit of Christ becomes the Spirit of the believer, uniting the Lord and His followers in one life, gradually transforming the life of the disciple until it be completely conformed to Christ. It is His work in effecting this conformity which we recognize when we call the Holy Spirit the "Spirit of adoption." It is as conformed to Christ by the Spirit that we ourselves can approach the Father, laying claim to what is, in Christ, now ours by right.

> ...You received the Spirit of sonship. And by him we cry 'Abba, Father.' The Spirit himself testifies that we are heirs—heirs of God and co-heirs with Christ if indeed we share in his sufferings in order that we may also share in his glory (Rom. 8:15-17).

The epistle to the Hebrews, writing of the exalted Lord, speaks of Him as priest and says:

...Because Jesus lives forever, he has a permanent priesthood. Therefore he is able to save completely those who come to God through him, because he always lives to intercede for them (Heb. 7:24-25).

The book of Revelation speaks of the same intercessory role of the risen Christ when it describes the "Lamb, looking as if it had been slain" (Rv. 5:6). It is the Lamb of Golgotha, living now in glory. He unites with His priestly intercession the priestly people (cf. 1 Pt. 2:5) when He unites them with Himself through Eucharist and Spirit. This mystery of the common priestly prayer was a truth dear to St. Augustine who saw all the Psalms as a prayer of Christ, Head and members.

It is Christ, therefore, who here speaks in the prophet; yes, I dare to affirm, Christ is speaking. The prophet will utter certain things in this Psalm which may seem impossible of application to Christ, to that excellence of our Head, above all to that Word which in the beginning was God abiding with God. Sometimes, too, certain other things will be said which seem scarcely relevant to Him who has taken the form of a servant, the form He took from the Virgin. And yet it is Christ speaking, because in Christ's members Christ Himself speaks.[101]

It was for the formation of this solidarity in Christ through the Spirit that it was good for us that Jesus departed (Jn. 16:7). The mystery of the Incarnation is complete only when what He has achieved becomes ours in Him through the Spirit who brings us to share His life.

3. Conceived by the Holy Spirit and Born of the Virgin Mary

In his letter to the Galatians, St. Paul compares his work as an Apostle to the pain of a woman in labor.

My dear children, for whom I am again in the pains of childbirth until Christ is formed in you... (Gal. 4:19).

The comparison is apt because, spiritually speaking, the history of mankind since the resurrection is the mystery of being born in Christ.

> ...Speaking the truth in love, we will in all things grow up into him who is the Head, that is, Christ. From him the whole body, joined and held together by every supporting ligament, grows and builds itself up in love, as each part does its work (Eph. 4:15-16).

The process by which the risen Lord joins to Himself all those who are His own will last until the consummation of earthly history. In the thought of Augustine, it is the coming to birth of one Man, the whole Christ, the Head and the Body.[102] In that process, the Holy Spirit and the Virgin Mother continue the work which started with her "Yes" at Nazareth to the angel Gabriel. Every person who comes in time to exist "in Christ" is "conceived by the Holy Spirit and born of the Virgin Mary," those who came to be "not of natural descent, nor of human decision or a husband's will, but born of God" (Jn. 1:13). A priestly people is begotten to exist in the one Priest who, in Himself and in His members, through the Spirit, intercedes now before God, praying as He has always prayed: "Abba, Father."

Frequently Used Abbreviations

I. *Versions of the Bible*

NIV — New International Version of the Holy Bible, Zondervan, Grand Rapids, Mich., 1979.

NAB — New American Bible.

RSV — Revised Standard Version of the Holy Bible

II. *Other*

Acta Synodalia *Acta Synodalia Sacrosancti Concilii Oecumenici* *Vaticani II*, Polyglot Press, Rome, 1978, 25 volumes.

DS Enchiridion Symbolorum, Editio XXXII, H. Denzinger and A. Schönmetzer, editors, Herder, Rome, 1963.

Enchiridion Patristicum editor M. J. Rouet de Journel, S.J., Herder, New York, 1962.

JBC *The Jerome Biblical Commentary*, Prentice-Hall, Inc., Englewood Cliffs, New Jersey, 1968.

S. Th. Summa Theologica of St. Thomas Aquinas, BAC, Madrid, 1951.
English translation of the Summa: *Summa Theologiae*, (Thomas Gilby, O.P. editor), McGraw-Hill Book Co., New York, 1964ff., 61 volumes.

TPS *The Pope Speaks*, a quarterly of Church Documents, OSV Press, Huntington, Ind.

Vorgrimler *Commentary on the Documents of Vatican II*, 5 vols. (H. Vorgrimler, editor), Herder and Herder, New York, 1969.

The Sacramentary (English Translation Prepared by the International Commission On English in the Liturgy), Catholic Book Publishing Co., N.Y., 1974.

III. *Documents of Vatican Council II*

Ad gentes Decree on the Missionary Activity of the Church

Dei Verbum Dogmatic Constitution on Divine Revelation

Gaudium et spes Pastoral Constitution on the Church in the Modern World

Lumen gentium Dogmatic Constitution on the Church

Nostra aetate Declaration on the Relationship of the Church to Non-Christians

Sacrosanctum concilium Constitution on the Sacred Liturgy

Full bibliographical material is found in Bibliography.

Notes for Introduction

1. *The Works of Flavius Josephus* (William Whiston, trans.), *Life*, (2), vol. II, p. 5.
2. *Idem.*, vol. IV, p. 11.
3. A recent appraisal of the *Testimonium Flavianum* by a Jewish historian can be found in Avi-Baras, *History of the Jewish People*, vol. 8, Appendix, pp. 303-313. Cf. C. K. Barrett, *The New Testament Background: Selected Documents*, pp. 197-199.
4. Tacitus, *The Annals of Imperial Rome* (Michael Grant, trans.), Penguin Books, London, 1981, p. 365.
5. Suetonius, *The Twelve Caesars* (Robert Graves, trans.), Penguin Books, London, 1970, p. 197.
6. A collection of such texts can be found in *The Other Gospels* (Ron Cameron, editor). Unfortunately, precise information concerning authorship, dating and origin of these texts is largely conjecture.
7. Eusebius, *Ecclesiastical History*, Bk. III, ch. 39.
8. Cf. J. Quasten, *Patrology*, vol. I, pp. 82ff.; R. Gundry, *Matthew*, pp. 609ff. has recently re-examined the dating, value and meaning of Papias' testimony. His argument for a dating prior to 110 A.D. is a strong one; his other conclusions are problematical.
9. Irenaeus, *Adversus Haereses*, Bk. III, ch. 1.
10. Irenaeus, *Letter to Florinus*, quoted in Eusebius' *Ecclesiastical History*, Bk. 5, ch. 20.
11. Quoted by Eusebius, *Ecclesiastical History*, Bk. VI, ch. 14.
12. F. W. Beare, *The Gospel According to Matthew*, p. 7.
13. C. Dickens, *Martin Chuzzlewit*, Penguin Edition, 1982, p. 53.
14. Robert Giroux, *The Book Known as Q: A Consideration of Shakespeare's Sonnets*, Atheneum, New York, 1982.
15. Alexis de Tocqueville, *Democracy in America*, vol. I (Phillips Bradley, trans. and editor), Vintage Books, New York, 1960, p. 451.
16. W. G. Kümmel, *The Theology of the New Testament*, p. 119. Cf. Beare, *Matthew*, p. 435; Peter F. Ellis, *Matthew: his mind and his message*, p. 5.
17. R. Gundry, *Matthew*, p. 436.
18. W. F. Albright and C. S. Mann, *Matthew*, p. 269.
19. Cf. Adolf Harnack, *The Date of Acts and of the Synoptic Tradition*. Harnack, who himself thought that Matthew was written shortly after the fall of Jerusalem says of Mt. 22:7: "...Here St. Matt. XXII, 7...is of special weight. And yet composition before the catastrophe cannot be excluded with absolute certainty"

(p. 134). He adds in a footnote, "I could sooner convince myself that Matthew was written before the destruction of Jerusalem than believe that one decade elapsed after the catastrophe before the book was written."

20. Cf. Peter Ellis, *op. cit.*, pp. 5-6; R. Brown, *John*, vol. I, pp. LXXIV *John*, vol. II, pp. 690-691. The text of the prayer can be found in C. K. Barrett, *The New Testament Background*, p. 167.

21. Flavius Josephus, *Antiquities*, Bk. XX, ch. IX, 1.

22. Cf. John Rist, *On the Independence of Matthew and Mark*, p. 5. Rist rejects the "post Jamnian" dating for Luke.

23. W. G. Kümmel, *op. cit.*, p. 120.

24. Thus, Kümmel, *op. cit.*, p. 121; Beare, *op. cit.*, p. 7, and many others.

25. Henry Owen, *Observations on the Four Gospels*, London, 1764.

26. Cf. especially, B. C. Butler, *The Originality of St. Matthew: A Critique of the Two-Document Hypothesis.*

27. Cf. William R. Farmer, *The Synoptic Problem: A Critical Analysis;* Hans-Herbert Stoldt, *History and Criticism of the Marcan Hypothesis;* A. M. Farrer, "On Dispensing with Q," *Studies in the Gospels: Essays* in Memory of R. H. Lightfoot (D. E. Nineham, editor), Oxford Univ. Press, Oxford, 1955; Bernard Orchard, *Matthew, Luke and Mark.*

28. J. Bernard Orchard (editor), *A Synopsis of the Four Gospels.*

29. John M. Rist, *On the Independence of Matthew and Mark.*

30. *Idem*, pp. 106-107.

31. *Idem*, p. 107. The charge that the thesis for Marcan priority has "ideological overtones" is also made by Stoldt *(op. cit.*, ch. 14) and seconded by the non-Catholic Wm. Farmer who writes, in the Introduction to Stoldt's work: "(The Marcan hypothesis)...may live on in the minds of those who believe in 'the Q community,' and it may thrive among those who are inspired by the vision of 'Mark's Galilean community' resisting the authoritarianism of the Jerusalem (read Vatican) hierarchy" *(op. cit.*, p. XVIII). M. Hengel, *Acts and the History of Earliest Christianity* (p. 129, no. 1 and 2). The "ideological overtones" mentioned by Rist, however, are quite other than any imagined anti-Roman ideology.

32. Rist, *op. cit.*, p. 104.

33. Cf. G. M. Styler, "The Priority of Mark," in C. F. D. Moule's *The Birth of the New Testament*, pp. 285ff.

34. Joseph Fitzmyer, *The Gospel According to Luke* I-IX, p. 63.

35. *Idem*, p. 65.

36. M. Hengel, *Acts and the History of Earliest Christianity*, p. 129, nos. 1, 2 and 3.

37. Cf. below, Part III, "The Easter Triduum," pp. 233 and note 70 and 77. Together with many others, Ratzinger has used the "priority-of-creedal-statements presupposition" in his *The God of Jesus Christ*, pp. 86ff.

38. E. Schillebeeckx's book, *Jesus*, is an example of a work where the literary and historical criterion are frequently confused. Cf. J. T. O'Connor "Edward Schillebeeckx's Jesus—an Experiment in Christology," *Christian Faith and Freedom* (Paul Williams, editor), Northeast Books, Scranton, Pa., 1982, pp. 99ff.

39. Cf., for example, the various commentaries on Matthew 10, the "Missionary Discourse." Of it, Beare, *Matthew*, writes: "...Matthew has arranged scattered sayings of Jesus in the form of a discourse.... Great parts of it are not at all compatible with the situation which Matthew has devised for its delivery. Most of the sayings, indeed, reflect conditions which did not exist in the lifetime of Jesus for His followers and must be seen rather as bearing upon the mission of those early years of the

Church, when it was still limiting its approach to Jews; some elements even reflect a later period when the movement is carried into Gentile territories..." (p. 241).

40. J.R.R. Tolkien, *The Fellowship of the Ring*, 2nd edition, Houghton Mifflin Co., Boston, 1965, p. 7.

41. C.S. Lewis, "Modern Theology and Biblical Criticism," *Christian Reflections*, p. 164.

42. *Constitution on Divine Revelation (Dei Verbum)*, no. 9.

43. Cf. Robert Grant, *A Short History of the Interpretation of the Bible:* "The real merit of form-criticism...lies partly in its identification of pre-literary forms and, more significantly, in its implicit recognition of the Gospels as books of the Church. They did not exist prior to or apart from the Church...; the Church, in and for which they were written, came into existence before they did."

44. K. Rahner, "I Believe in the Church," *Theological Investigations*, vol. III, pp. 112-113.

45. J. Ratzinger in *Vorgrimler*, II, p. 184.

46. *Dei Verbum*, nos. 18, 19.

47. Paul VI, Address "Siamo felici," *TPS*, vol. 10, no. 1, p. 20.

48. *Acta Synodalia*, vol. IV, pt. 5, p. 722. "Quidem Patres...proponunt ut scribatur 'ipsi *vel* apostolici viri'...ne dirimatur quaestio de auctoribus I et IV Evangelii."

The Response, refusing a change, reads: "De 'Apostolis *et* apostolicis viris' sensu patet ex contextu." The significance of the request is clear; the reason given for the denial is not so clear.

49. Hans Urs von Balthasar, "Theology and Aesthetic," *Communio*, vol. VIII, no. 1, p. 65.

50. J. Ratzinger has given a simple but accurate description of "A Modern Stock Idea of the 'Historical Jesus'" in *Introduction to Christianity*, pp. 157ff.

51. *TPS*, vol. 10, no. 1, p. 87.

52. *Acta Synodalia*, vol. IV, pt. 1, p. 367.

53. *Idem*, pp. 369-370. "...phrasis 'ut non ficta, ex creatrici potentia primaevae communitatis promantia' visa est non retinenda, quia verba haec nimium honorem tribuunt opinioni alicui in decursu obsoletae."

54. Beda Rigaux in *Vorgrimler III*, p. 277. The Council's hesitation about the words "history" and "historical" can be seen in *Acta Synodalia*, vol. IV, pt. 5, p. 723.

55. Cf. *Acta Synodalia*, vol. IV, pt. 5, p. 723. "Commissio scripsit 'tenuit ac tenet,' quia sic melius exprimitur hanc historicitatem teneri fide *et ratione*, et non tantum fide."

56. *Dei Verbum*, no. 11.

57. St. Thomas, *De Veritate*, qu. 12, a 2c. English translation: *Truth* (James V. McGlynn, trans.), Regnery, Chicago, 1953.

58. Some of these rationalistic presuppositions are listed in the *Instruction Sancta Mater Ecclesia:* "Some proponents of this method, motivated by rationalistic prejudices, refuse to recognize the existence of a supernatural order. They deny the intervention of a personal God in the world by means of revelation in the strict sense, and reject the possibility or actual occurrence of miracles and prophecies. Some start with an erroneous concept of faith, regarding faith as indifferent to, or even incompatible with, historical truth. Some deny, *a priori* as it were, the historical nature and historical value of the documents of revelation" *(TPS*, vol. 10, no. 1, p. 87).

59. "Some Observations of the Congregation for the Doctrine of the Faith on the Final Report of the Anglican-Roman Catholic International Commission (ARCIC)," *TPS*, vol. 27, no. 3, p. 262. The observation on the historico-critical method is made twice in this document.

60. It is postulated by some that "Christian prophets" delivered oracles from the risen Lord, which oracles were eventually mingled with words He spoke during His ministry, thus entering the Gospel narrative. Cf., among others, J. Jeremias, *New Testament Theology*, pp. 1-2. There is no evidence for this supposition. The book of Revelation certainly records words of the risen Lord, but in that context the words clearly come from the Risen One; there is no attempt to have them appear as words of His ministry. On the other hand, Paul, who claimed the gift of prophecy for himself, clearly differentiated between such gifts and the Lord's own earthly words (cf. 1 Cor. 7:10, 12, 25). The supposition is thus one of those possibilities which lack real supportive evidence.

61. Cf. Part I, p. 77 and notes.

62. St. Augustine, *City of God*, Bk. 10, ch. 23.

63. Jacques Maritain, *The Degrees of Knowledge*, pp. 261-262.

64. *Ibid.*

65. *Mysterium Ecclesiae*, no. 5; *TPS*, vol. 18, no. 2, p. 152.

66. *Ibid.*

67. *Ibid.* It should be noted that the Latin for "conceptions" is *cogitationes* throughout. The document is not speaking here of concepts or ideas in the technical sense.

68. Russell F. Aldwinckle, *More Than Man*, pp. 179-181.

69. Cf. K. Rahner, *The Trinity*, pp., 103ff.

70. Emile Mersch, *The Theology of the Mystical Body*, p. 533.

Notes for Part I

1. Cf. R. Brown, *The Birth of the Messiah*, with the ample bibliography therein contained. Also, E. Schillebeeckx, *Jesus*, esp. Part II, chapter 2; W. Pannenberg, *Jesus: God and Man*; J. Fitzmyer, *The Gospel According to Luke I-IX*; pp. 303-448.

2. By "theological construct" we mean that the infancy narratives manifest not so much historical tradition as they do a theological reflection conveyed in narrative form. Such an approach proceeds from the theory that there were different—and perhaps contradictory—ways of viewing Jesus and His work, and that there was a gradual development of theological thinking about Him, a development found reflected in the N.T. writings. Thus, for example, if one asks the question "When did Jesus become Lord and Messiah?" one can find specific and different answers in the N.T. For Mark, it would be at His baptism in the Jordan; for Matthew and Luke, it would have been at His conception; for John, it would have been "eternity" in His preexistence with the Father. Such a development would coincide rather nicely with the presumed order of the Gospels (Mark as first, then Matthew and Luke, finally John) and their dating.

Brown, *op. cit.*, pp. 29-33, gives his version of such a Christological development, in which a "conception Christology" as reflected in Matthew and Luke would be the penultimate step. Like others, Brown doubts any familial source behind the accounts of the virginal conception (cf. pp. 521 and 526) and sees the "conception Christology" as an alternative answer to adoptionism (the other alternative being a "preexistence Christology" which Brown views as being

Johannine—*op. cit.*, p. 141). Brown's understanding here is quite in conformity with that of Pannenberg. He does not, however, show the same conclusion as does Pannenberg, to wit: "In its content, the legend of Jesus' virgin birth stands in an irreconcilable contradiction to the Christology in the incarnation of the preexistent Son of God found in Paul and John" (*op. cit.*, p. 143). For Schillebeeckx, cf. *Jesus*, pp. 554-557.

For some, the development of these distinctive Christologies in the N.T. seems to necessitate the fact of ignorance or disagreement concerning the position held by another N.T. writer. Thus, it is suggested, for example, that Matthew and Luke did not know or rejected the "preexistence Christology" (cf. Brown, *op. cit.*, p. 31; James D. G. Dunn, *Christology in the Making*, pp. 49-50; Fitzmyer, *op. cit.*, p. 340).

3. The above hypothesis must be viewed as logically and theologically uncritical. Apart from the disputed premises about the priority and dating of the Gospels, it posits a linear development in the Christologies which cannot be substantiated. Preexistence is not the end of a developmental process, but is present already in Paul, and is even very likely pre-Pauline. This fact, viz. Pauline doctrine on preexistence, is seen by Schillebeeckx (*op. cit.*, p. 556) and Fitzmyer (*op. cit.*, p. 197) but contested by Brown (cf. his *The Community of the Beloved Disciple*, pp. 45-46 where he defends himself against criticism leveled at his neglect of Pauline preexistence doctrine in the *Birth of the Messiah*). The hypothesis also posits a relatively lengthy time span for the development of the various Christologies, a position admirably countered by Martin Hengel (*The Son of God*, esp. pp. 59ff.). The assertion that Luke and Matthew did not know of the preexistence Christology or even that their position is irreconcilable with it can be substantiated only by the argument from silence. It is a fact that they do not explicitly speak of preexistence. Nevertheless, even so unbiased a critic as Fred B. Craddock (unbiased in the sense that he understands all the preexistence language as mythological, revealing nothing more than the uniqueness of Jesus) asserts—rightly we think—that all the Synoptic Gospels are written from the viewpoint of the "pre- and post-existent dimensions of the story. The portrayals of Jesus' teaching, healing, doing mighty works, are drawn so as to impress clearly upon the reader that Jesus is not simply 'of Nazareth'; He can be understood only in the context of eternity" (*The Pre-existence of Christ in the New Testament*, p. 158).

Finally, from the point of view of Catholic doctrine which infallibly teaches the historical and biological facticity of the virginal conception, it appears almost ingenuous to say that our knowledge of such an historical event comes as the result of a theological conclusion on the part of Matthew and Luke instead of from a historical and ultimately familial source. It is a *Deus ex machina* solution.

4. Eusebius, *Ecclesiastical History*, III, 19-20. English trans. can be found in Nicene and Post-Nicene Fathers (Schraff and Wace, editors), Second Series, vol. I, pp. 148-149.

5. Cf. Emiliano Vallauri, "Natus in Bethlehem," *Laurentianum*, 19:3 pp. 413-441 (excerpt in *Theology Digest*, vol. 28, no. 1, pp. 39ff.); R. Brown, *The Gospel According to John*, vol. I, p. 330; *The Birth of the Messiah*, Appendices II and III. In the light of the evidence and the lack of clear evidence to the contrary, both authors are unduly tentative in affirming the historicity of the birth in Bethlehem, but they provide the spectrum of opinions.

6. Some idea of the malice of Herod can be gained from the following account of Josephus. "Herod sent for his sister Salome and her husband and said: 'I know the

Jews will greet my death with wild rejoicings; but I can be mourned on other people's account and make sure of a magnificent funeral if you will do as I tell you. These men under guard—as soon as I die, kill them all...; then all Judea and every family will weep for me—they can't help it'" *(The Jewish War,* trans. by G. A. Williamson, Penguin Classics, London, 1959, p. 110). This, too, is the man who killed his wife and his eldest son and heir and who, according to St. Matthew, is responsible for the death of the children in Bethlehem.

7. The article by Joseph Fitzmyer, S.J., "The Virginal Conception of Jesus in the New Testament" *(Theological Studies,* vol. 34, no. 1, pp. 541ff.), calling into question the traditional understanding that Luke teaches the virginal conception, found little favorable response. Fitzmyer himself has abandoned the view (cf. *The Gospel According to Luke* I-IX, p. 338).

8. Cf. R. Brown, *The Birth of the Messiah,* p. 521.

9. Cf. William Farmer, *The Synoptic Problem,* pp. 231-232. Farmer shows that Mark need not have been written from a lack of knowledge or rejection of virginal conception.

10. On the weight to be given such affirmations of the creeds, see the remarks directed by Joseph Ratzinger to Piet Schoonenberg in Ratzinger's *Introduction to Christianity,* p. 212, note 52: "The original form in which the Church states its faith in a binding fashion is the creed or symbolum," etc. As background for the reference to the virginal conception in the Creed of Paul VI, cf. AAS, 60 (1966) dealing with the disputes over the so-called Dutch Catechism *(A New Catechism,* Herder and Herder, 1967) and its original remarks on the virginal conception *(Idem.,* pp. 74-75).

11. *Enchiridion Patristicum,* no. 112.

12. D 993—"sed etiam ipsius fidei fundamenta negare paresumant...."

13. Cf. *A New Catechism, loc. cit.;* W. Pannenberg, *The Apostles' Creed,* pp. 71-77; Joseph Fitzmyer, "The Virginal Conception of Jesus in the New Testament," *op. cit.,* esp. pp. 548-550. Note Fitzmyer's definition of "Theologoumenon": "...a theological assertion that does not directly express a matter of Faith or an official teaching of the Church, and hence is in itself not normative, but that expresses in language that may prescind from factuality a notion which supports, enhances, or is related to a matter of faith."

14. Thomas Aquinas, *Compendium of Theology* (trans. by Cyril Vollert, S.J.) B. Herder Book Co., St. Louis, Mo., 1955, ch. 221, p. 259.

15. *S. Th.,* III, q. 28, a. 1 c. One finds this Thomistic reason reflected in the pastoral letter of the Bishops of the United States, *Behold Your Mother* (USCC, Washington, D.C., 1973), no. 48: "The glorious positive sign value of the Virgin birth is the merciful and free saving grace of the Father sending His Son, conceived by the Holy Spirit, born of the Virgin Mary, that we might receive the adoption of sons."

16. *S. Th.,* III, q. 28, a. 1 c.

17. *Phaedo* 76 A-77 E, in *Great Dialogues of Plato* (trans. by W. H. D. Rouse), A Mentor Book, New American Library, New York, 1960, p. 480. Cf. F. Copleston, S.J., *A History of Philosophy,* vol. I, part I, Image Books, Garden City, New York, 1960, p. 237.

18. Cf. Martin Hengel, *Jews, Greeks and Barbarians,* p. 113, where Hengel speaks of "the gradual invasion of Hellenistic civilization": even into Jewish Palestine. Cf. also his *Judaism and Hellenism* for a master study of this mixed culture.

19. Cf. Jack T. Sanders, *The New Testament Christological Hymns,* p. 96; Fred B. Craddock, *The Preexistence of Christ in the New Testament,* pp. 35-41; M. Hengel, *The Son of God,* pp. 51ff. Some of the dispute on the presence of a

preexistence theme in pre-Christian Jewish writings depends on the dating and evaluation made of the "Similitudes of Enoch" (chapters 37-71 of I Enoch). Noting the absence of these chapters from the Enoch literature found among the Dead Sea texts, James D. G. Dunn, following J. T. Milik, finds a pre-70 A.D. date improbable (*Christology in the Making*, pp. 76-77 and notes). The Jewish author George W. E. Nickelsburg finds such argumentation inconclusive and contends that the writings are Jewish, from a time close to the beginnings of the Christian era (*Jewish Literature Between the Bible and the Mishnah*, pp. 216-223). The writings themselves attribute preexistence to a Son of Man, and thus may be significant in helping to understand Jesus' use of that term, as well as the use made of it by the evangelists. M. Hengel, *Judaism and Hellenism*, vol. II, p. 120 and note 480 apparently agrees with a pre-Christian dating for the Similitudes, as does R. Schnackenburg, *John*, vol. I, Excursus II, pp. 494ff. Kümmel, *Theology of the New Testament*, p. 78 is apodictic: "In spite of much dispute, there is no doubt that this section of Enoch is of Jewish origin and arose at the latest at the beginning of the first Christian century." Cf. also D. S. Russell, *The Method and Message of Jewish Apocalyptic*, pp. 52 and 349-351; M. Hengel, *Judaism and Hellenism*, vol. I, pp. 153, 156, 166ff. for a general treatment on preexistence in pre-Christian Judaism.

20. The hymn in the epistle to the Colossians (1:15-20) develops the same theme, and is redolent with similarities to the Wisdom texts. The Pauline authorship of the epistle is disputed by some, but the thought is no more than a development of the text in Corinthians.

21. Dunn, *Christology in the Making*, pp. 183-184 claims that preexistence is not found in this text, but, among many others, the explanation of Schnackenburg, *John*, vol. I, p. 505, is much more probable.

22. From time to time opinions appear which deny that preexistence is being stated in the Philippian hymn. One should consult the commentaries for the various views. However, the overwhelming opinion of exegetes in every age supports the *prima facie* evidence of the text itself. Cf., for example, Jack T. Sanders, *The New Testament Christological Hymns*, pp. 58ff.; Hans Conzelmann, *I Corinthians*, p. 167. For the minority view, cf. Xavier Leon-Dufour, *Resurrection and the Message of Easter*, pp. 27-28; Jerome Murphy-O'Connor, "Christological Anthropology in Phil. 2:6-11," *Revue Biblique*, 83 (1976), pp. 25-50. Dunn, *Christology in the Making*, pp. 118ff., argues in a scholarly but ultimately non-persuasive manner that preexistence is not found in Paul at all, and that Phil. 2:6-11 is an example of the "Adam-Christ" comparison found elsewhere in Paul's writings. Unlike Adam who was created in the "image" of God but lost that image by disobediently grasping for more, Jesus, the New Adam, is in the form (image) of God but does not grasp. There is no evidence, however, that Paul is directly using the Adamic parallel in Phil., nor is there clear evidence that *morphe* (form) and *eikon* (image) are equivalent Greek terms for Paul, Murphy-O'Connor's efforts to show the opposite notwithstanding (*op. cit.*, pp. 41ff.). Indeed, Paul, when speaking of Jesus as "image" of God elsewhere uses *eikon*, not *morphe* (cf. 2 Cor. 4:4; Col. 1:15). A survey of the efforts to identify *morphe* and *eikon* can be found in R. P. Martin, *Carmen Christi*, pp. 106-120.

23. Cf. W. G. Kümmel, *Theology of the New Testament*, p. 170; M. Hengel, *The Son of God*, p. 11.

24. On Gal. 4:4, cf. Dunn, *Christology in the Making*, p. 283 for authors who see preexistence in the text. Dunn's own position is negative (pp. 38ff.)

25. Thus the Vulgate, Jerusalem Bible and NIV rendering of the Greek, where the punctuation is difficult and disputed. Cf. Joseph Fitzmyer's commentary in *The*

Jerome Biblical Commentary, (53:97). Origin read the text in the same way as the Vulgate (cf. *Enchiridion Patristicum*, 502).

26. M. Hengel, *The Son of God*, p. 2, has written: "...the 'apotheosis of the crucified Jesus' must already have taken place in the forties, and one is tempted to say that more *happened in this period of less than two decades than in the whole of the next seven centuries, up to the time when the doctrine of the early Church was completed.*" Also, "Paul's conception of the Son of God, which was certainly not his own creation but goes back to earlier community tradition before Paul's letters, thus proves to be quite unique" (p. 15).

Because their authenticity is disputed, we have not directly considered Paul's references to preexistence in Colossians and Ephesians. On the latter, cf. Marcus Barth, *Ephesians 1—3*, pp. 109ff. Barth argues for Pauline authorship, places the date c. 62, and explains its teaching on preexistence.

27. The usage is the same in Mt. 14:22-33. Luke does not record the scene.

28. Lk. 13:5-6 has the same usage in the same context; Mt. 24:26-28 has the context, but not the "I am" usage.

29. The parallels in Matthew and Luke do not have the same usage. Commentators recognize the peculiarity of the Marcan usage. Cf. Ernest Martinez, "The Identity of Jesus in Mark," *Communio*, Winter, 1974, pp. 323ff.; R. Brown, *The Gospel of John*, vol. I, p. 538; Vincent Taylor, *The Gospel According to St. Mark*, p. 330, and esp. p. 504.

30. Cf. notes 2 and 3 above.

31. By "contextual reading" we mean the attempt to understand a text or idea within the context of the entire book of the N.T. in which the text appears, and within the overall framework of the Church's understanding of the mystery of Christ. This form of reading is referred to by the Second Vatican Council's *Constitution on Divine Revelation*, no. 12.

32. Cf. K. Rahner, "Theos in the New Testament," *Theological Investigations*, vol. I, pp. 79ff.; Vincent Taylor, "Does the New Testament Call Jesus 'God,'" *New Testament Essays*, pp. 83ff.; R. Brown, *Jesus: God and Man*, pp. 1ff.; J. Fitzmyer, *The Gospel According to Luke*, pp. 218-219.

33. Ephesians 18. Trans. by Maxwell Staniforth, *Early Christian Writings*, p. 81.

34. *Idem.*, p. 103. Cf. also Ephesians 1; Smyrna 1, etc.

35. *Idem.*, Magnesians 6, p. 88. Likewise Magnesians 7, p. 89: "...Jesus Christ who came down from the one and only Father is eternally with that One, and to that One is now returned."

36. *Idem.*, Magnesians 11, p. 90. J. N. D. Kelly, *Early Christian Creeds*, pp. 68-70 finds here and in Ephesians 18, Trallians 9, and Smyrna 1 indications or echoes of early creedal formulae.

37. Ephesians 19.

38. Ephesians 1, *Idem.*, p. 75.

39. *Idem.*, p. 105.

40. Ephesians 7.

41. Some would read the text: "...the Church of God which He bought at the price of His Son's blood."

42. James M. Carmody, S.J. and Thomas Clarke, S.J., *Word and Redeemer*, p. 19.

43. St. Thomas later faced the problem posed by the Docetists and responded: "To be united to God in unity of person was not suitable to human nature because that is something beyond its dignity. However, it was suitable for God because of the

infinite excellence of His goodness to unite human nature to Himself for the sake of man's salvation" *(S. Th.,* III, q. 1, a. 1, ad. 2).

44. Cf. Magnesians 9, 11; Trallians 9, 10; Smyrna 7, etc.

45. The *De Carne Christi* (the Latin with English translation can be found in Ernest Evans, *Tertullian's Treatise on the Incarnation,* S.P.C.K., London, 1956) gives us those famous lines in defense of a God who has made flesh His own, and died and rose in that flesh: "Whatever is beneath God's dignity is for my advantage. I am saved if I am not ashamed of my Lord.... The Son of God was crucified: I am not ashamed—because it is shameful. The Son of God dies: it is immediately credible—because it is silly. He was buried and rose again: it is certain—because it is impossible" (p. 17).

46. The modern classic in this field still remains the work of Aloys Grill-meier, S.J., *Christ in Christian Tradition.* Cf. also Bernard Lonergan, *The Way to Nicea.*

47. *DS* 125.

48. *DS* 126.

49. St. Augustine in his *Tracts on the Gospel of John* has a fine explanation of what Nicea meant by saying "Light from Light": "Just as the Father is ageless, so the Son does not grow; the Father has not grown old, nor has the Son increased. Rather Equal begot Equal; the Eternal begot the Eternal. How, someone may ask, has the Eternal begotten the Eternal? Like a temporal flame generates a temporal light. The flame which generates the light is coterminous with the light which it generates. From the moment the flame begins, from that moment there is light. Show me a flame without light, and I will show you the Father without the Son" *(In Joh,* 20, 8).

50. Ephesians 18, *op. cit.,* p. 81.

51. Again it is a text from the writings of St. Luke which comes closest linguistically to the usage of the *communicatio idiomatum.* Cf., however, Fitzmyer, *The Gospel According to Luke* I-IX, p. 365 and pp. 200-204.

52. The Christian people of Ephesus enthusiastically hailed the decision in favor of the Theotokos. To note, however, the enthusiasm of the people of that same city, *almost four centuries earlier,* for the cult of the goddess Diana (cf. Acts 19:23ff.) and insinuate that this explains the conciliar definition in 431—as does Hans Küng in his *On Being a Christian,* p. 460—is not only anachronistic, but foolish. Is one to presume a hereditary, genetic disposition or an ethos in favor of the female which was transmitted for over three hundred years? In fact, it was not the people of Ephesus, but the bishop of Alexandria, Egypt, and his supporters who were instrumental in effecting the conciliar definition concerning the Mother of God.

53. *DS* 251.

54. The fact that "Mother of God" is said *properly* and *truly* (as opposed to improperly or in a restricted sense in comparison to the way other women are called mothers) of Mary is implied by the decree of Ephesus, but not said explicitly. Later, however, at Constantinople II in 553 *(DS* 427) and Constantinople III *(DS* 555) in 681, that fact is explicitly defined, and thus is a matter of Faith *de fide definita.* The importance of this for Christology can be seen by remembering that *Mother of God* is the most commonly used form of the *communicatio idiomatum,* a language which highlights the unity of the one Person who is both God and man. Because such language is true and proper, the recent reservation of Karl Rahner appears to be almost a throwback to the Nestorian dispute. Rahner has written: "But the meaning 'is' in statements involving an interchange of predicates in Christology is *not* based on such a real identification. It is based rather on a unique, otherwise unknown and deeply mysterious unity between realities which are really different and which are at

an infinite distance from each other. For in and according to the humanity which we see when we say 'Jesus,' Jesus 'is' not God, and in and according to His divinity God 'is' not man in the sense of a real identification. The Chalcedonian *adiairetos* (unseparated) which this 'is' intends to express *(DS 302)* expresses it in such a way that the *asynchytos* (unmixed) of the same formula does not come into expression. Consequently, the statement is always in danger of being understood in a 'monophysitic' sense, that is, as a formula which simply identifies the subject and predicate.... Hence as presumed parallels to 'is' statements elsewhere in our everyday language, the Christological 'is' formulas (for example, 'the same' person is God and man) are constantly in danger of being interpreted falsely, a danger which flows from these parallels" *(Foundations of Christian Faith*, pp. 290-291).

The remarks of W. Thüsing are even more perplexing: "The doctrine of the *communicatio idiomatum* was developed in a particular spiritual climate or context, in which the classical Christology with its ontic categories was current.... In fact, the doctrine of the *communicatio idiomatum* is nowadays only understood by a relatively small circle of specialists in dogmatic theology (and especially the history of that theology). It is no longer used in catechetics or in homilies and in these and related spheres other ways have to be found for safeguarding the unique significance of Jesus" (Rahner-Thüsing, *A New Christology*, pp. 180-181). Such remarks are surely misinformed since the use of the *communicatio idiomatum* antedates by a few centuries the appearance of "classical theology with its ontic categories" and since its use and understanding both in the *Hail Mary* and in the Christological sections of the Creed used weekly at Mass indicate that more than a "relatively small circle of specialists in dogmatic theology" understand it, granted the fact that most are completely unaware of the technical term. In regard to Rahner's reservations, A. Grillmeier's remarks on Nestorius are pertinent: "In some sense, of course, Nestorious failed...as the theological position of current Christology could have shown him that his metaphysical analyses did not fully succeed in doing justice to tradition. We mean the doctrine of *communicatio idiomatum* of which the famous Theotokos was the expression. It already contained a metaphysical intuition that the Logos was the final subject in Christ" *(op. cit.*, p. 518; cf. p. 546). Cardinal Höffner of Germany has challenged Rahner's interpretation of the *communicatio idiomatum* (cf. *The Month*, April, 1971, pp. 104-107, and *Theological Investigations*, vol. XVII, p. 37, note 14). Cf. J. T. O'Connor, "Modern Christologies and Mary's Place Therein," *Marian Studies*, vol. XXXII (1981), pp. 72-73; Jean Galot, *Who is Christ?*, pp. 282-283, esp. notes 7 and 8.

55. *PG* 77, 991-995; *Mansi*, IV, 1251-1258. The Marian sections of the homily form the second reading for the Office of Readings of the Roman Breviary for August 5, Feast of the Dedication of St. Mary Major.

56. The heresy of adoptionism in various forms reappears after Ephesus. It shows itself in Spain and then in Germany in the eighth century, and was frequently condemned. Cf. *DS* 595, 510-615, etc., and the Profession of Faith of the Eastern Emperor Michael Palaelogus at the Council of Vienna in 1274 *(DS* 852). Adoptionism has at times appeared under the "assumptus homo" theory of the Incarnation, according to which an ordinary man was gradually "divinized." Forms of this heretical notion have reappeared in our own day.

57. *DS* 301-302.

58. *DS* 556.

59. In the past fifty years alone, the following major documents of the Papal Magisterium have treated matters in Christology:

a) *Lux Veritatis*—Encyclical Letter of Pius XI, Dec. 25, 1931, on the Council of Ephesus.
b) *Mystici Corporis Christi*—Encyclical Letter of Pius XII, June, 1943, on the Church as Mystical Body of Christ.
c) *Orientalis Ecclesiae Decus*—Encyclical Letter of Pius XII, April, 1944, on 15th cen. of death of Cyril of Alexandria.
d) *Sempiternus Rex Christus*—Encyclical Letter of Pius XII, Sept., 1951, on 15th cen. of Chalcedon.
e) *Aeterna Dei Sapientia*—Encyclical Letter of John XXIII, Nov., 1961, on 5th cen. of death of Leo the Great.
f) Declaration of Congregation for Doctrine of the Faith of Feb., 1972.
g) Declaration of Congregation for Doctrine of the Faith of April, 1979, on a book by Jacques Pohier.
h) Declaration of Congregation for Doctrine of the Faith of Dec., 1979, on Fr. Hans Küng.

60. The necessity for reaffirming the distinction of Persons in the One God and the preexistence of Christ can be seen when one considers the following remark of Hans Küng:

"Why then were theological conclusions drawn, even in New Testament times, about the preexistence of God's Son in eternity? It was not in order to indulge in clever speculations about God and the world. The reason for it was to make clear and to justify in practice the *unique claim* of this crucified and yet living Jesus. We can no longer accept the mythical ideas of that age about a being descended from God, existing before time and beyond this world in a heavenly state; a 'story of gods,' in which two (or even three) divine beings are involved, is not for us. But we certainly have to consider in our very different climate just what the ideas of that time were meant to express" (*On Being a Christian*, p. 446).

In an effort to rethink the original message for our time, Küng and others attempt a demytholization of the Scriptural texts which in effect eviscerates the concept of the preexistence of Christ by making it the equivalent of the word "unique."

61. *Declaration for Safeguarding Belief in the Mysteries of the Incarnation and of the Most Holy Trinity Against Some Recent Errors*, Sacred Cong. for the Doctrine of the Faith, March 8, 1972. The actual text of the part of the statement cited reads: "Opinions which hold that it has not been revealed and made known to us that the Son of God subsists from all eternity in the mystery of the Godhead, distinct from the Father and the Holy Spirit, are in open conflict with (the Faith of the Church). The same is true of opinions which would abandon the notion of the one Person of Jesus Christ begotten in His divinity of the Father before all ages, and born in His humanity of the Virgin Mary in time; and, lastly, of the assertion that the humanity of Christ existed not as being assumed into the eternal Person of the Son of God, but existed rather of itself as a Person, and therefore that the mystery of Jesus Christ consists only in the fact that God, in revealing Himself, was present in the highest degree in the human Person of Christ" (*TPS*, vol. 17, no. 1, p. 65).

62. Cf. P. Schoonenberg, "From a Two-nature Christology to a Christology of Presence," *Christian Action and Openness to the World*, pp. 119-143, esp. p. 122. Also, P. Schoonenberg, *The Christ;* "He Emptied Himself," *Concilium*, vol. 11, Paulist Press, N.Y., 1966, pp. 47-66; "Process as History in God," *Theology Digest*, vol. 23, no. 1, pp. 38-44; *Letter of Schoonenberg to Theology Digest*, vol. 23, no. 3,

pp. 224-225. Schoonenberg claims to find the underpinnings of his position in the Trinitarian work of K. Rahner (cf. p. 224 of *Letter, op. cit.*) and the various elements of some of the "process" philosophies and theologies. The position set forth by Schoonenberg found some favorable response among Catholic writers. Cf. the tentative but generally favorable remarks by Bruce Vawter, *This Man Jesus* (pp. 166-175) and the article "Some Problems in Modern Christology," by Gerard Sloyan in *A World More Human: a Church More Christian* (George Divine, editor), Alba House, 1973.

63. Cf. Aloys Grillmeier, *op. cit.*, pp. 555-556: "On a closer inspection the Christological 'heresies' turn out to be a compromise between the original message of the Bible and the understanding of it in Hellenism and paganism. It is here that we have the real Hellenization of Christianity. The formulas of the Church, whether they are the *homoousios* of Nicea or the Chalcedonian Definition, represent the *lectio difficilior* of the Gospel, and maintain the demand for faith and the stumbling-block which Christ puts before men. This is a sign that they hand on the original message of Jesus. Nevertheless, the Hellenistic element in them, too, needs a thorough examination and demarcation." Likewise, Bernard Lonergan, *The Way to Nicea,* p. 130, writes: "There is no need, then, to speak of the importation of a hellenistic ontology. Indeed, the more carefully one examines the brands of hellenistic ontology that were actually available at the time, the more obviously superfluous does any such hypothesis appear." Cf. Jaroslav Pelikan, *The Emergence of the Catholic Tradition*, p. 45.

64. Cardinal Höffner of Germany noted this point when he commented on the Church's action against Hans Küng in the Declaration of Dec. 15, 1979, by the Cong. for the Doctrine of the Faith. Höffner said: "From ancient times the Christians professed: 'We believe...in one Lord, Jesus Christ, only-begotten Son of God, born of the Father before all ages: God from God, Light from Light, *true God from true God*—consubstantial with the Father....' This implies consequences for our salvation: if in Jesus Christ, God Himself has not given Himself for men, then the central point of Christian revelation falls.... When there is little clarity on fundamental points concerning the mystery of Jesus, the heart not only of the Catholic Faith but of Christian faith in general is threatened" (Origins, 9, no. 29, p. 465).

65. Cf. K. Rahner, "Current Problems in Christology," *Theological Investigations,* vol. I, pp. 149ff. for observations which, although now nearly thirty years old, are still remarkable for the questions raised.

66. *DS* 1330, *The Decree for the Jacobites.* The quotation included in the Decree is taken from St. Fulgentius of Ruspe, a disciple of Augustine.

67. St. Thomas Aquinas held that anyone of the Divine Persons *could* have assumed human nature (*S. Th.*, III, q. 3, a. 5 c). Some theologians do not consider this opinion correct. Cf. K. Rahner, *The Trinity*, pp. 28ff.; L. Bouyer, *The Eternal Son*, pp. 350-351. Determining, however, what God cannot do is a risky enterprise at best, and one likely to be met by "surprises." Whatever the case, St. Thomas thought that it was "most suitable" that the Son assume human nature. "The first creation was done by the power of the Father through the Word. Therefore the re-creation should be done through the Word by the power of the Father so that the re-creation would correspond to the first creation, as it says in 2 Cor. 5:19, 'God was in Christ reconciling the world to himself'" (*S. Th.*, III, q. 3, a. 8, ad. 2). Thomas notes elsewhere that, among the divine Persons, *only* the Son should properly be called

the Word (I, q. 34, a. 2 c) and that, since in the Word the Father perfectly knows Himself and all other things which He can do or create, the Word has a special connection with the created universe (I, q. 34, a. 3).

68. St. Thomas wrote: "The eternal act of existence *(esse)* of the Son of God, which is the divine nature itself, becomes the act of existence *(esse)* of a man, inasmuch as the human nature is assumed by the Son of God into the unity of person" *(S. Th.*, III, q. 17, a. 2, ad. 2). The difficulties and disputes among followers of St. Thomas and between them and other philosophical and theological approaches are numerous, technical and frequently abstruse. Cf. McGraw-Hill translation of *Summa Theologiae* (Thomas Gilby, O.P. and T. C. O'Brien, O.P., editors), vol. 50, *The One Mediator* (trans. and commentary by Coleman O'Neill), Appendix 2, pp. 221ff.; Michael Schmaus, *God and His Christ*, pp. 228ff.; J. Galot, *Who is Christ?*, pp. 289ff.

69. Cf. W. Pannenberg, *Jesus God and Man*, p. 338. The doctrine of the "anhypostasis," i.e., the absence of human personhood in Christ, was insisted upon by the Cong. for the Doctrine of the Faith in its Declaration of 1973 (cf. note 61 above) and in the *Letter from the Sacred Congregation for the Doctrine of the Faith to Fr. E. Schillebeeckx.* This latter document says, in part: "...to reject *anhypostasis* is not confined to denying any lacuna whatever in the humanity of Jesus, but it tends to show therein a distinct and independent reality in existence and to conjure up 'the unthinkable opposition between the man Jesus and the Son of God,' which Schillebeeckx himself wished to rule out..." *(L'Osservatore Romano*, English edition, 7/13/81, p. 5).

According to Catholic doctrine, the human nature of Christ is *enhypostatic*, i.e., it exists in the Person of the Word. Rejection of this understanding ultimately destroys the reality of the Incarnation, reducing the divinity of Jesus to some form of Adoptionism or Nestorianism.

70. *DS* 556. On the inability to sin in Jesus, Russell F. Aldwinckle, *More Than Man*, p. 175, has written: "As far as literal participation in certain kinds of experience, Jesus remains forever not one of us. If He were, He could never lift us out of ourselves. Modern man's difficulty at this point may not be primarily intellectual or even moral. It may spring from a pride which objects to the idea that a man could be good by nature and therefore different from us at this vital point of sin."

71. Epistle *Licet per nosotros* to Bishop Julian, June, 449: *DS* 299; English translation *The Nicene and Post-Nicene Fathers*, Second Series, vol. 12, pp. 48ff. The full letter is a masterpiece of dogmatic Christology.

72. On the nature of freedom, J. Galot, *(Who Is Christ?*, p. 390), using St. Augustine, has written well: "In response to Julian of Eclane who admitted the existence of freedom only where there was a faculty for choosing, i.e., 'the power to will the opposites,' Augustine declared: 'If no one is free unless he can will two things, that is to say, good and evil, then God is not free, for He cannot will evil. Is this the way you praise God, by stripping Him of His freedom?'

"The essence of freedom, therefore, is not to be sought in the faculty to choose between good and evil. It consists in self-determination or the faculty to determine one's voluntary acts for oneself. This is the freedom of God, and at a lower level, it is also the freedom of man."

73. Cf. *S. Th.*, III, q. 18, a. 5 and 6.

74. *Lumen gentium*, no. 56.

75. St. Augustine, *De virginitate*, no. 3.

76. That Mary's consent was intelligent and informed, i.e., that she was a *knowing* participant in the work of Redemption in which she was asked to cooperate, is pointed out several times by the Second Vatican Council in *Lumen gentium*, nos. 56 and 58.

As Archbishop of Cracow, Pope John Paul II wrote: "...The whole attitude of the ancient and modern Church to the Mother of God is based not only on the exceptional honor due to her divine maternity, but also on her awareness of the Redemption and her participation in the work of Christ" (K. Wojtyla, *Sources of Renewal: the Implementation of Vatican II*, p. 105).

St. Thomas, in citing his reasons as to why it was suitable that Mary should be informed that she was to conceive the Christ, wrote that it should have been done so that "she might offer to God the voluntary gift of her obedience..." *(S. Th.* III, q. 30, a. 1 c).

77. *S. Th.*, III, q. 30, a. 1 c.

78. *Idem.*

79. The doctrine of the "Virgin-birth" *(virginitas in partu)*, i.e., the physical integrity of Mary in the birth of her Son is traditional in the Church, taught by innumerable Fathers, by the Council of Chalcedon *(Mansi* 7, 462), the Ordinary Magisterium *(DS* 503, 1880; by Pius XII in his definition of the Assumption *AAS*, vol. XXXXII, p. 759), the Liturgy, and by the Second Vatican Council *(Lumen gentium*, no. 57: "This association was shown also at the birth of our Lord, who did not diminish but sanctified the virginal integrity of His mother"; cf. the official explanation of the text in *Acta synodalia*, vol. 3, part 1, p. 369, no. 213). Efforts previous to the Second Vatican Council to "reinterpret" or "spiritualize" the doctrine find no reflection in the Conciliar teaching. Cf. W. B. Smith, "The Theology of the Virginity *in Partu* and Its Consequences for the Church's Teaching on Chastity," *Marian Studies*, XXXI (1980), pp. 99ff.

80. Clarendon Press, Oxford, 1955.

81. For the ambiguity of *adelphos*, cf. J. Fitzmyer, *The Gospel According to Luke*, pp. 723-724.

82. Fitzmyer, *op. cit.*, p. 724, thinks they are the same people.

83. Cf. Johannes Quasten, *Patrology*, vol. I, p. 119.

84. *Idem.*, p. 114.

85. *P.G.*, XIII, 876B.

86. *P.G.*, XIII, 1818.

87. English translation in *Nicene and Post-Nicene Fathers*, second series, vol. VI, pp. 335ff.

88. *DS* 44.

89. *DS* 801; cf. Appendix.

90. Cf. Appendix.

91. *DS* 256.

92. *DS* 1880.

93. *Lumen gentium*, nos. 50 and 63.

94. *City of God*, XV, 16. Trans. by Henry Bettenson, Penguin Classics, London, England, 1972, p. 625.

95. *Lumen gentium*, no. 46.

96. *S. Th.*, III, q. 10, a. 1, ad. 2.

97. Cf. *S. Th.*, III, q. 46, a. 8.

98. Cf., among others, Leonardo Boff, *Jesus Christ Liberator*, pp. 34-35: "The Gospels contain little of the historical Jesus (what He was like and how He lived), but

a great deal concerning the reaction of faith among the first Christians who reflected on the words of Christ." And "The Gospels are not simply books concerning Jesus. They are primarily books that reflect the traditions and the dogmatic development of the primitive Church."

99. Cf., among others, Bruce Vawter, *This Man Jesus*, p. 135: "To say that Jesus in His earthly life knew and judged Himself to be God's natural Son and very God is to assert the unprovable and, from the perspective of the New Testament, the improbable."

100. Cf., among others, R. Brown, "Scripture as the Word of God," *Theological Studies*, vol. 42, no. 1, pp. 11-12: "Yet in the words of Jesus it is dubious that one encounters an unconditioned, timeless word spoken by God. The Son of God who speaks in the first three Gospels is a Jew of the first third of the first century who thinks in the images of His time, speaks in the idiom of His time, and shares much of the world view of His time. The Jesus of the fourth Gospel, who is preexistent, does claim to have heard words in the presence of His Father and to have brought them to earth (Jn. 3:31-32; 5:30; 8:26; 14:24; 15:15); but when one examines the words of the Johannine Jesus critically, they are often a variant form of the tradition known in the Synoptics. The very existence of diverse traditions of the words of Jesus reflected in the four Gospels testifies to the fact that His followers understood His words to be so time-conditioned and so locale-conditioned as to require adaptation as they were transmitted to new times and places."

Brown claims in a footnote that this position (that Jesus' words were "so time-conditioned and so locale-conditioned," etc.) is now formally acknowledged in Catholic Church doctrine in the 1964 document of the Pontifical Biblical Commission *Sancta Mater Ecclesia*. It would take an energetic exegesis of that document to substantiate such a claim, even when working from the selected excerpts cited by Brown.

101. Among others, K. Rahner in K. Rahner—W. Thüsing, *A New Christology*, p. 23: "I believe, however, that we are bound to react differently from Catholic Christians at the time of Pius X and frankly, sincerely, soberly and clearly admit that there was a temporally imminent expectation in the case of Jesus and this expectation was not fulfilled in the way in which He presented it to Himself and formulated it in words."

102. Cf., among others, Jon Sobrino, *Christology at the Crossroads*, p. 326: "Jesus, too, died as a prophet. But there was nothing beautiful about His death, nor was He just another martyr: 'Jesus' deathcry was not an expression of pious surrender; it welled up from His feeling that He had been abandoned by God.' His death differed from that of other martyrs and prophets, for they died with the intention that their death should serve as their last act in defense of their cause. Thus their death often stood in *continuity* with their life and cause. It had real meaning for them, and hence their psychic or physical suffering was secondary. By contrast Jesus dies in total *discontinuity* with His life and His cause."

103. Cf., among others, K. Rahner, *A New Christology*, p. 22: "Hans Küng can assert today that Jesus did not found a Church, and what is more, in saying this express a truth that can no longer be denied." Rahner makes that statement, however, with reservations, noting that Jesus did "found" a Church in the sense that the Church came from Jesus (*Idem.*, p. 24).

The above statements, cited here merely as examples, are to be weighed against hundreds of thousands of opinions about Jesus which have arisen since He first appeared. These are cited only to suggest some current tendencies, and it should be noted that not all the writers cited as exemplifying the various statements in the text would agree with all the five points as listed. There is as yet no full consensus on an overall picture of Jesus' human knowledge even within the general "revisionist" tendency. The individual conclusions, however, reflect elements in the growing "stock idea" of Jesus outlined by Ratzinger (*op. cit.*, pp. 157-159).

104. *DS* 419.
105. *DS* 474-476.
106. *DS* 3428.
107. *DS* 3432.
108. *DS* 3433.
109. *DS* 3434.
110. *DS* 3435.
111. *DS* 3438.
112. *DS* 3905.
113. *Puebla and Beyond*, Orbis Books, Maryknoll, N.T., 1980, pp. 145 and 151.

We have cited what we consider only the most significant of the Magisterial statements. For further reference, cf. William Most, *The Consciousness of Christ*.

To all such statements may be appended the following:

"Discussions of Jesus' human knowledge raise the question: was Jesus humanly aware of His personal self? It would go against Catholic tradition and teaching to suggest that Jesus did not know of His being the only-begotten, divine Son of God. This judgment is not based on individual scriptural texts or on whether and how Christ used one title or another. It relies rather on the interconnection and inner harmony of the truths of faith. A truly divine Person, Jesus was given, perhaps gradually and ever more clearly, a human awareness of His personal identity. He needed this especially if He was to accomplish the mission given Him by His Father.

"The collective force of these ecclesial memories of Jesus is to assure us that He was humanly aware that He was the Messiah, the Son of Man sent to establish the kingdom. More than that, it assures us that He was humanly aware of an even deeper mystery in Himself, that He was and is the true and only-begotten Son of God the Father" (Pastoral Letter of the Bishops of Canada, *Jesus Christ Center of the Christian Life*, Publication Service of the CCCB, Ottawa, Ontario, 1981, nos. 22-26).

"I know that you give careful attention to the need for healthy theology—and rightly so, at a time when we can see considerable revival of ancient brands of Gnosticism as well as bold denials of things that touch the very heart of Catholic Faith, such as for example, the absence of knowledge (or at least the uncertainty) in Christ Himself regarding His identity as Son of God, and many other points vital to our Credo" (John Paul II to Bishops of Belgium, Sept. 18, 1982, *L'Osservatore Romano*, English edition, Oct. 25, 1982, p. 4).

114. Hans Küng, with his amazing skill for saying explicitly what others only imply, wrote the following to Cardinal Höffner of Germany on Feb. 21, 1977:

"...This is the way in which to construct on solid historical foundations a Christology 'from below' as suggested by the whole historical research of the last 200 years. The Christology 'from above' is known to me.... I still regard it as a legitimate Christology. Yet I have already explained...why today it seems to me to be objectively right and pastorally appropriate to approach Christology 'from below.'

"...It makes a decisive difference..., methodologically, whether, in dealing with the interpretation of the New Testament witness, as well as with the traditional Christology from the Fathers to Karl Barth, a doctrine of the Trinity and of the Incarnation is the premise from which we start, and then move deductively from God ('from above') to the man Jesus of Nazareth; or whether I, as well as various other Catholic and Protestant theologians, begin by taking stock of modern exegetical discussions, and, placing ourselves time and again in the perspective of the first disciples of Jesus, as it were ('from below'), we systematically think our way to God, inductively and interpretatively. When one attempts an exact definition of the concepts, one cannot think with methodological consistency 'from above' and 'from below' at the same time. For a methodological point of view, we have here a genuine either/or" (*The Küng Dialogue*, USCC, Washington, D.C., 1980, p. 114).

One of the best critiques of the "Christology from above" and a defense of the "Christology from below" is given by Wolfhart Pannenberg, *Jesus—God and Man*, pp. 33-37. It cannot be denied that there is a defense to be made for it inasmuch as it serves as an apologetic approach to Christology. Nevertheless, apart from the fact that it still presupposes an ability to reach a Christ or Jesus whose historical reality lies "under" the Gospel presentation of Him, its overall value is dubious. In itself, it cannot give us a full treatment of Jesus as Christian faith knows Him or even as He knew and presented Himself. Walter Kasper, *Jesus the Christ*, while not adverse to all the elements entailed in a "Christology from below" concludes that "a Christology purely 'from below' is...condemned to failure" (p. 247). Joseph Fitzmyer, *The Gospel According to Luke, I-IX*, comments on the lack in Luke and Matthew of any such notion as a "Christology from below" (p. 447), and the same can be safely said of the entire New Testament. Enough has already been said about the ambiguity of "historical reconstructions" which, in essence, is what a Christology from below is.

115. A brief presentation of the "quest" for the historical Jesus, and the "new quest" launched by some of the disciples of Bultmann in the 1950's can be found in R. Brown and P. Joseph Cahill, *Biblical Tendencies Today: an Introduction to the Post-Bultmannians*, Corpus Books, Washington, D.C., 1969.

116. An example of how the individual words or "logia" of Jesus are disputed among the exegetes can be seen by examining the various approaches to the example given in the text, viz., Mt. 11:25-27. Some reject the authenticity of the text outright, seeing it as a construct of the later community; some accept its essential authenticity; others would accept it as is. Cf. R. Bultmann, *History of the Synoptic Tradition*, p. 166; Joachim Jeremias, *New Testament Theology*, pp. 56ff.; Oscar Culmann, *The Christology of the New Testament*, pp. 286ff.; R. Gundry, *Matthew*, pp. 215ff., etc. Marcus Barth, *Ephesians*, vol. I, p. 109, note 203, even sees the text as containing the notion of preexistence, thus placing himself in harmony with Craddock (cf. note 3 above).

117. *Dei Verbum*, no. 19.

118. *Idem.*, no. 11.

119. On *Abba*, cf. J. Jeremias, *op. cit.*, pp. 62ff.: "If we keep in mind this setting for *abba*, it will be clear why Palestinian Judaism does not use *abba* as a form of address to God. *Abba* was a children's word, used in everyday talk, an expression of courtesy. It would have seemed disrespectful, indeed unthinkable, to the sensibilities of Jesus' contemporaries to address God with this familiar word. Jesus dared to use *Abba* as a form of address to God. This Abba is the *ipsissima vox* Jesu" (p. 67). E. Schillebeeckx, *Jesus* (p. 266) writes: "Jesus' experience and awareness of the Father in prayer was also manifested in what for His listeners was an astonishing way of speaking about God, so much so that some took offense at it. It was not in His use of *Abba* as a way of addressing God that Jesus showed Himself to be forsaking late Judaism; but the *Abba* form of address (expressing a religious experience of a special color), when linked with the substance of Jesus' message, ministry and praxis, began

to prompt theological questions. The *Abba* experience would appear to be the source of the peculiar nature of Jesus' message and conduct, which without this religious experience, or apart from it, loses the distinctive meaning and content actually conferred on them by Jesus."

Schillebeeckx writes, however, that this Abba-experience of Jesus does not allow us "to build on it an awareness on Jesus' part of some 'transcendent' sonship and still less a Trinitarian doctrine.... For that more is needed. If we can find it, then in Jesus' unaffected intercourse with God as *Abba* we may justifiably perceive the natural consequences of it; not, however, the other way around" (p. 260).

120. Cf. the teaching of Vatican Council I in its Constitution *Dei Filius* on Divine Revelation, faith and human reason, especially chapter 4. See in particular DS 1315-1317.

121. *De praedestinatione sanctorum*, 15, 30-31 (PL 44, 781-983). It is the second reading of Roman Breviary for Friday of 13th week of Year.

122. St. Augustine, *In Johannem*, 21, 3.

123. Cf. above, pp. 39-41.

124. Cf. Juan Alfaro, *Mysterium Salutis*, III, I (Spanish Edition, Ediciones Cristiandad, Madrid, 1971, pp. 732-735: "As true man, Christ has a human consciousness which translates the ontological perfection of His humanity, hypostatically assumed by the Logos, into an internal experience.... The man Jesus could not have an awareness of Himself without an immediate knowledge of the Person of the Word, subsistent relation with the Father, that is to say, without the immediate vision of God, His Father.... In human experience Christ lives His divine filiation; in the most profound center of His psychic life He experiences God as His Father." Etc.

Although one need not agree in all particulars, Alfaro's treatment is among the best. In its turn, it is dependent—although clearer—on K. Rahner's "Dogmatic Reflections on the Knowledge and Self-Consciousness of Christ," *Theological Investigations*, vol. V, pp. 157ff. Rahner writes there: "This means, however, that this really existing direct vision of God is nothing other than the original unobjectified consciousness of divine sonship, which is present by the mere fact that there *is* a hypostatic union" (p. 208). We have tried to avoid the particularities about the beatific vision being "objectified" or "unobjectified" since the nature of the beatific vision in Christ is completely beyond our ability to comprehend.

Cf. also Frederick E. Crowe, "The Mind of Jesus," *Communio*, Winter, 1974, pp. 365ff. Crowe makes a valid and important conclusion: "A real religious need now in this very time of emphasis on the Lord's humanity, is to recognize that Jesus even as man has more than we have. I am sure the author of Hebrews could defend his use of the proposition that Jesus is like us in all things except sin, but I doubt that we can defend the varied use we make of it; Jesus is different, we have to face that and take account of it" (p. 384).

Emile Mersch, *Theology of the Mystical Body*, pp. 384ff., had long anticipated the thought of Rahner and Alfaro.

125. Cf. *S. Th.*, II, IIae, q. 45, a. 2 c.

126. Charles Dickens understood this truth when he had his heroine, Esther Summerson, write: "I had always rather a noticing way—not a quick way, oh, no!—a silent way of noticing what passed before men and thinking I should like to understand it better. I have not by any means a quick understanding. When I love a person very tenderly indeed, it seems to brighten" (*Bleak House*, Signet Classic, New American Library, Inc., New York, 1980, p. 31).

127. Cf. J. Maritain, *The Degrees of Knowledge*, pp. 259ff. Maritain studies "knowledge by connaturality" and its relation to the mystical element in prayer. What is said there would have to be said in an eminent way of the prayer of Christ.

128. St. Athanasius wrote of this *ekonomia*. Cf. for example, *Discourse II Against the Arians*, XX, no. 51, *Nicene and Post-Nicene Fathers*, second series, pp. 376ff. Athanasius himself, of course, admitted certain forms of ignorance in the humanity of Christ (cf. *Discourse I Against the Arians*, *Idem.*, ch. XIII, no. 62-63 where he attributes such ignorance to the *ekonomia*). Even if his views on ignorance should be rejected—and have been rejected—the notion of the *ekonomia* itself is valid as part of the *kenosis* of the Incarnation.

129. J. Alfaro, *op. cit.*: "The mystery of His divine filiation, Christ learned from no one but His Father.... The knowledge acquired by the man Jesus in His contact with the world and with men served to help Him conceptualize and thus express to Himself and to others in human signs His interior secret" (p. 734).

130. Vincent Taylor, *The Person of Christ*, correctly points out the limits of historical criticism in the area of Jesus' self-awareness, when he writes: "Restated, the conclusion is this: Within the limitation of the human life of Jesus His consciousness of Sonship was gained through the knowledge that God was His Father, mediated by prayer and communion with Him in a process of growth and development which begins before the opening of the historic ministry and is consummated in decisive experiences of revelation and intuition....

"The conclusion just stated appears to represent the furthest point to which historical criticism can go.... Nevertheless, it must be recognized that unless we are willing to consider the theological issues, we must confess that the problem of Christ's divine consciousness is insoluble" (p. 186).

Notes for Part II

1. *In Johannem*, XV, 6, 7. Trans., *Nicene and Post-Nicene Fathers*, series two, vol. VII, pp. 100-101.

2. There is general agreement among experts on the chronology, at least within a two year margin. One should consult the standard references and commentaries, as well as some of the older "Lives" of Christ which often treated the matter in greater detail than many of the more recent works.

3. It is such a compressed view of chronology and geography that may be said to account in part for the view of those who write and speak of the so-called "Galilean crisis" of Jesus. These authors would hold that, after initial successes in Galilee, Jesus sensed growing rejection and decided to entrust His fate to the capital city. Others modify this view and see the "Galilean crisis" as one of several, and one which prompted a change in focus of His mission, leading Him first to the "ten towns of the Decapolis" and the area in what is today Southern Lebanon (cf. Mk. 7:24, 31), and later to Jerusalem. Jon Sobrino goes so far as to parallel these geographic shifts with a type of "identity crisis" in Jesus. He has written:

"The end of the first stage comes with what is called the 'crisis in Galilee.' It is given that geographical label because Jesus abandons the heart of Galilee, heading first to Caesarea Philippi and then toward the ten towns of the Decapolis.... This geographical break in Jesus' activity expresses an even deeper break in the Person of Jesus Himself. Jesus comes to realize that He has failed in His mission as He had previously understood it. The crowds are abandoning Him, the religious leaders of the Jewish people will not accept Him, and God is not getting any closer with power to renovate reality. So there is a real break in both the internal awareness and external activity of Jesus" *(Christology at the Crossroads*, p. 93). Cf. also, L. Boff, *Jesus Christ, Liberator*, p. 116; X. Leon-Dufour, "Jesus face a la mort menacante," Nouvelle revue Theologique, 110: 6, pp. 803-821 (Eng. synopsis in *Theology Digest*, vol. 29, no. 1, pp. 57-60). Leon-Dufour describes the first six chapters of Mark's Gospel as a "true Galilean springtime" ("un veritable 'printemps Galileen'") and, while admitting with F. Mussner that we do not have a biography of the Lord, thinks that the literary sources impose some such chronological order as Mark seems to give in those chapters (p. 807).

As can be seen from our text, the entire construction is artificial, an artificiality probably deliberately chosen by the evangelists (almost certainly so by Luke), but being used by current writers for purposes far different than the evangelists'. It simply is not possible to construct a complete chronology from Mark's Gospel for the events of the ministry. To presume that one can, and then to construct a history of development in the ministry or, even more, a development in Jesus' human psychology, indicates that one is working with the literary genus called historical fiction.

4. There are similarities to be noted between this episode and Heb. 5:7-10, as well as to the Lord's prayer in Gethsemane (Mt. 26:38; Mk. 14:34).

5. It would seem that V. Taylor's comment *(The Gospel According to St. Mark*, p. 162) must be accepted as accurate: "The fundamental note in the saying (Mk. 1:11) is the filial status of Jesus, and the words are best understood as an assurance, or confirmation, of this relationship, rather than a disclosure or revelation." He also notes that Mark 1:11 "gives strong support to the contention of Harnack that 'our Lord's consciousness of Sonship must have preceded in time His consciousness of Messiahship, must indeed have formed a stepping-stone to the latter'" *(Ibid.)*.

6. *S. Th.*, II, IIae, q. 188, a. 6 c.

7. *Collected Letters of St. Thérèse of Lisieux* (Trans. F. J. Sheed), Sheed and Ward, London, 1972, p. 316.

8. *Idem.*, p. 292.

9. Epistle to Romans, 7. Eng. trans. in *Ancient Christian Writers*, vol. I (James Kleist, S.J.), Newman, Westminster, Md., p. 83.

10. Cf. Joachim Jeremias, *New Testament Theology*, pp. 133-134: "Even more, Jesus instructed His disciples to limit their activity to Israel and expressly forbade them to go to the Gentiles.... This does not mean that Jesus excluded the Gentiles from the *basileia*. It does mean, rather, He expected the eschatological pilgrimage of the peoples to Zion (Mt. 8:11 par., Luke 13:28ff.) as God's mighty act at the coming of His reign."

Hans Küng, *On Being a Christian*, p. 167: "...he could not have thought of any proclamation among the Gentiles."

Eduard Schweizer, *Jesus*, p. 42: "So strong is His desire to call all men to God that even the limits of Jewish nationality and Jewish religion are not absolute limits for Him (Mk. 7:15, 29; Mt. 8:11-12; etc.). The idea that slowly gained the upper hand in the Old Testament, contending against opposition and competing with other ideas...was namely the realization that, as the chosen People of God, Israel could never be an end in itself but only a representative and emissary for the entire world—this idea is embodied uniquely and astonishingly in Jesus."

11. Cf. Mt. 24:14; Mk. 13:10; 14:9. Jeremias considers these sayings inauthentic *(op. cit.,* p. 134). On the other hand, cf. V. Taylor, *The Gospel According to Mark,* pp. 507-508, 534.

12. Both R. Brown *(The Gospel of John,* vol. I, pp. 175-176) and R. Schnackenburn *(The Gospel of John,* vol. I, p. 420) argue for the historical plausibility of the Johannine account.

13. Whether Paul himself expected the end within his own lifetime is not easy to determine. Certain passages in his writings would seem to imply such an expectation (1 Thes. 4:15-17, etc.), but the *hemeis hoi zontes* ("those of us who are living") there can readily be understood as an indefinite, much as if one were to say while preaching to a congregation, "Those of us who see the turn of the century." Such language is both common and indefinite enough to preclude any certain reading of the speaker or writer's expectation for self. Furthermore, like Jesus, Paul stated definitely that he did not know the "times and seasons" of the end (1 Thes. 5:1).

14. Cf. Hal Lindsey, *The Late Great Planet Earth,* Zondervan Publ., Grand Rapids, Mich., 1970.

15. It was Albert Schweitzer in 1906 who set the tone for such views when he stressed the eschatological or apocalyptic element in the life of Jesus (cf. *The Quest of the Historical Jesus,* p. 370ff.). This work has had enormous influence as the frequent reprintings and translations since 1906 evidence. Schweitzer's approach can be said to be the basis for the talk of a "Galilean crisis" in the life of Jesus, to which reference has already been made. Modified in various ways since Schweitzer—especially by the tendency of Barth and Bultmann to remove the apocalyptic or futurist aspect from eschatology (cf. Jurgen Moltmann, *Theology of Hope,* pp. 37-93), its influence persists. Cf., for example, W. G. Kümmel, *The Theology of the New Testament,* pp. 32-33: "The threat of judgment on 'this generation' (Mt. 12:41-42 par.) and the reference to the sudden coming of the Son of Man in judgment (Mt. 24:43-44 par.; Mk. 8:38 par.) show unmistakably that Jesus also announced the *early* coming of the judgment day.... One cannot deny, without doing violence to the texts, that Jesus anticipated a temporally *very near approach* of the kingdom of God, yet it is only a few of the extant words of Jesus which speak of this temporally limited closeness."

Cf., also, Hans Küng, *On Being a Christian,* pp. 181, 216-218: "...it is clear from the oldest stratum of the Synoptic tradition that Jesus expects the kingdom of God in the immediate future" (p. 216). For K. Rahner, cf. note 101 of Part I above.

16. Cf. Hans Küng, *On Being a Christian,* p. 217: "...Jesus Himself did not speak of the imminence of God's rule merely with a kind of 'prophetic intensity,' but really believed in the immediate proximity of the kingdom. This belief alone can explain His extraordinarily urgent sayings about not being concerned for security of life, food, and clothing, about prayer being heard, the faith that moves mountains, the decision that cannot be deferred; the imagery of the great banquet and even the Our Father and the beatitudes."

Such an approach goes back to Schweitzer, and of it Ernst Käsemann has written appropriately: "Hardly any New Testament scholar will now be left who agrees with Schweitzer's answer—namely, that Jesus, inspired by a burning expectation of the end, sent His disciples out on a hasty mission to Palestine had Himself proclaimed an 'interim ethic'; then, finally, when His hopes proved ill-founded, sought to force divine intervention by His journey to Jerusalem and so perished" ("Primitive Christian Apocalyptic," *New Testament Questions of Today*, p. 111). W. G. Kümmel also views the notion of an "interim ethic" as incorrect. Cf. *The Theology of the New Testament*, pp. 48-49. It would seem, however, that some forms of stressing the "time-bound" aspect of Jesus' teaching will inevitably run the danger of reducing Jesus' teaching to an "interim ethic" (cf. note 100, Part I above).

17. Norman Perrin's conclusions about this matter are appropriate: "The conclusion to be drawn from this discussion of the teaching of Jesus concerning the future is, we believe, that Jesus did look toward a consummation of that which had begun in His own ministry, and that He did indicate various aspects of that consummation. But He did not offer any specific instruction as to its exact nature.... To do justice to this teaching we must hold fast to the conviction that the consummation of that which has begun in the ministry of Jesus *will be*.... How? When? Where? may be natural questions but they are illegitimate questions in view of the fact that the teaching of Jesus seems deliberately to avoid anything that could be construed as an answer to them..." (*The Kingdom of God in the Teaching of Jesus,* pp. 189-190).

E. Käsemann, *New Testament Questions of Today*, pp. 112-113, writes: "Jesus is obviously speaking of the coming of the *basileia* in a sense different from that of the Baptist and of contemporary Judaism; His reference is not only or primarily to an end of the world which can in principle be dated within chronological time. This means, however, that the alternative—so useful in other contexts—of a present or a future eschatology becomes, ultimately and in the strict sense, useless when applied to the message of Jesus.... Obviously in the mind of Jesus there is no separation between the God who is near and the God who is far off, because Creator and Judge cannot be separated without doing injury to the Godhead of God."

On E. Schillebeeckx's opinion on this matter—a view not all that clear—cf. *Jesus*, pp. 152 and 177.

18. Cf. St. Athanasius, *Discourse II Against the Arians*, 59 (PG 26, 273), English trans., *The Nicene and Post-Nicene Fathers*, series II, vol. 4, p. 380: "...for men, being by nature creatures, could not become sons except by receiving the Spirit of the true and natural Son. And so that this might be, 'the Word became flesh' so that He might make men capable of receiving divinity.... We are not sons by nature...and the Father is not our Father by nature, but is Father of that Word in us in whom and cause of whom we cry, 'Abba, Father.'"

19. Cf. Emile Mersch, S.J., *The Theology of the Mystical Body*, p. 364: "Through the hypostatic union, therefore, this human nature has the same relations as the second Person has.... The sacred humanity possesses, in the Word, all the relations of the Word."

20. The historicity of the temptation itself is generally accepted by exegetes, although certainly not universally. Cf. J. Jeremias, *New Testament Theology*, pp. 70-74. Worthy of special attention is the remark of Jeremias on the word *peirasmos* which we normally translate as "temptation": "The word *peirasmos* occurs

twenty-one times in the N.T. In no less than twenty of them, however, it has the meaning of 'trial,' 'testing,' 'ordeal'; only in one passage does it clearly denote 'temptation to sin' (1 Tm. 6:9).... For the meaning of the so-called 'temptation story' is not that Jesus was put in the way of sin and rejected it; rather the story is about Jesus' acceptance of His mission" (p. 74). The remarks are accurate, and should be noted by all those who use Hebrews 4:15 ("...he was tempted in every way that we are...") as a basis for ill-advised remarks on Jesus' inability to sin, for the word in that context is *peirasmos*. As 1 Tm. 6:9 demonstrates, the word can have the meaning we normally associate with "temptation," but so often the word takes on for us the association with a spiritual or psychological response to the "testing" which goes beyond the actual meaning of the Greek that it is not truly appropriate when applied to Jesus.

21. As such, a "Galilean springtime" which witnessed a ministry free of trial or struggle is unbiblical. Cf. note 3 above.

22. Paul VI, "Talk of Nov. 15, 1972," *TPS*, vol. 17, no. 4, pp. 315ff.

23. *Idem.*, p. 317.

24. On efforts to demythologize the devil, cf., among many others, T. McDermott, O.P., "The Devil and His Angels," *New Blackfriars*, vol. 48 (Oct. 1966), pp. 16-25; P. Schoonenberg, *God's World in the Making*, pp. 8ff., esp., note 16; *The New Catechism*, pp. 482ff.

25. The fundamental pronouncement of the Magisterium is the *Firmiter* of Lateran IV (*DS* 800-801; cf. Appendix). On the dogmatic value of the *Firmiter*, cf. Paul Quay, S.J., "Angels and Demons: The Teaching of Lateran IV," *Theological Studies*, vol. 42, no. 1, pp. 20ff.; Cong. for Doctrine of the Faith, "Christian Faith and Demonology," *TPS*, vol. 20, nos. 3-4, pp. 209ff. Cf. also *DS* 1511; the following documents of Vatican II: *Gaudium et spes*, nos. 2, 13; *Sacrosanctum concilium*, no. 6; *Ad gentes*, nos. 3, 9; *Lumen gentium*, no. 16. Also, Paul VI, "Talk of Nov. 15, 1972," *TPS*, vol. 17, no. 4, pp. 315ff.

Whether the existence of the devil is an infallible teaching of the Church from the ordinary or extraordinary Magisterium is disputed, depending on the evaluation made of the *Firmiter*. That the existence of the devil is infallibly taught *de fide* is certain. Even as far back as the time of the Council of Trent, Melchior Cano held that the *Firmiter* of Lateran IV did not directly define this matter (cf. A. Theiner, *Acta Genuina*, I, p. 493), but in light of the studies cited above his accuracy is to be doubted.

26. The final petition of the Lord's Prayer should perhaps be translated as "Deliver as from the Evil One."

27. "In the biblical testimony about Jesus Christ there is included, as an undeniable negative presupposition, the existence of a superhuman power of darkness, conquered by the death of Christ on the cross..." (Michael Seeman, *Mysterium Salutis*, II, 2, p. 1046). Cf. K. Rahner's article "Devil" in *Sacramentum Mundi*; H. Schlier, *Principalities and Powers in the New Testament*.

28. *Gaudium et spes*, no. 2.

29. Despite the translation of 1 Cor. 2:6 in the *NAB*, the *arkontes* (rulers) mentioned by Paul in verses 6, 7, and 8 are not to be understood as "men" but as angelic beings. Cf. 2 Cor. 4:4; Eph. 6:12, etc., and H. Schlier, *Principalities and Powers in the New Testament*, and *JBC*, 51:19.

30. *To the Ephesians*, 19. Trans. Cyril Richardson, *Early Christian Fathers*, p. 93.

31. Cf. Martin Hengel, *Judaism and Hellenism*, I, pp. 176, 253.

32. *Idem.*, pp. 143, 81 (Antigonus of Sacho, the reputed founder of the Sadducees).

33. "Zechariah son of Barachiah" has been something of an exegetical and theological problem (one not present in the Lucan parallel, 11:51, which does not contain the words). Most think that the Zechariah referred to is the man spoken of in 2 Chr. 24:20-22. If that is so, his father was not Barachiah, but Jehoiada. One should consult the commentaries for the various solutions proposed. The problem was known at least as far back as St. Jerome's time.

34. J. Jeremias, *The Parables of Jesus*, p. 21, makes the following remarks about the parables but which are appropriate for the general context of struggle for the kingdom: "...they were predominantly concerned with a situation of conflict. They correct, reprove, attack. For the greater part, though not exclusively, the parables are weapons of warfare."

35. Cf. D. S. Russell, *The Method and Message of Jewish Apocalyptic*, pp. 252ff.

36. Vatican Council II, *Gaudium et spes*, no. 13. Cf. *DS* 371-372; 1510-1516.

37. The teaching of Jesus on the eternity of hell as a consequence of one's own evil works has been repeated infallibly, at opportune times, by His Church. Cf. *Firmiter* of Lateran IV (*DS* 801; Appendix); the Council of Lyons (*DS* 858); Vatican Council II (*Lumen gentium*, no. 48). The discussions at Vatican II make it clear that the passage in *Lumen gentium*, no. 48 does not speak of the salvation of the entire human race and that it is to be presumed that some will actually be damned; hell is not merely a possibility. Cf. *Acta Synodalia*, vol. 3, part 8, pp. 140-145.

38. Teilhard de Chardin, *The Divine Milieu*, p. 147.

39. *Idem.*, p. 148.

40. The note on this verse in the *Jerusalem Bible* and in John Meier's *Matthew*, p. 274, indicate that the "how often" may reveal a knowledge in Matthew's tradition of more than one visit of the Lord to Jerusalem.

41. *The Jewish War*, trans., by G. A. Williamson, p. 325.

42. The *Jerusalem Bible*, commenting on Lk. 19:41ff. notes, with what would seem to be complete accuracy: "This whole prophecy is made up of O.T. references...and suggests the destruction of Jerusalem in 587 as much as, and more than, that of 70 A.D. of whose distinctive features it says nothing. It cannot, therefore, be concluded from this text that the destruction of 70 A.D. had already taken place." Cf. G. A. Williamson, *op. cit.*, "Introduction," esp. pp. 8-9.
As far as Mt. 22:1-14 with its reference to the king burning the city, cf. Introduction. There are parallels in the O.T. which, as in the case with the Lucan references, would be sufficient to explain any reference to a city, even Jerusalem, being burned. Cf. Neh. 1:3-4; Jer. 21:10; 22:7; Ps. 74:7-8; Ez. 24:9-11; 28:18-19; Lam. 2:3; 4:11; Zech. 9:4, etc.
At times people are so busy looking for *vaticinia ex eventu* in order to show that Jesus could not have predicted such and such that they miss the obvious: certain

types of foresight are not uncommon even among people far less endowed than the Lord. If a nonscientist and literary figure could "predict" in 1927 a destructive use for atomic energy and laser beams (cf. A. C. Mallowan, *The Big Four*, Dodd, Mead and Co., Inc., New York, 1927; reprinted 1972, Dell Pub. Co., p. 160), one should be very sober in what one denies as a possibility for Jesus.

43. Cf. Eusebius, *Ecclesiastical History* Book III, ch. V.

44. On Mt. 10:17 cf. Introduction. There is not sufficient reason to conclude that Jesus expected for His followers better treatment than He Himself received (cf. Lk. 4:28-30; Mk. 3:1-6; Jn. 7:20-24).

45. St. Thomas Aquinas, *Super Evangelium S. Joannis*, p. 68. Alan Richardson, *The Gospel According to St. John*, thinks the Cana account "is a parable, not an actual historical fact" (p. 56), but finds the meaning of the "parable" where St. Thomas does, except for the Marian aspect.

46. *S. Th.*, III, q. 43, a. 1 c; cf. Vatican Council II, *Dei Verbum*, no. 2.

47. *S. Th.*, III, q. 44, a. 4, ad 3.

48. Cf. *S. Th.*, III, q. 44, a. 1-4.

49. Cf. W. Kaspar, *Jesus the Christ*, pp. 89ff.; Alan Richardson, *An Introduction to the Theology of the New Testament*, pp. 95ff.; J. Jeremias, *New Testament Theology*, pp. 85ff.

50. John Meier, *Matthew*, p. 165, remarks on the "I am" statement: "Indeed, the divine ego eimi ("I am" or "it is I") probably means here what it meant in Ex. 3:14: "I am here to save you."

51. Cf. J. Jeremias, *New Testament Theology*, p. 87.

52. Cf. R. Brown's remarks on the *epi tes thalasses* in *The Gospel According to John*, I, p. 252, where he notes that translating the phrase as "on the seashore" would seem to make the story "pointless." That observation can be applied equally to the Matthean and Marcan narratives. Cf. A. Richardson, *The Gospel According to St. John*, p. 97.

53. Thus, for example, Kaspar, *Jesus the Christ*, p. 90.

54. The reasoning that goes into such conjectures is not always that of strict logic. The commentaries of R. Brown and R. Schnackenburg of John's Gospel offer a ready example of this when they treat the Johannine account of Christ's walking on the water. Both men agree that the Johannine account is more primitive than Mark's (and Matthew's) basically because of the terseness of John's treatment (cf. Brown, *op. cit.*, I, p. 254; Schnackenburg, *op. cit.*, II, p. 28). It should be noted, also, that Brown claims the Johannine account is more primitive because of its "lack of emphasis on the miraculous" while S. sees it as belonging to the primitive "semeia source" because "the account gives prominence...to the extraordinary and miraculous things."

The Marcan and Matthean accounts, being longer, would indicate greater theological development and so a less primitive retelling. That presupposition is not demonstrable, and often, in fact, the opposite can be demonstrated, viz., that the more elaborate account is more primitive. Terseness alone will not demonstrate that one account is more primitive than another (compare, for example, Mt. 8:28-34 and Mk. 5:1-20).

The different evaluation made by the two commentators concerning the importance of the miraculous in the Johannine account reminds one again of the subjective element in the argumentation from internal evidence, and also of the difficulty involved in drawing conclusions about conjectured sources.

55. W. Kaspar, *Jesus the Christ*, p. 91, puts this well. His suggestions on the particular miracles are not always as happy. Attempting to show, for example, how

the Gospels tend "to intensify, magnify and multiply the miracles," he cites Mark and Matthew's accounts of the raising of the daughter of Jairus (Mt. 9:18-26; Mk. 5:21-43) as what is presumably an example of "intensification." He writes: "In Mark Jairus' daughter is on the point of death; in Matthew she is already dead" *(Jesus the Christ,* p. 89). He presumes that Mark is the earlier written of the accounts. Even on that presumption, however, the observation is not pertinent. The account in Mark indeed begins by saying the girl is on the point of death (Mk. 5:23) while Matthew has the father saying that she is already dead (Mt. 9:18). However, before Jesus ever gets to the girl, Mark also reports that she has in fact died in the meantime (Mk. 5:35), and thus the whole point of Kaspar's observation about a tendency to intensify the miraculous is not *ad rem.*

56. St. Augustine, *In Johannem ad Parthos,* V, 7. An English trans. may be found in *The Nicene and Post-Nicene Fathers,* first series, vol. VII, p. 490.

57. C. S. Lewis, *Perelandra,* pp. 199-200.

58. For the meaning of the famous "exceptive clause" in Matthew's version of the teaching on divorce (Mt. 19:9; 5:32), cf. J. Meier, *Matthew,* pp. 52-53, 216. Correctly understood as prohibiting unions within certain degrees of consanguinity or affinity, the so-called Matthean "exception" is in fact no exception at all, and Matthew's version is in agreement with the absolute prohibition recorded in Mk. and Lk.

59. Cf. *Gaudium et spes* of Vatican Council II: "Marriage and conjugal love are by their nature ordained toward the begetting and educating of children" (no. 50).

60. At length and with great depth, Pope John Paul II has analyzed some of the implications of what Jesus is teaching about marriage when He refers back to creation: monogamous union, the purposes of that union as companionship and procreation, the meaning of the human body, the effects of the Fall on sexuality, etc. Cf. *Original Unity of Man and Woman.*

61. Jesus is citing Micah 7:5-6.

62. The NIV, NAB, the Jerusalem Bible and perhaps the Vulgate adopt this interpretation.

The word translated as "out of his mind" (Gk., *exeste,* from *existamai)* offers different connotations according to context. Cf. Mt. 12:23; Mk. 2:12; 5:42; 6:51; 2 Cor. 5:13, etc. The nearest one can come to a generalized sense for the word would seem to be our English expression "to be beside oneself." One can see the translation difficulties by comparing the different renderings of 2 Cor. 5:13:

NIV—"If we are out of our mind, it is for the sake of God; but if we are in our right mind it is for you."

NAB—"Indeed, if we are ever caught up out of ourselves, God is the reason; and when we are brought back to our senses, it is for your sakes."

Jerusalem Bible—"If we seemed out of our senses, it was for God; but if we are being reasonable now it is for your sake."

RSV—"For if we are beside ourselves, it is for God; if we are in our right mind, it is for you."

63. V. Taylor, *The Gospel According to St. Mark,* pp. 235-237, although indicating another possible reading as one defended by some, accepts this interpretation. J. Fitzmyer, *The Gospel According to Luke,* also reads it this way, seeing a "negative attitude" toward Mary which "would suggest a different view of her in the earlier tradition from what one finds here in the Lucan story" (p. 341). Indeed, for Fitzmyer, Luke completely changes the meaning of the logion in Mk.

3:31-35 so as to make Jesus speak in praise of His Mother and family (pp. 722-725). R. Brown, et al, *Mary in the New Testament*, pp. 51-54 hold the same understanding of the Marcan text, but, given the obvious difficulties of the Greek text, their "tone" is more certain than their actual statements (e.g., "...the Marcan context inclines us strongly"—it "is likely that for Mark the 'mother and brothers' of 3:31...are the same as 'his own' of 3:21 who set out [from Nazareth] to seize Him." "There are signs that Mark sees the events in 3:20-35 as a unit...," etc.).

64. Cf. V. Taylor, *The Gospel According to St. Mark*, pp. 235-237.

65. This is the reading given by M. Zerwick, *Analysis Philologica Novi Testamenti Graeci*, Rome, 1953, p. 84. The RSV, although adopting "family" as the meaning of *hoi par' autou*, translates the entire text so that it is the crowd, not the family, who claims Jesus is "beside Himself." All admit this is a possible reading of the Greek, but many would not consider it probable.

66. J. Fitzmyer, *The Gospel According to Luke*, I-IX, p. 725, is emphatic that Luke presents the text as praise of Mary and the brothers: "So runs the literal translation of Luke, other attempts to interpret these words notwithstanding." Cf. Brown *et al*, *op. cit.*, pp. 169-170.

67. St. Augustine, *Holy Virginity*, St. Paul Editions, Boston, MA, (John McQuade, translator), 1961, pp. 22-23. Cf. C. S. Lewis, "The Psalms," *Christian Reflections*, pp. 120-121 for an insightful comparison between the harshness of Jesus' language in respect to His family and the harshness of Mary's language in the *Magnificat*.

68. There are undoubtedly differences in emphasis between Luke and the other evangelists in respect to money and the poor, but it is one of emphasis, not of contradiction. "...the attitude toward wealth in the Lucan Gospel did not originate with Luke himself. There is no need to think that it is not rooted in the preaching of the historical Jesus" (J. Fitzmyer, *The Gospel According to Luke*, p. 248).

69. *S. Th.*, III, q. 1, a. 5 c.

70. Cf. Suetonius, *The Twelve Caesars* (Robert Graves, trans.), Penguin Books, London, 1970, p. 132.

71. Cf. Rudolf Schnackenburg, *The Moral Teaching of the New Testament*, pp. 118-119: "(Jesus) leaves the secular state and at that time the pagan state its rights in its own sphere, but only to the extent that the all-embracing rights of God over man are not thereby violated. This implies a reservation in regard to the state, but there is no reservation in regard to God."

72. Pope Paul VI, "Address to Wednesday Audience of Feb. 3, 1971"; cf. Oscar Cullmann, *Jesus and the Revolutionaries*.

73. Paul VI, "Address to Wednesday Audience of Jan. 27, 1971," reprinted in *Who Is Jesus?*, St. Paul Editions, Boston, 1972, p. 37.

74. This rejection of power, even when it could be used for a good end, is included in Jesus' rejection of "political messianism" (cf. O. Cullmann, *Jesus and the Revolutionaries*, pp. 10, 39).

75. Paul VI, *op. cit.*, p. 36.

76. It can be noted that the names of all the Twelve as listed by Mt., Mk., and Lk. are in full agreement with the exception of "Thaddeus" (Mt. and Mk.) and "Jude of James" (Lk.). John does not have a full list, but includes a Nathaniel not listed in the Synoptics. Tradition has identified Thaddeus with Jude and probably accurately (cf. J. Jeremias, *New Testament Theology*, pp. 232ff.). Nathaniel has long been identified with Bartholomew, but cf. R. Brown, *Gospel According to John*, I, p. 82, who thinks Nathaniel may not have been one of the Twelve.

77. The thought (as distinguished from the exact words) expressed here by Jesus is repeated variously by the evangelists. Matthew and John apply it directly to the Twelve; Luke to the mission of the seventy-two. Mark has only the second part of the saying, but likewise puts it in the context of the dignity or authority of the Twelve.

78. Cf. O. Cullmann, *Peter, Disciple, Apostle, Martyr;* R. Brown, K. Sonfried, J. Reumann (editors), *Peter in the New Testament.* The latter word speaks of a "trajectory of the images of Peter" (pp. 162ff.) in the N.T. writings. How much of such a "trajectory" is the actual historical fact and how much is "theological" reflection on Peter's role after his departure from the scene, and, indeed, whether the entire notion of such a "trajectory" is valid at all are questions which depend to a great extent on methodological conclusions and the authenticity and dates of the various documents.

79. Cf. J. Jeremias, *New Testament Theology,* pp. 167ff.; Brown *et al, Peter in the New Testament,* pp. 83ff.; H. Conzelmann, *An Outline of the Theology of the New Testament,* pp. 33-34; W. G. Kümmel, *The Theology of the New Testament,* p. 129.

80. Cf. note 113, Part I above.

81. Cf. *DS* 774, 3302; Vatican Council, *Lumen gentium,* no. 5 and *passim.*

That Jesus Himself intentionally and explicitly founded the Church has been—and is—frequently denied. Such a denial is allied with the impression that His preaching of the kingdom was not universalistic and that He expected an imminent end of the world. Hans Conzelmann expresses such views as follows:

"The group of disciples was not organized. It had no constitution, no fixed ordering of life. Even if the 'twelve' were in fact already constituted during the lifetime of Jesus, the very choosing of 'twelve' contains a claim on all Israel and a reference to the coming rule of God. It does not point to the founding of a church. Jesus' eschatological awareness of Himself excludes the idea of a present church.

"The recognition that here (Mt. 16:18-19) is no authentic saying of Jesus does not of course 'settle' the matter theologically. Liberal theology drew from its inauthenticity the conclusion that Loisy put so perversely: Jesus expected the kingdom of God and the Church came. This statement is historically correct. But what does it mean?" (*An Outline of the Theology of the New Testament,* pp. 33-34).

Hans Küng has accepted such a conclusion (*On Being a Christian,* pp. 167, 212, 284-285, 300), as has Kümmel, *Theology of the New Testament,* pp. 36-38, as has Karl Rahner, in a modified form (cf. note 103, Part I above). On the other hand, cf. J. Jeremias, *New Testament Theology,* pp. 167ff.

Along with the conclusions about Jesus' views on universality and the end of the world, part of the difficulty in this question concerns the varied criteria for what "founding the Church" entails. If "to found" means giving a "constitution" or *detailing* future structures, operation, etc., then Jesus did not "found" the Church. If, however, "to found" means intentionally to begin a community with discernible beliefs and structures, an "ethos" and ways of acting—as well as to give it a mission—then Jesus did indeed found the Church and did so during His public ministry.

82. Cf. R. Schnackenburg, *The Gospel According to St. John,* I, pp. 410-412 for a discussion of the meaning of this baptism.

83. St. Augustine, *In Johannem,* XV, 3. English trans. *Nicene and Post-Nicene Fathers,* VII, p. 100.

84. Cf. *S. Th.,* III, q. 83, a. 1, ad 3; Vatican Council II, *Sacrosanctum concilium,* no. 33; *Lumen gentium,* no. 10; Congregation for the Doctrine of the Faith, Declaration *Inter insigniores,* 1976, section V.

85. Certain sectors of German exegesis, working from a fairly rigid division between Palestinian Judaism and Hellenistic Judaism (and also between Palestinian Christianity and Hellenistic Christianity) viewed some of the titles (e.g., Son of God, Kyrios-Lord, Savior) as having originated in the Hellenistic milieu. Bultmann, following W. Bossuet, saw the Son of God title as having arisen in the Hellenistic myth of the "divine man" (cf. *Theology of the New Testament*, I, pp. 130-132). For him and many of his followers, these ideas were often viewed against the background of the so-called "Gnostic Redeemer Myth" (cf. *Idem.*, pp. 166ff.). This "redeemer myth," as well as other "gnostic" influences on N.T. Christology, has now been generally discredited (cf. M. Hengel, *Son of God*, p. 33, esp. note 66; James Dunn, *Christology in the Making*, pp. 99ff.), but its influence was pervasive. E. Schillebeeckx still makes some use of it in *Jesus*, pp. 424-429. Origins of the Logos-Word title in such a milieu were also advocated (cf. Kümmel, *Theology of the New Testament*, pp. 264-265, 280-281), but this, too, has been questioned (cf. R. Schnackenburg, *The Gospel According to John*, I, Excursus I, pp. 488ff.; R. Brown, *The Gospel According to John*, I, Appendix II, pp. 519ff.; James Dunn, *Christology in the Making*, pp. 215ff.).

It must be realized, however, that grounding the titles in the Old Testament and in inter-testamentary Jewish literature does not exclude a certain "cross-fertilization" of Jewish and Hellenistic influences; indeed, in some cases it presumes it.

86. Cf. R. Fuller, *The Foundations of N.T. Christology*, p. 50; O. Cullmann, *The Christology of the New Testament*, pp. 203-210.

87. Jesus' injunction against making His messianic dignity known appears so frequently in the Gospel of Mark that, since the time of W. Wrede in the early part of this century, one frequently sees mention of the Marcan "Messianic Secret." For all its frequency in Mark, however, it is not peculiar to him (cf. Mt. 8:4; 9:30; 17:9) and even John's Gospel reflects the unwillingness of Jesus to make open assertions about the matter (cf. Jn. 8:25; 10:25). Such reticence must be recognized as truly reflecting Jesus' own mode of acting (cf. V. Taylor, *The Gospel According to St. Mark*, pp. 122-125; O. Cullmann, *The Christology of the New Testament*, pp. 124-125) and not a later theological device of Mark, as some would still hold (cf. Kümmel, *Theology of the New Testament*, p. 64; Conzelmann, *Outline of Theology of the New Testament*, pp. 138ff.).

88. The matter is studied in J. Jeremias, *New Testament Theology*, pp. 262-264.

89. H. E. Todt, *The Son of Man in the Synoptic Tradition*, uses the threefold division to organize the central chapters (II, III, IV) of his treatment. Indeed, since Bultmann, the division has become almost traditional.

90. Thus, E. Schillebeeckx, *Jesus*, p. 468. He also writes: "The whole question has become technically so complex, it seems, that even some of the specialists in the subject have declared any further effort to investigate it pointless."

91. Thus, Bultmann, Todt, and, among Catholics, apparently both Hans Küng, *On Being a Christian*, p. 386, and E. Schillebeeckx, *Jesus*, pp. 471-472.

92. Cf. W. G. Kümmel, *The Theology of the New Testament*, pp. 76-85; E. Schweitzer, *Jesus*, pp. 19-22.

93. Cf. note 19, Part I above.

94. Hans Küng, *On Being a Christian*, p. 386, put this truth well: "But in any case Jesus did not get His authority from these ambiguous, misleading titles. He Himself...gave them authority and definite clarity. They were not simply transferred, but recoined. The title did not determine what He was. He Himself, His concrete, historical existence, His death and new life determined how they were to be freshly understood and gave them new meaning."

95. Note the variations in the synoptic accounts. Mark does not have the saying "If I drive out demons by the Spirit," etc. Luke has it, but instead of "Spirit of God" has "by the finger of God." E. Schweizer states, probably correctly, that by the statement Jesus is equating what He does with "God's finger" or God's Spirit, i.e., with God Himself (*Jesus*, p. 14).

96. J. Jeremias, *New Testament Theology*, p. 36, says of this: "The novelty of the usage, the way in which it is strictly confined to the sayings of Jesus, and the unanimous testimony of all the strata of tradition in the Gospels show that here we have the creation of a new expression by Jesus."

On the force and implications of Jesus' manner of teaching and acting, the words of Albert Schweitzer, *The Quest of the Historical Jesus*, pp. 372-373, are accurate and still relevant: "And yet in all His speech and action the messianic consciousness shines forth. One might, indeed, speak of the acts of His messianic consciousness. The beatitudes, nay, the whole of the Sermon on the Mount, with the authoritative 'I' for ever breaking through, bear witness to the high dignity which He ascribed to Himself. Did not this 'I' set the people thinking?

"What must they have thought when, at the close of this discourse, He spoke of people who, at the day of judgment, would call upon Him as Lord, and appeal to the works that they had done in His name, and who yet were destined to be rejected because He would not recognize them (Mt. 7:21-23)?

"What must they have thought of Him when He pronounced those blessed who were persecuted and despised for His sake (Mt. 5:11)? By what authority did this man forgive sins (Mk. 2:5ff.)?

"In the discourse at the sending forth of the disciples the 'I' is still more prominent. He demands of men that in the trials to come they shall confess Him, that they shall love Him more than father or mother, bear their cross after Him, and follow Him to the death.... We have still to ask who was He whose yea or nay should prevail with God to determine the fate of men at the judgment."

97. P. Benoit, *Jesus and the Gospel*, I, p. 69, writes: "Could He have said more?... Certainly not.... Leaving the growth of the crop to the future (Mk. 4:26-29; cf. 4:30-32), He scattered the seed for it widely in a form in which the field could accept it. Even minted thus in insights taken from the tradition of His people, His Word was difficult enough to understand. It was a 'mystery,' a 'secret' which could only be grasped through a revelation from the Father (Mk. 4:11 and par.; Mt. 11:27f. and Lk. 10:22f.; Mt. 16:17). There were many who 'took offense' at Him...and they were to some extent pardonable (Mt. 12:32 and Lk. 12:10) by reason of the veil of humanity which cloaked the mystery of His being."

98. R. Schnackenburg, *The Gospel According to St. John*, II, p. 101, writes, for example: "At Jesus' own time, the Jews could not come to such a conclusion, because Jesus had not publicly called Himself the Son of God, at least according to the synoptic presentation. The dispute presupposes the understanding of the Christian community...." S. does not seem to have considered the possibility that the Jews could have made the charge because of Jesus' whole mode of speaking and acting, something more significant than the use or nonuse of one title.

99. Cf. A. Schweitzer, *The Quest of the Historical Jesus*, pp. 393ff.; J. Jeremias, *New Testament Theology*, pp. 254-255; W. G. Kümmel, *Theology of the New Testament*, pp. 72, 83-85.

These commentators are talking directly about Jesus' messianic claim. The difficulty in seeing how such a claim merited the charge of blasphemy comes from too juridical or exacting an exegesis of the High Priest's remarks at Jesus' trial. It was not just a claim to a title (or various titles) which the High Priest reacted to, but rather to all that was implied when this particular individual acknowledged a title. On the lips of Jesus, a messianic title, non-blasphemous in itself, might well be seen as blasphemy because of its association with the way He deported Himself generally.

100. P. Benoit, *Jesus and the Gospel*, I, p. 55, writes: "(In claiming to forgive sins), He assumed to Himself a divine attribute in a way which should have caused them to ponder deeply, if they did not reject it immediately as a blasphemy."

101. William Farmer's remarks in *The Synoptic Problem*, p. 230, are pertinent in this regard and appear to be logically unassailable: "...there is no reliable way in which to adjudge the Christology of Mark as earlier or later than that of Matthew or Luke. All three Gospels came from the post-Pauline period of the early Church, about which very little is known apart from inferences derived from the Gospels themselves. Apart from the Gospels there is no objective basis upon which to reconstruct a scheme of Christological development in this period against which to measure the relative date of a specific Christological reference in the Gospels. For this reason, the Christology of a given passage offers no secure criteria by which it can be judged primary or secondary to a related Christology in a parallel passage."

102. R. Brown gives examples of this type of hypothetical reconstruction. Cf. *The Community of the Beloved Disciple;* "New Testament Background for the Concept of Local Church," *Proceedings* of the 36th annual convention of the Catholic Theological Society of America, vol. 36, pp. 1-14. Although Brown admits that "after the death of the great apostles in the 60's, our knowledge of Christian Church life is drawn from reading between the lines of Christian writings of the last third of the first century and restructuring the communities for whom such works would make sense" (*Proceedings*, p. 9), he is able, through such "reading between the lines," to reconstruct the post-Pauline communities reflected in the pastoral epistles, two forms of Johannine communities, a community related to 1 Peter, a community related to the epistle of James, etc. (pp. 9-12).

103. Cf. J. Jeremias, *New Testament Theology*, p. 262. Jeremias himself, however, opts for the certain authenticity of only the first type of Son of Man sayings, viz., the eschatological Son of Man. Kümmel, *Theology of the New Testament*, p. 82, shows there is no necessity for such reductionism.

104. One can cite as example of this tendency that which is frequently asserted of Romans 1:3-4, and some of the speeches in the Acts of the Apostles (e.g., Acts 2:32-36). Cf. R. Brown, *The Birth of the Messiah*, p. 30.

To claim that such texts reveal a period of time when there existed *only* a Resurrection Christology (i.e., that Jesus became Messiah and Son of God only at the resurrection) is to presume that such statements intended to be a fully adequate presentation of who Jesus is, at least for the speaker or author. Such a presumption cannot be demonstrated and is, in fact, unlikely. When Paul VI spoke of Jesus as the "Man for others" and John Paul II speaks of Him as "Son of Mary," we are certainly not safe in presuming that either expression is saying all that one or the other Pope has to say about Jesus. Indeed, the very Peter who said that "God has made both Lord and Christ this Jesus who has been raised up" is the same Peter who had confessed, during the public ministry, that Jesus was even then the Christ.

It is the same postulate of a gradual development in Christological thinking—one not completed until the end of the first century—which underlies a work such as James Dunn's *Christology in the Making.* Whatever may be the overall value of his book and the accuracy of his efforts at dating the N.T. documents, J. A. T. Robinson (*Redating the New Testament*, p. 344) has wisely observed: "...nothing is so slippery as the relation between Christology and chronology.... The assumption that it was slow or steady is purely arbitrary. In fact it is inherently probable, as in the creative ferment of any new movement, that it was swift and took place in spurts—with periods of retrenchment and consolidation in between." Cf. note 101 above and note 26 of Part I.

105. *DS* 3427 and 3431.

106. *Creed of Paul VI*, Appendix.

Notes for Part III

1. Many writings of Teilhard de Chardin develop this Christological point of view. Cf. "Christology and Evolution," *Christianity and Evolution*, pp. 76-95, an essay which reflects the grandeur but also some of the more theologically objectionable aspects of his work, especially as regards God's freedom in creating, and the nature of sin, especially original sin. Cf., also, K. Rahner, "Christology Within an Evolutionary View of the World," *Theological Investigations*, V, pp. 158-192. Rahner writes: "In the Catholic Church it is freely permitted to see the Incarnation first of all, in God's primary intention, as the summit and height of the divine plan of creation, and not primarily and in the first place as the act of a mere restoration of a divine world-order destroyed by the sins of mankind, an order which God had conceived, in itself, without any Incarnation" (p. 185).

2. "Super Iam Epistolam ad Timotheum Lectura," I, lec. IV, *Super Epistolas S. Pauli*, II, p. 219.

3. *S. Th.*, III, q. 1, a. 3, ad. 3.

4. Roman Breviary, Hymn for Office of Readings during Holy Week. Trans. by J. M. Neale in M. Britt, *The Hymns of the Breviary and Missal*.

5. Cf., above, note 102, Part I.

6. Cf. *DS* 423, 442, 502, 1364.

7. *Nostra aetate*, no. 4. This teaching was subsequently confirmed in the 1979 Declaration of the Cong. for the Doctrine of the Faith concerning the book *Quand je di Dieu* of Rev. Jacques Pohier, O.P. "Among the more evident errors of this book are denials of the following truths: Christ's intention of giving His passion a redemptive and sacrificial value..." (*TPS*, vol. 24, no. 3, p. 227).

8. The injunction on bearing the cross is found also in Mt. 10:38 and Lk. 14:27.

9. Cf., for example, "The Martyrdom of Isaiah," in *Apocrypha and Pseudepigrapha of the Old Testament*, II, R. H. Charles, editor, pp. 155-162. The date of the "Martyrdom" is first century A.D.

10. Cf. W. G. Kümmel, *The Theology of the New Testament*, pp. 87-88: "On the basis of these testimonies it may be regarded as certain that Jesus viewed His violent death as the way ordained for Him by God, even though we obviously do not know whether He had always had this certainty or had only reached it in the course of His activity."

11. J. Fitzmyer, *The Gospel According to Luke*, I-IX, p. 785, seems to use this type of *a priori* reasoning in his commentary on Lk. 9:23. He writes: "The saying becomes intelligible once Jesus had carried 'his own cross' (Jn. 19:17) or simply been crucified.... But what meaning would it have had on the lips of Jesus prior to His crucifixion?... Since it is only the joining of Jesus' own messiahship with the cross on which He was crucified that makes the metaphor have any sense, the saying, as we now have it, must come from the early Christian community."

V. Taylor, *The Gospel According to St. Mark*, p. 381, writes: "The idea is metaphorical.... The last risk to be taken. It is by no means necessary to suppose that the metaphor is 'Christian' in the sense that the crucifixion of Christ is implied.... Death by crucifixion under the Romans was a sufficiently familiar sight in Palestine to be the basis of the saying...."

In response, Fitzmyer writes that the "problem is to explain why Jesus would ever use such an image for *following* Him.... (Would a modern community leader, seeking to instill self-denial and dedication to himself and his followers, get the idea across by telling them to face the firing line or strap themselves into an electric chair—using a modern mode of execution?)" (p. 785)

The answer to that rhetorical question of Fitzmyer could well be: given the proper leader and an important enough cause, why not? History is filled with leaders, good and evil, who have asked their followers to accept death, Jonestown being only a relatively recent example.

As for the word crucifixion in Mt. 20:19, Beare, *Matthew*, pp. 404-405, working from the priority of Mark and the Two Source theory, writes that Mt. changes Mk. by "substituting 'crucify' for the more general 'put to death' of Mark. There is evident here a tendency to make the prediction more specific." But what if Mt. is not working from Mk., or if the dependence is not as absolute as Beare seems to imply?

12. St. Paul would later use the perduring differences between the Pharisees and Sadducees over the resurrection of the dead to help extricate himself from a threatening situation. Cf. Acts 23:6ff.

13. For the relation between the accounts of Jesus' raising of the dead to life and the wonders of the same sort attributed to Apollonius of Tyana, cf. J. Fitzmyer, *The Gospel According to Luke*, pp. 656-677.

14. Thus, for example, W. G. Kümmel, *The Theology of the New Testament*, p. 94; Todt, *The Son of Man in the Synoptic Tradition*, pp. 144ff.

15. K. Rahner, "Knowledge and Self-Consciousness of Christ," *Theological Investigations*, V, p. 205, has written: "We start then from the axiom of the Thomistic metaphysics of knowledge according to which being and self-awareness are elements of the one reality which condition each other immanently. Hence, something which exists is present to itself, to the extent in which it has or is being." Assuming the truth of the axiom, one can perhaps extend it from the being and self-awareness of Jesus to the purpose for which the Son assumed His humanity, viz., that of dying and rising to save mankind. That purpose constitutes part of the being, then, of the humanity, and, by the same reasoning, should be an element of consciousness as well as of being.

16. Moses Hadas, *The Third and Fourth Books of Maccabees*, p. 96, dates the work 30-41 A.D.; R. H. Charles, *The Apocrypha and Pseudepigrapha*, II, places it at 63 B.C. to 38 A.D. (p. 654); G. Nickelsburg, *Jewish Literature Between the Bible and the Mishnah*, follows Hades (p. 226 and note 40); M. Hengel, *Judaism and Hellenism*, I, p. 167, dates it as "beginning of the first century A.D."

17. Moses Hadas, *The Third and Fourth Books of Maccabees*, p. 181.

18. *Idem.*, p. 237.

19. Cf. M. Hengel, *The Atonement*.

20. The authenticity of Mk. 10:45 (Mt. 20:27-28) is frequently questioned. Thus, Kümmel, *The Theology of the New Testament*, p. 89, writes: "Therefore, Mk. 10:45 par. in its version as handed down hardly belongs to the earliest Jesus tradition..."; R. Bultmann, *Theology of the New Testament*, I, p. 29; R. Fuller, *Foundations of N.T. Christology*, p. 106, writes: "The majority of Jesus' sayings

about His death contain either an explicit Christology...or an explicit soteriology (so Mk. 10:45b and the cup word at the supper, Mk. 14:24). They must therefore on grounds of traditio-historical criticism be assigned to the early Church, rather than to Jesus Himself"; H. Conzelmann, *An Outline of the Theology of the New Testament*, p. 134.

On the other hand, O. Cullmann, *The Christology of the New Testament*, p. 65: "There is no valid argument for contesting the genuineness of Mk. 10:45.... Jesus consciously united in His Person the two central concepts of the Jewish faith, *barnasha* and *ebed Yahweh*"; J. Jeremias, *New Testament Theology*, pp. 292-294; V. Taylor, *The Gospel According to St. Mark*, pp. 445-446; M. Hengel, *The Atonement*, p. 53, writes: "As we find it in Mk. 10:45, the surrender formula indicates an original Semitic form which must come either from the Aramaic-speaking community or from Jesus Himself."

What Hengel writes in the same context of Mk. 10:45 is appropriate for the entire discussion: "By contrast, the allegedly independent, decidedly post-Easter 'theologies' of the so-called Q or Marcan 'communities,' detached completely from the Person of Jesus, are artificial products of modern exegesis.... Q and Mark did not set out to present 'community theology,' but primarily the message and work of Jesus" (p. 35).

It should be noted that the word translated as "ransom" in IV Maccabees is *antipsychon* and is not the same as that in Mt. 20:28 (Mk. 10:45) where the word is *lutron*. The idea in *antipsychon* is really that of substitution, not a payment or ransom properly speaking. They are,, of course, both metaphors, and the general idea is the same.

21. Beare, *Matthew*, p. 409, writes correctly: The verbal form of *lutron* "(in LXX) comes to be used figuratively in the more general sense of *rescue*.... There is no question of a ransom to be paid to anyone. So then it is wrong to ask to whom Christ pays His life as a ransom."

Some of the early Fathers of the Church forgot the metaphorical nature of *lutron* and spoke of a ransom being paid to the devil in order to win mankind back from him for God.

22. For the relation between the Johannine text and the Synoptics and the relation of both to the passion, cf. R. Brown, *John I*, pp. 471-474; and R. Schnackenburg, *John II*, pp. 383-384.

23. Cf. Mk. 14:12-16 for a similar expression of the extraordinary knowledge which Jesus had of what was before Him.

24. Cf. *Dei verbum*, no. 11.

25. The NAB and others translate 13:1 as "He had loved his own in this world, and would show his love for them to the end." In fact, the *eis telos egapesen* can mean "to the limit," "completely," or "to the end" (of His life). Cf. R. Brown, *The Gospel According to John*, II, p. 550.

26. Some have questioned the historicity of both the Supper itself and the institution of the Eucharist. The Supper accounts as we have them would have arisen—so it is claimed—out of the celebrations held by the early Christians in remembrance of Jesus and in remembrance of His table fellowship with His disciples, as well as with social outcasts and the ritually unclean. The Christians would have been aware of Jesus' own presence in their midst at such celebrations. In time the presence was "located" in the elements of bread and wine as these were eaten in remembrance of His meals. Gradually a connection with His death and resurrection was made—especially to His body broken and blood shed. Interpretive words were used, then spoken over the bread and wine. Etc. Cf. Willi Marxsen, *The*

Beginnings of Christology, pp. 88ff.; H. Conzelmann, *Outline of the Theology of the New Testament*, pp. 50-59; H. Küng, *On Being a Christian*, pp. 322ff.

Even Karl Rahner could cite with approval, in a 1971 essay, the idea that Protestant exegetes and theologians "will no longer assert with boldness and apodictic certainty that the institution of baptism and the Eucharist in the New Testament goes back to explicit words of institution on the part of the historical Jesus" ("What Is a Sacrament?", *Theological Investigations*, XIV, p. 136).

The opinions are many and varied. In their more extreme forms they have little claim to serious consideration. If we do not know with certainty the dating of Matthew, Mark and Luke, it is, nevertheless, universally agreed that Paul wrote 1 Cor. in the mid-fifties. It is clear from 1 Cor. 11:23 that he had previously taught the faithful at Corinth what he was recalling to them. Furthermore, Paul claims that the Lord Himself is the origin of the facts which Paul recalls, and he states clearly that this reminder of his is a recalling of what Jesus did "on the night he was betrayed." Paul's account concords in all substantials with that of the Synoptics, and his testimony dates to about twenty years from the date of the Supper itself. By norms of reasonable historical research, the N.T. accounts of the Supper are most trustworthy.

27. Jeremias, *New Testament Theology*, p. 289, is surely correct when he observes that "our texts go back to pre-liturgical narrative tradition. At their beginning we do not find liturgy, but a historical account."

In fact, the frequent assertion that the accounts as we have them are *liturgical* formulae is a non-verifiable hypothesis. We have no documentary evidence for the "order of celebration" of the Christian community in the period in question, except perhaps the *Didache* (nos. 8 and 9) which itself does not support the claim that the N.T. accounts are "extracts" from a liturgy.

28. The repugnance at drinking blood was such that Jeremias, *New Testament Theology*, p. 289, thinks that it may explain the "more complicated formulation" of the word over the cup as it is found in Paul and Luke, blunting the notion of drinking blood.

29. Cf. note 20 above for remarks of R. Fuller. Also, O. Cullmann, *Christology of the New Testament*, pp. 64-69. Cullmann, unlike Fuller, holds that it was Jesus Himself and not the early Church which united the fundamental concepts of Servant of Yahweh and Son of Man.

30. Cyril of Jerusalem, *Mistagogic Catechesis*, 22, IV, 3-6, 9. Roman Breviary, Second Reading for Office of Readings for Saturday within Octave of Easter. English trans. in *The Nicene and Post-Nicene Fathers*, second series, vol. 7, pp. 153-157.

31. Cf. *DS* 1637-1638, 1651-1652; Vatican Council II, *Sacrosanctum concilium*, no. 47; *Creed of the People of God* (cf. Appendix).

32. *DS* 1740-1741. The Council of Trent also issued one of the Church's relatively rare definitions of the meaning of a Scriptural text when it said, "if anyone should say that by the words 'Do this in memory of me' (Lk. 22:19; 1 Cor. 11:24) Christ did not institute the Apostles as priests or did not ordain that they and other priests offer His body and blood, A.S." (*DS* 1752).

33. Cf. St. Thomas Aquinas, *Super Evangelium S. Joannis*, 17, lec. IV, I, p. 420; R. Brown, *The Gospel According to John*, II, pp. 765-767; NIV, explanatory note on Jn. 17:17 and 19.

34. The "God has reigned from a Tree" is an ancient version of Ps. 96[95]:10, found in the Old Latin and some LXX manuscripts. Fortunatus refers to it in his hymn to the cross: the *Pange Lingua:*

Impleta sunt quae concinit (Those things are now fulfilled,
David fideli carmine Which David spoke in faithful song,
Dicendo a nationibus Saying to the nations,
Regnavit a ligno Deus. "God has reigned from a tree.")

Cf. Hymn of *Liturgia horarum* for Matins of Passiontide, although in present Breviary the above verse is now omitted. Trans. in Dom Matthew Britt (editor), *The Hymns of the Breviary and Missal.*

35. The word "author" (Gk. *arkegos*) is used in Acts 3:15; 5:31 and in Heb. 2:10 and 12:2. On its meaning, cf. Ernst Haenchen, *The Acts of the Apostles,* p. 206 (although his contention in note 5 that this is a "liturgical formula" is not convincing); J. Fitzmyer, *The Gospel According to Luke,* I-IX, p. 217.

36. Hans Conzelmann, *1 Corinthians,* p. 63, writes of this text: "A divine predicate is here transferred to the 'Lord' Jesus"; Dunn, *Christology in the Making,* p. 177, denies this, consistent with his views denying any notion of preexistence in Paul.

37. While the bishops at Ephesus approved the Twelve Anathemas of St. Cyril, there is doubt as to whether they intended to accept them as actual definitions of the Faith. Some of the terminology found in them is not as clear as some later usage, but the doctrine itself is accurate and subsequently approved frequently, although in terminology which is different.

38. Apollinarianism, named after Bishop Apollinaris of Laodicea (b. around 300—d. about 390), taught that, in becoming man, the Word Himself took the part of the rational soul and that Christ, therefore, did not have a human spirit. The doctrine was condemned by Pope Damasus I in 377 and at Constantinople I in 381. Some of Apollinaris' language was accepted and used by St. Athanasius in his conflict with the Arians and by St. Cyril in combatting Nestorianism. The affinity of Apollinaris' thought with that of Eutyches is readily seen.

39. J. Pelikan, *The Emergence of the Catholic Tradition,* p. 229, writes: "...the early Christian picture of God was controlled by the self-evident axiom, accepted by all, of the absoluteness and impassibility of the divine nature."

40. Cf. *Firmiter,* Appendix I; Vatican Council I, *Dei Filius,* DS 3001.

41. S. Th., III, q. 35, a. 5 c; cf. III, q. 2, a. 7.

42. Karl Rahner has placed such objections clearly and forcefully in his essay "Current Problems in Christology," *Theological Investigations,* I, pp. 173-184. His own answer is that God, while remaining immutable *in Himself* is able to come to be in the other, viz., in that which He causes to be united to Him, while still diverse from Him (p. 181). "For it is true, come what may, and a dogma, that the Logos Himself has become man: thus that He Himself has become something that He has not always been (formaliter); and therefore that what has so become is, as just itself and of itself, God's reality. Now if this is a truth of Faith, ontology must allow itself to be guided by it...must seek enlightenment from it, and grant that while God remains immutable 'in Himself,' He can come to be 'in the other,' and that *both* assertions must really and truly be made of the same God as God" (note 3, p. 181).

Here he is clearly emphasizing the "undivided and inseparable" union of the two natures in the Chalcedonian definition of the Hypostatic Union, defending the reality of the Incarnation. How this emphasis is to be reconciled with his statement on the *communicatio idiomatum* (cf. note 54, Part I) when his (later) concern is to defend the "unconfused and unmixed" union of the two natures is not clear, although both emphases are apparently his way of underlining the mystery. Nor is it clear what the formula "unchanged in Himself—coming to be in the other" is actually saying. It promises more than it delivers since the traditional Thomistic position can assent to it on the basis that all change is "in the other" (i.e., in the human nature) and not in God Himself. If it means literally that God comes to be not just in the other but in Himself, i.e., that God changes, then, linguistically at least, he is close to the unacceptable categories in which process philosophers speak of God.

Jean Galot, *Who Is Christ?*, pp. 268-279, has attempted to go beyond Rahner, asserting a real relation of the Word to His humanity, a relation in which "God does not eschew a certain dependence with respect to man, since He is affected by their behavior" (p. 277), including a real relation and dependence of the Word *vis à vis* Mary (p. 278). E. L. Mascall has called this position one of "voluntary real relations" on the part of God (as distinguished from necessary real relations, i.e., the Trinitarian relations, and logical relations) (*Theology and the Gospel of Christ*, p. 182).

43. St. Ignatius of Antioch, Part I, p. 64 above. Aquinas, too, answers affirmatively the question as to whether the passion of Christ is to be attributed to His divinity. The reason he gives is that the divine and human natures subsist in the Divine Person of the Son, and the passion is to be attributed to the Divine Person by reason, not of His divinity, but of His humanity (*S. Th.*, III, q. 46, a. 12).

44. As translated by the NIV the text in Titus is one of the relatively few in the N.T. which applies the word "God" to Jesus. For other examples of the "redemption" terminology, cf. Mt. 20:28; Lk. 1:68; 2:36; 24:21; Heb. 9:12; 1 Cor. 1:30 *(apolutrosis)*.

45. English translation of *Cur Deus Homo* is *Why God Became Man*, trans. with notes by Joseph M. Colleran.

46. *Why God Became Man*, Bk. II, ch. 19, p. 155. The perennial value of the main elements in Anselm's theology is defended by Colleran in his Introduction, pp. 23-48, and by Walter Kasper, *Jesus the Christ*, pp. 219-225.

47. St. Thomas Aquinas, *Compendium of Theology*, chapter 196, p. 212.

48. *Idem.*, p. 215 (ch. 200).

49. *S. Th.*, I, q. 21, a. 4 c; cf. I, q. 25, a. 3, ad 3.

50. Vatican Council II, *Lumen gentium*, no. 62.

51. *Idem.*, nos. 61 and 62; cf. Part I, note 76 above.

52. Office of Readings, *Liturgia Horarum*. Trans. by J. M. Neale in *The Hymns of the Roman Breviary and Missal*, p. 119.

53. *S. Th.*, III, q. 46, a. 4, ad 3; cf. St. Anselm, *op. cit.*, Bk. I, ch. 3, p. 68.

54. *DS* 1739-1740; cf. 1743, 1753.

55. *Why God Became Man*, Bk. I, ch. 9, pp. 76-77.

56. Jurgen Moltmann in *The Crucified God*, p. 276, writes: "When God becomes man in Jesus of Nazareth, He not only enters into the finitude of man, but in His death also enters into the situation of man's godforsakenness.... The suffering in the passion of Jesus is abandonment, rejection by God, His Father."

57. *DS* 16.

58. Cf. J. N. D. Kelly, *Early Christian Creeds*, pp. 378ff. Kelly's contention, however, that reference to the descent into hell is found in Ignatius of Antioch's epistle to the Magnesians, no. 4, is to be questioned. It is likely that the reference there is to the event recorded in Mt. 27:52, which need not be understood as being connected with the descent.

59. *DS* 76 (Appendix).

60. *DS* 801 (Appendix).

61. St. Thomas cites John Damascene as interpreting the text as a reference to the descent into hell. Augustine did not so interpret it, and Aquinas agrees with Augustine (cf. *S. Th.*, III, q. 52, a. 2, ad 3). Among modern commentators,

J. Fitzmyer, *JBC* 58:19-20, also holds against Damascene's view. Bo Reicke, *The Epistles of James, Peter, and Jude*, pp. 110-111, and Claude Holmes Thompson (*The Interpreter's One-Volume Commentary on the Bible*, Abingdon Press, Nashville and New York, 1971, p. 929) tend to agree with Damascene.

62. Cf. J. N. D. Kelly, *Early Christian Creeds*, p. 378. Karl Rahner, "He Descended into Hell," *Theological Investigations*, VII, pp. 145ff., seems to hold this view as being the only meaning of the creedal article. Whether J. Ratzinger, *Introduction to Christianity*, pp. 229-230, is saying more than Rahner is not clear. The same may be said of W. Kasper, *Jesus the Christ*, p. 224.

63. Second Reading, Office of Readings, Holy Saturday, *Liturgia Horarum*.

64. Cf. the definition of the Immaculate Conception, *Ineffabilis Deus*, DS 2803.

65. Vatican Council II, *Lumen gentium*, no. 16. Wolfhart Pannenberg, *The Apostles' Creed*, pp. 94-95, rightly saw the depth of meaning in the mystery of the descent into hell when he wrote: "What, finally, is to happen to the people who have certainly heard the message of Christ but who—perhaps through the fault of those very Christians who have been charged with its proclamation—have never come face to face with its truth? Are all these people delivered over to damnation?...

"The Christian faith can say 'no' to this urgent question. That is the meaning of the phrase about Christ's descent into hell in the creed.... What took place for mankind in Jesus also applies to the people who either never came into contact with Jesus and the message about Him, or who have never really caught sight of the truth of His Person and His story. In a way that is hidden from us—and in a way hidden even from themselves—the lives of these people may yet be related to the revelation of God which appeared in Jesus.... And this relationship means for them, too, salvation or judgment. We have, it is true, no guarantee of their salvation. Salvation is only guaranteed to the man who has definite communion with Jesus.... But all other men, too, even those who died before Jesus' ministry, can achieve the salvation which appeared in Him—even if in ways beyond our comprehension. The meaning of the Christian acknowledgment of the conquest of the kingdom of death and Jesus Christ's descent into hell lies in the universal scope of salvation. Anyone who has grasped this can only regret that this particular article of the Apostles' Creed has recently come up against such special lack of understanding...."

66. The historical value to be placed on Peter's speech is disputed. C. H. Dodd, *The Apostolic Preaching and Its Development*, held that it represents, if not Peter himself, the "Kerygma of the Church in Jerusalem at an early period" (p. 21). E. Haenchen, *The Acts of the Apostles*, pp. 185ff., notes that the speech presupposes the LXX text of the O.T. and thus "Hellenistic Christianity," and is therefore a composition of the author of Acts. Johannes Munck, *The Acts of the Apostles*, holds for a pre-70 A.D. for the composition of Acts and in general rejects Haenchen's whole approach to Lk. as a *creator*-author (pp. XXXVIII-XXXIX). Martin Hengel, *Acts and the History of Earliest Christianity*, has also written in general agreement with Dodd. For Hengel, "to deny in principle the presence of earlier traditions in the speeches composed by Luke makes them incomprehensible and is no more than an interpreter's whim" (p. 104).

67. V. Taylor, *The Gospel According to St. Mark*, argues in favor of the Petrine connection (p. 30) as does M. Hengel, *Acts and the History of Earliest Christianity*, pp. 92-98.

68. In light of Mark 16:7, E. Schillebeeckx's assertions that the original Marcan Gospel does not refer to Jesus' appearances (*Jesus*, pp. 332, 352, 357) are simply erroneous. For the hypothesis that Mk. 16:7 refers not to a resurrection appearance,

but to the Parousia, cf. C. F. Evans, *Resurrection and the New Testament*, pp. 80-81; R. Fuller, *The Formation of the Resurrection Narratives*, pp. 62-64.

69. Some see Lk. 24:12, 24 and Jn. 20:3-8 as reflecting a tradition earlier than Mark's account in 16:1-8. Cf. J. Jeremias, *New Testament Theology*, pp. 304-305; on the other hand, R. Brown, *John*, II, pp. 1000ff.

70. An alternate understanding of the role of the appearances would be this: The sight of the empty tomb (or some other experience) led Peter to the conclusion that Jesus lives. This conviction of Peter, and subsequently of others, is soon described as a manifestation of the "Incorrupt One," depicted in the language of "seeing."

Willi Marxsen, *The Resurrection of Jesus of Nazareth*, is an example of one who would hold that the appearances are linguistic symbols used to describe the experience whereby Peter (and the others) became convinced that, after His death, the "activity of Jesus goes on" (pp. 77, 96, 127). For Marxsen, Jesus is really dead in the normal sense of that word.

E. Schillebeeckx, *Jesus*, holds that Jesus lives and that it is He who, from heaven, causes an experience of forgiveness in Peter, a "conversion experience." This experience is then expressed in the language of vision, and thus the appearances are "an extrapolation of the grace characterizing" them (p. 358). Schillebeeckx attempts to substantiate this hypothesis by a literary analysis of the "Jewish conversion model" (p. 358). This conversion model—a literary model—explains for Schillebeeckx the construction of the account of Paul's conversion on the road to Damascus, and is then applied to what supposedly happened to Peter. It is a classic case of the confusion of historical and literary criteria of analysis (cf. J. O'Connor, "Edward Schillebeeckx's *Jesus—An Experiment in Christology*," *Christian Faith and Freedom*, Northeast Books, Scranton, Penn., 1982, pp. 85ff.).

In his dialogue with the Congregation for the Doctrine of the Faith over his work *Jesus*, Schillebeeckx admitted that his talk of conversion model perhaps "lends itself to misunderstanding," and declared that for him "in this terminology of 'conversion,' Christophany is essential" (*Letter from the Sacred Congregation for the Doctrine of the Faith to Fr. E. Schillebeeckx*, *L'Osservatore Romano*, English edition, July 13, 1981, p. 5). Taking note of this clarification, the Congregation states that "ambiguity remains" as to what Schillebeeckx actually is saying *vis à vis* the appearances and the role they have as foundation of the Easter faith (cf. *Idem.*).

71. This is frequently stated. Cf. R. Brown, *The Virginal Conception and Bodily Resurrection of Jesus*, p. 78: "Our earliest material consists of short formulas about the risen Jesus that were current in the preaching, the catechesis, the liturgy, and the confessions of faith of the early Christians." R. Fuller, *The Formation of the Resurrection Narratives*, p. 48, writes: "The oldest available traditions of the Easter events are to be found not in the stories at the end of the Gospels, but in 1 Cor. 15:3-8." B. Vawter, *This Man Jesus*, p. 36, writes: "There seems to be no doubt at all that the very earliest witness to the resurrection that we possess is the one recorded by Paul in the fifteenth chapter of his first letter to the Corinthians." Others, more cautiously, note that 1 Cor. 15 is the "earliest written or literary testimony." Such a way of putting it would allow for the fact that what is first to be written down need not represent what is first to exist.

72. Cf. R. Fuller, *Formation of the Resurrection Narratives*, p. 52; B. Vawter, *This Man Jesus*, p. 44; Kümmel, *Theology of the New Testament*, pp. 101-102; H. Conzelman, *An Outline of the Theology of the New Testament*, p. 67, states flatly, "The empty tomb is unknown to the early Kerygma." Cf. also, C. F. Evans, *Resurrection and the New Testament*, p. 75.

73. The variations on the "aetiological cult legend" approach to the tomb are many. Cf. Bas van Iersel, "The Resurrection of Jesus—Information or Interpretation?" *Immortality and Resurrection* (Benoit and Murphy, editors), pp. 54ff., esp. pp. 62-63, 66; Jean Delorme, "The Resurrection and Jesus' Tomb," *The Resurrection and Modern Biblical Thought* (Paul DeSurgy, editor), pp. 74ff., esp. pp. 87ff.; E. Schillebeeckx, *Jesus*, pp. 331-339. Schillebeeckx, however, has had second thoughts about this totally hypothetical construction. Cf. *Interim Report on the Books Jesus and Christ*, pp. 86-87. Cf. also, W. Kasper, *Jesus the Christ*, p. 127.

74. The historical value of Mt.'s account about the guards is fairly generally questioned or denied. Cf. Beare, *The Gospel According to Matthew*, p. 539, who calls it "Surely one of the most extravagant of inventions." Also, van Iersel, *op. cit.*, p. 60; Evans, *Resurrection and the New Testament*, p. 82; Marxsen, *The Resurrection of Jesus of Nazareth*, pp. 46-47; J. Meier, *Matthew*, pp. 356-357.

75. O. Cullmann, *The Christology of the New Testament*, writes: "We may even assert that this is probably the oldest known solution to the Christological problem" (p. 73).

76. E. Haenchen, *The Acts of the Apostles*, thinks that the author composed the Petrine speeches and that the so-called primitive titles in the Petrine speeches reflect "Gentile Christian missionary preaching" (p. 130), there being no "conscious intention to write in an archaic manner" (p. 186).

77. Ulrich Wilckens, *Resurrection*, is an example of one who holds that kerygmatic formulae precede the resurrection narratives: "At the earliest stage in the transmission of the tradition, previous to Paul and contemporary with Paul, the appearances of Jesus are recorded in short formulaic sentences.... In this sense, Christ's appearances to Peter, James, and Paul were reported in the whole of primitive Christianity only in the short form, in which only the bare fact is mentioned. They were not complete stories" (p. 63).

78. Citing some of the differences in the accounts, W. Kasper, *Jesus the Christ*, p. 127, concludes: "These and other differences which cannot be harmonized show that the events of Easter morning can no longer be reconstructed: indeed that a purely historical account is not what matters in the Easter stories." Like some others, he sees only the differences, not the agreements. Not everything can be historically harmonized, but some things certainly can.

Kasper notes next that all the Gospel accounts depend on Mk. 16:1-8. R. Brown sees six Gospel "sources," not just one. Cf. *The Virginal Conception and Bodily Resurrection of Jesus*, p. 99 and chart on p. 100.

79. On the evangelists and the empty tomb, Marxsen, *The Resurrection of Jesus of Nazareth*, p. 43, writes: "...whether the tomb was empty or not. One answer at least can be considered as certain: Mark was convinced it was. And we might add that the other evangelists were equally sure, for all of them mention the empty tomb."

80. E. Schweizer, *Jesus*, p. 48, makes this observation, while also pointing out the ambiguous nature of an empty tomb as historical evidence. Without the appearances, the empty tomb would be only "one-half" an indication.

81. To Smyrna, 3. The citation may be to Lk. 24:39.

82. Pope Pelagius I (561 A.D.), *DS* 442.

83. *DS* 801; Appendix.

84. The *Ave Verum* is a hymn, author unknown, of the late 14th century.

85. "place of rest": So translate the NIV, and the New American Standard. The Vulgate used *sepulcrum* (tomb) and the LXX used *anapausis* (rest). The Hebrew means resting place or place of rest, the same word found in Ps. 95:11 ("...they shall

not enter into my rest"). The meaning of Isaiah probably is that the royal city, the king's place of rest, Jerusalem, would be glorious.

86. Cf. Beare, *Matthew*, pp. 540ff.; Bas van Iersel, *op. cit.*, p. 64-66; R. Fuller, *The Formation of the Resurrection Narratives*, pp. 78-79.

87. On the relationship among the various formularies, cf. X. Leon-Dufour, *Resurrection and the Message of Easter*, pp. 24, 40ff.; R. Brown, *The Virginal Conception and Bodily Resurrection of Jesus*, pp. 73-80; C. F. Evans, *Resurrection and the New Testament*, pp. 133ff.; P. Benoit, *Jesus and the Gospel*, I, pp. 222ff.

88. Pope Paul VI, Catechesis of April 5, 1974, *L'Osservatore Romano*, English edition.

89. Cf. Pierre Benoit, "The Ascension," *Jesus and the Gospel*, I, pp. 209-253.

90. Cf. X. Leon-Dufour's discussion, *Resurrection and the Message of Easter*, pp. 190ff.

91. The paramount role of Peter is one of the generally agreed-upon facts of modern criticism. Cf. Marxsen, *The Resurrection of Jesus of Nazareth*, p. 89: "There is really no reason to doubt that Peter really was the first to believe in Jesus after Good Friday." Marxsen, to be sure, does not think that Peter actually saw the Risen One. X. Leon-Dufour, *Resurrection and the Message of Easter*, p. 203: "Most critics accept that Peter was the first to see the risen Christ."

92. Cf. George W. E. Nickelsburg, *Jewish Literature Between the Bible and the Mishnah*, pp. 2-3.

93. *The Sacramentary*, Liturgy of the Easter Vigil.

94. Paul VI, *Creed of the People of God* (Appendix).

95. *S. Th.*, III, q. 49, a. 6 c.

96. Roman Breviary, Hymn at the Hour of Reading for the time after Ascension. The song is from the School of St. Ambrose, fifth century.

97. *S. Th.*, Ia, IIae, q. 109, a. 1, ad. 1.

98. *Dei verbum*, nos. 15-16.

99. Emile Mersch, *The Theology of the Mystical Body*, pp. 415-416.

100. St. Thomas, *Super Evangelium S. Joannis*, ch. VI, lec. VII, nos. III and IV, p. 183.

101. St. Augustine, "Second Discourse on Psalm 30," *Ancient Christian Writers*, vol. 11 (Johannes Quasten and Waltar Burghardt, editors), trans. and annotated by Dame Scholastica Hebgin and Dame Felicitas Corrigan, Newman Press, Westminster, Md, 1961, p. 13.

102. Cf. Emile Mersch, *The Whole Christ*, pp. 384-440 for a fine treatment of Augustine's theology of the Body of Christ. Cf. also the fine presentation of the role of the Holy Spirit and Mary in Luis M. Martinez's *The Sanctifier* (St. Paul Editions, Boston, 1982), pp. 3-7.

Bibliography

Albright, W. F. and Mann, C. S. *Matthew*, The Anchor Bible, Doubleday, Garden City., New York, 1971.

Aldwinckle, Russell F. *More than Man*, Wm. B. Eerdmans, Grand Rapids, Michigan, 1976.

Anselm, St. *Cur Deus Homo: Why God Became Man*, trans. and notes by Joseph M. Colleran, Magi Books, Inc., Albany, New York, 1969.

Aquinas, St. Thomas. *Compendium of Theology*, trans. by Cyril Vollert, S.J., B. Herder Book Co., St. Louis, Mo., 1955.

——————. *Super Epistolas S. Pauli*, II, Marietti, Rome, 1951.

——————. Super Evangelium S. Joannis, Marietti, Rome, 1952.

——————. *Super Evangelium S. Matthaei*, Marietti, Rome, 1951.

Avi-Yonah, Michael and Baras, Zvi (editors), *The World History of the Jewish People*, vol. 8, Masada Pub. Ltd., Jerusalem, 1977.

Barrett, C. K. *The New Testament Background: Selected Documents*, Harper and Row, New York, 1961.

Barth, Marcus. *Ephesians 1-3*, Doubleday, Garden City, N.Y., 1974.

Beare, F.W. *The Gospel According to Matthew*, Harper and Row, New York, 1981.

Benoit, Pierre. *Jesus and the Gospel*, I, Seabury, New York, 1973.

——————. *Jesus and the Gospel*, II, Seabury, New York, 1974.

Benoit and Murphy (editors). *Immorality and Resurrection*, Concilium Series, vol. 60, Herder and Herder, N.Y., 1970.

Boff, Leonardo. *Jesus Christ Liberator*, Orbis Books, Maryknoll, N.Y., 1979.

Bouyer, Louis. *The Eternal Son*, Our Sunday Visitor, Inc., Huntington, Ind., 1978.

Britt, Dom Matthew, O.S.B. (editor), *The Hymns of the Breviary and Missal*, Benziger Bros., New York, 1955.

Brown, Raymond. *The Birth of the Messiah*, Doubleday, Garden City, N.Y. 1977.

——————. *The Community of the Beloved Disciple*, Paulist Press, N.Y., 1978.

——————. *The Gospel According to John*, I, Doubleday, Garden City, N.Y., 1966.

——————. *The Gospel According to John*, II, Doubleday, Garden City, N.Y., 1970.

——————. *Jesus: God and Man*, Bruce Pub. Co., Milwaukee, 1967.

——————. *The Virginal Conception and Bodily Resurrection of Jesus*, Paulist Press, N.Y., 1973.

Brown, Raymond *et al.* (editors), *Mary in the New Testament*, Paulist Press, N.Y., 1978.

_____. *Peter in the New Testament*, Paulist Press, N.Y., 1973.

Bultmann, Rudolf, *History of the Synoptic Tradition*, Harper and Row, N.Y., 1968.

_____. *Theology of the New Testament*, vol. I, SCM Press, London, 1959.

_____. *Theology of the New Testament*, II, SCM Press, London, 1958.

Butler, B.C. *The Originality of St. Matthew: A Critique of the Two-Document Hypothesis*, Cambridge Univ. Press, Cambridge, 1951.

Cameron, Ron (editor). *The Other Gospels*, Westminster Press, Philadelphia, 1982.

Carmody, James M. and Clarke, Thomas. *Word and Redeemer*, Paulist Press, Glen Rock, N.Y., 1966.

Charles, R. H. (editor), *Apocrypha and Pseudepigrapha of the Old Testament*, II, Clarenden Press, Oxford, 1913.

Conzelmann, Hans. *1 Corinthians*, (trans. J. W. Leitch), Fortress Press, Phila., 1975.

_____. *An Outline of the Theology of the New Testament*, SCM Press, London, 1969.

Cook, Michael, S.J. *The Jesus of Faith*, Paulist Press, N.Y., 1981.

Craddock, Fred B. *The Preexistence of Christ in the New Testament*, Abingdon Press, N.Y., 1968.

Cullmann, Oscar. *The Christology of the New Testament*, Westminster Press, Phila., 1958.

_____. *Jesus and the Revolutionaries*, Harper and Row, N.Y., 1970.

_____. *Peter, Disciple, Apostle, Martyr*, Westminster Press, Phila., 1962.

de Chardin, Pierre Teilhard. *The Divine Milieu*, Harper Torchbooks, Harper and Row, N.Y., 1968.

_____. *Christianity and Evolution*, Harcourt, Brace, Jovanovich, N.Y., 1971.

De Lubac, Henri. *The Sources of Revelation*, Herder and Herder, N.Y., 1968.

De Surgy, Paul (editor). *The Resurrection and Modern Biblical Thought*, Corpus Books, N.Y., 1970.

Dodd, C. H. *The Apostolic Preaching and Its Development*, Hodder and Stoughton, London, 1963.

Dunn, James D. G. *Christology in the Making*, Westminster Press, Phila., 1980.

Ellis, Peter F. *Matthew: His Mind and His Message*, Liturgical Press, Collegeville, Minn., 1974.

Evans, C. F. *Resurrection and the New Testament*, Alec R. Allenson, Inc., Naperville, Ill., 1970.

Farmer, William. *The Synoptic Problem*, Mercer Univ. Press, Macon, Ga., 1976.

Fitzmyer, Joseph A. *The Gospel According to Luke I-IX*, Doubleday and Co., Garden City, N.Y., 1981.

Fuller, Reginald. *The Foundations of New Testament Christology*, Charles Scribner's Sons, N.Y., 1965.

_____. *The Formation of the Resurrection Narratives*, Macmillan, N.Y., 1971.

Galot, Jean, S.J. *Who Is Christ?*, Franciscan Herald Press, Chicago, Ill., 1981.

Grant, Robert. *A Short History of the Interpretation of the Bible*, Macmillan Paperbooks, Macmillan, N.Y., 1966.

Grillmeier, Aloys, S.J. *Christ in Christian Tradition*, I, John Knox Press, Atlanta, Ga., 1975.

Gundry, Robert. *Matthew*, Wm. B. Eerdmans Pub. Co., Grand Rapids, Mich., 1982.

Hadas, Moses. *The Third and Fourth Books of Maccabees*, Harper and Bros., N.Y., 1953.
Haenchen, Ernst. *The Acts of the Apostles*, Westminster Press, Phila., 1971.
Harnack, Adolf *The Date of the Acts and of the Synoptic Gospels*, G. P. Putnam's Sons, N.Y., 1911.
Hengel, Martin *The Son of God*, Fortress Press, Phila., 1976.
——————. *Judaism and Hellenism*, I and II, Fortress Press, Phila., 1981.
——————. *Jews, Greeks and Barbarians*, Fortress Press, Phila., 1980.
——————. *The Atonement*, Fortress Press, Philadelphia, 1981.
——————. *Acts and the History of Earliest Christianity*, Fortress Press, Phila., 1980.
Jeremias, Joachim. *The Parables of Jesus*, Charles Scribner's Sons, N.Y., 1963.
——————. *New Testament Theology*, Charles Scribner's Sons, N.Y., 1971.
Josephus, Flavius. *The Jewish War* (trans., G. A. Williamson), Penguin Classics, London, 1959.
——————. *The Works of Flavius Josephus*, 4 vol., trans. by William Whiston, Baker Book House, Grand Rapids, Mich., 1980.
Käsemann, Ernst. *New Testament Questions of Today*, SCM Press, London, 1969.
Kasper, Walter. *Jesus the Christ*, Paulist Press, N.Y., 1981.
Kelly, J.N.D. *Early Christian Creeds*, McKay, N.Y., 1964.
Knox, Wilfred. *The Sources of the Synoptic Gospels*, Cambridge Univ. Press, Cambridge, 1953.
Kümmel, W. G. *The Theology of the New Testament*, SCM Press, London, 1974.
——————. *Introduction to the New Testament*, Abingdon Press, Nashville-New York, 1975.
Küng, Hans. *On Being a Christian*, Doubleday and Co., Garden City, N.Y., 1976.
Leon-Dufour, Xavier. *Resurrection and the Message of Easter*, Holt, Rinehart and Winston, N.Y., 1971.
Lewis, C.S. *Perelandra*, Macmillan Pub. Co., N.Y., 1973.
——————. *Christian Reflections*, Wm. B. Eerdmans Pub. Co., Grand Rapids, Mich., reprinted 1982.
Lonergan, Bernard. *The Way to Nicea* (trans. Conn O'Donovan), Westminster Press, Phila., 1976.
Maritain, Jacques. *The Degrees of Knowledge*, Charles Scribner's Sons, N.Y., 1959.
——————. *On the Grace and Humanity of Jesus*. Herder and Herder, N.Y., 1969.
Marshall, I. Howard (editor). *New Testament Interpretation*, The Paternoster Press, Exeter, England, 1977.
Martin, R. P. *Carmen Christi*, Cambridge Univ. Press, Cambridge, 1967.
Marxsen, Willi. *The Beginnings of Christology*, Fortress Press, Phila., 1979.
——————. *The Resurrection of Jesus of Nazareth*, Fortress Press, Phila., 1971.
Meier, John. *Matthew*, Michael Glazier, Inc., Wilmington, Del., 1980.
Mersch, Emile, S.J. *The Whole Christ*, Bruce Pub. Co., Milwaukee, 1938.
——————. *The Theology of the Mystical Body*, B. Herder Book Co., St. Louis, Mo., 1958.
Moltmann, Jügen. *Theology of Hope*, Harper and Row, New York, 1967.
——————. *The Crucified God*, Harper and Row, N.Y., 1974.
Moule, C. F. D. *The Birth of the New Testament*, Harper and Row, San Francisco, 1982.
Munck, Johannes. *The Acts of the Apostles*, Doubleday, Garden City, 1967.
——————. *A New Catechism*, Herder and Herder, N.Y., 1967.

Nickelsburg, George W. E. *Jewish Literature Between the Bible and the Mishnah*, Fortress Press, Phila., 1981.

Orchard, J. Bernard. *Matthew, Luke and Mark*, Koinonia, Manchester, England, 1977.

——————. *A Synopsis of the Four Gospels*, Mercer Univ. Press, Macon, Ga., 1982.

Pannenberg, Wolfhart. *Jesus, God and Man*, Westminster Press, Phila., 1968.

——————. *The Apostles' Creed*, Westminster Press, Phila., 1972.

Pelikan, Jaroslav. *The Emergence of the Catholic Tradition*, Univ. of Chicago Press, Chicago, 1971.

Perrin, Norman. *The Kingdom of God in the Teaching of Jesus*, SCM Press, London, 1963.

Plato. *Phaedo, Great Dialogues of Plato* (trans. by W. H. D. Rouse), New American Library, N. Y., 1960.

Pope John Paul II. *Original Unity of Man and Woman*, St. Paul Editions, Boston, 1981

Quasten, Johannes. *Patrology*, 3 vol., Newman Press, Westminster, Md., 1962.

Rahner, Karl. *The Trinity*, Burns and Oates, London, 1970.

——————. *Foundations of Christian Faith*, Seabury Press, N.Y., 1978.

——————. *Theological Investigations*,I, Helicon Press, Balt., Md., 1963.
V, Helicon Press, Balt., Md., 1966.
VII, Herder and Herder, N.Y., 1971.
XIV, Seabury Press, N.Y., 1976.
XVII, Crossroad, N.Y., 1981.

Rahner, K. and Thüsing, W. *A New Christology*, Seabury Press. N.Y., 1980.

Ratzinger, Joseph. *Introduction to Christianity*, Seabury Press, N.Y., 1969.

——————. *The God of Jesus Christ*, Franciscan Herald Press, Chicago, Ill., 1979.

Reicke, Bo. *The Epistles of James, Peter, and Jude*, Doubleday, Garden City, N.Y., 1964.

Richardson, Alan. *An Introduction to the Theology of the New Testament*, Harper and Row, N.Y., 1958.

——————. *The Gospel According to St. John*, Collier Books, N.Y., 1962.

Richardson, Cyril (translator). *Early Christian Fathers*, Macmillan Co., N.Y., 1970.

Rist, John M. *On the Independence of Matthew and Mark*, Society for New Testament Studies, Monograph Series, 32, Cambridge Univ. Press, Cambridge, 1978.

Robinson, J. A. T. *Redating the New Testament*, the Westminster Press, Phila., 1976.

Russell, D. S. *The Method and Message of Jewish Apocalyptic*, Westminster Press, Phila., 1964.

Sanders, Jack. *The New Testament Christological Hymns*, Cambridge Univ. Press, London, 1971.

Schaff, P. and Wace, H. (editors). *The Nicene and Post-Nicene Fathers*, the Christian Literature Co., N.Y., 1890ff.

Schillebeeckx, Edward. *Jesus: An Experiment in Christology*, Seabury Press, N.Y., 1979.

——————. *Interim Report on the Books Jesus and Christ*, Crossroad Pub. Co., N.Y., 1981.

Schlier, H. *Principalities and Powers in the New Testament*, Herder and Herder, N.Y., 1966.

Schmaus, Michael. *God and His Christ*, Sheed and Ward, N.Y., 1971.

Schnackenburg, Rudolf. *The Gospel According to St. John*,
   I, Herder and Herder, N.Y., 1968.
   II, Seabury Press, N.Y., 1980.
   _____. *The Moral Teaching of the New Testament*, Herder and Herder,
      N.Y., 1965.

Schoonenberg, Piet. *God's World in the Making*, Duquesne Univ. Press, Pittsburgh,
   Pa., 1964.
   _____. "From a Two-Nature Christology to a Christology of Presence,"
      Christian Action and Openness to the World (J. Papin, editor), Villanova
      Univ. Press, 1970.
   _____. *The Christ*, Herder and Herder, N.Y., 1971.

Schweitzer, Albert. *The Quest of the Historical Jesus*, Macmillan, N.Y., 1971.

Schweizer, Edward. *Jesus*, SCM Press, London, 1971.

Sobrino, Jon. *Christology at the Crossroads*, Orbis Books, Maryknoll, N.Y., 1978.
   Staniforth, Maxwell (trans.). *Early Christian Writings*, Penguin Books,
      London, 1968.

Stoldt, Hans-Herbert. *History and Criticism of the Marcan Hypothesis* (Donald
   Niewyk, trans. and ed.), Mercer Univ. Press, Macon, Ga., 1980.

Taylor, Vincent. *The Gospel According to St. Mark* (2nd ed.), Macmillan, London,
   1969.
   _____. *New Testament Essays*, Eerdmans Pub. Co., Grand Rapids,
      Mich., 1972.
   _____. *The Person of Christ in New Testament Teaching*, Macmillan,
      London, 1958.

Tertullian. *De Carne Christi* (Eng. Trans.: *Treatise on the Incarnation*, trans. by
   Ernest Evans, S.P.C.K., London, 1956).

Tixeront, J. *History of Dogmas*, Dr. E. Pannico, (editor) Christian Classics,
   Westminster, Md., 1984.

Tödt, H. E. *The Son of Man in the Synoptic Tradition*, SCM Press, London, 1965.

Vawter, Bruce. *This Man Jesus*, Doubleday and Co., Garden City, N.Y., 1973.

Wilckens, Ulrich. *Resurrection*, John Knox Press, Atlanta, 1978.

Wojtyla, Karol. *Sources of Renewal: The Implementation of Vatican II*, Harper and
   Row, N.Y., 1980.

Appendix: The Creeds
The Quicumque
The Firmiter
The Creed of the People of God

THE QUICUMQUE
OR ATHANASIAN CREED

DS 75   Whoever wants to be saved has the task, above all else, of holding the Catholic Faith. Unless anyone has preserved it whole and entire, he will without doubt perish forever.

Now the Catholic Faith is this: we venerate One God in Trinity and Trinity in unity, neither confusing the Persons nor separating the substance. Distinct is the Person of the Father, distinct that of the Son, distinct that of the Holy Spirit, but the Father and the Son and the Holy Spirit have one divinity, equal glory, co-eternal majesty.

As is the Father, so the Son, so the Holy Spirit: the Father uncreated, the Son uncreated, the Holy Spirit uncreated; the Father immense, the Son immense, the Holy Spirit immense; the Father eternal, the Son eternal, the Holy Spirit eternal. Nevertheless, there are not three eternal ones, but one Eternal One, just as there are not three uncreated nor three immense, but One Uncreated and One Immense. Likewise, the Father is all-powerful, the Son all-powerful, the Holy Spirit all-powerful. Nevertheless, there are not three all-powerful, but One all-powerful. Thus, the Father is God, the Son is God, the Holy Spirit is God. Nevertheless there are not three gods, but one God. Thus, the Father is Lord, the Son is Lord, the Holy Spirit is Lord. Nevertheless there are not three lords, but One Lord, because, just as we are obliged by Catholic truth to confess

each Person individually as God and Lord, so we are
forbidden by the Catholic religion to speak of three gods or
three lords.

The Father is neither made nor created nor begotten by
anyone; the Son is from the Father Alone, neither made nor
created, but begotten; the Holy Spirit is from the Father and
the Son, neither made nor created nor begotten, but
proceeding. Therefore there is One Father, not three
fathers; One Son, not three sons; One Holy Spirit, not three
holy spirits. In this Trinity there is neither before nor after,
nor lesser nor greater, but all Three Persons are co-eternal
and co-equal. Thus, in all things, as we said above, Unity in
Trinity and Trinity in Unity must be venerated. Therefore,
whoever wishes to be saved must think thus of the Trinity.

DS 76   But it is necessary for eternal salvation that one also
faithfully believe in the incarnation of our Lord Jesus Christ.
Thus, it is correct faith that we believe and profess that our
Lord Jesus Christ, the Son of God, is both God and man. He
is God begotten of the substance of the Father before time,
and born as man of the substance of His Mother in time;
perfect God, perfect man subsisting in a rational soul and
human flesh; equal to the Father according to divinity, less
than the Father according to humanity. Although He is God
and man, Christ is not two but One. He is One not by the
conversion of the divinity into flesh, but by the assumption
of humanity into God. He is completely One, not in a
confusion of substance but in a unity of Person. For, as the
rational soul and the flesh form one man, so God and man is
the One Christ. He suffered for our salvation, descended
into hell, rose on the third day from the dead, ascended into
heaven, sits at the right hand of the Father, whence He will
come to judge the living and the dead. At His coming, all
must rise in their bodies and give an account of their own
deeds. Those who have done good things will go to eternal
life, those who have done evil to eternal fire.

This is the Catholic Faith. Unless anyone faithfully and
firmly believes it, he cannot be saved.

FIRMITER OF LATERAN IV
— 1215 —

DS 800   Firmly we believe and simply we confess that One Alone is the true God, eternal, immense and unchangeable, incomprehensible, all-powerful and ineffable, Father, Son and Holy Spirit: Three Persons indeed but one essence, substance or completely simple nature. The Father is from no one, the Son from the Father alone and the Holy Spirit is equally from Both: without beginning, always, and without end: the Father generating, the Son begotten, and the Holy Spirit proceeding: consubstantial and co-equal and co-omnipotent and co-eternal, the One Principle of all things: Creator of all things visible and invisible, of things spiritual and corporeal. By His almighty power He created from the very beginning of time both the spiritual and corporeal creation, i.e., the angelic and the earthly, and, then, the human order, common to both spiritual and material as constituted of spirit and body. The devil indeed and the other demons were created by God as good according to nature but through their own fault became evil. Man sinned at the suggestion of the devil. This Holy Trinity, undivided according to the common essence and distinct according to personal properties, gave saving doctrine to the human race, first through Moses and the holy prophets and His other servants according to a perfectly ordered distribution of times.

DS 801   Finally, Jesus Christ, the only-begotten Son of God, incarnate by power common to the Trinity, conceived by the ever Virgin Mary with the cooperation of the Holy Spirit, and made true man of a rational soul and human flesh, one Person in two natures, taught the way of life more clearly. He who according to His divinity is immortal and incapable of suffering is the same One who according to His humanity is mortal and capable of suffering. For the salvation of the human race He suffered and died on the wood of the cross, descended into hell, rose from the dead and ascended into heaven. He descended in His soul, and rose in His flesh, and ascended in soul and flesh. He will come at the end of the ages to judge the living and the dead and to render to each, both damned and elect, according to their works. All of these will rise with their own bodies which they now possess in order to receive according to their works, whether good or bad. The evil will receive perpetual punishment with the devil, the good eternal glory with Christ.

DS 802   There is one universal Church of the faithful, outside of which no one at all is saved. In this Church, Jesus Christ is both priest and sacrifice. In the Sacrament of the Altar, under the species of bread and wine, His Body and Blood are truly contained, the bread having been transubstantiated into His Body and the wine into His Blood by the divine power. In order to complete the mystery of unity, we receive from Him what He received from us. And no one is able to confect this sacrament except the priest·who is properly ordained according to the keys of the Church which Jesus Christ Himself gave to the Apostles and their successors. The Sacrament of Baptism (which by the invocation of God and the individual Trinity, i.e., of the Father and of the Son and of the Holy Spirit) is consecrated in water and avails to salvation both for children and adults when conferred in the form of the Church of whatever rite. And if, after the reception of Baptism, anyone falls again into sin, he is always able to be redeemed through true penance. Moreover, not only virgins and celibates, but spouses as well, through a proper faith and good works pleasing to God, merit to arrive at eternal happiness.

CREED OF THE PEOPLE OF GOD
— Pope Paul VI — June 30, 1968

We believe in One God, Father, Son and Holy Spirit, the Creator of all things visible—such as this world where we pass our brief life—

and of things invisible—to which belong the pure spirits whom we also call angels. He is likewise the Creator in each man of a spiritual and immortal soul.

We believe that this Only God is absolutely One in His most holy Essence, as He is in His other perfections: in His omnipotence, in His infinite knowledge, in His providence, in His will and love. "He is who is," as He revealed Himself to Moses; He is Love, as John the Apostle teaches us. Thus these two names, Being and Love, ineffably express the same divine Essence of Him who willed to manifest Himself to us, and who, dwelling in inaccessible light, is in Himself above every name and above all things and created intelligences. God alone is able to grant to us a correct and full knowledge of Himself, revealing Himself as Father, Son and Holy Spirit. We are called to share His eternal life through grace, in the obscurity of faith here on earth and in everlasting light after death. The mutual bonds which constitute from all eternity the Three Persons, Each of Whom is One and the same Divine Being, are the intimate and blessed life of the Most Holy God, and infinitely surpass everything we can understand in a human manner. Nevertheless, we give thanks to the Divine Goodness that so many believers are able to testify with us to the Divine Unity, although they do not know the mystery of the Most Holy Trinity.

We believe therefore in God who, in all eternity, begets the Son; we believe in the Son, the Word of God, who is eternally begotten; we believe in the Holy Spirit, Uncreated Person, who proceeds from the Father and the Son as their Eternal Love. Thus, the life and happiness of the completely One God abound and are consummated in Three Divine Persons, who are co-equal and co-eternal, with the excellence and glory proper to the Uncreated Essence. And so a "Unity in Trinity and Trinity in Unity must be venerated."

We believe in our Lord Jesus Christ, the Son of God. He is the eternal Word, born of the Father before all ages and consubstantial with the Father, *homoousios to Patri.* Through Him all things were made. And He became flesh by the Holy Spirit of the Virgin Mary, and was made man. He is therefore equal to the Father according to divinity, less than the Father according to humanity. He is completely One, not by a confusion of natures (which is not able to happen), but by a unity of Person. He lived among us full of grace and truth. He announced and set up the kingdom of God, manifesting the Father to us in Himself. He gave us His new commandment, that we love one another as He has loved us. He taught us the way of the Gospel beatitudes: namely, to be poor in spirit and meek, to bear sorrow in patience, to thirst for justice, to be merciful, pure of heart, peacemakers, and to suffer persecution for the sake of justice. As the Lamb of God, carrying the sins of the world, He suffered under Pontius Pilate. He died for us, nailed to the cross, giving us salvation by His redeeming blood. He was buried, and by His own power rose on the third day, drawing us by His resurrection to a share in the divine life, which is grace. He ascended into heaven, whence He shall come again with glory to judge the living and the dead, each receiving according to his own merits. Those who have responded to the Love and Mercy of God will go to eternal life; those who have rejected that Love and Mercy to the end will go to the fire which will have no end.

And His kingdom will have no end.

We believe in the Holy Spirit, the Lord and Life-giver, who is adored and glorified together with the Father and the Son. He spoke through the prophets. He was sent to us by Christ after He rose and ascended to the Father. He illumines, vivifies, protects and rules the Church, whose members He purifies as long as they do not turn away from grace. His works, which reach to the depth of the soul, make one capable of responding to the precept of Christ: "Be perfect, as your Heavenly Father is perfect."

We believe that Blessed Mary, who always remained a Virgin, was the Mother of the Incarnate Word, our God and Savior Jesus Christ. We believe that she, because of her singular election "and redeemed in a more sublime manner in view of the merits of her Son, was preserved immune from every stain of original sin, and that she surpasses all other creatures by the gift of most special grace." Joined by a close and unbreakable link to the mystery of the Incarnation and Redemption, the Most Blessed Virgin Mary Immaculate, "having completed the course of her earthly life, was assumed body and soul into heavenly glory." Made like to her Son, who rose from the dead, she received by anticipation the reward of all the just.

We believe that the Most Holy Mother of God, the new Eve, the Mother of the Church, "continues to exercise now from heaven her maternal function toward the members of Christ, and so helps to bring to birth and foster the divine life in the souls of each of those who have been redeemed."

We believe that all have sinned in Adam. This means that the original fault committed by Adam has brought it about that human nature, common to all men, has fallen into such a state that it suffers the consequences of his fault. This state is no longer that in which it was found in our first parents, that is as constituted in holiness and justice, and in which man was exempt from evil and death. Therefore, this human nature, thus fallen, is passed on to all men— a nature destitute of the grace with which it was formerly adorned, a nature wounded in its natural powers and subject to the dominion of death. In this sense, every man is born in sin. Therefore, following the Council of Trent, we hold that original sin, together with human nature, is passed on "by propagation, not by imitation," and that it "is present in each one as his own."

We believe that our Lord Jesus Christ, by the Sacrifice of the Cross, has redeemed us from original sin and from all the personal sins committed by each one of us, and thus the words of the Apostle remain true: "Where sin abounded, grace has more abounded."

As believers, we confess one Baptism instituted by our Lord Jesus Christ unto the remission of sins. Indeed, Baptism is to be conferred on infants "who have not yet committed any sins of their own." In this way, deprived of supernatural grace at their birth, they are reborn of water and the Holy Spirit to divine life in Christ Jesus.

We believe in one, holy, catholic and apostolic Church, founded by Jesus Christ on the rock which is Peter. She is the Mystical Body of Christ, a visible society, hierarchically constructed and simultaneously a spiritual community. She is "the earthly Church, the People of God" on pilgrimage here on earth, "and the Church enriched with heavenly goods," the "seed and beginning of the kingdom of God." Through the Church, the work and the sufferings of the Redemption are continued for all ages of mankind, and with all her strength she hopes for that perfect fulfillment, to be gained in heavenly glory at the end of time. In the course of time, the Lord Jesus forms His Church by means of the Sacraments which flow from His fullness.

By means of these sacraments, the Church brings it about that her members participate in the mystery of the death and resurrection of Jesus Christ, through the grace of the Holy Spirit who vivifies and moves her. The Church is holy, although she embraces sinners in her bosom. She is holy because she enjoys no other life than that of grace. If they are nourished by this life, her members are made holy; if they remove themselves from this life, they contract sins and stains which serve as obstacles to the radiation of her holiness. Therefore she is afflicted and does penance for these sins, since she has the power of freeing her children from them through the Blood of Christ and the gift of the Holy Spirit.

The Church is the heiress of the divine promises, and the daughter of Abraham according to the Spirit, through that Israel, whose sacred Books she lovingly guards and whose patriarchs and prophets she piously venerates. Founded on the Apostles, she faithfully passes on through the course of the ages both their ever-living words and their own power as pastors in the Successor of Peter and in the bishops who preserve communion with him. Finally, enjoying the perpetual assistance of the Holy Spirit, the Church has the duty of preserving, teaching, expounding and spreading that truth which God fully revealed to men through the Lord Jesus, a truth foreshadowed to a certain point through the prophets. We believe all those things "Which are contained in the Word of God written or handed down, and which are set forth by the Church as being divinely revealed, whether she does this by solemn judgment or by her ordinary and universal Magisterium." We believe in that infallibility which is enjoyed by the Successor of Peter when as pastor and teacher of all Christians "he speaks *ex cathedra.*" This infallibility is present in the Body of Bishops also when it exercises its supreme Magisterium with the Successor of Peter.

We believe that the Church, which Christ established and for which He offered prayers, is indefectibly one in faith and cult and in the bond of hierarchical communion. In the bosom of this Church, neither the very rich variety of liturgical rites nor the legitimate difference of theological and spiritual patrimony and of particular disciplines harm this unity; rather they make it more evident.

Acknowledging that outside the structure of the Church of Christ there are found very many elements of sanctification and truth, which, as gifts belonging to the same Church, impel to Catholic unity, and believing in the action of the Holy Spirit who arouses in all followers of Christ a desire for this unity, we hope that it will come about that Christians who do not yet enjoy full communion with the unique Church will finally be united in one flock with one Shepherd.

We believe that the Church is necessary for salvation. For Christ is the One Mediator and Way of salvation and He becomes present to us in His Body which is the Church. But the divine purpose for salvation embraces all men, and those "who are ignorant of the Gospel of Christ and His Church, through no fault of their own, and who seek God with a sincere heart and recognize His will through the dictates of conscience and who, under the influence of grace, strive to fulfill it by their works," such as these, also, in a number which only God knows, "are able to attain salvation."

We believe that the Mass which is celebrated by a priest acting *in persona Christi,* by the power received through the Sacrament of Orders, and which is offered by the priest in the name of Christ and of the members of His Mystical Body, is truly the Sacrifice of Calvary which is made sacramentally present on our altars. We believe that the bread and wine consecrated by the Lord at His Last Supper were changed into His Body and Blood which were to be offered for us on the cross. Likewise the bread and wine consecrated by the priest are changed into the Body and Blood of Christ, now gloriously seated in heaven. And we believe that the presence of the Lord—hidden under the appearance of these realities, which continue to appear to our senses as they were before—is truly, really and substantially present.

Therefore in this Sacrament, Christ is not able to be present other than through a change of the whole substance of bread into His Body and a change of the whole substance of wine into His Blood, while the properties of bread and wine which appear to our senses remain intact. This hidden change is fittingly and properly called transubstantiation by the Church. Thus, if it is to be in harmony with Catholic faith, any interpretation of theologians which seeks some understanding of this mystery, must preserve the truth that, in the very nature of the things themselves, that is as separate from our mind, the bread and wine cease to exist after the consecration. After the consecration, under the sacramental species of bread and wine, there is present for our adoration the Body and Blood of the Lord Jesus, just as He Himself wished, so that He might offer Himself to us as food and associate us in the unity of His Mystical Body.

The one and individual existence of Christ the Lord, glorious in heaven, is not multiplied, but is made present in this Sacrament in the various places throughout the world where the Eucharistic Sacrifice is enacted. Moreover, the same Existence remains present in the most Blessed Sacrament after the Sacrifice has been celebrated. In the tabernacle on the altar this most holy Sacrament is the living heart of our churches. Because of this, we have the pleasant duty of offering honor and adoration in the Sacred Host upon which our eyes gaze, to the Word Incarnate Himself, whom our eyes are not able to see and who has become present before us without leaving heaven.

Likewise we profess that the kingdom of God, which has its beginnings here on earth in the Church of Christ, is not of this world whose figure is passing away. The proper growth of this Church is not able to be judged as being identical with the progress of human culture or of the sciences or of technical skills. Her proper growth rather consists in this: that the vast riches of Christ be more deeply known, that hope may be more constantly placed in eternal goods, that there may be a more ardent response to the love of God, and that grace and holiness may be more widely diffused among men. By that same love, the Church is impelled to have constantly at heart the true temporal good of mankind. While she does not cease to warn her children that they have here on earth no lasting city, she also urges each one, according to his condition of life and resources, to foster the growth of a truly human society, to promote justice, peace and fraternal harmony among men, and to come generously to the aid of one's brother, especially the poor and unhappy. Therefore, this great concern with which the Church attends to the needs of mankind—that is, to their joys and expectations, their sorrows and labors—is nothing else than the eagerness which so vehemently impels her to be present to mankind with this goal in mind: to enlighten men with the light of Christ, and to bring together and join all men in Him who is their only Savior. Indeed, this concern must never be understood as meaning that the Church is conforming herself to the reality of this world, or is losing the ardor with which she awaits her Lord and His eternal kingdom.

We believe in life everlasting. We believe that the souls of all those who have died in the grace of Christ—both those who still must be purified in the fire of purgatory and those who are taken into paradise by Jesus as soon as separated from their bodies, as was the Good Thief—constitute the People of God after death, which itself will be completely destroyed on the day of the resurrection when these souls will be joined to their bodies.

We believe that the multitude of these souls, who are joined in paradise with Jesus and Mary, make up the Church of heaven where, enjoying eternal happiness, they see God as He is. They participate, surely in different degrees and manner, together with the holy angels in the divine governance of reality exercised by the glorified Christ. This they do when they intercede for us and greatly help our weakness by their fraternal concern.

We believe in the communion of all Christ's faithful, that is, of those who are pilgrims on earth, of those who have died and are being purified, and of those who enjoy heavenly happiness; we believe that all of them form the one Church. We also believe that in this communion there is present to us the merciful love of God and of His saints, who always listen to our prayers, as Jesus Himself assured us: "Ask and you will receive." Professing this faith and resting on this hope, we await the resurrection of the dead and the life of the world to come.

Blessed be the thrice-holy God. Amen.

Index